Readings in Psychosynthesis
Theory, Process, and Practice

Volume 2

Readings in Psychosynthesis: Theory, Process, & Practice

Volume 2

Psychotherapy
Self-Care
Education
Health
Religion
Organizational Development
World Order

Edited by: John Weiser and Thomas Yeomans

Published in Canada by The Department of Applied Psychology/The Ontario Institute for Studies in Education, 252 Bloor Street West, Toronto, Ontario M5S 1V6

Canadian Cataloguing in Publication Data

Main entry under title:
Readings in psychosynthesis

Includes bibliographies.
ISBN 0-7744-9803-X (v. 1). – ISBN 0-7744-9809-9 (v. 2)

1. Psychology. 2. Psychotherapy. 3. Psychology, Applied. I. Weiser, John, 1929-   . II. Yeomans, Thomas, 1940-   . III. Ontario Institute for Studies in Education. Dept. of Applied Psychology.

RC489.P8R42 1985   616.89'14   C85-099391-1

Editorial/Design—H. Berkeley/H. Solar
Typesetting—Webcom
Printing—Webcom

CONTENTS

World Order

Introduction: Psychosynthesis in North America

John Weiser and Thomas Yeomans

It is fundamental to the history of ideas that as an idea takes root in a particular culture it adapts itself to that culture in order to be understood and useful. At the same time, it introduces an innovation in thought and behavior that is needed if the culture is to grow. A recent example of this phenomenon is the emergence of Buddhism in the West. Though in essence still akin to Buddhism in the East, it has in many ways changed to fit the concerns and cultural orientation of practitioners on this continent.

This has been true of the emergence of Psychosynthesis in North America. Though rooted in Europe in the original vision of Roberto Assagioli (whose centennial we celebrate this year), it has developed in ways particularly North American. As we look back over these last 30 years of developments in Psychosynthesis, we can begin to recognize both how it has contributed to North American culture and how it has been changed and transformed through interaction with it.

This book of readings is one expression of this transformative journey. In it are articles which span work that includes both person and planet. The articles address major sources of suffering and dysfunction in this culture as well as areas of innovation and creative response. Here, by way of introduction, we would like to reflect briefly on some of the salient characteristics of Psychosynthesis that have emerged over the last three decades in North America.

Initially, the Psychosynthesis Research Foundation was established in New York City in 1958 at the request of Roberto Assagioli. It was a small research foundation that hosted colloquia for a modest following among members of the various helping professions. This was a good beginning, but it was not until ten years later that Psychosynthesis gained greater visibility—mostly on the West Coast and predominately through its association with Humanistic and Transpersonal Psychology and the strong counter-cultural movement for alternative approaches to healing and human development. This turn of events temporarily separated Psychosynthesis from the mainstream of traditional psychological thought—something that did not happen in Europe—and, as a result, it became known on this continent as an alternative psychology in the Human Potential movement rather than as a traditional depth psychology. This period (1968–1980), however,

1

brought great variety and richness to the practice of Psychosynthesis; many new techniques were developed to support the underlying process of psycho-spiritual growth and Psychosynthesis became a major school in the alternative culture for work with the spiritual search that engaged so many people at the time.

This period ended in the early 1980s. Bringing with them the wealth of experience gained in the previous period of experimentation, many practitioners have been reconnecting the field to its more traditional roots. As the eighties draw to a close, Psychosynthesis in North America is beginning to integrate the diverse cultural streams that have been a part of its history on this continent. Hopefully, in the nineties, a synthesis can be forged that includes the best of both orientations—a union which Roberto Assagioli envisioned from the beginning—and, if all goes well, the next century will see Psychosynthesis emerge as one of a number of truly global psychologies of the Spirit.

What, then, are some of the qualities that have come to characterize Psychosynthesis on this continent? Below we list the major ones.

Pragmatic—Pragmatism, expressed in an emphasis on real change in behavior as a result of expansion of consciousness, has brought to the fore work with the personal will and its alignment with the will of the Self. More generally, it has meant the development of a grounded, practical, almost behavioral approach to spiritual work, and an insistence that spiritual awakening lead not only to expanded consciousness, but also to changed conditions, both personal and social, in daily life.

Rich in Techniques—North American practitioners have vastly increased the range of techniques for working with the process of psychosynthesis. To do this, they have drawn on many schools of psychological practice, from neuro-muscular body work to advanced forms of meditative practice. At its best, a panoply of techniques now exists to serve the underlying principles of psychological and spiritual growth; at its worst, technique becomes an end in itself. But the point is that technical options now far exceed what was previously available, and the practice of Psychosynthesis has been enriched many fold.

Democratic—In its early years on this continent, Psychosynthesis enjoyed the freedom of growing in an open, egalitarian political climate. However, in the late seventies, it underwent some very intense encounters with the autocratic distortions that emerge in groups when freedom is misused. This was a painful chapter, but learning from it has led in recent years to a renewed emphasis on decentralized relationships and a fuller appreciation of democratic principles in group formation. This characteristic has also manifested itself in the work of some theorists in placing relatively less emphasis on a hierarchical relationship between Self and personality. For these theorists, the Self is seen as "embedded" in human experience rather than as "above" it and as something that can be reached only through transcendence. This orientation has been accompanied in practice by a stronger affirmation of the inherent dignity of each person and his or her experience, whatever the level of development, and a respect for the unconscious life process, as a means to Self-realization. It has also led to both a more systemic and a less structural/hierarchical analysis of personal psychodynamics and the relationship of Self and personality. Another result has been a stronger emphasis on direct access to Self, with less need for intermediaries—be they teachers, therapists, or priests. Therapeutically, it has led to a more co-operative relationship between client and guide; organizationally, to "networking" among centres and an egalitarian structuring of a growing community of co-workers.

Experimental—This characteristic has produced a "frontier" spirit in Psychosynthesis which includes a willingness to take risks and to question traditional ideas. Though, at times, this spirit has generated ungrounded experience and the rejection of the findings of the past, something which happened particularly during the counter-cultural period, it has, at its best, been a catalyst to continued exploration and to the significant development of the field. The articles in this book attest to the existence of a grounded *and* fresh approach to the problems we face in this culture.

Exoteric—Because of Roberto Assagioli's interest in the esoteric teachings of the Tibetans and of Alice Bailey, Psychosynthesis was initially associated with, and influenced by, this body of material. While a few practitioners still study these religious teachings, the majority in North America approach Psychosynthesis as an exoteric psycho-spiritual discipline and school of thought which draws on many psychological and spiritual traditions to understand human development from a spiritual perspective. This, in fact, was Assagioli's original intention—that Psychosynthesis not be associated with his personal involvement with this, or any, school of religious thought, but stay free, undogmatic, and scientifically empirical so as to be able to grow with the new discoveries in psycho-spiritual science of this century and the next.

These five characteristics—pragmatic, rich in techniques, democratic, experimental, and exoteric—suggest the flavor of North American Psychosynthesis as it has developed so far. These have been rich decades. Yet, in the year of Roberto Assagioli's centennial, we can also say that we are only beginning. Whole areas remain uncharted, and only the first fruits of writing and research have been harvested.

During these decades, also, Psychosynthesis has become established worldwide, so that these findings, both present and future, will need to be integrated with those from other cultures around the globe. This is particularly true in relation to the work of a new generation of psychosynthesists in Europe who have also taken the field in many new directions. The international conference in Italy this year, hopefully, will be the beginning of a new level of collaboration between Europe, North America, and the other continents. This shared work should take us well into the 21st century.

Finally, it is fair to say that the contribution of Psychosynthesis to this culture, and to the world, still lies ahead. In these decades, we have seen among a growing number of people an awakening to spiritual reality and a desire to integrate this experience with psychological and daily life. This number grows yearly, and as we confront the political, economic, ecological, and social crises in which we increasingly find ourselves, it is likely that many more will turn to a deeper search for Self. Psychosynthesis is one of a number of integrative approaches that have already been immensely useful for this purpose, and, if we do our work well, this field, along with others, will be able to meet this need even more fully in the future.

We, therefore, offer this book in the spirit of beginning and in gratitude that North America has had a part to play in the development of Psychosynthesis so far. We look forward to growing contact and co-operation with psychosynthesists all over the world as we move forward together, "from the eternal, in the present, for the future."

Counselling/Therapy

Family of Origin: Land of Opportunity for Transpersonal Therapists

Penelope Young

For the past ten years, I have worked to synthesize Family Systems Therapy and Psychosynthesis. In this article, I would like to share the basics of Family Systems Therapy, as proposed by Dr. Murray Bowen, and highlight the similarities with Psychosynthesis. Drawing from personal and professional experience, I will demonstrate the opportunities family systems work offers transpersonal therapy practitioners.

In 1975, I completed a four-year training program in Family Studies at Albert Einstein College of Medicine, where I studied with Dr. Tom Fogarty, a Bowen proponent. A major demand of the program was that students work intensively with the relationships in *their own families* of origin. I began a process of profound healing with my parents and brother and laid the foundation for a deep and abiding friendship with the man who was then my husband, and is the father of my son.

I propose that working directly with parents and siblings provides an exquisite opportunity for grounding transpersonal work.

Theoretical Contexts

Family Systems Therapy and Psychosynthesis both take place in the context of identifying and strengthening the personal self. The difference is that in family therapy the "I" is almost indistinguishable from thinking processes and is not directly linked to higher consciousness (Bowen, 1971).

In Psychosynthesis, the personal self is the integrating centre of awareness and will for the personality (Crampton, 1981, p. 712) and includes feelings and body as well as mind and the psychological functions of sensation, emotion, impulse, imagination, thought, intuition, and will (Ferrucci, 1984, p. 45). In Psychosynthesis, the sources of the personal self are our higher feelings of love and compassion; our higher thoughts of clarity, intuition, and inspiration; and our experience of illumination and unity (Assagioli, 1965).

While Family Systems Therapy doesn't directly speak of the transpersonal, the words "value," "conviction" and "belief" are commonly used to define self, and they certainly suggest a higher realm. Bowen himself often said the "I" position represented the beliefs one would die for.

Both Family Systems Therapy and Psychosynthesis take place in the context of the will. Although Family Systems never directly addresses will, it is permeated with the sense of it. Bowen, for example, defines self as a "definite quantity illustrated by such 'I' position stances as: 'These are my beliefs and convictions; this is what I am, and who I am, and what I will do or not do'. The basic self may be changed from *within* self on the basis of new knowledge and experience. That basic self *is not negotiable in the relationship system* in that it is not changed by coercion or pressure, or to gain approval, or enhance one's stand with others" (1971, p. 118).

For Psychosynthesis, the will is the force of manifestation in the Universe and includes strength, skill, and goodness united in love (Brown, 1983).

The intention of Family Systems Therapy is to enable the client to experience him or herself as a differentiated "I" within the family of origin *while developing and maintaining effective and satisfying relationships with family members*. For family systems theory, "the core of emotional dysfunction is fusion . . . the blending of one self into another . . . " (Fogarty, 1975, p. 88). Bowen and Fogarty are very clear that handling disturbing family interactions by distancing physically or emotionally is not a sign of integration or maturity. Distancing is not the opposite of fusion, rather, as is intense conflict, it is *indicative* of fusion. Bowen, states, "The more intense the cutoff with the past, the more likely the individual [is] to have an exaggerated version of his parental family problem in his own marriage and the more likely [are] his own children to do a more intense cutoff with him in the next generation" (1976, p. 85).

The concept of fusion is similar to the psychosynthesis concept of identification: "We are identified with something when we are unable to separate ourselves from that thing, when our identity is bound up in it" (Crampton, 1981, p. 715). Handling our identifications by trying to rid ourselves of our dysfunctional aspects does not work any better for personality systems than do cutoffs for family systems.

The cornerstones of the family systems method for facilitating differentiation are coaching, the genogram, detriangulation, and the "I" position.

Methods

Coaching—In Family Systems, the therapeutic process is called "coaching" and involves teaching the theory of family systems as well as guiding the clients through work with their families of origin. Coaching may involve an individual client or an entire family. As in Psychosynthesis, the therapist has a respect for clients and deliberately avoids a transference relationship. In the coaching process, the therapist attempts to "read the automatic emotional responsiveness [of the family system] so as to control [his or her] own automatic emotional participation in the emotional process . . . while staying emotionally in contact with the family" (Bowen, 1976, p. 53).

Bowen and Fogarty propose that Family Systems Therapy can be done as effectively with only one family member present, usually the most motivated one. Family Systems Therapy is, for them, a point of view rather than a description of who actually attends sessions. Bowen himself prefers to work with the marital couple, coaching each partner in the presence of the other. The couple finds that as work progresses in their families of origin, their marriage begins to heal. A mother bringing her daughter in for evaluation as a result of school problems may, on the other hand, find Dr. Bowen sending the daughter home and inviting the mother to bring in *her mother* for conjoint therapy or for coaching on that relationship. Again, without direct intervention, the daughter's problems subside.

Coaching clients to work back a generation is also used strategically by family systems therapists who directly address marital or family issues in cases where the immediate situation is reactively hot or contractedly blocked. I have successfully used this strategy when dealing with troubled relationships between parents and rebellious or recalcitrant adolescents. I invite the adolescents to attend the sessions and sit in on the work I do with their parent(s) concerning their parents' relationships with their parents during adolescence. Hostilities subside and hearts open as parents emerge as real people and as adolescent traumas are recalled empathetically.

Working back a generation has similarities to the psychosynthesis concept of disidentification which refers to our ability to "stand back from our subpersonalities in order to see them more clearly and to find the vantage point from which we can do something to transmute them" (Crampton, 1981, p. 715). Subpersonalities are derived from distortions of qualities which the Self is trying to manifest but which are split off from the whole personality (Crampton, 1981).

Family Systems Therapy works to help an individual differentiate his or her "I" from the various pulls of his or her family system. The client is then helped to be in *better relation to family members*. Psychosynthesis works to bring energies of the Higher Self into the personality (or the "I") and to differentiate this energy from the pulls of the subpersonalities. The client is helped to be in *better relation to subpersonalities*, releasing the positive energy at his or her core and making it available for integration into the personality. Subpersonalities are often projected onto family members, and, conversely, family members are often the models for the introjects from which the subpersonality configurations are formed.

A psychosynthesis parallel to *working back a generation* is that of *working up a level*. When working with parental images or images of significant others, the psychosynthesis guide often asks the client to become the other in order to increase understanding and empathy. If the relationship is too reactively hot, he or she is asked to speak to or to become the *Higher Self* of the estranged significant other or family member.

Polt (1983) creatively blended back-a-generation and up-a-level strategies by devising a visualization process in which clients first imagine themselves experiencing an unmet need in the presence of their parents and then imagine their *parents as children* experiencing *similar unmet needs* with their parents. Once this process is completed, the client returns to each image and focusses on having the need fulfilled.

The Genogram—Family of origin work begins by having the individual or couple draw up a "genogram," a three-generational map of family relationships graphically depicting births, deaths, marriages, divorces, and sibling order (Guerin & Fogarty, 1972, p. 449).

When I drew up my own genogram, I was amazed to discover that my mother's mother died during World War II three months before I was born, and that six months after I was born my father was shipped to Okinawa. The moment I considered what such a birth must have been like for a new mother, facing not only the loss of her mother but also the absence of her husband, I began to experience a transformation of this painfully reactive relationship. My heart opened on the spot to this person who also happened to be my mother.

The rationale for working directly with parents is described by prominent family therapist John Framo (1976): "The client, by having sessions with his or her family of origin, takes the problems to where they began, thereby making available a direct route to etiological factions. Dealing with the real external parental figures is designed to loosen the grip of the internal representatives of these figures and expose them to reality considerations and their live derivatives. Having gone backward in time, the individual can then move forward in dealing with the spouse and children in more appropriate fashion since their transference meaning has changed."

Everyone doing transpersonal therapy (or anyone on a spiritual path) has encountered difficulty in translating profound insights into guidelines for practical situations. Psychosynthesis has been in the vanguard of those insisting on the importance of "grounding" (Brown, 1983). The challenge of grounding is continually highlighted in my sessions. I find myself sharing an experience of breath-taking radiance and expansion with a client. And then the moment arises when I say, "Now, staying connected with this experience, imagine that you are facing the problem you brought up earlier and that your [mother, husband, lover, boss, inner judge, etc.] is before you. What do you need now to communicate to that person or part of you?" The client often struggles with contraction and separation at just the thought of facing the matter.

Early in my family therapy training, I would plan my approaches to my own parents months before I was able to fly back to California to see them. Within minutes of arriving, I would find myself caught in the same old dysfunctional patterns. Yet I know that powerful inner work has a powerful correspondence in the outer world. I, too, have received a long distance phone call from someone with whom I've just moments earlier completed an inner healing. Working in the flesh with parents and siblings exponentially *increases* our ability to embody in daily life the most powerful truths of our Higher Selves.

If you doubt this, take a look at your reaction. Is fear present? How much resistance? It has been my experience that the biggest problem in using this method is that of finding willing clients. According to Framo, "it is difficult to communicate in words the almost instinctive, aversive response of people to this idea" (1976, p. 197). His view is that "when adults relate to their parents of today, they are, in part, still viewing the parents as they did when they were children, when they were small and more vulnerable, and when their feelings were experienced in gross categories" (p. 108).

The choice of which arena in which to work, inner or outer, depends on the needs of the client at the moment, the willingness of both client and guide, and the availability of family members. However, at the end of an intense piece of work with the family of origin, one is left with not only a greater sense of "I" but also fulfilling relationships with those people most significant in one's life.

During my second year of training, my mother, a courageous woman devoted to finding and manifesting truth in her life, agreed to participate in a videotaped session in which we would be coached by a fellow trainee. At one point, I heard her speak of being proud of me for my commitments to world peace and to ending hunger. But I heard her say these things in a tone I had always experienced as sarcastic and critical. I commented that I thought she was being sarcastic. The coach intervened and I heard my mother repeat her words with increased conviction and admiration. I heard her that time. I've reviewed this video many times and have seen my introject of the "critical mother" dissolve before my eyes.

As my learning continued, I tried to reach out to my father. My first attempt consisted of walking around the block with him five minutes before I was due to leave for the airport to fly home.

Since my father is a reserved, private person, I attempted to fill in a picture of him by talking with his sisters and brother. (An important aspect of family of origin work involves interviewing and researching the family network to obtain information not available from parents and grandparents personally.) Another introject dissolved on the spot when I began talking with my father's closest sister, Dorothy. I mentioned that I thought my father was very puritanical and not interested in sex. She could hardly stop laughing as she recounted that when they were youngsters in Kansas he was so interested in sex that he suggested they "practise" together. I began to see the twinkle in my father's eye for the first time.

After two years of training, I told my father I had struggled a lot with feeling that he wasn't really interested in me. "Had he ever felt," I asked him, "that I wasn't interested in him?" To my great surprise, he said, "Once when you were a little girl, shortly after I came home from Okinawa, you and I were going for a walk and I was telling you about something; you turned to me and said, 'Daddy, stop talking'."

I was at least 32 years old when I had this discussion with my dad. I was astonished that he had carried that memory for 28 years. From that moment, I began to see my father as a real person with feelings and sensitivities, as a person who cared very much what I felt about him.

Detriangulation—The primary instruction to trainees working with family members is to find the main "triangle" and then to "detriangulate" it. For Bowen, the triangle is the "basic building block of any emotional system, whether it is in the family or any other group. The triangle is the smallest stable relationship system. A two-person system may be stable as long as it is calm, but when anxiety increases, it immediately involves the most vulnerable other person to become a triangle. When tension in the triangle is too great for the threesome, it involves others to become a series of interlocking triangles" (1976, p. 76).

Triangulation is the way human beings habitually handle the anxiety which arises in the face of intimacy. Intimacy brings up issues of autonomy, fear of loss and of abandonment, in the vulnerable context of a primary relationship. Only in the last 20 years have we begun to attain the clarity and increased consciousness to work through these issues.

Triangles are not always dysfunctional. They are dysfunctional only to the extent that they represent intimacy. Rather than relating one to one and facing conflict, people focus on a third person, object, or activity. Fogarty joked frequently that the average length of time any two people relate directly to one another ranges from thirty seconds to two minutes. Common triangles include parents focussing on an acting-out child; a marital couple focussing on in-laws or on an extra-marital affair; a marital couple focussing on one partner's drinking or drug problem; a boss and an employee focussing on sports or business; or friends focussing on gossip. An early uneasy alliance between Freud and Jung, for example, was maintained by their focus on their common disagreement and mistrust of Alfred Adler. William McGuire, in the *Freud/Jung Letters* (1974), describes how they avoided dealing with their major disagreements in this way for years. When Jung finally took an "I" position and challenged some of Freud's views, their friendship and correspondence ended.

Bowen describes the shifting of alliances within triangles. "In periods of calm, the triangle is made up of a comfortably close twosome and a less comfortable outsider. The twosome works to preserve the togetherness, lest one become uncomfortable and form a better togetherness else-where. . . . in periods of stress, the outside position is the most comfortable and desired position. . . . in stress, each works to get the outside position to escape tension in the twosome. . . . when available tensions are very high in families and available family triangles are exhausted, the family system triangles in people from outside the family, such as police and social agencies. A successful externalization of the tension occurs when outside workers are in conflict about the family, while the family is calmer" (1976, p. 76).

In my family, the major triangle found my mother and myself in the close, conflictual position and either my father or my brother in the distant posi-tion. As my mother and I began to have a rewarding relationship, I suggested that my dad and I take a short vacation in Arizona to play tennis (something we both enjoyed and could "triangulate" enough with to keep us from being too anxious to relate at all). In order to bring this about, I had to "operate the triangle" (Bowen, 1971) by enlisting my mother's full co-operation. Once I did this, she actively encouraged my dad to take the trip.

This was the first time I had my father "all to myself" and an opportunity to really know him. We played lots of tennis, talked, laughed, got cranky, and when the weekend was over, I found myself full of pain about ending this special time. I shared this with my father and found him to be as tender and understanding as I had wished all of my life. Our relationship continues to be full of subtlety and sensitivity.

According to Bowen, the work of detriangulation is so powerful that "when the triangular emotional pattern is modified in a single important triangle in the family, and the members of this triangle remain in emotional contact with the rest of the family, other triangles will automatically change in relation to the first" (Bowen, 1971, p. 125). This was true for my relationship with my brother which became more intimate even before I directly ad-dressed it (or him). My work with my brother involved taking a ten-day trip across the U.S. during which we visited all the important living relatives in my mother's family. I had a twofold purpose for this trip. The first was to spend time with my brother. The second was to bring to life my maternal grandparents. My grandfather had been cut off from the family when my mother was a baby and died when she was 12; and, as mentioned, my grandmother died shortly before I was born.

As my brother and I spent those days trekking across the country, we began to sort through our misperceptions of each other. As we explored our different experiences growing up in the same family, we forged a path of caring and clarity between us.

My research on my mother's family during that trip led me to a very important piece of information. I was tracing the theme of the distant or cutoff father/daughter relationship through two generations (my mother's and mine). My mother's father had a nervous breakdown shortly after her birth and couldn't maintain his law practice in Chicago. He went to O'Neill, Nebraska, then still somewhat a frontier town in 1918, resumed his practice, and ultimately became the mayor. The story was that my grandmother didn't want to move to the Wild West, so she and my mother remained in Chicago with only infrequent visits from grandfather.

In O'Neill, I found a picture of my grandfather sitting in front of his big roll-top desk which prominently displayed a picture of my mother as a little girl. The moment I saw that picture, I sensed a love and connection between father and daughter that could not be separated by any distance of miles. At that moment, I also became connected with my grandfather, and through that connection, experienced an increased sense of self-worth.

"I" Position—In preparation for writing this article, I contacted several clients whom I had coached over the past ten years with family of origin work. I asked them to recall the most profound aspects of this work as it affected them now.

One woman, Judith T., now a professor at a major eastern university, recalled a letter she had written to her father to begin a dialogue about her recurrent feelings of unworthiness. She had considered herself selfish, a notion with which she felt sure her father would agree. As soon as her father received the letter, he called, full of concern for her. Judith reported that what he said to her, which did not correspond to her imaginings, was not as important as the deeply experienced realization that "my father loves me and loves me a lot." She added that this letter represented the first time she had ever approached her father from an "I" position, rather than a reaction, and that it has provided a framework for a fulfilling relationship for the past ten years.

The "I" position, in addition to being the definition of one's beliefs and values, is also "the responsible 'I' which assumes responsibility for one's own happiness, comfort and well being, and avoids blaming others for any discomfort and unhappiness" (Cain, 1976, p. 68). The "I" position in action assumes responsibility and is a key operation in the differentiation process. In the above example, Judith did not approach her father by *blaming him* for "making her feel unworthy," which she had certainly done in the past. She took responsibility for her reaction, and in this case, her projection, and by writing to her father she created the opportunity for her father to approach her with love and compassion.

Much of the coaching and guiding I do is concerned with helping clients reveal for themselves, and thereby diminish the power of, the dysfunctional belief systems out of which they subconsciously operate. I then encourage clients to take full responsibility for the process of incorporating these beliefs *even if the process has been largely or totally unconscious, and even if the outer messages had initiated the dysfunctional belief*. This may not seem fair to the personality, yet for the Higher Self, it is a reflection of unity with the energy of Cause in the Universe. And, practically speaking, who else could or would take responsibility? In 1948, in an essay entitled *General Aspects of Dream Psychology*, Carl Jung expressed this beautifully:

> If we dissolve the time honoured and sacrosanct identity between image and object the concequences for our psychology, too, can scarcely be imagined: we would no longer have anybody to rail against, nobody whom we could make responsible, nobody to instruct, improve and punish. On the contrary we would have to begin, in all things with ourselves; we would have to demand of ourselves, and of no one else, all the things which we habitually demand of others.

Conclusion

The opportunities found in a synthesis of Family Systems Therapy and Psychosynthesis are myriad. These range from providing experiences of self-worth, clarity, and compassion, of personal responsibility and unity consciousness, to deep and fulfilling relationships with parents and siblings.

My present relationships with my mother, father, and brother are now reaping the harvest of this synthesis. These connections are so rewarding, mutually supportive, and just plain fun that I am eternally grateful I have lived long enough to experience our love, our remarkable individuality, and our choice to be a family. My greatest joy now comes from the opportunities my work provides to share this harvest.

References

Anonymous. (1972). Toward the differentiation of self in one's own family. In J. Framo (Ed.), *Family interaction* (p. 111–173). New York: Spring.

Assagioli, R. (1965). *Psychosynthesis*. New York: Penguin.

Bowen, M. (1976). Theory in the practice of psychotherapy. In P. J. Guerin (Ed.), *Family therapy theory and practice* (pp. 42–90). New York: Gardner.

Brown, M. Y. (1983). *The unfolding self: Psychosynthesis and counseling*. Los Angeles: Psychosynthesis Press.

Cain, A. (1976). The role of the therapist in Family Systems Therapy. *The Family*, 3(2), 65–71.

Ferrucci, P. (1982). *What we may be: Techniques for psychological and spiritual growth*. Los Angeles: J. P. Tarcher.

Fogarty, T. F. (1975). The family emotional self system. *Family Therapy*, 2(1), 79–97.

Fogarty, T. F. (1976). Systems concepts and the dimensions of self. In P. J. Guerin (Ed.), *Family therapy theory and practice* (pp. 145–153). New York: Gardner.

Fogarty, T. F. (1979). Operating principles. *The Family*, 7(1), 48–54.

Framo, J. L. (1976). Family of origin as a therapeutic resource for adults in marital and family therapy: You can and should go home again. *Family Process*, 193–210.

Guerin, P., & Fogarty, T. F. (1972). Study your own family. In A. Ferber, M. Mendelsohn, & A. Napier (Eds.), *The book of family therapy* (pp. 445–457). New York: Science House.

Polt, W. (1980). *A generational healing experience: Connecting family systems theory and psychosynthesis*. Paper presented at the Psychosynthesis Conference, Florence, Italy.

McGuire, W. (1974). *Freud/Jung letters: The correspondence between Sigmund Freud and C. G. Jung* (R. Manheim & R. F. C. Hull, Trans.). Princeton: Princeton University Press.

Treating Mental and Emotional Abuse

Victoria Tackett

Much clinical counselling work consists of alleviating the mental anguish and emotional suffering inflicted on individuals in their interpersonal relationships. If the client is female, her self-esteem has very often been damaged by a multitude of sexist insults and societal misassumptions about her appearance, ability, potential, and worth. If the client is male, he may have been judged as lacking, measured against stereotypically high expectations, or emotionally injured by the cultural admonition against the male expression of a full range of feelings. In a society that claims to value and encourage individuality, individuals are denied their inalienable rights at home, at school, and at work—sometimes in subtle and insidious ways. In a society that claims to love its children and support the family unit, homes and families are dissolving at an alarming rate. Add to this the overwhelming visage of nuclear destruction, planetary pollution, and economic instability and it is no wonder that the stress has made us apathetic toward one another. And yet, the problem of psychological abuse and alienation in America is of such major proportions that it must be addressed if life is to be worth living at all.

Socially inflicted hurts and rejections occur with such frequency that they are now considered an expected part of daily life. Marriages have become battlegrounds. Children are not adequately cared for. Authoritarian professors, physicians, and bosses are endured. Politicians are assumed to be dishonest. Television producers parody these situations and sell them as entertainment. Comedians attempt to make us laugh about it. And we all know, from our own experience, that the situation is critical.

The problems of physical separation, loneliness, and alienation have become extreme—so much so that Ma Bell has found it necessary, as well as lucrative, to encourage us to "reach out and touch someone." The problem of mental abuse is so commonplace that a nation-wide bank promotes its services with the statement: "We'll treat you with respect, concern, and understanding. But don't worry, you'll get used to it." And the dire problem of emotional abuse of children in the United States prompted a national media campaign to remind us that "it shouldn't hurt to be a child." Apparently, we had forgotten.

To anesthetize these interpersonal wounds, we are rapidly becoming a nation of addicts. Across the nation people confess addictions to everything from alcohol, to cigarettes, to illicit and prescription drugs of all kinds, to food, to work, to jogging and other sports, to power, to sex, and even to

15

love—all attempting to ease the need for personal support and spiritual sustenance and block the psychological pain of alienation and abuse. When this pain cannot be suppressed, some react by becoming even more psychologically abusive, while others, seeing no solution for their pain, take their own lives. Human beings are much more sensitive and complex than we care to admit.

Although our courts do not, as yet, consider mental and emotional abuse as crime, counsellors see the crippling results in their offices on a daily basis. Even when physical or sexual abuse is also reported, the associated mental and emotional injury is often what lingers on and remains in need of healing. The matter-of-fact way in which innocent young hearts and minds are ridiculed, hurt, and betrayed results in producing apparently functional adults who are unable to trust, love, or provide stable home environments for their own children.

It is difficult to admit the extent of this problem in human relations because we have all been wounded, and we have all hurt someone else at some point in our lives. We are able to admit complicity after we have changed our point of view and can re-examine the interaction, and our participation, in a new light. Then we may experience shame, remorse, and the desire for forgiveness or reconciliation. Only then can honest apologies and amends be made to those we have hurt through ignorance. When we are humbled by the recognition of our past mistakes toward others, to have our apology accepted acts as a natural healing agent for ourselves and for those we have hurt. These wounds do not seem to heal simply with time. Interpersonally inflicted wounds are best healed within an interpersonal context of love and genuine care.

Forms of Abuse

Ultimately, the line between healthy and abusive interaction is not merely one of degree, but of quality and kind. Healthy interactions are different from abusive ones; that difference can be felt and understood. However, acknowledging that difference is a matter of social awareness, education, personal sensitivity, and environmental support. Those social assaults to the mind and feelings that are inflicted intentionally, those that are extreme or acute, or those that are subtly insidious and are repeated over time can all be defined in the clinical setting, without question, as psychological "abuse."

For purposes of clarification and study, psychological abuse can be stated as taking two forms: (1) mental abuse and (2) emotional abuse. In daily interactions, mental and emotional abuse most often occur simultaneously, and may be expressed either verbally or non-verbally. As well as being a betrayal of the body, physical abuse, rape, and sexual molestation always have with them a psychologically abusive component. Alternatively, when one's highest ideals, religious convictions, or spiritual experiences are ridiculed or refuted, this increases self-doubt and it is then that spiritual orthodoxy becomes psychological abuse. Below, examples of mentally abusive tactics are given, followed by examples of emotionally abusive behavior.

In mentally abusive interactions, people are harmed by being treated as objects, or by being lied to or otherwise deceived. Mental abusiveness creates extreme cognitive dissonance. It is often based on things that individuals cannot change such as their race, gender, sexual orientation, appearance, weight, body type, age, disability, intelligence, financial status, or ethnic heritage. Racism, sexism, homophobia, bigotry, and other class distinctions are all forms of mental abuse. They are used to rationalize mistreatment, unfair employment practices, and inequity. At best, this prejudice is personally demeaning; at worst, it leads to genocide, homocide, and suicide.

The Western overvaluation of the scientific method, rationality, and analytic thinking—besides limiting creative possibilities—becomes abusive when it is used to discredit visionary or intuitive functioning. Many minds are wounded in our educational institutions: bright and intelligent people are judged as stupid because they are able to think synthetically, seeing first the whole, then extrapolating the relationship between levels and parts, rather than coming to conclusions in a step-by-step analytic fashion. Intuitive thinking is often met with scepticism and misgiving, causing considerable pain and rejection of visionary insight at a time when the world is in need of new visions.

Lies and deceptions are the most common form of mental abuse used in everyday interpersonal interactions. Being blatantly lied to—whether by advertisers, politicians, or loved ones—is a cause of confusion, anguish, and mistrust. Lying behavior may also take indirect forms such as evasiveness, secrecy, duplicity, withholding information, chronic ambivalence, and the use of covert statements that make the truth hard to ascertain. Not knowing the truth, it is difficult to take affirmative action. Widespread fear, uncertainty, and insecurity may be a natural reaction to this pervasive cultural habit of lying.

Other techniques of mental abuse include extreme mental dominance, callous arrogance, and unrelenting one-upmanship. Overcontrol, the enforcement of impossibly rigorous expectations, obsessive or convoluted stories designed to "win" at all costs, brainwashing methods, and semantic rigidity used against another to limit inquiry are but a few more examples.

To be lied to, or persecuted, or refused respect is very damaging. Such mental abuses, commonplace in interpersonal relationships, educational and professional institutions, and social groups of all kinds, are unjust and painful. In our culture, this pain is seldom acknowledged. Yet widespread mental abuse points to a crisis in our personal and cultural values. If, as individuals and as a society, we value only youth, then one automatically loses one's value early, after youth has passed. If it is popular to believe that one can be neither too rich nor too thin, then we look down on those without money and create a climate where cosmetic surgery and fad diets are a major industry and young girls die of anorexia. As a nation we spend millions of dollars on non-essentials while many of our neighbors are homeless, hungry, and destitute. If we remain intent on looking out for "Number One," then who is to care for the children and for those who are temporarily unable to care for themselves? If we only value life in the fast lane, then we are bound by frenetic activity in which there is no place for a rich and meaningful inner life. As we lose a sense of deeper values, addictions and abuses flourish. In this context, the existence of pervasive mental abuse demands a conscious re-examination of, and change in, popular cultural values.

While mental abuses tend to discount, confuse, or demean, emotional abuses are experienced more personally—on the feeling level. They are frequently described in the same language and metaphors used to describe physical wounds. This may be due, in part, to the fact that emotionally abusive interactions evoke and are accompanied by physical indicators such as instantaneous headache, nausea, the breath being held, a feeling of being "hit" in the solar plexus, the heart "breaking," or heartbeat racing in fear. Why is it that emotional abuse has such an overall effect? It is because humans are feeling beings.

In emotionally abusive interactions, the natural feeling bond that takes place between human beings is either denied, misused, severed, ignored, or negated. Some studies indicate that this human bonding is necessary for survival. Infants have been known to die without it. In adulthood, the lack of such bonds appears to weaken the immune system. We are indeed feeling beings, and as such are bonded to one another—for better or for worse.

Emotional abuse is particularly hurtful and unsettling when it occurs within the intimate bonds of trust inherent in marital and familial relationships. We are harmed when we experience threats to these emotional bonds in the form of insults, degradation, cruelty, ridicule, criticism, "put-downs," verbal assaults, and intimidation from those who are supposed to love us. It is unfortunate that the family is often the place where emotionally abusive behavior is first learned. Emotional abuses experienced in childhood become a devastating legacy for the entire nation—for the betrayal of trust between parent and child leads the abused child to re-create similarly dysfunctional relationships in adult life, and the problem of emotional abuse expands exponentially.

Dominance and forced submission, harassment, and public or private humiliations are psychologically abusive and lower self-esteem. Both mental abuses and emotional threats may seem relatively minor when assessed incident by incident; they may even seem a normal part of growing up. But when taken collectively, or when repeated with recurrent frequency over time, they definitely become injurious. Emotion-laden projection, volatility, moodiness, inconsistencies, emotional manipulation, violent, chaotic, and unpredictable behavior are all ways in which the emotional bonding between individuals is misused. The withholding of love or approval, ignoring another, refusing affection, threats of abandonment, forced isolation, and other emotional deprivations are examples of how this natural human bond is negated or denied.

In situations or relationships in which emotional abuse is prevalent, there are typically periodic demonstrations of the abuser's superiority, of coldness, of anger, or of the potential for violence. These displays are coupled with occasional indulgences and periods of kindness and affection. Unfortunately, in the context of emotional tyranny, these indulgences prove to be abusive rather than kind—they feed the illusion that the emotional bonding has not actually been damaged or severed by the abuse, when, in fact, it has.

The pervasiveness of psychological abuse in our culture calls us to reexamine not only our societal values, but all of our social relations—whether between governments, co-workers, family members, or women and men—in light of our socially moral and ethical stance. Throughout the world, the United States is defined, not as a democratic society, but as a capitalistic society that values money above all else. It is revealing that most of the words in the English language that exemplify an ethical or moral commitment to other human beings have fallen into disuse in everyday conversation. Words like *loyal, kind, courteous, just, moral, conscientious, decent, principled, honorable, faithful, reliable, ethical, constant, integrity*—all seem to describe a bygone era in which life was both simple and (to us?) boring. Aré we, as a people, so addicted to the new, the improved, and the exciting that we have lost a sense of interpersonal ethics? Have we become blind to the effects on human life of our self-gratifying choices? If we are to put an end to further psychological abuse so that the quality of our lives is improved, these questions must be honestly answered.

It is now recognized that psychological abuse can occur in any human interaction in which there is a real, or perceived, power difference. Mental and emotional abusiveness by those seen as more powerful, and compliance by the others in the system, has been widely accepted as the norm. In counselling offices across the country, a multitude of abuses of social and personal power are being revealed by those who have been personally injured and are in need of healing. Resignation to the "pecking-order" is currently being challenged, and hierarchical structures of all kinds are being scrutinized for abuses of power.

When amends are not made, understanding and compassion are often sought by individuals in counselling sessions. Sadly, mentally and emotionally abused clients also report abuses from professionals they have previously consulted. It is therefore extremely important that the therapist, teacher, priest, physician, attorney, or other professional, acting for a time as mentor, take great care not to further victimize the client through a misguided (though well-meaning) attitude, belief system, language, style, or approach.

Treating Abused Clients

An individual whose trust has been repeatedly betrayed by being lied to, humiliated or demeaned is no longer sure of what is true. Once labelled as "neurotic," the abused client comes to counselling in a state of pained confusion and low self-esteem now clinically defined as "learned helplessness." Self-esteem is a result of having confidence in one's own perceptions, feelings, and sensations. Psychologically abused individuals who live within a culture that denies abuse commonly enter treatment with low self-esteem.

Some presenting symptoms that can alert the clinician to possible psychological abuse are self-condemnation, doubt, hopelessness, depression, lack of confidence, low energy, lack of direction and motivation, and a variety of physical complaints such as breathing difficulties, headaches, or digestion problems. These symptoms may appear to the professional to be due to any number of personal intrapsychic problems. Often, these clients have already consulted physicians who can find no physiological basis for their symptoms. They may have been prescribed mood-altering medications as a palliative measure. The possibility of psychological abuse has probably been ignored. All of the presenting symptoms may, however, appear wholly as a result of abusive acculturation, and are not necessarily a sign of neurosis or personal psychological disturbance. In these cases, the counsellor would do well to inquire into the possibility of mental or emotional abuse as a causative factor.

If abuse is suspected, the counsellor should begin whatever detective work is necessary to uncover the source of the difficulty. It is important to find out who abused the client—parent, spouse, sibling, co-worker, friend, therapist, boss, neighbor, or other intimate—when, and how. It is then valuable to acknowledge the source of abuse and actually name it as abuse so that denial can be overcome and the client can know that his or her report is believed. This acknowledgement builds self-esteem because, when correctly ascertained, it corresponds to the client's lived experience, thus providing the previously missing validation. Only after the outer abuse is acknowledged can questions of inner compliance be intelligently addressed.

The validation of factual information is empowering simply because it acknowledges the truth of what actually happened. From admitting the truth, the client again begins to build trust and self-esteem. Feelings of self-worth re-emerge. The power that the abuse has held over the individual's life is recognized, thus enabling him or her to become the "survivor" of the situation. He or she no longer feels compelled to be a part of the cultural conspiracy of silence that surrounds psychological abuse. Sometimes the client is able to confront the abuser. Even when confrontation is not possible or appropriate, these clients learn that they need no longer tolerate psychological abuse from others.

Stages of Healing

The social interactions of modern life afford many opportunities both for psychological enrichment and for psychological injury. Some people are able to withstand such injuries to a greater degree than are others. These people generally have a support system of understanding friends to help them through difficult times. Others, however, reach a limit in which their former ability to cope with recurrent insults and rejections is no longer adequate. As a general rule, these people close down emotionally, become cynical, withdraw from intimate social contacts, or become abusive themselves. Or they seek help through counselling hoping to deal with their problems and put an end to the pain.

Like those with physical wounds, those with psychological wounds go through various stages in the process of healing. In treatment, an individual may stay several months (or even years) in one stage, be in a different stage from one session to the next, or change stages within a single counselling session. Counselling interventions, to be helpful, must be stage-specific, as will be explained below. I have observed seven distinct stages of healing in my 15 years of practice as a psychosynthesis guide. They are offered here as a guideline for psychologically abused individuals, as well as for those who counsel them. The need for mental and emotional healing that is being addressed here presupposes the occurrence of an intolerable number of interpersonal wounds in an individual's life.

Stage 1—The first stage of healing can be called "Coping." This is the stage in which survival is the major motivator. Typical in this stage is a sense of overresponsibility, self-blame, denial, guilt, shame, fear, silent grief, extreme stress, attempts to gain control, or an inappropriate grandiosity in which the abused individual imagines having greater power over the situation than is possible. When clients enter counselling at this stage, the issues to be addressed are very basic ones: personal safety, elimination of self-blame, physical health, nutrition, exercise, social support systems, work, and financial stability.

Stage 2—The second stage is that of "Awakening" to the abuse. In this stage, there is a need for a great deal of honest self-disclosure, and for a reporting of wounding experiences in a non-judgmental environment. In Stage 2, clients admit, perhaps for the first time, that they have been abused. They often need to ventilate feelings of anger, outrage, and sadness. In this stage of the healing process, it is appropriate for clients to condemn the abuser, become active on behalf of themselves and others in similar situations, and express open grief for what has been lost. Self-validation is begun at this point. New injuries experienced when the client is in this stage of healing are deeply felt, and can serve to keep the client in Stage 2 for an extended length of time. This stage of emerging awareness is clearly marked by a recognition that things are not the way they seem. This is the stage that breaks through the pattern of denial.

Stage 3—In the third stage, "Patterning," the intrapsychic patterns of the client's life are recognized and addressed. These can include issues of truthfulness, trust, control, co-dependence, responsibility, love, self-esteem, boundaries, spontaneity, risk, commitment, will, assertion, spiritual surrender, patience, forgiveness, and self-nurture. This is the stage in which the major personal therapeutic work is done, assisting abused clients to discover their own self-limiting patterns and to come to an understanding of their own truths.

Stage 4—The fourth stage can be called "Transformation." This is the stage in which the slow process of self-acceptance is begun in earnest. The client comes to accept both limitation and potential in Stage 4. Forgiveness toward the abuser may occur, accompanied by the realization that this forgiveness releases resentment and is a part of the healing process. A spiritual perspective naturally emerges when this stage is not prematurely forced. With this comes a suspension of old belief systems and a greater acceptance of life as it is.

Stage 5—In the fifth stage, "Integration," the patterns worked through in Stage 3 come up again to be fully integrated into the client's daily life, but in a new way. This stage can be disheartening when it is not understood. There is a tendency to mistake it for a setback. In fact, in psychosynthesis counselling work, the fifth stage results in active co-operation with the will of the Self and is considered quite positive. At this stage of healing, it is useful for the counsellor to help the client cultivate a sense of proportion and the capacity to hold paradox.

Stage 6—The sixth stage is that of "Synthesis." In this stage, individuals who have been mentally and emotionally abused begin to see their relationship to the abuse in a new way, and the problem is then perceived as the "gift" that has led them on the path of self-discovery. The former abuse, though remembered and important, is no longer an issue. At the sixth stage, there is a gratitude for the truth and the new life that has emerged from the abusive experience. There is a deepening and greater appreciation of life. Here real acceptance takes place.

Stage 7—In the last stage, "Healing," the abuse is just one of many events of the past. The client's focus is now on the present and the future. Taking the lessons learned about themselves, other people, and the world, clients go forward, with greater wisdom, acceptance, and capacities for discernment. At this stage, the healing cycle is complete.

However well-meaning, counsellors can be harmful to psychologically damaged clients by remaining unaware of the stages outlined here. Some approaches to therapy that utilize a specific technique or method are excellent for clients in a particular stage of healing, but may prove detrimental if the client is in another stage. For instance, a Stage 3 therapy intervention is not really useful for a client still at Stage 1, as it only magnifies the tendency to overresponsibility and self-blame. In addition, interventions appropriate for a client at Stage 6 are wholly inappropriate for a client currently at Stage 2. Counselling is rarely initiated at Stage 4 or 6, so methods useful at these stages are not immediately beneficial for beginning work—even when the client aspires to view life from a "spiritual" perspective. It is important to remember that an intervention which is not stage-specific can, in fact, be harmful.

When we contemplate abuses in counselling, we first think of sexual seduction or financial misconduct. However, clients more often report abuses of a psycho-social nature. Counsellors are only human. In a sexist society, they must be consciously trained to view social interaction in non-sexist terms. In a hierarchical society, they must learn egalitarianism. These things are not often learned in the context of professional training, nor are they required for licensing. They must be learned in the field.

Some counselling trainees are still taught in school that the recipient of abuse is, in all probability, the covert victimizer. Those who are abused are considered responsible for the abuse by "asking for," encouraging, or, in the popular theory of secondary gain, even enjoying being abused. The social inequity in which the abuse is taking place is not seen as relevant. If not considered directly responsible for their own abuse, mentally and emotionally abused clients are judged responsible indirectly for putting up with it. Those who "blame the victim," as this attitude is now termed, subtly collude with the abuser, and by doing so, further damage the self-esteem of an already psychologically abused individual. Such outdated notions are not in line with current findings and are in need of revision.

Even in the newer transpersonally-oriented counsellor training, there are certain philosophical assumptions that prove detrimental to clients who have been previously mentally or emotionally abused. Particularly troublesome is the concept, "there is no victim, no victimizer." The idea of no-fault abuse is, for the wounded client, blatantly untrue and adds to the ever-present tendency to deny and repress. This idea is often elaborated to suggest that all experiences, no matter how horrible, were, in fact, "chosen" by the client, and that he or she is 100 percent responsible for creating the abusive reality. The intention of this philosophy is self-empowerment. However, in practice with psychologically wounded clients, this attitude actually is the spiritualized version of "blaming the victim." For those clients not yet free from the effects of abuse, this concept leads to further self-flagellation, frustration, depression, self-doubt, guilt, diminished self-esteem, and feeds into the inappropriate grandiosity common within the early coping mechanisms that deny that abuse is a problem. Others question why they have chosen to "draw to themselves" such abuse. Accepting the idea of a completely self-created reality, abused clients label themselves hopelessly neurotic. As part of the denial, they may continue an abusive relationship, imagining quite unrealistically that they have the power to change it since they created it, that they can transcend the pain, or that when they "get" what they need to learn from the situation, the abuse will stop. While a positive attitude can always be of help, the truth is that with greater tolerance, psychological abuse does not stop—it escalates over time. Psychosynthesis theory would suggest that *total* responsibility is simply the polarity of *no* responsibility, and that the truth is found elsewhere.

Responsibility is said to be "response-ability," or the ability to respond. Clients who have been chronically abused have a weakened or diminished ability to respond on their own behalf, and so they seek assistance. They must be listened to and given appropriate help, without imposed concepts.

Victim-blaming attitudes are not new. They were originally incorporated into Western psychology by Freud, who blamed incest victims for their own seduction, and discounted reports of familial rape as fantasized wish-fulfillment, leaving the more powerful adult beyond reproach, and the child-victim psychologically victimized as well. We now know that forced incest is a social reality, yet the absurd conclusion that the child is somehow responsible for its occurrence is still held as valid in orthodox psychoanalytic practice. Even more insidious, and more difficult to prove otherwise, are victim-blaming attitudes toward those who have been psychologically raped. Unfortunately, in our society, and therefore in our traditional graduate training of professional counsellors, those who exploit the less powerful are not usually considered the problem.

There is never any reasonable justification for mental or emotional abuse, no matter how provocative one might judge the child or adult victim to be. It makes us all uncomfortable to admit the possibility that there might be abusive people among us, that our own abusiveness may not have been justified, that as adults we really are accountable for our own behavior. We seem to have a kind of "emperor's new clothes" mentality, protecting powerful individuals by denying their nakedness. Because of this, attitudes which blame the less powerful for their own abuse are pervasive in our culture. Those who are called upon to intervene therapeutically, in abuse cases in particular, must be completely free of all victim-blaming attitudes.

Similarly, because mentally and emotionally abused clients have been injured by those who have taken a position of dominance over them, approaches in which the counsellor acts as the "expert," the authority, the harsh confronter, or the behavior-modifier are not useful. Abused clients need to be drawn out with compassion and respect, not pushed, confronted, or told what do do. They must learn to become their own authority.

The Psychosynthesis Approach

Because mental and emotional abuse is so pervasive, and because its scars are invisible except in times of stress, it is not easy to recognize or to understand it. Through its broad-based, client-centred, non-judgmental approach, psychosynthesis counselling can provide this understanding. In Psychosynthesis, the client remains his or her own expert. Over 75 years of clinical research continues to convince psychosynthesis practitioners that even the most eloquent theories are only guidelines for actual clinical work. Every case is unique; practitioners learn from each client.

Psychosynthesis practitioners are called "guides," as that most accurately describes the facilitative work that is done. The guide simultaneously leads and follows the healing process, being actively present to this process without attempting to modify or control it. In addition to clinical counselling and psychotherapy, psychosynthesis-oriented consultants work within many vocations such as education, medicine, business, the arts, law, social services, international relations, and the clergy. If we are to alleviate mental and emotional abuse, this multidisciplinary approach is invaluable.

Psychosynthesis guides are trained to evoke and to trust the individual's inner guiding principle, called the Self, as the expert witness in his or her life. By referring to the Self, the guide is always able to see hope, no matter how frightening, painful, or horrific the client's experience of abuse. The guide remains aware that there is much more to the individual than his or her history of victimization. For psychologically abused clients, this perspective itself, which accommodates the pain of abuse while adding a broader context, is healing.[1]

The characteristically broad perspective of Psychosynthesis encourages self-help through self-acceptance. The elimination of denial and the development of self-acceptance are crucial in healing psychological wounds for both victims and perpetrators of abuse. With recognition and acceptance, the stages of the healing process are allowed to unfold in their own time and in their own way. Trusting the individual process of each client rather than following one particular method proves, paradoxically, to be an efficient method of treatment. Change has been observed to occur in a timely fashion when the natural rhythm of each person is honored. Clients who have been repeatedly mentally and emotionally battered are not accustomed to this degree of loving interest and respect. They are nourished by such treatment and are quick to respond.

Because the psychological wounds of each person are different, there is no universal formula for treatment. The psychosynthesis approach proves especially effective for victims of mental and emotional abuse in its recognition of this fact and in the multiplicity of techniques available for use within the counselling session. The techniques specific to Psychosynthesis, learning self-trust and disidentification, balancing and synthesizing polarities, and developing a sense of personal values, are particularly meaningful to these clients. Guides are taught many methods for centring the Self and for accessing their own inner guidance. These techniques are described in the psychosynthesis training literature.

Though individual guides may be more proficient with, or prefer using, some techniques over others, they are not wedded to a specific method and to its limitations. Inner dialogue, visualization, meditation, guided imagery, grief work, assertion training, gestalt technique, couples counselling, interpersonal communication, family systems work, art therapy, feminist education, massage, will training, spiritual development, and existential dialogue have all been used successfully in the treatment of the wounds of psychological abuse.

I have also had success with the few self-defined abusers I have had the opportunity to counsel. As they proved to have been abused as children, they benefitted from comparable methods of treatment in their psychosynthesis sessions. Their greatest need was to heal from the psychological scars of their own childhoods. Except in cases of genuine social pathology or dire biochemical imbalance, abusive behavior may be a reaction to previous abuse, and can be considered a learned behavior. Some of these clients also displayed addictive/co-dependent tendencies. Both addictive and enabling behaviors may be ineffective means for trying to cope with psychological abuse and alienation. Through psychological introjection, this could also be the case with psychologically self-abusive behaviors such as excessive self-criticism, guilt, and perfectionism. When these wounds are healed, positive changes take place.

Stopping Abusive Interactions

Mental and emotional abuse is ultimately stopped by a change within the abuser, not by a change within the abused. As in any system, change on the part of one participant does have some effect; when abusers are reported or rejected by their victims, they do take notice of that fact. However, victims of abuse do not have the power themselves to change abusers or to change their psychologically abusive behaviors.

In cases of reported physical or sexual abuse, the perpetrator is most often an adult male. However, in cases of mental and emotional abuse, both men and women have been shown to be abusive. They may justify their abusiveness by seeing themselves at the mercy of outside provocation, or of uncontrollable moods. They believe that if others acted in line with their often unreasonable demands, there would be no need to be abusive to them. With this belief system in place, those who are repeatedly abusive continue to injure loved ones, employees, and even strangers, denying the need for change and refusing offers for intervention. This leaves those who must deal with them in a difficult position: stay and be abused, or leave the relationship. There is rarely room for negotiation.

Psychosynthesis may view the abusive individual as "stuck," perhaps for very understandable reasons, in a limiting personal identification. The pattern may often be one of emotional abuse in childhood resulting in a lost sense of integrity, values, and meaning. While seeking respect and needing love, they become isolated from others and are atheistic or spiritually empty as a result of their experience. They display either frozen or volatile feelings, causing others to act fearfully around them, offering co-dependent contrition. Rarely are they met straightforwardly as persons. Those abusers I have seen were very outwardly focussed and seemed to lack introspection. They were reared in dysfunctional families or attended schools where they were severely punished or abused in the ways they abuse others. Those who become abusive are in need of deep healing. For most, unfortunately, this healing never takes place.

One abusive client who was assisted through a psychosynthesis approach was a black male in his forties, initially referred to me for counselling with his wife who complained of his violent temper, and worried that his harsh punishment of their adolescent son might cause permanent psychological scars. At work, the man was competent and personable, a top salesman for a major company, and reported no interpersonal problems there. Since the problem of his abusive behavior seemed to be focussed on his family, counselling was done with this man individually, with him and his wife together, and with their 7-year-old daughter. The adolescent son refused to come.

The turning point occurred in a session in which a spontaneous form of guided hypno-therapeutic regression was utilized to access the history of the client's abusive behavior. In deep relaxation, he recalled that he had been physically and emotionally abused as a child. With deep feeling, he fully accepted this wounded Inner Child. He then remembered that his parents had been similarly abused, as were his grandparents on his mother's side of the family. (This information came from piecing together personal experience, family stories, and subconscious connections.) He revealed that both his great-grandparents and his great-great-grandparents were African slaves of American Confederate tobacco plantation owners in the South. As slaves, they were beaten and degraded and were, in turn, abusive to their own children. He then realized that the abusive behavior of his ancestors served their children as a form of insurance for survival on the plantation and in the slave markets into which they were sold or abducted. Those blacks who were strong-willed, independent, outspoken, or otherwise "uppity" were, in fact, killed. The client further became aware of the fact that, although the Emancipation Proclamation was signed over a century ago, his children were, in actuality, the first generation of his family to have the education, freedom of speech, and equality promised by the Constitution. His own children, unlike himself, were at last freed from the restraints of segregation and it was, therefore, no longer necessary for their survival to keep them "down." He experienced deep relief when he received this internal message.

Through the awareness gained in this psychosynthesis session, this client was able to stop his abusive behavior and ask forgiveness of his wife and children. It must be emphasized that this man had been personally damaged by cultural racism and that this most certainly contributed to his behavior toward his family. Recognition of that fact served to raise his self-esteem, allowed him to acknowledge his abusive behavior, and gave him more control over his own life.

Abusive interactions can sometimes be stopped by helping abusers become accountable for their mentally and emotionally abusive behaviors. Although not responsible for the abuse they received in childhood, they become responsible for the abuse they inflict on others in adulthood. Avoidance and denial serve no one. Some among us have become unwitting tyrants. If given socially sanctioned alternatives, a percentage of these people do take the opportunity to change unworkable patterns. Psychosynthesis, with its emphasis on developing potential, proves to be a particularly useful approach for those ready for self-responsible change.

Case Study

The case history that follows is taken from a psychosynthesis session with a 32-year-old woman who had a long history of both mental and emotional abuse. The woman had recently relocated to the area following a particularly difficult divorce, and had not, as yet, established a support system of friends. She was an active Catholic, and a feminist, and had already spent several years in Stage 2 of her healing process.

This was her fourth psychosynthesis session, and the first session in which she was able to imagine the healing of her psychological wounds. At this juncture, the technique of guided affective imagery was used. As this excerpt illustrates graphically, it is not atypical for those who have been mentally and emotionally abused to experience their wounds as though they were physical injuries. Psyche and soma are more intertwined than we generally acknowledge.

Guide: Close your eyes and allow an image to come of your injured self . . .

Client: Female, my age, and all bent over on herself, holding her entire front body, from chin to knees . . . it is all injured.

Guide: Would she be willing to allow us to see the extent of her injuries?

Client: Yes. She opens up just to show us. Ooow! It is all red and raw, all the flesh from chin to knees. Seems just like a shark or some huge beast had taken a bite right out of the front of her! (pause) It really is a bad open wound. She needs to close up now because the air makes the wound sting.

Guide: Does actually seeing the wound give you any further information?

Client: Just one thing. About rejection. And my mother. Seeing the wound somehow made me see that my mother rejected everyone, not just me—that the rejection wasn't personally directed at me. I understand that now, but that doesn't really change the wound. It's too late for that . . .

Guide: Yes, it is a bad wound. (pause) Can it be healed?

Client: No, it can't. It's a fatal wound.

Guide: I see. (pause) Has there ever been a cure for such a wound, or will there be a cure in the future?

Client: Well, yes. There will be a cure in the future. Medical technology will one day be able to extract from fatality victims the pure essence of love, just as they now take eyes and hearts and lungs for transplant. . . . Love is the only cure for a wound like mine. Just as they can tell the good eyes and lungs from the bad ones, they will be able to tell which people have good love—like children and loving parents—and they can remove it from the person and distill it into its pure essence. Then injured people, like me, can be treated with this pure essence of love.

Guide: Can you imagine that you are in that future time and receive the love treatment for your wounds?

Client: Yes. (pause) Yes. The treatment works so that I live. I am left with rather thick scar tissue, but I am alive.

Guide: What's it like to have this scar tissue?

Client: Well, it's rather sobering to know that I'll never be as freely joyful, as open, as trusting, as naïve, or as vulnerable as I was before. It's as though my childhood purity is really gone for good now. (pause) They have been gone for a long time, actually. I feel a little sad about that. But mostly, I'm glad to be alive—even with the scar tissue . . . and loss of innocence.

Guide: What is sad about the loss of innocence?

Client: Well, you know. (pause) It would be better if we could live in a world that lets us stay innocent and pure. It's such a sweet feeling. But it seems that isn't really possible in this world, so I'm glad to be alive.

Guide: Even with the loss of innocence, you are grateful to be alive.

Client: Yes, very grateful. Very thankful. I know I'm going to be okay now.

And she was right. The full extent of her mental and emotional wounds were then recognized and acknowledged. She realized for the first time that these wounds were not fatal, and began moving through further stages of healing.

After five months of psychosynthesis counselling, this client, who had been repeatedly psychologically abused and betrayed both in childhood and as an adult, went on to establish new and supportive relationships. She was able, at last, to allow herself to be loved and then love in return. By reaching out in her own way, she once again began to trust in love. By coming to psychosynthesis counselling as her own best expert, she initiated the process that would eventually cure her wounds. With guidance, and the support of her friends, she was able to move through all seven stages of the healing process in a relatively short time. As her counsellor, I must conclude that she seemed to have known all along, "Love is the only cure for a wound like mine."

It is our clients that make the view from the counsellor's chair one of hope rather than despair. Though the pain is difficult to witness, the fact that mental and emotional abuses are beginning to be acknowledged and healed gives hope for a brighter future. Perhaps psychological abuses will not be routinely passed down to future generations if we continue the work of healing the wounds of those who have been abused—and if we encourage abusers to change their behavior and make amends—now.

Surveying the popular press and media, there are a few examples of groups and individuals beginning to work together in mutually empowering ways. In addition, the therapeutic and educational work of psychosynthesis guides and other consultants, the socially supportive work of various 12-Step programs, and the work of a few popular entertainers and musicians give nation-wide exposure to the ethic of positive human values and relation-ships. We need more healing and more popular examples if we are to change our cultural values and personal ethics in such a way that we may freely relate to one another, without fear of being oppressed or psychologically abused.

I end this article with a pertinent reminder from the originator of Psychosynthesis, the late Dr. Roberto Assagioli:

We are constantly influencing others, whether we are conscious of doing so or not, whether we desire to do so or not. And the more we are aware of this, the more we can see to it that our influence is beneficent and constructive.

Note

1. Guides must be careful not to minimize the problem by treating victims of mental and emotional abuse as though the problem were merely an unruly victim subpersonality to be integrated. The client may have developed certain subpersonalities to cope with aspects of the abusive situation. These can be worked with in Stage 3. Prior to that, victimization can be considered a social reality, not just an intrapsychic phenomenon. One must be very sensitive to those who have become mentally and emotionally disabled through psychological abuse in their interpersonal relationships, and take care not to minimize the problem.

The Addict Meditation

Jonathan P. Kessler

Truth is what the addict searches for . . . and as painful and perverse as the way may be, the addiction is their way to truth. It is the opening to themselves, profoundly committed to becoming conscious, they will not, cannot, give up until they know what it means. In the addiction is hidden the treasure—the knowledge of themselves—and they can take no other path toward it. It is their particular sacred journey, their tao, their way.

MARION WOODMAN (1985)

Individuals who are seeking recovery from an addiction, whether it be alcohol, drugs, food, sex, or gambling, must begin by acknowledging that the problem of their addiction exists. The first step in any self-help process includes these words, "We admitted we were powerless over alcohol, drugs, etc. . . . that our lives had become unmanageable" (Alcoholics Anonymous World Services, p. 1). We who are in the field of helping substance abusers must be committed to the idea that this recognition precedes an individual's exploration to find the hidden treasure within the addiction. In our culture, the stereotypes surrounding the addict have crystallized and have forced individuals to hide their own processes of self-discovery and emotional growth. Stereotypes which easily come to mind include "the obnoxious drunk," "the drug addict who would steal from his own family to get a fix," "the mousy introverted anorexic," "the greasy gambler who smokes fiendishly as he rolls the dice." Richard Knox states that "a broader view of addiction . . . must emerge which can embrace a whole spectrum of drugs and perhaps compulsive behaviors as well" (1986, p. 5). A comprehensive theory of addiction which can bring to light the dedicated search of the addict for his or her truth must be forthcoming in order to break the destructive cycles of addiction in our society.

Basic Concepts

In using the Addict Meditation, several basic premises must be established. First, one must consider that many individuals who become drug or alcohol dependent have adopted cyclical forms of behavior which inhibit their emotional growth. These people have stumbled into a repetitive pattern of existence in order to ward off their emotional pain. One could make the claim that the addiction is not merely to the substance itself, but to the fear of growth and change. It is my experience that during the course of recovery these individuals demonstrate a deep and unresting need for emotional healing and spiritual enlightenment. According to Marion Woodman, "An

30

addict attempts to fill a terrible emptiness inside. But it is a spiritual emptiness, not a physical one" (1985, p. 4).

Arthur Deikman in *The Observing Self* makes the point that "the pervasive use of alcohol, sedatives and narcotics in our society might well reflect many people's attempts to suppress despair at their purposelessness, and to substitute heightened sensation for meaning" (1982, p. 7). E. F. Schumacher adds that "human beings need meaning. Without it, they suffer boredom, depression, and despair." He continues, "Man's happiness is to move higher, to develop his highest faculties, to gain knowledge of the highest things, and if possible to 'see God.' If he moves lower, develops only his lower faculties, which he shares with the animals, then he makes himself deeply unhappy, even to the point of despair" (1977, p. 12). For the addict, reaching "the highest" seems to be an impossible undertaking. It is easier to maintain a lifestyle which is familiar though painful. The addict, according to Frank Haronian, "fears growth because it means abandoning the familiar for the unknown and that always involves risk" (1972, p. 2). Abraham Maslow stated it this way: "We are generally afraid to become that which we glimpse in our most perfect moments, under the most perfect conditions. . . . we enjoy and even thrill to the godlike possibilities we see in ourselves at such peak moments. And yet we simultaneously shiver with weakness, awe and fear before these same possibilities" (1966, p. 4).

The concept of reaching for the higher qualities of life is the basis to the self-help recovery programs in existence today. These programs include Alcoholics Anonymous, Narcotics Anonymous, and Sex and Love Addicts Anonymous. The first tenet (or step) in these programs is *admitting* that due to the addiction or the addictive behavior the individual's life has become unmanageable. The second step emphasizes the higher reaches that the addict is searching for. For example, the second step of the Alcoholics Anonymous 12-step program is, "I came to believe that a power greater than myself could restore me to sanity." This is followed by a third step which is, "I made a decision to turn my will and my life over to the care of God as I understand him" (Alcoholics Anonymous World Services, p. 1).

The first three steps provide an opportunity for the addicted individual to lay the foundation for later spiritual development. The basic tenets of these programs can thus be seen to parallel James Vargiu's five phases of subpersonality integration.

The Addict Meditation may be seen to assist the individual in identifying subpersonalities that play a part in his or her addiction. In his article "Subpersonalities," Vargiu claims that "the solution lies not in disowning but in including the subpersonality" (1974, p. 58). For years, we have shut out the addict as being of no value. But we should hold to a second truth, which is that those individuals who are addicted to compulsive forms of behavior are operating on a limited self-definition.

One can see this at, for example, Narcotics Anonymous meetings when an individual introduces himself and says, "Hello, my name is Joe, I'm an addict." This is, in fact, a falsehood. Joe may have many selves. Joe may have within him a subpersonality which is a Seeker of Truth, a Scared Child, a Critic, a Father, a Son. This distinction is vital in assisting the addict with an opportunity for recovery. Though it is a simple concept, it can be the most difficult to grasp. An addict who is involved in a program may come to rely on the definition of himself as an alcoholic or drug addict so as to avoid looking deeper into his own mirror of fear and confronting the pain/joy of growth.

To sum up, then, the theoretical base of the Addict Meditation relies on the concept of subpersonalities. It is only through the meeting, recognition, acceptance, and eventual synthesis of the addict within the soul that a person can recover. The Addict Meditation offers the individual in recovery an opportunity for deeper exploration into his many selves. It is the responsibility of the therapist to provide an environment of healing and light in which the addict is encouraged to take a deep look into himself and his gift. The therapist must recognize, however, that a dynamic between the Addict, Critic, and the Scared Child may also be present and may take the form of a secret agreement between these three subpersonalities.

The Process

If one evaluates the triangulated relationship between the subpersonalities with an eye toward the power of each, one can see the change which may occur during the process of substance use. When the individual is not under the influence, the Critic maintains the overriding power within the system. The Child, left unprotected by the Addict, experiences the least amount of power. The Child may recognize many needs and fears, and a great deal of dissatisfaction, as its opportunities for self-expression are consistently thwarted by the Critic.

In response, the Child takes refuge within the Addict which gradually becomes a separate force to be reckoned with. The Addict becomes increasingly capable of dominating the Critic—in the guise of providing the Child with more and more opportunities for expression. (This is particularly true for those individuals who suffer from physical forms of addiction, e.g., heroin, cocaine, and other kinds of narcotics.) Once this occurs, there is a constant push by the Addict-Child to return to using [the substance], thus increasing disequilibrium in the system.

During the initial phase of getting high, the Child may experience a quieting of the Critic's overbearing presence. However, for many users, the experience of guilt and increased pain after use re-empowers the Critic. Thus, the Child who initially felt scared and powerless, has now inadvertently given the Critic even more fuel. These feelings of powerlessness are repeatedly reinforced by the Critic while the Addict abandons the Child once again to the familiar harassment.

To demonstrate, let us take an example of an individual who smokes pot three to five times a week. She recognizes that she is unsure why she uses marijuana and acknowledges some desire to stop. She claims that she is aware that she enjoys getting high, and yet there is a degree of discomfort that she experiences both while under the influence and afterward.

If we dissect this experience, we can see that, initially, the Scared Child may be neglected and in extreme cases totally dominated by the Critic. In this case, one can see that the addict and the critic subpersonalities are embroiled in a power struggle for domination of the system. The Addict has in some way convinced the Child that while under the influence there is nothing to worry about, that performance doesn't matter, that relief is only found through the use of the substance. The Addict-Child, thus, uses the substance to dis-empower the Critic and then experiences this as a false sense of freedom, integrity, and power. Michael Elkin in *Families Under the Influence* states, "Alcohol becomes a short-term cure for rejection and loneliness. This, combined with its ability to cure powerless feelings, certainly makes it seem a boon to an alienated and insecure [individual]" (1984, p. 45).

The Process Explained

Vargiu (1974) bases his theory of subpersonalities on five phases: (1) recognition, (2) acceptance, (3) co-ordination, (4) integration, and (5) the synthesis of the subpersonalities. In the Addict Meditation, one provides an opportunity for individuals to meet, greet, and explore various parts of themselves. It is a directive meditation which can be used repeatedly or singularly to facilitate the healing of an individual. It is my personal belief that all of us have within us an addict subpersonality—a part of ourselves that is addicted to emotional experiences which inhibit our true expression of soul and psychic energy.

In the Addict Meditation, individuals introduce (1) a part of themselves which they know very well and present to the world, (2) the critic subpersonality which generally maintains power within the system, and (3) the addict subpersonality which is responsible for the care, protection, and expression of the Scared Child's needs. A separate meeting of the child subpersonality is not indicated within the meditation. However, it is important for the guide to note that the Child may, in fact, be found within the Addict as the meditation process unfolds. It is vital that the guide provide the individual with an environment of safety. This kind of exploration into the psyche can promote growth as well as frighten the individual.

The first subpersonality individuals will meet is a part of themselves that they know very well. This provides individuals with an understanding of the basic assumptions which they make about themselves. It is a part which is familiar and yet helps to assure later recognition of other subpersonalities within the system.

The second subpersonality which the client will be asked to meet is the Judge-Critic. The Critic prevents the individual from growth. While trying to protect the Child from harm, the Critic also may provide the Addict-Child with an irrational reason to continue use (e.g., using out of spite). With the use of a substance, the Critic becomes quiet and allows the Child's freedom of expression. This can be seen among individuals who have an afternoon drink or joint, and then are able to "relax." Generally, these individuals overidentify with the critic subpersonality. The denial of the fear of growth helps, in many ways, to foster the continued use of the substance . Through disidentification from the Critic, one can begin to recognize the imbalance within the system.

The third and final aspect of this meditation involves the introduction of the individual to their addict subpersonality. The Addict-Child is often seen as the scapegoat for problems and may suffer over issues of self-worth and self-esteem. The paradox is that as the individual continues to try to disown the Addict, the Addict fights back harder for life. First viewing the Addict from a distance, then making eye-contact, and then bringing the Addict inside may show individuals the Child who is looking for power and relief. The question which may be raised by that Scared Child is, "Am I really worthy of love and attention?" Clearly, the Child wants growth, but is terribly afraid of taking the step toward health without the protection of the Addict. The therapist must gently move the individual away from this experience by asking the individual that he or she be ready to receive the gift the Addict may bring. With repeated use of the meditation, one may find that the Addict's gift, originally a symbol or word, is the integration and eventual synthesis of the subpersonality into the psyche.

The Addict Meditation

1. Begin by asking the client to sit with both feet on the floor in a comfortable position with eyes closed.

2. Guide the client through a body-, feeling-, and thinking-relaxation exercise. (This helps to create a sense of calmness and of inner balance for the journey.)

3. Ask the client to find a place of safety and comfort. This should be done by suggesting a place of his or her own choosing where he or she feels secure, comfortable, nurtured, and loved.

4. Suggest that the client imagine this sanctuary being lifted to a beautiful field of open grass. The sun is shining, a blue sky dominates, a light breeze is blowing . . .

5. In this space, ask the client to become aware of the part of him or herself that is watching the process unfold. Suggest that this is their Observer, a non-judgmental part just watching the process unfold.

6. Having established the Observer, suggest to the client that a familiar part of him or herself is beginning to move toward the sanctuary. Guide the client through the different stages of awareness as this subpersonality moves closer. Take the time to assist the client in registering the experience on a physical, emotional, and mental level.

7. Allow for this part to move past the Observer, guiding the client to notice any of his or her reactions. Throughout the exercise, it is important to help the client to process verbally what is going on. The guide should encourage individuals to share their reactions on a physical, emotional, and mental level as they are being guided.

8. Suggest to the client that he or she allow for the familiar part to move off into the distance. Guide the client back to his or her sanctuary. Allow for any discharge of emotion or physical discomfort to be released by asking the client to return to the state of equilibrium noted by the Observer.

9. After this calmness has been acknowledged, ask the client to turn again to the horizon to observe another part of him or herself approaching. Suggest

that this is an extremely critical part which has qualities of both self-depre-cation and the ability to criticize and judge others.

10. As this subpersonality begins to move toward the sanctuary, ask the client to focus on his or her physical, emotional, and mental experiences. Allow a significant period of time for this meeting to take place and then suggest that the client let the Critic move on.

11. Assist the client in returning to the sanctuary, to a state of equilibrium.

12. Again, suggest that the client look to the horizon and be aware of another part of him or herself moving closer. Suggest that this aspect is their Addict. Begin this exploration from a distance. Ask the client to be conscious of what is experienced when the Addict is viewed from afar. Assist the client by asking for a physical description—what he or she is wearing, how he or she is standing.

13. Slowly guide the client to bring the Addict toward the Observer and to a place of safety. It may be too threatening for the individual to experience the Addict close up. Guide the client, again, through reactions in his or her physical, emotional, and mental body. From whatever distance seems safe, suggest to the client that he or she make eye-contact with the Addict. Once eye-contact is established, assist the client, again, by processing the experi-ence on the three levels of existence. Suggest to the client that he or she deepen that contact by allowing the Addict an opportunity to say what it is that the Addict is experiencing. Provide the client with an opportunity to share with the Addict what the experience of viewing is like.

14. If possible, guide the client to bring the addict subpersonality within the sanctuary of safety. Suggest to the client that the Addict has a gift. Suggest that this is an opportunity to receive this gift. (You may suggest that the gift may come in the form of a feeling, symbol, word, or a statement.)

15. Again, help the client to process the experience on a physical, emo-tional, and mental level.

16. Allow ample time for this process to flow and gradually suggest to the client that it is time to move on. However, you may also suggest that the client has an option to allow the Addict to move on or to stay. Help the client to process what the experience brings up, in either case.

17. Suggest to the client that he or she return to a state of security, calm-ness, and equilibrium within the sanctuary. Allow enough time to feel safe and comfortable.

18. Gradually, in the client's own time, suggest that he or she open his (or her) eyes and then process the experience with you.

The meditation may take anywhere from 20 to 45 minutes. It is suggested that ample time be allowed for processing the experience after the medita-tion has been completed. The debriefing should process what each indi-vidual subpersonality has brought up for the client, with particular attention to the Addict. As with any meditation, repeated use helps to bring about the healing process.

References

Alcoholics Anonymous World Services. *Twelve steps and twelve traditions*. New York: Author.

Deikman, A. J. (1982). *The observing self, mysticism and psychotherapy*. Boston: Beacon Press.

Elkin, M. (1984). *Families under the influence: Changing alcoholic patterns*. New York: W. W. Norton.

Haronian, F. (1972). The repression of the sublime. *P.R.F.*, **30**. (The Institute of Psychosynthesis, London).

Knox, R. A. (1986, Dec. 10). Cocaine's psychological addiction. *The Boston Globe*.

Maslow, A. H. (1966). Neurosis as a failure of personal growth. *Humanities*, **III**.

Schumacher, E. F. (1977). *A guide for the perplexed*. New York: Harper Colophon.

Vargiu, J. (1974). Subpersonalities. *Synthesis Journal*, **I**. (Redwood City).

Woodman, M. (1981, Dec./1986, Jan.). The Tarrytown letter.

Woodman, M. (1985). *The pregnant virgin*. Toronto: Inner City Books.

Setting the Captives Free: A New Approach

Kathleen Denison

Individuals who have been imprisoned are usually thought of as society's untouchables. Persons convicted of crimes such as murder, rape, child abuse, drug sales, theft, and embezzlement are incarcerated with little expectation of rehabilitation, let alone healing. The "lockup" serves its purpose and removes the offender from the streets. Until released, the offender is far removed from the mind and heart of the average person.

My work as prison chaplain the last few years has brought me into the heart of the reality that exists behind the bars. Not only have I walked into the physical environment that is called prison, but I have also walked into inner prison cells, and explored the depths of the psyche imprisoned there. This has been an exploration of the heart and of healing.

My work with prisoners has led to profound and dramatic changes in men and women who have been labelled "unredeemable." As I developed this work, I found that principles of Psychosynthesis assisted them in a process of psychic "liberation" which opened their inner selves to healing and enabled them to step from the darkness of their inner cells.[1]

In reflecting upon the relationship of the prisoner to the prison, it became clear that the outer prison environment actually mirrored the inner psychic environment of the inmates. Similarly, the inner psychic environment was reinforced by the outer setting.

The Outer Prison

A typical jail or prison environment is characterized by isolation from the outside world. Most jails or prisons are located in secluded spots and are surrounded by high barbed wire fences which clearly define the area that is set apart from the rest of society. Most inmates cannot see outside the prison building itself, since the bars on the windows and the frosted glass are intended to prevent any visibility to the outside. This seclusion is even more pronounced in some facilities which are designed to provide "outside recreation" in an entirely enclosed courtyard. Areas within the prison setting are securely locked and movement is limited. Visits from immediate family members are arranged for only a few hours on set days and phone calls are restricted. Incoming and outgoing mail is carefully monitored.

Inmates are classified according to their crimes and behavior, and are assigned to different levels of security. As an inmate becomes more threatening to the system, through a disregard of certain rules, greater isolation is imposed. A high security facility, for example, imposes the greatest isolation so that the risk of escape is minimized. Within the correctional system, segregation provides maximum seclusion as a form of punishment. An inmate is placed in a cold, dark cell with only a bed and a toilet. Visits from family are denied.

Almost all jails or prisons are devoid of beauty and natural light. Visually, prisons are ugly. Inappropriate color combinations assault the eye upon entering. A building may be painted yellow with black trim, or walls may be painted bright orange. Generally there are no trees, plants, or flowers within or around the building. The inmates are encased within smoke-filled rooms, surrounded by steel, concrete, and fluorescent lighting. There is no access to the healing aspects of nature. There is no room for beauty.

The sounds within the prison setting also assault the senses. The bang of steel doors or the loud clang of the bars sliding back into a locked position is constant. The barrage of abusive language is continual. Noise blares endlessly from multiple TVs. Loud speaker announcements successfully interrupt any meaningful speaking or listening. The buzz of fluorescent lights is constant. Solitude is not an option.

The prison environment is highly structured and highly controlled. Security is primary. Rules which safeguard this security dominate the needs of individual persons. The guards enforce the rules. These officers are predominantly young with minimal education and undeveloped social skills. They take their power seriously. In order to safeguard their own security, their power must be equated with control. The guards control the movement and monitor the behavior of the inmates. They carry the keys which can open or lock an area. The degree of an inmate's freedom, therefore, is dependent upon the co-operation of the guards. The inmates must acquiesce to the defined structure of rules and power in order to survive.

The prison culture is characterized by a lack of the feminine—a lack of feelings, sensitivity, and compassion. This is true for the inmates as well as the guards. Caring and sensitivity are considered a sign of weakness. Since such "weakness" results in the loss of power and status, toughness and hardness become the norm. Guards who are too compassionate cannot enforce the rules and are disdainfully considered by colleagues to be "inmate lovers." Inmates who do not have a tough exterior are easy prey to the demands of the tougher inmates. Their few commissary supplies are stolen and they are subject to constant harassment by other inmates.

Key to the prison culture is the attitude of the "keepers" toward the "kept." The attitude toward the inmate is often punitive and demeaning. Little respect is shown the inmate. Incarceration is seen as a just punishment. Verbal abuse and physical abuse between inmate and inmate and between guard and inmate are common. The inmates are treated like children, punished for the slightest disregard of a rule no matter how insignificant it is. Since everything is taken away from the inmate, anything needed must be requested from the guards or administration. There is no room for initiative or autonomy. The inmate is constantly told what to do and how to do it. The inmate no longer has to make any choices. All food, clothing, and shelter are provided. Dependency is fostered. Autonomy is neither encouraged nor tolerated.

As I worked with inmates, I discovered that although the dehumanized and dependent setting of the prison system is on one level highly uncomfortable, on another level it is familiar. Such a destructive and regressive environment is chosen by the individual on an unconscious level because it is familiar and therefore safe. Most inmates have experienced profound dehumanization in their own families, and the prison environment simply replays that history. Dependency is also chosen on an unconscious level because it means that care is finally being provided. In addition, the external pressures of life are temporarily removed. The inmate no longer has to deal with paying the rent or negotiating family and child demands.

The Inner Prison

Mirrored in the external environment of the prison setting, the inner prison begins to take shape. The parts of the individual that are considered unacceptable are repressed, isolated, and locked up. As in the external environment, the more threatening the aspect of the personality, the more restricted it becomes. The most dangerous subpersonalities are locked away, doing time in segregation and isolated from other aspects of the personality.

The inner prison environment is also highly structured and controlled. The inner psyche sets up rules to guarantee safety and appoints guards to monitor and enforce the rules and maintain control. Just as in the outer prison, the degree of freedom becomes dependent upon co-operation with the guards and acquiescence to the rules.

The inner guards take their positions very seriously. They will not allow themselves to experience compassion and sensitivity lest they lose power or become too identified with the "prisoner." In order to keep the prisoner in line, the inner guards may be punitive and demeaning. Internal verbal abuse may go on constantly.

Consequently, the core attitude toward the Self becomes punitive, restrictive, and harsh. Self-hate is predominant, and guilt and fear reinforce the hate. There is no room for compassion. There is virtually no real sense of self-worth and no experience of self-acceptance. There is also an innate distrust of Self, just as the prison guard distrusts the inmate.

Because the psychic guards carry the keys and hold the power, they become the "visible self" of the inmate, which is tough, macho, and intolerant of weakness. In essence, the outer system, the prison guards, and the inner guards collude to keep the "inner self safe." Ostensibly, the world is being kept safe and protected from the inner "monster."

But who lives in the inner cell? Each of my experiences with inmates has demonstrated that a Wounded Child lives behind the bars. This child is in pain. As I have progressed through this work, a consistent pattern has emerged. The inmates have usually experienced some sort of profound loss, rejection, abuse, or abandonment at a point of critical emotional vulnerability. This usually occurred when the inmate was a small child or young adolescent and experienced feelings of loss, abandonment, loneliness, terror, rejection, or emptiness. The psychic pain became so overwhelming that this part of the self was locked up to be kept safe from pain; the ability to feel was, and continues to be, anesthetized. The Child becomes isolated behind a wall of frozen feeling. He or she is placed in segregation. No one comes in and no one goes out. The Child is trapped and held hostage by the psyche's fear of pain. The walls are thick, cold, and unfeeling. The inner cell is dark and lonely.

Just as the inmate in the outer prison environment is subjected to a constant barrage of noise and abusive language, so too the inner child is constantly harassed by inner messages taken from parents and society. These messages interrupt any positive sense of worth and reaffirm feelings of worthlessness. The inner child begins to connect only with other psychic inmates who are also imprisoned and who have grown up with the same inner messages. The messages from the psychic prison culture are clear and consistent: "You are no good"; "I will not let you forget what you have done"; "You do not deserve to be trusted, loved, or cared for"; "You are worthless"; "You get what you deserve"; "It was something you did that got you here"; "You are an animal."

Time and time again, however, as I work with the Child imprisoned within, I discover that the Child is basically good—sensitive, spontaneous, and linked to the positive aspects of the Self. The Child is not a monster, but a victim who has been traumatized at a crucial development stage. In fact, it is acute psychic sensitivity that made the early formative experiences so traumatic.

In order to ensure the Child's survival, a Benevolent Judge orders protective custody. The original intention is one of survival and concern. The Child is put in a place where it will not be hurt again. This action is a direct indication of the psyche's drive toward health and wholeness. Although the protection is originally a loving act, what protects eventually imprisons. The protective mechanism cuts the Child off from further nourishment and he or she cannot grow. The positive aspects of the Self cannot be sufficiently developed.

The jailers, or guards, in the psyche simply carry out the sentence issued by the Benevolent Judge. The inner cell is tightly monitored so that the Child cannot leave, lest the pain be touched again. Security is primary and the jailers are constantly on guard for danger to the system. The Benevolent Judge is removed from the scene and the Child has no advocate.

My work with Philip, a 24-year-old man in prison, helps to illustrate the power of the jailer and the vulnerability of the Wounded Child within. I first met Philip in segregation. He was a victim of repeated beatings by his alcoholic father. He witnessed his father rape his mother and sister—both at his father's insistence that he watch. When Philip was 8, his mother turned her children over to the state since she planned to remarry. From that point on, Philip lived in numerous children's institutions. As he grew older, he began skipping school regularly. He became a chronic truant who was continually ordered by the court to spend time in a centre for juvenile delinquents. He would escape from the centre, steal a car for a joy ride, and then end up serving additional time in the correctional centre. This pattern matured into incarceration for car theft and drug usage. At the time I met him, Philip had served more than two years in medium security at a state prison. Shortly after we began to work together, he wrote me:

I don't really know if I can write you without you or myself getting into trouble. See, I've been here for two years and ten months and all of the time I never talked to anyone about my problems because I am scared to get close to anyone in here. . . . I can write my problems and my feelings down on paper better than I can talk about them. Because I am so used to it and after I write them down I read it over and over and then I throw it away so no one will find it. Some of the time I feel like crying but I hold it in, and hide it. And now that I am down here in lockup, I can think a lot better now because I'm alone and if I don't want to talk to anyone, I can just lie here and pretend like I'm sleeping.

I don't really know why I am writing you this letter cause I've been here so long! Have you ever heard of the saying that when you get hurt so many times you put up a wall so no one can get in? Well, my wall is up so high that it even scares me because if I don't open up to someone, then when I get out of here, I'm still going to have everything still inside of me, and believe me, I don't want to come back to this place.

After Philip was returned to the prison dorm, I was able to meet with him in a private room. I was concerned about his appearance. He looked hardened and unkempt. He explained that he had stayed in bed the last three days—not wanting to eat or even take a shower. He talked about his rage at his father. He had just learned that his father was coming back to live with his sister (the one the father had raped). All he could do was think about getting out and beating up his father. Nothing else mattered.

Philip and I began to work in meditation and guided imagery. He imagined an 8-year-old boy who was kept in a room by an older angry youth who would bully him. The younger boy felt lost, lonely, and rejected. He was sitting slumped in a dark corner. The younger boy wanted to talk to the bully, but his attempts were met with anger and physical abuse. The bully didn't want anyone to get near the boy. He kept him in the room and made it impossible for him to get out.

Philip's story is very typical of those told by the men I encountered at the prison. It illustrates the premise that the positive aspects of the psyche are imprisoned within inner cells, just as the individual is imprisoned within the institution. The wounded parts of the person contain incredible potential but he is too fearful and feels these parts are too despicable to approach or retrieve.

Another inmate, sentenced for selling drugs, wrote:

I feel like crying a lot, fighting back the pain and hurt I feel so much of . . . not willing to deal with the parts in me that are rotten, that I feel ashamed of. . . . The guilt is so overwhelming, so terrifying . . . I'm always thinking, can I find what of me is lost, or what is broken? I'm really just a child with so much to learn, so much to do, with no time, no freedom.

Given the main components of the inner prison, it becomes quite apparent that the set-up of the prison not only reinforces the inner wound but also makes real rehabilitation almost impossible. Ironically, the prison system seems to successfully re-create the inmate's past childhood environment of severe confinement and abuse. It gives credibility to the voices of self-negation, and encourages the power of the inner jailer. The inner child feels that the abuse is deserved. The prison system acts like a magnetic pull dragging the inmates back into what is most worthless and condemned within themselves. They are not trusted or believed. They are kept in their place within the inner prison. One 30-year-old male in a high security facility asked, "Why does this place put so much energy into making you feel like a nobody—an animal who can't escape his past? Why don't they put energy into making you feel human—giving you another shot? It's so frustrating in here because even though I change inside, I'm still treated the same way."

The Healing Process

Since the early world of the inmates was so unsafe, the introduction of a new inner environment which is safe is essential to the healing process. Inmates are first taught to imagine an environment where they feel safe and accepted. Often built upon childhood memories of a favorite place, their new place becomes a haven to which they can return, through imagination, at any time. Because it's safe, eventually this place becomes the inmate's "home base." As one inmate put it, "I'm in touch with who I really am. There are no cons. Wherever I am inside, I'm faced with it immediately. In this place I can only be myself."

Many imagine this place to be outside, in a setting of natural beauty such as at the ocean, or on a mountain. Others remember grandfather's attic, or their own bedrooms. The place provides a protective, serene environment where an individual can be alone, if desired, and content, without fear of intrusion. The unmasked self begins to have a place to "be." The place provides the security previously found only within the inner cell. Unlike the prison environment, the safe place emerges with color, light, warmth, and beauty.

Once the safe place is established, the inmate can begin to explore memories of past pain and rejection. What is wounded within can begin to be faced. Structured imagery sequences and attention to feeling begin to evoke this.

Working with inmates, I discovered that following a feeling was essential to the process of finding a wound. The frozen feeling, or wall of pain, insulates the wound within the psyche. As long as feelings are shut down, wounds can be ignored, even if life continues to be controlled by them. In an accepting environment where feelings are welcomed, the pain can begin to be experienced. Through the attention of compassionate listening, the frozen wall of feelings melts and flows to the source of the wound like a healing stream.

In ministering to individual inmates, I listen to the feelings under their words and their stories. I then invite them to explore a particular feeling such as anger, guilt, or loneliness, and encourage them to express it through words, images, or drawings. For example, the inmate is invited to explore an image evoked in response to the question, "What is the hurting part of you?" or "Who is the part of you that feels guilty, angry, lonely, etc.?" Invariably, the image evoked is that of a hurting child or adolescent. The inmate is then encouraged to dialogue with the hurting part and to listen to the feelings of the Child who has been isolated within the psyche.

Eventually, when it is safe enough, the inmate is able to actually *feel* the feelings and not just identify them. The use of imagery gives the inmate a means to explore the intensity of feelings that have long been buried. At the same time, imagery bypasses a mental exploration, which can define but does not feel. The combination of feeling and image is a very powerful means of arriving quickly at what is most in need of healing and acceptance within the psyche.

Part of the structured imagery process also involves re-creating former experiences of loss, abandonment, and rejection. Through guided imagery, the inmate is taught to step back and to begin to feel compassion for the part that is hurting. The inmates are given very explicit directions on how to take the Wounded Child to the safe place, and to image holding him, allowing tears to come. They are told to "give the child what is needed." The Child guides the inmate in the healing process.

After the inmate has identified the Wounded Child, he or she is taught to form a relationship with the Child. A bond is established which is compassionate and tender. After this relationship is firmly established, a new relationship is introduced. The inmate is invited to call in a Divine Friend to work with the Wounded Child. This Friend is experienced as unconditionally loving and accepting. The Friend will be either masculine or feminine depending upon the inner psychic needs of the individual. The gender is not prescribed but emerges through the meditation exercises. The Divine Friend image reinforces the channel of love developed through the relationship with the Child.

The Divine Friend becomes an outer figure which offers unconditional acceptance and love. The Friend is unafraid of feelings, encourages their expression, and makes no judgment about the outer self. Most frequently, the Divine Friend is experienced as Jesus or as Mary, the mother of Jesus. Many of the inmates have had early Christian training, and the request to call the Friend evokes these images. Crucial to this process is the visualization of a *personal* divinity.

This figure is not equivalent to the traditional guide in Psychosynthesis. The Divine Friend brings love rather than wisdom. It is an image used to reinforce a healing relationship and to evoke a renewed relationship to divine energy. The divine is invited to enter the core of the wounded self. The Divine Friend is able to model an ideal of loving acceptance. Healing proceeds as that core is further energized. The Divine Friend brings both light and warmth to the darkness of the inner prison. The inmate experiences the healing, the light, and the warmth. Change takes place from the centre outward.

The impact of this work on inmates has been striking. Most noticeable is the melting effect outlined above. The Divine Friend provides a deeper dimension of safety so that frozen feelings can be softened. An example of this is shown in the story of Karen.

Karen, an inmate in a women's correctional facility, was charged with sexually molesting her child. As is usually the case, she herself was the victim of incest. Through imagery, Karen visualized the 7-year-old victim of incest who was imprisoned within her. This child felt dirty, guilty, and unlovable. Since Karen was in need of feminine support and understanding,

I suggested that she invite Mary the mother of Jesus to come and be with her. Karen agreed to this. Mary came as a Divine Friend and gently invited Karen to allow herself to feel the guilt and pain of the child. As she began to cry from experiencing the pain, she also experienced the love and tenderness of Mary who held the 7-year-old child in her arms.

Previously, Karen had had difficulty getting close to the pain within her. With Mary present, she could let herself feel it because she felt safe. Tears came as they had never come before. After this experience, Karen struggled with why Mary would love her when her own mother hadn't. I encouraged her to express her struggle to Mary directly. She did this and her relationship with her Divine Friend deepened. On her own, she began to spend time with her inner 7-year-old in her safe place. Often she asked Mary to be present. Over a short period of time, Karen became less anxious, more connected to feeling, and more at peace with herself. She began to possess a new inner strength and softness. Equipped with a new sense of self-worth, she began to ask her Divine Friend to explore with her the parts of herself which she had imprisoned because they were unacceptable.

Later she wrote to me,

> I learned that there are many parts of yourself you can count on when you need them. They are always there and you cannot try to suppress them or pretend they do not exist . . . I have met many of these personalities and I have found I enjoyed meeting them and getting to know them. I saw that if I cannot like them, I can at least accept them. I grew to like these parts of myself and in doing so, grew to like me.
>
> I have never trusted a woman completely before this time. It was surprising for me to trust a woman. I also learned that I could trust myself, that there are limits to my anger and other such emotions. In dealing with what I have always considered violent emotions, I now figure I can deal with all the emotions. The most important thing I learned is to feel. Sometimes I do not like what I am feeling but I could never go back to not feeling at all.
>
> I have found a freedom and peace I have never had before this time.

There is no question that this system evokes deep inner healing. The core is found, brought to a safe place, and engaged in a process that allows feelings to be felt. The reactivation of the feelings allows the inmate to move into a healing relationship with the wounded self. The introduction of the Divine Friend reinforces that healing relationship and evokes connection with the core self. The net effect is liberation from the inner prison.

Externally observed positive changes in behavior are corroborated by the inmates' own experience of themselves. Each of them has reported a significant improvement in the ability to accept who they are and what they have done. Since it is the deepest core which has been energized, the process does not stop with the end of the actual work an inmate may have done with me. The process continues with the life of its own that comes from the inner relationships to the Wounded Child and the Divine Friend. The inmates speak, "When you open, you get pain . . . but you feel the warmth and love that is inside . . . Who could go back? Something else is coming out . . . it cannot be stopped because it is so real."

Note

1. This is not to say that major systemic penal reform is not also necessary. Rather, my intention in this article is to focus upon the inner prisoner who can be touched, healed, and liberated. This can be achieved through the use of imagery, drawing, careful attention to feelings, the establishment of an inner safe place, and a relationship with an inner Divine Friend.

Transference and Counter-Transference in Psychosynthesis Psychotherapy

Will Friedman

My purpose in writing on the place of transference and counter-transference in Psychosynthesis is to try to articulate more clearly my approach to a vital area of therapeutic work. Assagioli, perhaps because he assumed a familiarity on the part of his readers with the fundamental contributions of psychoanalysis, spent very little time discussing transference. He focussed his attention on the new contributions Psychosynthesis was making to the therapeutic endeavor while reminding us, "Psychosynthesis presupposes psychoanalysis" (Assagioli, 1965b). However, Psychosynthesis has, I think, somewhat lost touch with its analytic roots in recent years, and this may have contributed to what I feel is too little attention being paid to such basics as transference and counter-transference. In any event, the specifically *psychosynthetic* perspective on transference and counter-transference has yet to be clarified.

In preface, it should be noted that in Psychosynthesis the heart of the therapeutic relationship is the attitudinal factor often referred to as "presence" (see Brown, 1983; or Rogers, 1961, and related work). By presence is meant the therapist's attitude toward the client and the quality that is brought to that relationship—a matter of both the therapist's world view and his or her psychological and spiritual practice.

If we place the therapeutic relationship in the context of the psychosynthesis model of the psyche—the "egg diagram" delineating three broad dimensions of consciousness (the lower unconscious, the middle unconscious, and the superconscious)—we can begin to clarify a theoretical perspective on this relationship. On *the superconscious level*, in addition to the factor of presence, we also find shared peak experiences, synchronisms, I-Thou experiences of authentic, spiritual relatedness, "grace" (Peck, 1978), and so on.

On the level of *the middle unconscious*, we have the more or less conscious feelings, intentions, and perceptions of both parties, and at least a large measure of what analysts call the "therapeutic alliance"—which involves the establishment of a minimal bond of communication, co-operation, and commitment. Without this, ongoing, intensive psychotherapy is difficult at best.[1]

On the level of *the lower unconscious,* we encounter those dynamics

46

within the therapeutic relationship which can be discussed under the headings of transference and counter-transference, the focus of this article. In order to delineate the specific approach of Psychosynthesis, as I see it, I will compare it to that of psychoanalysis.

Transference and Counter-Transference

According to Assagioli, "[Transference] projections have to be analyzed and dissolved. Here there is agreement between psychoanalysis and psychosynthesis" (1967). While there is this basic agreement, there are also some major differences relating to the emphasis placed on the transference and the techniques used to work with it. *In psychoanalysis, the analysis of the transference is the centrepiece of the therapy.* In Freud's words, "Finally every conflict has to fought out in the sphere of the transference" (1943). In Psychosynthesis, as we shall see, transference work may be considered as *one part* of a larger, or more varied, overall approach.

Specifically, in psychoanalysis, the approach to working through neurotic conflict is to encourage, or, as some theorists prefer, to "allow" the development of what is often referred to as a full, regressive "transference neurosis" (e.g., Fine, 1979; Menninger, 1958). The client's neurotic pattern is admitted "into the transference as a playground in which it is allowed to expand in almost complete freedom" (Freud, 1943). In other words, the analyst's therapeutic posture (non-gratifying, "blank screen," etc.) encourages the client to become emotionally and psycho-sexually fixated on the therapist and "regressively" play out childhood patterns *vis à vis* the therapist. Following the establishment of the transference neurosis, the transference is interpreted and analyzed. Experiencing formerly unconscious patterns consciously, the client gains insight and works through his or her issues via the therapeutic relationship.[2]

In Psychosynthesis, we do not specifically encourage or seek the development of a full-fledged transference neurosis, nor do we consider the analysis of transference as necessarily the core of the therapeutic process. Instead, we treat (or should treat) transference dynamics, *as they arise,* as *one of many ways* of learning about the client and helping the client confront his or her issues. In this, we are in agreement with Jung, who, in *The Psychology of the Transference* (1954), writes:

> The great importance of the transference has often led to the mistaken idea that it is absolutely indispensible for a cure, that it must be demanded from the patient, so to speak. But a thing like that can no more be demanded than faith, which is only valuable when it is spontaneous. . . . Anyone who thinks that he must "demand" a transference is forgetting that this is only one of the therapeutic factors. . . . I personally am always glad when there is only a mild transference or when it is practically unnoticeable. Far less claim is then made upon one as a person, and one can be satisfied with other therapeutically effective factors.

In Psychosynthesis, these "other therapeutically effective factors" include an array of *intrapsychic* (in contrast to interpersonal) techniques which actively and experimentally engage the client in the therapeutic process and which attain the same ends as transference work—that is, dealing with the unconscious, intrapsychic, "neurotic" conflicts, and strengthening the ego or personal self. I am referring to such techniques as subpersonality work, disidentification, dialogic imagery with the parental imagoes, catharsis techniques, and so on (Assagioli, 1965a; Crampton, 1981, 1985; Ferrucci, 1982). This point is supported by Fromm (1980) who points out, "It is the child in the analysand who is transferring." Thus, inner child subpersonality work and dialogic imagery with the parental imagoes, along with the abreactive emotional component, are getting at exactly the same material that the analyst is seeking to access through the transference. Analyzing the process from a psychosynthesis perspective, typically what happens in the course of the transference neurosis is that the client progressively identifies with the child subpersonality and projects the parental imagoes (the introjects) onto the therapist. This is certainly one way to access this material—the question is whether it is the only way or the most effective way in all cases. In my opinion, the more active intrapsychic techniques that are often used in Psychosynthesis allow many clients to access the material in a way that is very direct, efficient, and effective.[3] In this regard, Assagioli felt that "no mere analytic treatment is sufficient to bring about true integration and growth, which require the use of active techniques" (1965a). It should be noted, however, that the use of active, intrapsychic techniques in no way downplays the importance of the therapeutic relationship. Assagioli goes on to emphasize in the same passage "the decisive importance . . . of the living interpersonal relation between the therapist and patient."

Thus, instead of a long-term process of confronting unconscious material through the regression of the transference neurosis, techniques such as subpersonality work and imagery allow us to assist the client in regressing *as needed* in a given session or series of sessions, so as to "make the unconscious conscious" and work through inner conflicts. The following is a brief example of such "focussed regression" via an intrapsychic technique (in this case, dialogic imagery). The client is a middle-aged woman working on self-assertion issues. Earlier in the session we had been discussing a pattern which she had associated with childhood of ignoring her own needs while attending to those around her. In this vignette, we are exploring one of these childhood incidents:

Therapist: Let's go back to that scene again that you were describing when you were playing with that man. . . . Just see it. See yourself at that age, 5 or 6. See him. And describe to me what you see.

Client: (sigh, voice choked up) I used to see him and it was so much joy, I used to *run* to him, like this (extends arms). He would pick me up, hug me, and throw me up in the air. [Client has eyes closed, is visualizing the scene.]

Therapist: Just allow the feelings that come with this to be there.

Client: And sometimes you see people doing that with kids and they seem to get tired of it, like they liked to do it a couple of times. But he never seemed to get tired. Throwing me in the air, or doing his little tricks. And he always did it enough so that I was happy, you know, and was able to go about my business afterward. It was kind of perfect. . . . He made me feel smart. . . . It was always like there was a crowd of adults around, that's when we saw him, at these parties. And, um, I was the centre of his attention (sniffling, sighs). And it felt good until that day [the details discussed earlier in the session aren't crucial here]. And it was like I closed the door (voice choking, crying). And I wasn't going to open it up ever again.

Therapist: Just allow the feelings. . . .

Client: They're so sad. It's like something died. It's worse because when something dies it's the end.

Therapist: mm hmm

Client: The door wasn't closed so that I couldn't see on the other side. But I wasn't going to open it. A lot of disbelief, like, how could he do that to me? And the other thing is, like, he wasn't really my friend, he was *her* friend [i.e., mother's]. And like, I had no friends (crying). The people who seemed to be my friends weren't my friends. I feel so alone. I feel alone, I feel there's nobody I can trust and nobody I can believe. Very confused. And sad. . . . And he just notices [in the imagery, she perceives that he notices her reaction]. Nobody seems to care, they laugh. It's like a big joke. And the only one who knows it's not a big joke is me and him.

Therapist: He knows.

Client: He knows. He knows I closed that door. And he can't do anything about it. He tries. But it's too late.

Therapist: So what are you saying to him right now? Underneath that?

Client: I don't trust him. [To him in the imagery:] I don't trust you, I don't believe you. You're not my friend. I don't believe you were *ever* my friend. You're *her* friend (laughing a bit). Any friend of hers is not a friend of mine. . . . I get a kind of sense like that was the end of an era. The end of hope.

Therapist: And not only did you close the door, you said, I don't think you were *ever* my friend.

Client: Right.

Therapist: So you rewrote the past there.

Client: Right. Negated all the good . . .

One can easily imagine the same material coming up via transference. From the psychosynthesis point of view, one of the virtues of the intrapsychic approach, which explores the unconscious "in installments," as Assagioli put it, in contrast to an exclusive reliance on transference, is that it avoids the danger of *unnecessarily* energizing the client's lower unconscious dynamics. As Assagioli frequently pointed out, "energy follows thought," and if we focus on the transference strongly enough we are sure to find lots of it, and may even end up energizing it out of proportion to what is needed to work it through (see Assagioli, 1965a, pp. 99–100).

It is also worth considering here whether the so-called neutral, blank-screen, non-interactive stance of classical psychoanalytic couch work is really so neutral after all. One might question whether such an artificial mode of relating, while certainly conducive to eliciting transference, is as telling as seeing what transference dynamics emerge when the therapist relates and interacts somewhat more naturally. Quite possibly, transference dynamics that arise in the latter case have more to do with the client's real-life blocks and issues than with those which come to the fore in the somewhat more withheld and artificial mode of classical analysis.

Actually, there are a number of factors in Psychosynthesis that tend to *dissolve* the transference as it emerges rather than letting it build into a full-fledged transference neurosis. These include: (1) the tendency to relate to the client in a somewhat less mysterious and withheld manner than in classical analysis; (2) the use of intrapsychic techniques (such as subpersonalities) which focus the therapeutic action on what is going on *within* the client rather than between the client and the therapist; and (3) the tendency to work through the transference material *as it arises* and then to go on to other techniques rather than focussing on the transference as the centrepiece of the therapy and *seeking* the development of a transference neurosis.[4] These factors, along with the relatively more active and experiential engagement of the client in the process and the inclusion, where appropriate, of the healing and integrative use of superconscious experience and techniques (see, e.g., Assagioli, 1965a; Ferrucci, 1982, 1984) help account for the fact that a typical course of psychosynthesis therapy requires a shorter period of time than a typical psychoanalysis.

However, while from the standpoint of Psychosynthesis, psychoanalysis can be criticized for an overreliance and overemphasis on transference, I think many psychosynthesis practitioners are limited because they underemphasize the importance of interpersonal dynamics in therapy. My observation is that many of the binds that psychosynthesists run into in their work can be attributed to not paying close enough attention to transference and counter-transference.

Too often, for example, the client goes along with a psychosynthesis intrapsychic technique *for transference reasons* (e.g., to please the therapist/parent figure), and therefore the technique may look good in the execution but fail to effect any real change in core patterns. Or the client may be resistant to using the technique, which psychosynthesists may conceive of as a lack of "will alignment"—which is true enough—but pay too little attention to the interpersonal (transference) issues of power, control, fear, and so on which may be at the heart of what is happening.

One of my clients who did beautiful subpersonality work would continually leave the sessions saying that she was going to pay attention to her needy Little Girl subpersonality during the coming week. Inevitably, she would report at the next session that she hadn't done so. Eventually, I started feeling annoyed about this and realized that until I clarified what was happening between us interpersonally I could strategize with her forever without penetrating the real issue. I felt, subjectively, that she was throwing her failure to take care of her Little Girl in my face. As we discussed what was going on, we realized that just as she "failed" in her life—to be successful, to be happy—as a way to make her parents "crazy," she was failing in the therapy as a way to make *me* crazy. At this point, we were able to shift the focus to less self-destructive ways for her to express her anger. Thus, attending to the transference and counter-transference allowed us to shift to the real issues and got us out of what was becoming a non-productive power struggle that was an *expression* of her conflicts rather than a way of working them through. Therefore, paying attention to transference can add a dimension to intrapsychic techniques that can make them more effective.

Having both intrapsychic (e.g., imagery and subpersonalities) and inter-personal (transference) techniques available makes all sorts of combinations possible. I have already given the example of a client whose subpersonality work had been affected by transference dynamics. In this case, we worked from the intrapsychic (subpersonality) to the interpersonal (transference) and back again. In other instances, one can bridge the transference and the intrapsychic levels. An example of this would be a client who repeatedly felt uncomfortable about what the therapist was thinking when there was a silence in the session. After discussing the feelings and fantasies involved, the therapist could move the work into an intrapsychic mode by asking the client about the part of himself that had these feelings and fantasies and then focussing the session on imagistic subpersonality work:

Client: I feel like a kid who's been bad waiting for his father to come home.

Therapist: Tell me about this kid. What does he look like?

I think moving between modalities can be very effective, but I would also add that the movement into the intrapsychic, as in the previous example, can sometimes be driven by the therapist's counter-transference rather than being a creative therapeutic response to the client's unfolding process. Spec-ifically, if the transference feels too hot for the therapist to handle, he or she might, as a defence, suggest imagery work, silently sighing with relief when the client's eyes are closed. This isn't the end of the world—it strikes me as roughly equivalent to Freud's developing "couch work" partly because he didn't like having to make eye contact all day long—but it should be conscious if it is to remain relatively harmless.

The discussion of the ways in which transference and counter-transference dynamics can either interfere with or augment psychosynthesis therapy could go on almost indefinitely. I'll restrict myself to a final observation about a particular category of transference that we have to be especially aware of in Psychosynthesis. We might call it "transpersonal transference," at least one version of which involves a kind of guru making. Any therapist is prone to being idealized by clients, but when the therapist represents an explicitly transpersonal approach the pitfalls are magnified. It's so easy to feel special, and evolved, and subtly gratified by *transpersonal* idealization that it bears attention. Ferrucci (1982) provides a good example of the sort of thing I'm talking about in the following anecdote:

I will never forget the disillusioned expression on the face of a client of mine when he met me at a soccer match. The angelic image he had projected onto me—I later discovered—clashed violently in his mind with such a prosaic reality as the one he saw in me on that occasion.

Summary and Conclusion

In my view, a psychosynthesis approach to transference and counter-trans-ference can be summarized as follows.

Without seeking to elicit a full transference neurosis, we need to pay attention to whatever transference and counter-transference dynamics arise naturally in the course of psychosynthesis psychotherapy. At the minimum, these give us valuable insight into the client's patterns as they emerge in the here and now of therapy. Also, we need to pay attention to transference in order to avoid distortions in the use of intrapsychic techniques. Beyond this, transference and counter-transference can provide an entry into the client's process, either through direct exploration and interpretation (psychoanalysis) or by using them as a jumping-off place for intrapsychic work.

I would also like to suggest that transference and counter-transference dynamics are not only important in terms of effectiveness, but they also add an exciting and creative dimension to the work. Working with the transference is a here and now process that demands a creative aliveness and rigorous self-inquiry on the part of the therapist. Thus, while I am by no means suggesting that we work in the analytic mode and make the analysis of the transference neurosis the core of the therapy, I do believe that it is both essential and rewarding for psychosynthesists to pay a good deal of creative attention to transference and counter-transference issues. In this article, I have attempted to define a specifically psychosynthetic position on these issues, and I look forward to further refinements as other practitioners take up the discussion.

Notes

1. It is largely because of the difficulty in establishing a real therapeutic alliance, as opposed to a regressive symbiotic relationship, that therapy with a client with a weak sense of self (e.g., "borderline") is so challenging. For a brief discussion of this point within a psychosynthesis context, see Friedman (1984).

2. From the standpoint of theoretical clarity, it should be noted that the regression which the transference neurosis involves is not meant to be an *ego* regression (it shouldn't make the client psychotic). The regression of the transference neurosis is restricted to the *emotional/psycho-sexual* domain, and is contra-indicated for someone who lacks the ego strength to avoid ego regression during therapy. In the words of Blanck and Blanck (1974), "In psychoanalysis, it is the deliberate purpose to promote regression. The structure of the analysand is such [i.e., the ego is stable enough] that regression is along psychosexual lines only, the ego remains intact. Regression is in the service of the ego, therefore reversible."

3. Some analysts with whom I've discussed these ideas agree that one can indeed access the unconscious with techniques such as imagery, but they raise some objections. Interestingly, I've heard some argue that you can't go as deeply into the psyche with techniques like imagery as you can with transference, while others have taken the somewhat opposite position that such techniques go *too* deeply too soon. This latter position argues that through transference the analyst gets to the same material, but several months later, when the client has worked through the intervening layers and is more ready for it. I think it would be most fruitful to engage this debate seriously, comparing case studies and attempting to understand the variables involved. See Grof (1985, p. 349), where he briefly contrasts transference analysis and "experiential therapy." I, by the way, disagree with the way Grof dismisses the relevance of transference in the light of his own "experiential" techniques.

4. In contrast, Saretsky (1978) points out that one of the ways in which the analyst elicits the transference neurosis is by "avoiding dealing with unrealistic attitudes toward the therapist until these have built up to overwhelming proportions." The approach typical of Psychosynthesis is that of continuously dissolving the transference instead of letting it build to the point of a transference neurosis. This is similar to the way in which analysts work with "borderline" as opposed to healthier, neurotic "normal" clients. With the borderline client, the analyst avoids the development of a full transference neurosis because of its tendency to devolve into a "transference psychosis" (Blanck & Blanck, 1974). (In a psychotic transference, rather than treating the therapist as someone who *reminds* him of his mother, the client treats the therapist as if he or she really *were* his mother.) It is only when the client's observing ego is healthy enough to be able to handle the transference neurosis that the analyst allows it to develop. My own observation is that if a client has a strong enough ego to deal with a transference neurosis, he or she has enough ego strength to utilize effectively the active, intrapsychic techniques that tend to make up a large part of the psychosynthesist's repertoire.

References

Assagioli, R. (1965a). *Psychosynthesis*. New York: Viking Press.

Assagioli, R. (1965b). *Psychosynthesis: Individual and social*. New York: Psychosynthesis Research Foundation.

Assagioli, R. (1967). *Jung and psychosynthesis*. New York: Psychosynthesis Research Foundation.

Assagioli, R. (1973). *The act of will*. Baltimore: Penguin.

Blanck, G., & Blanck, R. (1974). *Ego psychology: Theory and practice*. New York: Columbia University Press.

Brown, M. (1983). *The unfolding self: Psychosynthesis and counseling*. Los Angeles: Psychosynthesis Press.

Crampton, M. (1981). Psychosynthesis. In R. J. Corsini (Ed.), *Innovative psychotherapies*. New York: Wiley.

Crampton, M. (1985). *An historical survey of mental imagery techniques and description of dialogic imagery method* (revised ed.). London: Institute of Psychosynthesis.

Ferrucci, P. (1982). *What may be may be*. Los Angeles: J. P. Tarcher.

Ferrucci, P. (1984). The untrodden regions of the mind. In J. Weiser & T. Yeomans (Eds.), *Psychosynthesis in the helping professions*. Toronto: Department of Applied Psychology, Ontario Institute for Studies in Education.

Fine, R. (1979). *A history of psychoanalysis*. New York: Columbia University Press.

Freud, S. (1943). *A general introduction to psychoanalysis*. Garden City: Garden City Publishing.

Friedman, W. (1984). Psychosynthesis, psychoanalysis, and the emerging developmental perspective in psychotherapy. In J. Weiser & T. Yeomans (Eds.), *Psychosynthesis in the helping professions*. Toronto: Department of Applied Psychology, Ontario Institute for Studies in Education.

Fromm, E. (1980). *Greatness and limitations of Freud's thought*. New York: Mentor.

Grof, S. (1985). *Beyond the brain: Birth, death and transcendence in psychotherapy*. Albany: State University of New York.

Jung, C. (1954). *The psychology of the transference*. Princeton: Princeton University Press.

Menninger, K. (1958). *Theory and psychoanalytic technique*. New York: Harper Torchbooks.

Peck, M. S. (1978). *The road less traveled*. New York: Touchstone/Simon and Schuster.

Rogers, C. (1961). *On becoming a person*. Boston: Houghton Mifflin.

Saretsky, L. (1978). Transference. In G. Goldman & D. Milman (Eds.), *Psychoanalytic psychotherapy*. Reading, MA: Addison-Wesley.

Alcoholics Anonymous and Psychosynthesis

Bonnie Gulino Schaub and Richard Schaub

Alcoholics Anonymous (AA) is a worldwide, self-supporting, self-help organization devoted to (1) helping people stop drinking (abstinence) and (2) helping the abstainer achieve increasingly deeper levels of sobriety. To accomplish these goals, AA advocates the Twelve Steps, a program of psycho-spiritual development that asks for attitudinal and behavioral transformations.

In AA terminology, "working the program" refers to the inner psychological work described by the steps. Resistance to working the program, resistance to attitudinal and behavioral transformations, is seen as a danger signal in the abstainer's recovering process. (Please note the use of the term "recovering" rather than "recovery." As is reflected in the AA phrase, "The further you are from the last drink, the closer you are to the next one," AA views sobriety and the recovering process as a life-long issue.) If resistance becomes impacted, the abstainer is considered a "dry drunk," that is, someone who is not currently drinking but who retains all of the self-defeating attitudes of the active alcoholic. Attention to the Twelve Steps is therefore strongly encouraged in order to avoid a relapse. These Twelve Steps are listed below as originally articulated by Bill Wilson (Alcoholics Anonymous, 1955), one of AA's founders, in describing his own path to sobriety:

1. We admitted we were powerless over alcohol—our lives had become unmanageable;

2. Came to believe that a Power greater than ourselves could restore us to sanity;

3. Made a decision to turn our will and our lives over to the care of God *as we understood Him*;

4. Made a searching and fearless moral inventory of ourselves;

5. Admitted to God, to ourselves and to another human being the exact nature of our wrongs;

6. Were entirely ready to have God remove all these defects of character;

7. Humbly asked Him to remove our shortcomings;

8. Made a list of all persons we had harmed and became willing to make amends to them all;

9. Made direct amends to such people wherever possible, except when to do so would injure them or others;

55

10. Continued to take personal inventory, and when we were wrong promptly admitted it;

11. Sought through prayer and meditation to improve our conscious contact with God *as we understood Him,* praying only for knowledge of His will for us and the power to carry that out;

12. Having had a spiritual awakening as the result of these steps, we tried to carry this message to alcoholics and to practise these principles in all our affairs.

The "spiritual awakening" mentioned by Bill Wilson was that of a "great white light" (Alcoholics Anonymous, 1957), an experience consistent with cross-cultural mystical accounts of unitive consciousness (see, for example, Ring, 1984, pp. 227–228). As can be readily noted, the Twelve Steps ask the person recovering from alcohol and/or chemical dependency to adopt a spiritual overview and value system. However, this aspect of AA presents a dilemma for many people because of both their own spiritual repression and the general spiritual repression in our culture. In the least, this dilemma results in their not experiencing the depth of the AA program; in the extreme, it results in their rejecting AA as a support system in the struggle for sobriety and mental health.

Resistance to Spirituality

In our extensive professional experience working with people who are recovering from alcohol and/or chemical dependency, AA has proven to be *the* essential therapeutic intervention. Spiritually oriented psychotherapy, because of its compatibility with AA, has proven to be an important secondary intervention. To provide psychotherapeutic services to persons with alcohol and/or chemical dependency who are not in AA is a naïve and probably grandiose clinical endeavor; no single therapist can provide the reinforcement and support needed in the recovering process. The therapist, therefore, must be mindful of the degree of the client's participation in AA—a participation often marred by resistance to AA's spirituality.

In psychosynthesis terminology, resistance to spirituality is referred to as "repression of the sublime" (Haronian, 1974). While this repression is culturally inherent at present, it can also be traced to intrapsychic causes. Some of the intrapsychic variables that can contribute to spiritual repression include negative childhood experiences with traditional religious practice; negative transference to God as Father; overidentification with subpersonality patterns such as rebellion and cynicism; fear of loss of control (which can in some cases be related to unintegrated experiences of altered states of consciousness); fear of loss of identity; unresolved grief (which can result in continual anger at the world, at God, at life, at the way things are); and irrational thoughts about spirituality (e.g., that spirituality makes one ignore social and political realities).

Working Through the Resistance

Assagioli's model (1965) of human consciousness provides a number of principles which suggest ways to assist clients in lifting spiritual repression. This article, of course, relates specifically to working through resistance to spirituality in the recovering person so that he or she can fully benefit from AA. The principles, however, can be applied to any case of spiritual repression and may also be of use to helping professionals who themselves face spiritual repression as an issue. We make this point because it is genuinely difficult for spiritually repressed psychotherapists to assist clients who are working through AA's Twelve Steps. Below, we illustrate Assagioli's general principles in the context of assisting such clients. In each clinical anecdote, the client (1) recently entered therapy, (2) had been evaluated as alcoholic and/or chemically dependent, (3) had been referred by the therapist to AA, and (4) had rejected AA because of its spiritual component.

The first principle suggested in Assagioli's model is that spirituality is an innate aspect of human nature existing above and beyond specific dogmas, beliefs, rituals. This principle was helpful in working with a client who rejected all spirituality because, despite her prayers, God had failed to protect her from her own abusive, alcoholic father. She eventually came to view God as unresponsive and indifferent, a male persona with no real credibility.

Through discussion and education, the client was freed to consider various cultural forms and expressions of spirituality. The possibility of spirituality without God (e.g., Buddhism) particularly appealed to her and allowed her to approach spirituality again, in turn allowing her to listen to AA's message in a less reactive way. The cognitive restructuring of this client's "belief system" about spirituality was facilitated by developing a more open view of spirituality.

A second principle in the model is that lack of knowledge of one's innate spirituality may simply be a matter of failing to try out a course of "definite inner experimentation" (Assagioli, 1965, p. 12). This principle was applied to a client who complained that he felt no evidence of spirituality within himself and so rejected AA's "God talk."

The client was trained in relaxation induction and was then introduced to several of Assagioli's techniques for tapping the intuitive and transpersonal levels of emotion and thought. What he found most intriguing was the experience of a personal self (also referred to as the observing self or the observing ego) which was an outcome for him of the "Who Is Aware" technique (Ferrucci, 1982, p. 66). He clearly had a strong experience of being "so much more" than the patterns in his personality. This experience allowed the client to open himself to the possibilities of other new experiences. While he still felt uncomfortable about AA's talk of God or Higher Power, he felt he could at least consider that there were unknown and mysterious aspects to his life. As White (1979) indicates, such peak or transcendent experiences are a significant aspect of the recovering process, particularly in that they give the recovering person a sense of participation in a "meaningful universe. . . . the person no longer views the larger system within which he/she lives as chaotic, painful and meaningless" (p. 126).

A third principle is that people reach blocks in their spiritual development just as they reach blocks in their ego development. (For a current discussion of this developmental perspective, see Wilber, 1986.) This principle was applied to a client who had begun drinking in his adult years in order to "fill the hole," the hole being a sense of frustration and despair, a crisis of meaning, which is clinically different from a depression. AA's spirituality infuriated him because he felt so remote from its potential to help him. Upon exploration, it was discovered that the client could accept Step One ("We admitted we were powerless over alcohol. . .") but was blocked by the implications of Step Two ("Came to believe that a Power greater than ourselves could restore us to sanity") because it asked him to take the mental and emotional risk of trusting in something beyond himself. On an intellectual level, "a Power greater than ourselves" sounded irrational. On an emotional level, the client feared disappearing into this "Power" and losing his identity. At the same time, he was vaguely aware that his identity was at least one source of his suffering, a suffering that had been blunted by drinking until drinking itself became a source of suffering.

As Friedman (1984) points out, "On [the] existential level of development, we are confronted with the need for a deeper, more authentic sense of identity and purpose than that provided by the ego and superego" (p. 35). Thus, the client was blocked in his spiritual development to a degree that he could not "work" AA's second step. We worked through the client's concern that "a Power greater than ourselves" sounded irrational by discussing various powers in nature. He was able to acknowledge the possibility that such powers as electricity, wind, the turning of the planets, and so on are neither rational nor irrational but require some other category of explanation. We were able to work through his other concern, that of losing his identity, by exploring this fear, finding its irrational core cognitions, and engaging in a course of study that included practising insight meditation and reading Ernest Becker's *Denial of Death* (1973) and Aldous Huxley's *The Perennial Philosophy* (1944). Concurrent with these educative and therapeutic approaches, the client began to hear in the "rooms" (AA meetings) how other members were gaining, rather than losing, their identity by "working" the second step.

A fourth principle is that human consciousness includes "lower" unconscious drives *and* "higher" unconscious drives. This principle was applied to a client who felt that the continued presence of anger in her emotions meant that AA's spirituality wasn't effective. In her interpretation, the anger was due to some essential flaw in her character.

Through the use of Assagioli's "map" of consciousness (1965, p. 26), the client was able to consider the possibility that "lower" drives, such as aggression and sexuality, co-exist with "higher" drives, such as meaning, creativity, and unity, and that her anger did not rule out her spirituality.

A fifth principle is that the "higher" unconscious drives manifest themselves in emotions and behavior just as the "lower" drives do. This principle was applied to clients who were unconscious about their motivations to be involved in various activities (such as the anti-nuclear movement) or who were unconscious about the implications of their reactions to things around them (such as crying when listening to sacred music). By interpreting such behavior as possible evidence of "higher" drives, they were able to acknowledge the possibility that spirituality was not remote or exotic but rather something that motivated them without their conscious awareness.

A sixth principle is that the therapist should undergo a training analysis including both personal and spiritual psychosynthesis. This principle was borne out by a client who resisted AA's spirituality because he associated spirituality with being "flaky" and weak. But because of the therapist's own training analysis, spirituality became a comfortable subject that could be examined directly and thoroughly. The therapist therefore served as a good role model capable of grounding spirituality in real, human terms.

Summary

The Twelve Steps of AA seek to strengthen the level of sobriety in the recovering person. However, the problem of the repression of the sublime, or the resistance to spirituality, can hinder the recovering person's use of AA. Psychosynthesis provides an extensive system of principles and techniques that can help clients effectively work through their resistance to an innate spirituality. By combining Alcoholics Anonymous with Psychosynthesis, the recovering process can be significantly enhanced.

References

Alcoholics Anonymous World Services. (1955). *Alcoholics Anonymous*. New York: Author.

Alcoholics Anonymous World Services. (1957). *Alcoholics Anonymous comes of age: A brief history of AA*. New York: Author.

Assagioli, R. (1965). *Psychosynthesis: A collection of basic writings*. New York: Viking Press.

Becker, E. (1973). *The denial of death*. New York: Macmillan.

Ferrucci, P. (1982). *What we may be*. Los Angeles: Tarcher.

Friedman, W. (1984). Psychosynthesis, psychoanalysis and the emerging developmental perspective in psychotherapy. In J. Weiser and T. Yeomans (Eds.), *Psychosynthesis in the helping professions*. Toronto: The Department of Applied Psychology, The Ontario Institute for Studies in Education.

Haronian, F. (1974). The repression of the sublime. *Synthesis, 1,* 51–62.

Huxley, A. (1944). *The perennial philosophy*. New York: Harper.

Ring, K. (1984). *Heading toward omega*. New York: Morrow.

White, L. (1979). Recovery from alcoholism: Transpersonal dimensions. *Journal of Transpersonal Psychology,* 11 (2), 117–128.

Wilber, K. (1986). Treatment modalities. In D. Brown, J. Engler, & K. Wilber (Eds.), *Transformations of consciousness*. Boston: New Science Library.

Healing the Wounds of Adults Abused as Children: A Transpersonal Approach

Therese A. Caveney

My purpose here is to share with other helping professionals a powerful and effective process for working with women who have been abused as children and/or adolescents. A full discussion of the issues and patterns for such women is not included because they have been well covered elsewhere (see, for example, Eliana Gil's book *Outgrowing the Pain*). This article focusses on the process of healing the wounds of abuse.

Two years ago, I began working with a woman who had been severely abused—emotionally, physically, and sexually—from early childhood into adolescence. She had a long history of disturbance, depression, and many hospitalizations. The majority of those who had treated her believed that her condition could not be treated successfully—that her panic attacks, depression, and self-destructive behavior were chronic. Yet the psychosynthesis process was so effective for her that after a year's time she urged me to put together a group.[1] As a result of her suggestion, we facilitated an initial group of women—she as peer counsellor and I as licensed therapist. The group was called Healing the Wounds. We met weekly for a period of one year, and are now meeting every three weeks.

The group was offered to women who had been abused either physically, or emotionally, or sexually. This proved to be a fortuitous decision because some women who had entered the group believing that only one form of abuse had occurred discovered through flashbacks, dreams, and so on that they had also suffered from other forms of abuse. On the other hand, if we consider the many shades or degrees of abuse, is there anyone who doesn't fall into one of the categories? My experience is that the process described below works equally well, regardless of how much or what kind of abuse has been experienced.

The progress of Healing the Wounds was dramatic and exciting. Perhaps the following excerpt from a letter written by one participant conveys the essence of what happened. The author of this letter had suffered from chronic depression and suicidal ideation for the past 20 years.

> When I joined the group I had "outside" help, but no "inside" help. This group has given me the tools to make that inside help constantly available. During the group sessions I was able to identify clearly and specifically the parts of me that needed healing . . . and I was able to help [them] *myself*.

I was living my life like a constantly frightened child in an adult suit! . . .
I lived my adult life believing I had to continue to use the childhood tactics
of survival with everyone until the day I died. . . . I still have some trouble
with trust, forgiveness, anger, others' disapproval, my own assertiveness, but
now at least I can identify exactly what's going on inside and my panicky little
wounded child no longer needs to "run the show" all the time. I have choices
I can make now as an adult. I believe I am learning as a result of caring for
her how to do more than just survive.

I no longer believe I am worthless, ugly, guilty, helpless, and unworthy of
love. I just plain do not experience the deeply depressed, suicidal feelings any
more. . . . I have a Blue Lady [a loving Presence that emerged during a
guided visualization] and a new sense, through the *experience* of her, of God's
unconditional love for me. I am beginning to open up more to experience the
love that significant people in my life give me. I have an inner source of hope
and strength and comforting. I have a set of skills to draw upon to relax, to
identify what's really going on deeply inside me, to feel healing and relief,
and a sense of centring to keep from going overboard emotionally. . . . I'm
beginning to experience a kind of love that I don't have to earn or be afraid
of or suspicious of, both human and spiritual.

All of the women in the group (there were six) were very creative people;
however, their creativity had been stifled because of the vast amount of
energy required to cope with the effects of their early abuse. One year after
the start of the group, their creative flow gained momentum. They began
to turn out poetry, stories, and art, to clear up dysfunctional relationships,
and to pursue their interests and careers. They now require little guidance
and do an excellent job of counselling each other.

A series of steps or stages involving some transgenerational work—not
only with the inner child but also with the inner child/adolescent of parental
introjects—emerged from working with this group. We found that these
steps did not necessarily occur in linear fashion but that there was a frequent
overlapping and a moving back and forth between stages. They might all
occur, symbolically, during one session, or over many sessions. Obviously,
the integration into life experience and expression required a longer period
of time. Often the process needed to be repeated with another inner child/
adolescent (a 5 year old, a 10 year old, a 16 year old) and with another
child/adolescent of the client's inner parents. This was not so complicated
as it might sound because the client's life experience, as it unfolded, highlighted what was needed. There are, essentially, three stages that I would
like to discuss below:

- Healing the Inner Family
- Letting Go: Stepping Out of the Family System
- Choice for Life: Discovering and Expressing Purpose.

For the sake of simplicity, I use the word "child" to indicate both child
and adolescent. Also, for simplicity, I use feminine pronouns since the discussion is mainly about my work with women. (The process appears to be
equally effective for men, although I do not have experience applying it with
men in the group setting.) For readers familiar with Psychosynthesis, much
of this will be familiar. However, I offer, I believe, some subtle but important additions to traditional psychosynthesis practice.

Stage 1—Healing the Inner Family

1. Establish a Connection With the Wounded Child—There are many ways to establish this connection. A few are offered here. It may be accomplished directly by asking clients to talk about their childhood and then facilitating a dialogue with the Child they describe. Another way is to say something like this:

> Imagine a door. Behind the door lives the Child within you that is in need of healing. When you are ready, allow the door to open and allow this Child to come out to meet you.

A less direct approach is to listen while a current situation is being described and then evoke awareness of the roots of that experience by using such interventions as:

> When have you experienced this before . . . and before that? What is your earliest memory of this experience? Allow your awareness now to move back in time to the origin of this experience . . . to your earliest or most acute memory of this experience.

Or you may say to clients:

> Close your eyes and allow an image to emerge for what you are experiencing right now—the first image, without censoring.

If the image turns out to be something symbolic or abstract, the following short cut often reveals the roots in childhood or adolescent experience. After listening to and dialoguing with the image, instruct clients in the following way:

> Ask the image how old it is. Go with the first number that comes to you—even if it makes no sense at all.

Then continue:

> See yourself at that age and describe what's happening. Listen to this Child. Allow her to tell you about what's going on in her life and how that is affecting her.

With a little imagination, it is usually not difficult to guide clients toward an encounter with their inner child. Often, however, especially where there has been childhood abuse, there is an immediate aversion to this meeting. This aversion can be manifested as judgment, disgust, anger, distance, or fear. Sometimes, even, the Child may appear unwilling to meet *them*. At this point, a simple intervention is usually immediately helpful:

> Imagine now that you can see your parents somewhere . . . at whatever distance feels right to you. [One woman initially could not make any contact with her inner child until she could see her parents miles away, behind a cyclone fence!] And now turn your attention to your Child. How do you feel toward that Child now?

It is often very difficult to maintain this perspective and it may be necessary, periodically, to ask if the parents are still out there somewhere where they can be seen.

It is important to listen to the Child's feelings, beliefs, and decisions:

They don't love me.
There must be something wrong with me.
I deserve to be punished.
It's not safe to be needy.
There is no love for little Jenny.

Next determine what she did or the life stance she assumed as a result of such decisions—for example, "I'm tough. I won't let anyone know that I need. I'll give a lot, and then maybe they'll like me, but I won't allow myself to receive." And then determine what the client does now in her current life situation that reflects those early decisions—for example, "I keep finding myself in abusive relationships".

It is important to evoke awareness of the benefits and limitations of such a stance. Holding the belief "There is no love," for instance, is safe in the sense that it is familiar and that it protects one from the possibility of opening to love and then having it ripped away. One client said, "If I don't let love in, then I won't get hurt." Alternatively, although such a stance may have meant survival in earlier years, it may perpetuate loneliness when survival is no longer an issue. In fact, another kind of survival issue may be present if an adult is ill or disabled and cannot ask for or accept the help that is needed.

Often a conflict between two inner children is revealed at this stage—one disowning or suppressing the behavior of the other because she feels threatened in some way—as was the case for one woman who at 4 years old was very bright, creative, and exuberantly expressive. Her grandfather was her loving, patient friend and teacher in an otherwise abusive environment. She learned quickly and soon was able to beat him regularly at the game of Kings. She was often told that she should let him win so he wouldn't feel bad. When her beloved grandfather died, she believed it was her fault. That bright, ebullient child was despised and suppressed by an older inner child who adopted the belief: "If I show how smart I am, I will lose my friend, my source of learning and comfort." In her adult life, this woman finds herself holding back what she knows with friends and employers.

2. Determine and Respond to the Child's Needs—As one proceeds, it is essential to ask the client to become aware of her feelings toward her inner child. If they are not benevolent, or at least neutral, make sure her parents are still out there where she can see them. The following interventions, with appropriate pacing and timing, are helpful:

> Listen to the Child. Invite her to communicate with you about what's happening, what she is feeling. Find out what beliefs she holds and what decisions she has made in relation to her experience. Ask her what she wants from you; and, at a deeper level, what she needs *most essentially*. Go for the bottom line—for example, "*Be* with me." "See me." "Recognize me." "Confirm my capability, creativity."
>
> Take time now to consider your willingness to meet those needs expressed by the Child. Determine how they can be met—for example, "How can I *be* with you? How will you know that I'm here?" Or, "What can I do or say so that you will know that you are loved?"

Responses include statements like "Hold me." "Just close your eyes and see me with you as you are doing now." Sometimes touching is helpful, such as a pat on the thigh (indicating that the Child is on her lap) or twirling a lock of hair. It is also helpful to choose some form of reminder for contacting the inner child. Consulting the Child will usually reveal something appropriate—perhaps a favorite color, animal, or object. Stickers (which have been so popular and can be found at almost any stationary or card shop) are very useful for this purpose—for example, puppies, kittens, butterflies, or just colored dots. Suggest that your client put one on the kitchen window, bathroom mirror, telephone, or steering wheel of the car and that each time she sees it she takes just a moment to make contact. One woman got herself a locket and inside were the words of her Child: "Be with me."

It must be emphasized that the amount of time spent with the Child is not nearly so important as frequent and consistent contact which is essential for integration into daily life. One of the problems often encountered at this stage is the refusal of the inner child to communicate her needs or to receive what is needed when it is offered. This is usually because of the pain she has experienced in having once trusted and then having had that trust violated; or, because she has learned that it is not safe to make her needs known. One woman, who at 2 years old ended up in the hospital because she had asked for attention when her mother had been at "the end of her rope", found it safer *not* to be aware of her needs, *not* to communicate her needs, *not* to allow herself to receive attention in the first place.

More than occasionally, a client has said, "The image keeps changing into my daughter," indicating that the dynamics between her and her own daughter are similar to those between herself as a child and her parents. (For an excellent treatment of this subject, see *The Drama of the Gifted Child*, by Alice Miller.) It is usually best to hold that discussion until the dialogue with her own inner child has been completed. You might suggest the following:

> Just allow her [your daughter] to be there and now refocus on your own inner child. We'll come back to your daughter.

When the question arises, "Will I have to do this for the rest of my life?", the answer you should provide is no. I use the example of a flower that receives ample water, sunlight, and nutrients from the soil and grows into the beautiful flower that it innately is. So it is with one's inner child. But, to take a delightful phrase from the poet Dale Mead, "you can't grow a flower with a hammer." Nor will pulling it up make it grow any faster. I suggest to clients that there is another similarity to the flower: the flower is unable to select the environment in which it grows. As adults, however, we can provide the nourishment, protection, and guidance that were missing in our early upbringings—both within ourselves and from without. As we relate to others, not as our inner child would, but as one who has brought about the confidence of our own inner children, we can begin to attract and to find the support and guidance that we need.

Traditional psychosynthesis practice evokes the image of sunlight to illuminate what needs to happen further between or among the subpersonalities that the client is working with. I do that too. In addition, however, I usually end a session by suggesting the following:

Imagine a sphere of light surrounding you—you, your child, and anyone else who may be there—beautiful light, of whatever color. This light represents the presence of Unconditional Love. Within this sphere of Unconditional Love, allow anything further that needs to happen, just for now, anything that needs to be communicated between or among you, verbally or non-verbally. Allow Love to reveal the right relationship between and among you, to heal what needs healing, to release what needs releasing.

If you have any questions or concerns, tell them to Love and be available to Love's response, allowing Unconditional Love to bring about whatever closure you need, just for now.

The use of the sphere to symbolize the presence of Unconditional Love has proven to be an important step in the healing process because its all-inclusiveness supports the revelation of the right relationship between and among all those who are consciously being held within it. This is the essence of healing—the restoration of wholeness. So, in holding such a context, we are activating the will to heal. If there is enormous resistance to the word "Love," a sphere symbolizing Universal Truth often works as well.

3. Establish a Connection with the Inner Child of the Inner Parents—The easiest and most natural way of doing this is to assist the client when she is talking about a parent to articulate what that relationship was like for her as a child (at the age you are working with). Ask her what she knows about the background of this parent which may have resulted in his or her inability to parent in the way that her inner child needed. Occasionally, someone will say, "If you are trying to make me feel compassion for my parents, forget it! I'll never forgive them for what they did." Your response should be:

The point is that what we are dealing with here is a part of *yourself* that is affecting you *now*. The end result may or may not significantly alter your relationship with your external parents, though it often does.

At this stage, a powerful visualization is:

Imagine now that your mother's (or father's) outer form begins to fade and you begin to see her at the age when, because of her own unmet needs, she lost her capacity to give and receive love and/or to offer guidance in the way which this child of yours needed it. Ask her what was happening in her life at this time. What kind of relationship did she have with the significant people in her life, and how did that affect her? Go with your first impressions or intuitions without censoring them, even if they are vague or don't make much sense.

I have not yet found anyone who could not do this. Clients always come up with something that appears to be significant in that positive change occurs as a result of dealing with what this visualization brings up. I tell them not to worry about accuracy because facts *per se* have nothing to do with their experience; it is what they have perceived from the perspective held as a child that has affected them over the years.

Another objection to making contact with the inner child of the inner parents is, "But I don't want to blame my parents for all my problems. After all, they did the best they could." Your answer should be:

That's true. And from this perspective in your life you know that. From the perspective of your inner child, you simply needed what you needed, and you were dependent on your parents (or surrogates) to provide for those needs.

Next, facilitate a dialogue with the mother's inner child, much as you would with the client's inner child. Using the mother's name helps to avoid confusion about which child you are talking to.

4. Determine and Respond to the Needs of the Inner Parent's Inner Child

—In this discussion, to avoid confusion, I refer to the client as "Jennifer", her inner child as "Jenny," her mother as "Martha," and her father as "Fred." One might proceed with the following:

> What would little Martha have needed at that time? [Go for the basic needs. Often clients will respond with what their own child needed to *do*.] What would she have needed to *receive*? How would she have been different if she had received what she really needed? "How would that have affected your growing up?"

This is where the process changes somewhat from what I described above in relation to working with the *client's* inner child. Here we have another child (Martha) with unmet needs. These needs must be met in some way if Jennifer is to be released from the limitations and/or destructiveness of the old familiar patterns of behavior—that is, if she is to be released from the constraints of her internal family system. The question is, "Who is going to do it?"

Most likely, Jennifer's whole life has centred around trying to anticipate her mother's needs, and catering to or avoiding the consequences of Martha's unmet needs. Moreover, at this stage, it is unlikely that Jennifer is sufficiently disidentified from little Jenny (or from her internal father and his dynamics) to respond positively to the suggestion that she consider Martha's needs. This is usually met with something like, "No way! It's my turn now!" At other times, the client may feel okay about caring for both Children. This works well as long as she is able to experience that she is caring for a *part of herself* and that it is not the same thing as a child taking responsibility for her mother. It appears to be best to offer some options and allow the client to choose which ones seem right for her. You might say something like this:

> Imagine a point of light way off in the distance. Gradually, as it approaches, it becomes brighter and larger and more and more beautiful. From the centre of that light there appears the image of a very Loving, very Kind, and very Wise Being or Presence—someone who knows little Martha well and has come to be just with her. [Note the emphasis on Love instead of Wisdom which is usual in traditional Psychosynthesis. People who have suffered abuse are much more immediately in need of Love than they are of Wisdom.] This being knows exactly what Martha needs and exactly how to provide for those needs. It may appear as a Being of Light, or a religious symbol, something from nature or it may have human form—male or female. Whatever comes is what is right for you.
>
> Notice how little Martha responds to this presence. *There is no need for you to do anything.* Just watch their interaction and allow the Being or Presence to handle whatever is going on with Martha. It knows what to do.

The following dialogue is an example of how this visualization works:

Jennifer: Martha won't have anything to do with the Loving Presence. She doesn't trust it.

Guide: And what does the Loving Presence do?

Jennifer: It just stands there.

Guide: And now what's happening?

Jennifer: Martha runs and hides.

Guide: And the Loving Presence?

Jennifer: It stays there. It's not doing anything.

Guide: Keep watching.

Jennifer: Martha is peeking. She wonders why it doesn't go away. She's going closer. She climbs up on its lap. She's crying and telling it she's afraid it will go away. The Loving Presence says it will always be there.

And it will—so long as *Jennifer* evokes the image of the Loving Presence with little Martha.

It is important to ask Jennifer to observe the response of little Jenny, just as she has observed the interaction between Martha and the Loving Presence. Usually, there is an experience of much relief, a lightening of the burden carried for many years. At this point, it is useful to suggest the following:

Consider now that Jenny never really had a mother, at least not with respect to what we're dealing with here. She had someone who was emotionally still a child—a needy child who was not capable of meeting Jenny's needs because she still had unmet needs of her own.

Take a moment to tell Jenny that it was not her responsibility to meet little Martha's needs, especially not at the expense of her own; and that, indeed, she couldn't, then or now! Reassure her that someone else will do that now. Notice how she responds.

Allow Jenny to tell you what it's like for her to watch as little Martha is being cared for. Ask her what she needs at this time—and from whom she needs to receive it.

Most often, the Child answers, "From you!" (in this case, Jennifer). Sometimes, she says, "I want one of those!" (her own Loving, Kind, and Wise Presence). At other times, she wants to share her mother's Presence. This is especially true if the image turns out to be a universal image such as Jesus or Mary (mother of Jesus). Whatever works is what is right! And so you must adjust your directions in accordance with what the Child communicates as her need and allow some time for Jennifer to visualize and to experience doing whatever seems necessary. It really doesn't matter which images are chosen. Jennifer is doing the healing either way, because *she* is the one who evokes and holds the healing images. Allow plenty of time for this. When this is done, conclude with the following:

Once again become aware of the sphere of Unconditional Love that surrounds you—you, Jenny, Martha, and the Loving Presence (or Presences, as the case may be). And within that sphere of Unconditional Love, allow anything further that needs to happen to bring about whatever closure you need, just for now, allowing Love to reveal what needs revealing, to heal what needs healing, to release what needs releasing.

Valuable new insights and experiences often emerge at this step. Significant memories may surface. There is a deepening of experience, a growing awareness of how one has alternately identified with an inner child (Jenny) and an introjected mother's inner child (Martha) and of how the competition has resulted in neither one getting their needs met. This, I believe, accounts for why so many clients work very hard to have affection for an inner child only to experience a bottomless pit. Thus, negative projections onto the Sphere of Unconditional Love may surface, echoing the feelings, thoughts, and beliefs which the client has had in relation to parents or other significant figures. Such projections are best handled by Love. You should encourage the client to share her feelings, thoughts, and concerns with the Sphere of Unconditional Love and to be open to Love's response.

There is usually a mixture of joy and sadness—joy for the healing, the hope, the release from the pain of unfulfilled needs; and sadness for the realization of what never was. ("I never had a mother. She was only—emotionally—a child!") So there is mourning for the wasted years—not only for what was lost, but also for what will never be! And that brings us to the next stage.

Stage 2—Letting Go: Stepping Out of the Family System

Needless to say, the above is only a phase of the whole process. It needs to be repeated with respect to the introjected father and his inner child—and sometimes with grandparents or other significant figures (foster parents and so on). At some point, holding all of these persons within the Sphere of Unconditional Love is very helpful—asking Love to reveal the right relationship between and among them. (There's plenty of room for all! Unconditional Love extends in all directions. The beauty of all this, I tell clients, is that you don't have to believe it for it to work! You just have to do it.)

The process of letting go is truly a death and rebirth experience and it includes all the stages of dying as described by Elizabeth Kubler Ross in *Death and Dying:* denial, anger, bargaining, depression, and acceptance. Stanislav Grof's (see *Realms of the Human Unconscious*) four basic perinatal matrices are also apparent in this process.

1. Denial—There is denial of the extent to which an internal family system is contributing to the havoc in one's life, be this depression, substance abuse, eating disorders, physiological problems, suicidal tendencies, self-mutilation, sexual dysfunction, anxiety and panic attacks, repeated victimization, dysfunctional relationships, inhibition of creativity, or difficulty holding a job. There is also denial of how one is projecting the patterns of an internal family system onto current personal and work relationships and of how one is playing out the familiar roles. Clients often protest, "But those people are really doing those things to me!" And of course they are. The point is as the client steps out of the internal family system and identifies with her own essence, her own Self, she will have the courage to affect changes in those relationships or to remove herself from environments which are destructive or tend to reinforce old survival patterns, the value of which have long ceased to exist. She will begin to approach people with openness and trust and warmth, to attract people who are capable of supporting her, encouraging her in the way that she desires and needs. She will search out and find guidance and avenues for her creative expression. But until she acknowledges her part in the system, and lets go of the old familiar way of relating, it is unlikely that she will be able to receive what she needs even when it is offered to her.

2. Anger—The client needs encouragement to experience and express her anger about having been violated, about having been deprived, about the loss, about all the wasted years. Often, this extends beyond anger about the pain and indignities inflicted by human beings and is directed toward God for bringing her into such an existence and for not bailing her out.

Several of the women in our group had previously been in groups which had urged them to use cathartic techniques to release their anger. This, apparently, led to too much intensity, too soon, and was so frightening that they left the group. It is essential to assist the client in finding a safe context and an optimum time for releasing profound rage. For many, their safety has depended upon withholding anger such that they fear that any release will result in violent outbursts toward others or themselves.

A useful technique is to have the client tell her inner child/adolescent that she sees that anger, that it was not safe for her to express it back then, but that she is willing to hear it now. Then, instruct the client to ask the Child:

> How angry are you? If you were safe and had all the power, what would you have said? What would you have liked to do? What would you have done?

A verbal outburst may follow, or the acting-out child may be visualized in a way which feels safe, such as at a distance or through a telescope. It is sometimes necessary to assure the client that you know she would not do such violent things and that this is only a way to release all that pent-up emotion. Often, this will leave the Child with a sense of empowerment. At other times, she will get in touch with her grief. Usually, the Child will need some form of support after such a catharsis. (See Harriet Goldhor Lerner, *The Dance of Anger*, for practical guidance on the acceptance and practical use of anger.)

3. Bargaining—As the old system begins to disintegrate, there is a desperate clinging to the dream of "Someday . . ." and a grasping for whatever threads can be found. The old system clearly wasn't working, but the new is unknown and therefore scary. The undercurrent of fear is not necessarily conscious, but it is nonetheless powerful:

> I can't take care of myself.
> I don't want to take care of myself.
> I won't take care of myself.
> I'll make you take care of me.

Please take care of me.
It must be *my* fault (old self-blame).
Maybe if I just . . . (bargaining).

4. Depression—This stage includes sadness for what might have been, for the abandonment of the dream, "Someday . . . if I'm just good enough or do enough then my mother (or father) will love me and take care of me. Someday they will recognize me, acknowledge who I am, what I know, what I can do." The truth is that the client herself *is the only one who can* decide that she is "enough." Often, she realizes that "I've lived my whole life trying to do something that can't be done!", and the anger now turns inward against herself.

5. Acceptance—Letting Go is not complete until there is acceptance of the fact that we are *the only ones who can provide for our well-being*. Even if all those others were willing to do it for us, they get sick, they have their own emotional upheavals, they sometimes die. We can count on only ourselves to be available to ourselves for the duration of our lives. With acceptance comes the realization that nothing is ever wasted and we appreciate what we have learned and developed through all our pain (though, of course, we wouldn't wish it on anyone!). There is acceptance of the fact that the external universe supports our choices, that we maintain our suffering by the choices we make, or we create our joy.[3] There is acceptance of the fact that no amount of bargaining will ever earn us what we most essentially need—Unconditional Love.

The following excerpts from an edited transcript of an actual session illustrate the stages discussed thus far. For clarity, the same names are used that were used above:

> I'm seeing three figures: Jennifer (the adult), my father (little Freddy), and my adult father (Fred). It's in flux . . . they're getting smaller. I see that both my mother and my father need to be looked after. It has nothing to do with age. . . . I'm making it on my own. [To parents:] You can't understand. I'm angry. I don't feel like looking after you. . . . Yes, I do . . . I'm still doing the traditional things in hope that you'll give back.
>
> I see a triangle: Jennifer/Jenny; Fred/Freddy, Martha/little Martha.
>
> I'm angry! I want to look after myself. I don't want to look after my mother and father. I don't need my parents to look after me. I can look after myself . . . I need *something* . . . from them . . . acknowledgement. That sounds trivial . . . then I'm holding back . . . it's a bonding thing then. It's almost like a checkmate. I have this feeling that they can't . . . they don't know how. That's the way they are. They just can't change.
>
> I feel sorry for them. The whole family is there now . . . brothers and sisters. The parents can't enter into communication with us. They have themselves locked up . . . the two of them. They can't say they're wrong. They can't say, "that's a great job," that the children have done well. They can't acknowledge.
>
> I feel sorry for them. It's sad . . . I want to shake them. I really feel like just walking off. I don't feel like taking on two more children. I'm involved with *my* family . . . looking after *my* children and after myself.
>
> Right now I don't feel guilty. I feel sad about it. I want to say I'll do it. But I can't now . . . because I've learned that there's only so much I can do. I just

can't do it now (not said angrily). I can just say that . . . without guilt on my part or resentment or . . . I want to hang up the phone and say, "I'll talk to you later! I'm still sad, but there's other things I have to do. I'm not ready to talk to you yet. You don't have to understand that."

[Surrounding all with a sphere of Unconditional Love:] I see my parents like Japanese dolls—little people trapped inside this wooden person.

[To parents:] It's a whole lot nicer outside. I'm going to be fine. I've gotten smarter . . . I'll see you some time.

It's so lonely for them. I'm feeling okay. I'm doing things I like to do . . . have time for myself . . . I'm feeling comfortable with my life. I feel sad because I know they're not. "I'll just have to get through to you another time."

I feel as though I'm closing a door . . . walking to another door . . . not ready to open it yet. I'll know when I'm ready. The path I've been on started a long time ago. You know there's a path. You don't always see what's around the bend, but you know it's there. The sphere of light is around the entire path.

I feel really quiet and comfortable . . . equipped! I don't feel confidence or not confidence. Just okay. Whatever comes up, I'll be able to handle it. If I don't know how, I'll learn how. I won't have to be waiting for something or someone to tell me how to handle it."

[Following a discussion about the stages of letting go:] Acceptance comes in two stages. First there is the awareness that you were not able to give me that. *OK*, I survived it. But I still expect something. Letting go of the expectations comes more gradually. It could be a long time . . . with a lot of bouncing back and forth.

Note in the transcript how the speaker bounces back and forth between expectations and letting go of them. Also, note how her awareness of her parents shifts between perceiving them as introjected parts of herself and as separate entities.

Often there is much confusion, disorientation, and frustration during the period between closing one door and opening another. The new vistas are still blurry: "I don't know who I am anymore!" "I don't seem to fit anywhere!" It is important to help, not force, the client to settle the confusion and to focus on the new orientation while affirming her choice to move on and to assume responsibility for her own support and guidance. In taking the last step, she will need to draw upon both inner resources and appropriate external resources (teachers, books, friends, and so on) with the conviction that, "If I don't know how, I'll learn how."

Stage 3—Choice for Life: Discovery and Expression of Purpose

Inevitably, as the client experiences that the old system can no longer contain her expanded sense of self (much as the womb can no longer contain the full-term baby), she begins to shift her focus away from a dependency/survival orientation. Hers is truly an experience of rebirth as she looks beyond the door that is closing. There is both excitement and fear, and often it is difficult to distinguish beteen them. Feelings and beliefs associated with prenatal and perinatal experiences are evoked.[4] Trust emerges, again as a central issue, not trust in any particular person, but in a Divine Order of Life, a life that supports the beliefs she holds and the choices she makes.

Quite often, this trust is blocked by fundamental decisions made very early in her life about her own desire. An infant whose cries are met with rejection or harsh treatment may decide, for example, "It's not safe for me to want what *I* want." This is probably the deepest wound of all, for *where there is no desire, life stops*. It's important to understand that the issue is not that the child can't have *what* she wants, but that she *can't even want it*. Without a redemption of her desire, the client cannot even want from Life, much less receive, the fruits of all her hard work.

Processes that evoke clarity concerning *what* the client wants to express and *to whom* are most helpful. Suggested reading may also be useful, such as *Work With Passion* by Nancy Anderson, or works which offer guidance in matching skills and talents with what one finds exciting or troublesome. New skills can be developed as a sense of purpose comes into view.

Concluding Remarks

It is helpful to consider other dynamics and to make use of exercises and processes in addition to the work described above. For example, catharsis should be encouraged, but not forced, and exercises are recommended that use art, imagery, and dialogue for balancing polarities, creating an "ideal model," and evoking positive qualities. All of these are amply described in the available psychosynthesis literature. Exploring the four basic questions— Where am I coming from? Where am I going? What's in my way? What do I need?—is a gentle but effective way to begin the group process. It is also valuable to repeat this exploration occasionally. At some time, it will be important to explore the relation between elements of the *internal* Victim/ Persecutor/Rescuer triangle and to facilitate disidentification and transformation of this system. (For a more complete description of these dynamics, see *Born to Win* by Muriel James.)

Perhaps this is an appropriate place to add a word about confrontation with the abuser. In much of the literature about dealing with child abuse, there is an emphasis on the importance of confronting abusers with what they did and the effects of their behavior. It cannot be overemphasized that the essence of healing the wounds of abuse has to do with the restoration of the *right relationship* between and among members of the *inner family* and/or surrogates. Reconciliation with external family members may or may not occur and is not essential to the healing process. This is good news for those whose parents are no longer living or who are set in their defences. Those who want to be reconciled with their families will be more likely to achieve their desired results if they make the attempt from a perspective that consciously holds awareness of their inner child and their inner family system. In so doing, they will be less likely to become a child again in relation to their family, which only results in the re-enactment of old dys-functional patterns.

The early results of applying the process described above to relationship therapy are also exciting. Identifying the wounded inner child/adolescent in each partner and in their relationship is helpful in unhooking the lower unconscious connection which is the source of so much distress. During the romantic phase of a relationship, there is a very powerful lower unconscious attraction. One Wounded Child recognizes and sympathizes with the

Wounded Child of the other, resulting in a very tight bonding—an unspoken, unconscious contract to comfort each other. This is a natural thing for two children and/or adolescents to do since they cannot meet either their own or each other's needs. To the degree that partners have completed the Letting Go phase and have entered the Choice for Life phase, they are able to choose freely an adult-to-adult way of relating to each other versus a dependency-oriented relationship. This latter way of being in Love (versus "in love") honors both the individuality and the needs to belong of each partner.

Rollo May has said that "violence is the explosion of powerlessness." If anything is clear from working with adults who have been abused as children it is that those who have been violated are likely to perpetuate that violence in some way upon themselves or upon others. (For a convincing study of this phenomenon, see Alice Miller, *For Your Own Good*.) No wonder that our prisons are so full; and no wonder that there is so much violence between nations. No wonder that mere incarceration does not deter the repetition of violent acts. Such treatment, while perhaps necessary in the absence of more effective means, only further constrains the unconstrainable.

When one considers the statistics that one in four adults have been sexually abused as children—and that this is considered to be a conservative estimate—it does not take a very large leap of imagination to see the effects that the healing of these wounds could have in bringing about a non-violent world. It seems reasonable to assume that those who experience the healing power of Love may become, instead of perpetrators of violence, "sowers of love," described in the Prayer of St. Francis of Assisi. Gradually the seeds of violence will have no room to grow.

Notes

1. Readers will recognize Assagioli's stages in the following pages: (1) thorough knowledge of one's personality; (2) control of its various elements; (3) realization of one's Self—the creation of a unifying centre; and (4) psychosynthesis—the formation of one's personality around the new centre.

2. This objection may be indicative of a role assumed by the child to protect the parents from the pain of their imperfection (so that they won't abandon or hurt the child in some way). It may also arise from the need of the child to see her parents as good and capable care-givers. In this case, the child assumes that there is something wrong with *her*. This position is often tenaciously adhered to because of the need to see her parents as capable of meeting her survival needs.

3. At some point, it is necessary to facilitate an acceptance of both joy and pain. The tendency is either to (1) identify with the pain and block out joy (because, for example, at some level a decision has been made that it hurts less to keep joy out in the first place rather than to let it in and have it ripped away again) or to (2) identify with the joy, which doesn't work too well either. In the first instance, one is always "waiting for the other shoe to drop," never appreciating periods of joy. The latter approach requires tremendous energy to block out awareness of pain and it deprives one of the opportunity to learn from or to protect oneself from the effects of the painful experience.
   A more useful position is that of "I am not my pain or my joy. Sometimes I

am in pain and sometimes I am in joy. I can chose which of these I want to explore." It is only from this perspective that healing becomes possible.

4.   For more information on how to heal the effects of these very early experiences, contact Dr. Tom Verny, Prenatal and Perinatal Psychology Association of North America, 36 Madison Avenue, Toronto, Ontario M5R 2S1; or Dr. Anne Maiden, Marina Counseling Center, 2137 Lombard Street, San Francisco, California 94123.

The Core Personality: Treatment Strategies for Multiple Personality Disorder

Vincent Dummer and Mary Greene

Practitioners of Psychosynthesis are familiar with a perspective of the personality which holds that it is a constellation of subpersonalities centred around an "I." James Vargiu's (1974) article "Subpersonalities" gives an excellent account of the inner multiplicity of an individual and the therapeutic process leading toward integration and synthesis. Therapeutic principles such as accepting the subpersonalities and meeting their needs have also been found to be applicable to clients with Multiple Personality Disorder (MPD). The subpersonalities in these clients take the form of alternate personalities (alters).

Our experience in working with subpersonalities has been very helpful in our work with alters. At the same time, our work with alters has helped us to better understand our work with subpersonalities. In this article, we would like to share our findings, some of which affirm ideas developed in Psychosynthesis and some of which tentatively expand the view of the personality and the healing process.

Characteristics of Multiple Personality Disorder

MPD is unusual, but contrary to common belief not rare. Probably each full-time therapist is seeing at this moment one or more clients with this disorder. The condition is frequently misdiagnosed because of lack of experience with the symptoms. Once therapists at our centre, for example, learned to diagnose the condition, they found at least one person in their client load who fit the diagnosis.

The difference between clients with subpersonalities and clients with alters is largely a matter of degree. Alters have more autonomy and are more distinct but can be more difficult to recognize because of the presence of an amnesic barrier. Many clients with MPD are unconscious of their alters and have learned to ignore the symptoms that indicate their existence. Some of these symptoms might be finding themselves somewhere and not knowing how they got there or finding articles of clothing, food, and so on they do not remember buying. They may be told by friends of things they said or did that they do not remember saying or doing and they may even be aware of spans of time elapsing for which they cannot account. Headaches and other psychosomatic symptoms are commonly reported by individuals

75

with alters as well as periods of extreme emotional disturbance for which they have no adequate explanation. In interacting with the individual, one can sometimes observe dramatic changes in facial expression, voice, movement, and handwriting.

Alters are apparently formed in the same manner as subpersonalities, but when the individual must dissociate either the emotional, mental, or physical content of an experience in order to survive or to maintain sanity, then an alter is formed. In general, dissociation occurs only under extremely stressful or traumatic circumstances and continues when adequate support is not given the individual following the trauma.

An example of dissociation could be the shock that people experience after an accident. The mind dissociates into separate parts which are capable of dealing with a specific aspect of the event but not with the total event. For instance, one part may hold the terror of anticipating the accident, another may hold the anger at the driver of the other car, and another may hold the pain and hurt. There might be another part that has no feelings at all but was able to get out of the car and get some help. And then one part may just be numb, not be able to remember anything of the accident, and eager to go on with life as if nothing had happened. By distinguishing the parts of the personality which deal with an aspect of the experience versus the experience as a whole and integral part of life, we can distinguish and identify the core personality. In this particular example, the one who does not remember anything of the accident would be the core personality.

We hypothesize that most individuals with MPD have, at least potentially, a core personality, a "state of mind," relatively free of defence mechanisms. For example, if someone suggests that we are rationalizing or projecting our experience, we can either become defensive or we can step back and sincerely acknowledge our behavior. It is possible, in other words, to move into a relatively centred, balanced state which is more than observational and which brings with it an increased awareness. This state includes mind, feelings, and physical sensations and is accompanied by an experience of being able to make and act on choices. In this state, we can check our experience to see whether or not it is influenced by defence mechanisms. Just as we can distinguish between being "real" and being controlled by defence mechanisms, people with MPD can distinguish between their core personality and the alters that have resulted from dissociation. We are not implying that alters cannot be genuine, centred, and objective, but that it is more difficult for them to stay this way.

Relating to Alters

In treating MPD, it is essential to consider all of the alters as important and valuable, even though they differ in characteristics, capabilities, and functions. Whereas the alters may have originally served an adaptive, survival, or defence function, the original personality has a broader function which is to live, love, be aware, and choose as a human being. We hypothesize that the essence of this function may be replicable but not transferable and that it is therefore continued in the core personality. The core personality is uniquely able to perform this function because it has the best capacity to experience fully and realistically both the inner life and the external world.

Some Inner Self Helpers may be more aware of certain values and better able to act on them than other alters, but we believe that the core personality is potentially best equipped to relate to the total picture and to act accordingly.

A careful history of the dissociations, with the help of the "memory trace" (Wilbur, 1984), usually reveals the core personality. If an individual's personality is not dormant, he or she experiences him or herself realistically as to age, gender, and physical appearance; he or she recognizes him or herself in a mirror or from a photograph while alters may not. A high sense of morality is frequently manifested as in a caring for the family, a general social awareness and concern for other people's feelings, a strong awareness of parental responsibilities, a striving for honesty, and feelings of existential shame and guilt. At the beginning of therapy, the core personality is mostly amnesic of the alters, and may confabulate to maintain a sense of continuity. Alters, however, are often aware of the core personality and strongly affected by its experiences (Ludwig, 1972). For example, experiences that the core personality has, such as seeing an instrument that was used in abuse, can easily stir up traumatic experiences in the alters. This may cause the alter to take over and act out the emotional experience, or covertly create emotional turmoil which makes the core personality feel "crazy." The core personality is generally willing to learn and to take responsibility for actions and mistakes. However, the core personality is easily overwhelmed and has a tendency to give up, requiring the alters to take over.

It is not unusual for the core personality to be depleted and for some alters to be stronger, better adjusted, more aware, and more energetic. That is, it is not the actual ability to cope that determines the core personality, but historical development and the potential to function fully and realistically. In cases of a dormant or weak core personality, one or more alters may stand in for or represent the core personality until it is able to develop. The core personality usually emerges as the strength of the whole person increases.

Alters may take on any imaginable form or identity. They frequently see themselves as having the age and appearance of the individual at the time of dissociation. They take on the identity of the aggressor in an abusive situation. Or they develop an imaginary identity consistent with an aspect of the experience of the trauma. Yet alters tend to relate to the core personality in three ways.

First, there are alters that present themselves as predominantly independent and power oriented (or yang). Second, there are alters that present themselves as oriented toward love and harmony (or yin). "Yang-alters" are initially more dominated by feelings of anger, rage, pride, or jealousy, whereas "yin-alters" are initially more controlled by feelings of fear, hurt, depression, or inadequacy. Although the yin-alters may be needy and helpless, they tend to accept and co-operate with the core personality. The yang-alters, however, can be very resistant to working on their traumas and tend to intimidate and reject others, including the core personality and the therapist. These alters can be better accepted if perceived as protectors. They almost always protect or stand up for some higher good or value, even though this may not be apparent at first sight. For instance, one of the infant alters of a client who had suffered severe infant abuse always appeared to be hitting "the baby" in the belief that if she hurt the baby enough the abuser would stop. Another alter tried to die in an effort to preserve the existential choice to live or to die. This alter would say: "Me die—him not die, me".

Third, there are the Inner Self Helpers, a unique group of alters which have a special relationship with the core personality. They are known for their knowledge of the system, their wise comments, and their loyalty to the individual (Comstock, 1985). Some of the Inner Self Helpers never come into the body. Their function is similar to that of the Wise Person and they can learn to perform any mental function that can be accomplished through hypnosis. But these Inner Self Helpers should not be confused with the Higher Self, since they have specific limitations related to the life experience of the individual and the functions for which they were developed. There are other Inner Self Helpers that hold little or no emotional aspects of the trauma. They have more inner awareness and serve helpful functions both intrapsychically and in the life of the individual.

Distinguishing the Core Personality

While the therapist is getting to know and understand the different alters and helping them to work through their traumas and deal with their conflicts, he or she starts experiencing each alter as a separate entity. Distinguishing the core personality is helpful in understanding how the reactions of the alters actually represent the complex intrapsychic dynamics of a single individual. Distinguishing a core personality also helps the therapist to structure and evaluate the progress of therapy. The strength of the core personality can be used as a prognosis for the mental health of the individual. For heuristic purposes, we propose distinguishing core personalities in terms of their strength and coping capacity. We have found three groups of core personalities which are representations on a dimension ranging from minimum strength to maximum strength. While a person's core personality may belong to one group, circumstances and stress can temporarily place that person in a different group.

The first group contains individuals with a *dormant* core personality. The core personality has had little real life experience and is absent most of the time. Sometimes prenatal or massive dissociation, followed by continued trauma, can keep a core personality from further development. The core personality may have tried at times to emerge, but was not successful due to a lack of strength. In these cases, the alters must make all of the decisions in life to the best of their abilities and understanding. It can, however, be hard to implement any long-term decision because of switching. The alters are often aware of the absence of a core personality and are, to some extent, psychologically ill-prepared for the core personality to develop. For instance, yang-alters can be convinced that the core personality cannot survive in this world, and they try to stop the emergence at all costs.

In the second group are individuals with a *functional* core personality. The core personality has developed a true identity and is able to cope with ordinary life situations. However, the core personality has not enough awareness and ability to relate to the alters from a position of acceptance and strength. When situations become too difficult, the core personality lets an alter take over, thus avoiding any emotional impact. Alters may be disdainful of or perceive the core personality as a threat to their existence.

In the third group are individuals with a *responsible* core personality. Individuals in this group have a core personality which is able to relate to the alters and can help them meet their needs in a constructive way. Usually enough co-operation has been achieved to make the individual's multiplicity appear both less obvious and less problematic. The core personality has developed the ability to express and to tolerate a wide range of emotions and to implement decisions guided by inner values. The core personality in this group may start experiencing the alters as parts of the self, as subpersonalities, or as "ego states" (Watkins, 1979) rather than as independent and autonomous alters.

We have learned from clinical experience to adjust the therapeutic strategies and the pacing of the therapy to the strength of the core personality. Depending on the client, we may prefer *not* to introduce the concept of a core personality until he or she has reached a certain stage of acceptance of the alters. Yet we have found that it is not necessary to discuss the core personality with the client in order to work with the concept. Essentially, the therapy is conceptualized as a process of strengthening the core personality: as therapy progresses, a core personality becomes stronger, and the individual moves to the next group.

Therapeutic Interventions

Clients with a dormant core personality may need a guardian or a hospital to rely on. Trust needs to be developed in both tangible and intangible ways and the trustworthiness of the therapist is subjected to numerous tests. The therapist must stand in for the core personality when working with the alters. Much of the work involves reclaiming and working through traumas. This work includes the release and acceptance of emotions, reframing attitudes, and learning new ways of coping. Essential skills and attitudes of relating to themselves, each other, and other people may also need to be taught. Alters can learn to monitor the therapy session so that they can benefit from one another's therapeutic experience.

The integration of the alters may be accomplished, especially in cases where this involves an integration of personality fragments. When the alters start making progress in dealing with their emotions, and the stress on the whole person diminishes, energy becomes available for the core personality to develop. The development of the core personality needs to be planned by the therapist. For instance, if the core personality is a fetus, it may be best to work through the infant and early childhood traumas before introducing the core personality to the world. Advice and recommendations from Inner Self Helpers can be helpful in this matter. Once the core personality has emerged, sometimes with the use of a birth ritual, the core personality may need age-appropriate forms of parenting and education in order to facilitate emotional growth. This may include bottle feeding, comforting, learning to play, and so on for a limited period of time. In this stage, some alters may need help in adjusting to the presence of the core personality.

Clients with a functional core personality have had some positive experiences and have learned to cope with ordinary life situations. Therefore, they require less effort on the part of the therapist in providing for a protective and nurturing environment. Hospitalizations can be avoided with this group by timely recognition and by working through traumas from the past that are triggered by present events. The therapist needs to help the core personality understand and accept MPD. It is helpful for the core personality to know about the symptoms of MPD, the presence of alters, and the reasons for switching. Facilitation of an emotional acceptance of MPD is frequently an ongoing process related to an increase in the strength of the core personality. It is useful for some of the therapeutic interventions to deal directly with strengthening the core personality. The core personality needs to be made aware of the tendency to give up as a way of coping with an intolerable situation. It needs to learn alternative ways of coping, to become aware of moments of choice, and to practise making choices using the new coping skills. The core personality benefits from an increased awareness of positive inner qualities.

In working directly with the core personality, the therapist needs to consider its limitations so that it is not overwhelmed with new responsibilities. The therapist continues helping the alters work through their traumas and improve their relations with each other. This work is not only beneficial for the alters but is also a vicarious learning experience for the core personality. The therapist needs to encourage the core personality toward co-consciousness and to cultivate the ability to deal with emotions that arise as a result of working with the alters. Teaching ways in which the core personality can help the alters greatly improves mutual acceptance. For example, the core personality may buy a stuffed animal for a child alter and give him or her time to play with it in a safe situation.

Clients with a responsible core personality may still have problems with their emotions but they are less likely to act them out in a harmful way. They can take more responsibility for their life and for the work done in the therapy sessions. Their dissociations are often intentional and are done for a therapeutic purpose. Generally, enough spiritual development is present for the core personality to be aware of and willing to act on values such as altruism, love, honesty, and courage. In combination with increased coping skills, this greatly enhances the self-acceptance and strength of the individual.

In this group, the experience of the alters is more available to the core personality. Usually, the core personality can begin learning to image the alters instead of dissociating into them. Through the image, the core personality is able to share in the experiences of the alters, reparent them, provide them with the needed nurturing and protection, and help them reframe their attitudes. Thus the alters can come to be experienced by the core personality as its parts, or subpersonalities, with wants and needs that the core personality can meet. When these needs are met, the alters become more co-operative and more united in their intentions. At this point, integration and fusion occur naturally.

Summary

We have conceptualized an approach to MPD that focusses on strengthening the core personality. If the core personality gains enough strength to cope with the traumatic history on an emotional, attitudinal, and behavioral level, the defence mechanism of dissociation is no longer needed. The person regains the freedom to make life decisions and to express him or herself in ways that are both aligned with inner values and appropriate to external circumstances.

References

Comstock, C. (1985). *Internal self helpers or centers*. Paper presented at the Second International Conference on Multiple Personalities and Dissociative States, Chicago.

Ludwig, A. M., Brandsma, J. M., Wilbur, C. B., Bendefeldt, F., & Jameson, D. H. (1972). The objective study of multiple personality. *Archives of General Psychiatry*, **26**, 298–310.

Vargiu, J. (1974). Subpersonalities. *Synthesis*, **1**, 59–90.

Watkins, J. G., & Watkins, H. H. (1979). Ego states and hidden observers. *Journal of Altered States of Consciousness*, **5**, 27–31.

Wilbur, C. B. (1984). Treatment of multiple personality. *Psychiatric Annals*, **14**, 27–31.

Suggested Reading

Diagnosis

Coons, P. M. (1980). Multiple personality: Diagnostic considerations. *Journal of Clinical Psychiatry*, **41**, 330–336.

Schafer, D. W. (1986). Recognizing multiple personality patients. *American Journal of Psychotherapy*, **4**, 500–510.

Treatment

Kluft, R. P. (1984). Treatment of multiple personality disorder. *Psychiatric Clinics of North America*, **7**(1), 9–29.

Braun, B. G. (1986). *Treatment of multiple personality disorder*. Washington, DC: American Psychiatric Press. (For copies write to: APA, 1400 K St. NW, Washington, DC 20005.)

Etiology

Kluft, R. P. (1985). Childhood antecedents of multiple personality. Washington, DC: American Psychiatric Press.

General

Proceedings of the International Conference on Multiple Personality and Dissociative States. (1984/85/86/87). (For copies write to: Dissociative Disorders Program, Department of Psychiatry, Rush University, 1720 West Polk St., Chicago, IL 60612.)

Grief Is More Than Crying

Kay Lynne Sherman

Several years ago my fiancé was murdered, apparently by burglars who entered the house. I was in another town at the time, and when the police called to notify me, my initial reaction was overwhelmingly physical. I walked into the bathroom and the entire contents of my digestive system turned to diarrhea. Then the convulsive shaking began, and alternate cold chills and hot sweats lasted for days and nights. I felt as though someone had whirled around with a very heavy board and had caught me in the mid-section with it; it took my breath away for months. Tears were the last thing on my mind. Rather, I felt as though I were riding a bucking bronco called my body, with a new surprising symptom every few minutes.

The ensuing months were no less of a surprise. Total numbness set in. Fear stalked me as I realized in agony that the police were in fact not going to catch the culprits. The world no longer seemed to make sense. If someone could murder a kind and gentle man such as John, how could anything make sense? What had I done to bring this into my life? The questions were deep and endless. My family and friends tried to do what they thought would help, which in many cases definitely did not help, but in fact added to my pain. Then I began the process of rebuilding myself and my life.

John Bowlby makes this observation:

> Loss of a loved person is one of the most intensely painful experiences any human being can suffer. And not only is it painful to experience but it is also painful to witness, if only because we are so impotent to help. To the bereaved nothing but the return of the lost person can bring true comfort; should what we provide fall short of that it is felt almost as an insult. That, perhaps, explains a bias that runs through so much of the older literature on how human beings respond to loss. Whether an author is discussing the effects of loss on an adult or a child, there is a tendency to underestimate how intensely distressing and disabling loss usually is and for how long the distress, and often the disablement, commonly lasts. Conversely, there is a tendency to suppose that a normal healthy person can and should get over a bereavement not only fairly rapidly, but also completely.

In this article, I would like to offer to the psychosynthesis community my understanding of the process that grief takes, based on my personal experience, my work with grieving clients, and on the research I have done in the area. I believe that this is a timely subject for us, because I see some essential changes occurring in Psychosynthesis.

Historically, writers and practitioners in the field have tended to emphasize the spiritual qualities of the work, out of excitement for a psychotherapy which acknowledges and co-operates with Spirit. Much of the work has been connected to the growth movement, guiding people to greater awareness of Self and of purpose in life. Recently, psychosynthesists with whom I have been in contact have been looking at ways in which we can deepen our understanding of Assagioli's work and apply it to the serious crises and pathologies that present themselves in clinical practice.

In my practice, and in my area of research, I have concentrated on the issues of bereavement and the grief process. I have found it interesting that grief, which is such a universal human experience, is absent in many training programs for therapists. In addition, it is an area of great ignorance and discomfort for most people in our culture. Grief work at its best can result in an experience of transformation and an expansion of the Self; Psychosynthesis offers a very suitable framework in which to do this work.

I pay particular attention below to the symptoms of grief since these often appear without conscious connection to loss. Recognizing the symptoms for what they are can open the door to healing and transformation in our personal lives and in our work with clients. Following a description of the phases or "tasks" of grieving, I discuss therapeutic approaches to the grief process and how they relate to the psychosynthesis approach.

The Grief Process

After the death of her husband Prince Albert, Queen Victoria continued to order servants to lay out his clothing and shaving gear daily, and often she was seen speaking to "him" as she made her palace rounds. As a model for behavior in her time, she no doubt influenced mourning practices greatly. To what extent do we continue to be influenced by her model? Where today do we look for guidelines on how to grieve?

Traditionally, mourning rituals have been determined by the dominant culture; priests and priestesses handled the ceremonies as well as the counselling. However, as our own culture changes, it no longer provides clear guidelines for mourning, and the bereaved are without wise counsel. Queen Victoria's behavior is as likely a model for mourning as were the awkward responses of those around her a standard guideline for sympathy. In much of Western culture, where the subjects of death and loss are generally avoided, the bereaved not only are deprived of guidelines on how to handle their loss but are also apt to find themselves a social embarrassment. The grieving person, with no information or guidelines, may regard symptoms as signs of physical or psychological illness, and in an attempt to suppress the process may indeed manifest illness.

How would we, as helping professionals or as friends, have responded to the Queen in her grief? How do we respond to our own friends and clients? How, in fact, do we deal with our own grief? It is sometimes difficult to know what to do or say when we come in contact with someone who has been bereaved. Conflicting ideas about what healthy grieving consists of, as well as our own lack of comfort with the subject, can immobilize us. Often we are really not sure that our actions have been appropriate or helpful.

Much has been done in recent years to transform dying into a meaningful rite of passage. Now, what of those who are left to grieve the death? And what of those who have suddenly lost a loved one through homicide or suicide and face their mourning with an additional burden to bear? By recognizing that the grief process itself has the potential to be a truly transformative experience, we can better understand and provide a caring response to those facing this crucial passage.

Attachment

[For the greylag goose], the first response to the disappearance of the partner consists in the anxious attempt to find him again. The goose moves about restlessly by day and night, uttering all the time the penetrating trisyllabic long-distance call. . . . The searching expeditions are extended farther and farther and quite often the searcher itself gets lost, or succumbs to an accident. . . . All the objective observable characteristics of the goose's behavior on losing its mate are roughly identical with human grief. (Lorenz, as quoted in Parkes, 1972, p. 40)

At the root of mourning is attachment to another human being. If we were not deeply connected, the loss of a loved one would not matter. British psychiatrist John Bowlby has produced a monumental work on the subject of attachment and loss. He sees attachment as a normal form of behavior, distinct from feeding behavior and sexual behavior and of at least equal significance (1980, pp. 39–41). Among all species, attachments develop for survival reasons. Obviously, our attachments to one another have motivations and aspects other than survival, but I think it is helpful to realize that the pain which is felt at separation has very deep instinctual roots.

According to Bowlby, attachment behavior in humans is any form of behavior which has to do with attaining proximity to a preferred person. Affective bonds and attachments are present throughout the life cycle and are closely connected to our emotions of joy or sorrow. Attachment behavior is mediated by behavioral systems which early in development become goal corrected; the baby soon learns which behavior best elicits the affection of the care-giver. In many species, mourning responses arise out of specific attachment behavior; we can better understand the response if we appreciate the attachment behavior which is behind it. So the bereaved greylag goose continues to search for its dead mate because in earlier experiences that searching brought forth reunion. Many widows continue to search for their husbands long after there is any rational hope of finding them, feeling compelled to do so and at the same time fearing that they may in fact be going mad.

To better understand the normal human reactions to loss, let us first explore the typical grief symptoms.

Physical Expressions of Grief

No one ever told me that grief felt so like fear. I am not afraid, but the sensation is like being afraid. The same fluttering in the stomach, the same restlessness, the yawning. I keep on swallowing. (C. S. Lewis, 1961)

In one of the earliest works on the subject, Erich Lindemann (1979) describes the symptoms experienced by 101 bereaved people, many of whom were survivors of those lost in a disastrous fire at The Coconut Grove night club. He describes acute grief as consisting of sensations of somatic distress occurring in waves lasting from 20 minutes to an hour at a time, a feeling of tightness in the throat, choking with shortness of breath, need for sighing, an empty feeling in the abdomen, lack of muscular power, and an intense subjective distress described as tension or mental pain.

In his highly sensitive work describing the many aspects of bereavement, Colin Murray Parkes (1972) quotes an Australian study which found the following symptoms: headaches, dizziness, fainting spells, blurred vision, skin rashes, excessive sweating, indigestion, difficulty in swallowing, vomiting, heavy menstrual periods, palpitations, chest pains, shortness of breath, frequent infections, and general aching. In his own study of London widows, Parkes observed alarm reaction, an urge to search for the lost person in some form, anger and guilt, feelings of internal loss of self, and identification phenomena—the adoption of traits, mannerisms, or symptoms of the lost person.

It is possible that the physical symptoms caused by grief are due in part to the poor diet and disturbed schedule that often follow the death of a loved one. Occasionally after bereavement, however, physical symptoms become chronic or serious and, indeed, can become cause for concern. Bowlby first became interested in grief and loss when he noticed that the majority of the patients in a study he was doing on colitis were recently bereaved. Parkes quotes several studies which show that the incidence of death is higher among the bereaved (1972, p. 16). Interestingly enough, as Parkes points out, the most frequent cause of death among the recently bereaved is heart disease. Perhaps it is possible to die of a broken heart.

Occasionally, people enter therapy directly after a loss, particularly if the loss has been a sudden or shocking one. In general, however, it is more common for people to enter therapy or to seek medical help considerably later, and it is very likely that the connection is not made between the loss and the current physical symptoms. Using an in-take questionnaire does not always serve to discover significant losses because they have actually disappeared from the conscious mind. A client I was working with who had been experiencing an extended depression mentioned to me in one session that she had been suffering from colitis attacks. Knowing that colitis has been observed as an indication of repressed grief reaction, I asked her whether she had lost anyone close to her recently. Initially she responded that she hadn't; then suddenly her face changed, and she began sobbing. She recalled that shortly after her husband and she had separated, her mother-in-law, whom she loved very deeply, had died of cancer. Because of the somewhat bitter circumstances of the divorce, she had not been able to attend the funeral, see her mother-in-law's body, or express her grief. We began working at that point on her grief, which was a part of what had contributed to her feelings of depression. By being aware of the physical symptoms of grief, we can sometimes discover grief that has been repressed and that would otherwise have gone unnoticed.

Cognitive Expressions of Grief

In addition to physical symptoms, cognitive changes also occur. Worden describes these as disbelief, confusion, preoccupation, sense of presence, and hallucinations (1982, p. 24). Particularly in the first hours and days, a sense of disbelief, of unreality, is prominent. If the death has been sudden, the disbelief is stronger; if it has been a violent death, stronger still. Even though persons of authority have said that a loved one has died, even though the body has been viewed and bid *adieu,* the sense remains that some mistake has been made and that the beloved person will somehow (joyously!) still be alive. Each day the bereaved person must let in a little more of the reality that the lost one is truly gone. The dissonance between the moment-ous change the bereaved is undergoing in his or her own life and the normal progression of the world can be highly disorienting. As one of my clients said after the death of her father, "You go to the supermarket and you can't believe that everyone is just buying their food as normal. Don't they know that the whole world has changed?"

Confusion takes hold as the mind struggles to process the overwhelming impact of the change. The job of healing the wound caused by a death initially takes every bit of available thought. The necessary decisions regard-ing such things as funeral arrangements, personal belongings, and business affairs may deplete all of the decision-making ability. Preoccupation with thoughts about the dead person may nearly amount to an obsession. Often these thoughts centre around how to recover the lost person. In some cases, the confusion and disorientation may last well beyond those intense first days. This seems to be a diagnostic sign that the grief work is still in process and that it is necessary and appropriate for the bereaved person to continue drawing inward for a while longer.

A sense of the presence of the lost person is often reported by the grieving person. This may include actual hallucinations of both the visual and audit-ory type. In light of the results of recent research on near-death experiences in which participants report a continuation of existence after death, it is entirely possible that the dead loved one might in fact be available for completion of the relationship and that those grieving, and the alert prac-titioner, may be able to sense this presence. It is also possible that the sense of the loved one's presence after death may be the result of a desperate wish that it be so. Whatever the cause, in my own work as a therapist, I have indeed on occasion felt a presence in the room while working with a grieving client and have used the opportunity to help him work on any unfinished relationship issues with the deceased. Common themes that emerge are anger, apology, and forgiveness.

Richard Kalish refers to another cognitive expression of grief: the ten-dency to go over again and again all the events that led up to the death:

"When I saw him last Saturday, he looked as though he were rallying."
   "Yes, but the next morning, the nurse told me he had had a bad night."
   "Do you think it might have had something to do with his sister's illness?"
   "I doubt it, but I heard from an aide that he fell going to the bathroom that morning."
   "That explains that bruise on his elbow."
   "No wonder he told me he was angry because he couldn't seem to do anything right."
   And so it goes, the attempt to understand why someone who was rallying on Saturday was dead on Wednesday. (1985, p. 189)

Kalish continues by remarking:

> When a death is caused by an accident or a disaster, the effort to make sense of it is pursued more vigorously. The bereaved want to put the death into a perspective they can understand and accept—divine intervention, a curse from a neighboring tribe, a logical sequence of cause and effect, whatever it may be.

I would add two additional aspects to this need to make sense of a death. The first is a form of magical thinking: if we can discover why the person died, perhaps we can avoid such a fate in our own lives. The kidnap and murder of a child in a presumably safe neighborhood threaten the security of many people, and minds race to try to find a reason why this particular child met that fate. There is the sense that if we can find a reason for the tragedy, and if the reason cannot possibly apply to us in any way, then we may be able to avoid such an event in our own lives. Senseless events give us a sense of impotence, and it becomes very important to re-order our world so that it seems predictable and controllable once again.

Second, in some cases, a death can severely disrupt the bereaved's entire world view, and the need to make sense of the event is intense. When people have been loving, gentle, and kind, a violent death is not supposed to befall them. Good children who are loved and cared for are not supposed to die. People who meditate every day and surround themselves with light are supposed to be protected from harm. The discovery that life doesn't abide by these standards can be shattering.

Behavioral Expressions of Grief

Worden has listed major changes in behavior accompanying grief: sleep disturbances, appetite disturbances, absent-minded behavior, social withdrawal, dreams of the deceased, avoiding reminders of the deceased, searching and calling out, sighing, restless overactivity, crying, or visiting places or carrying objects that belonged to the deceased (1982, p. 24).

It is almost predictable that a person who is suffering from a grief reaction will awaken every morning at around 5 o'clock, often just after a dream of the deceased. Usually, their thoughts will be centred around the lost loved one and the events of the death. It is possible that the tendency to awaken early in times of crisis is healthy, and that those hours are in fact the best time for doing the transformative work of the grief process. Monastic orders of the world religions make a practice of rising in the early morning hours to pray or to meditate. Perhaps the body tells the grieving person to wake up and partake of that very special time, when spiritual energy seems most available, to write of dreams and thoughts, to cry undisturbed, to pray or meditate, to begin to say good-bye.

Appetite disturbances are also common for the grieving person. One of my clearest memories of the day after my fiancé was killed involved absolute lack of appetite. A friend had come to take me to spend the next night with his wife and family, and before we left my house, he made some breakfast for us. I took the first bite and found that I could not taste it at all—I who for years had found one of life's greatest joys in preparing and eating food. I looked at my friend and said, "This tastes like straw." Sorrowfully, he nodded his agreement. It was weeks before I could taste again and actually about two years before I could do any decent cooking.

Absent-minded behavior is very much a part of the grief process. Worden tells the story of a patient who on three separate occasions drove across the city in her car, and by the time she had completed her business, had forgotten that she had driven herself and returned home via public transportation (1982, p. 25). For people who are accustomed to maintaining very demanding schedules, this sort of absent-mindedness can be especially exasperating and at times frightening.

Social withdrawal is a common phenomenon among the grieving, and to a certain exent it can even serve the healing process. There are people who should be avoided after a loss, and often the grieving person has a very acute sense of who those people are; friends and family who are insensitive to the issues of grief may cause further pain. In addition, the grieving person often simply does not feel very social and finds a great incongruity between his mood and that of others on social occasions. If friends are uncomfortable with death and grief issues, there may also be a tendency on their part to try to negate the reality of what has happened for the sake of their own comfort. Under such circumstances, it is understandable for the grieving person to isolate him or herself. However, it can be, and very often is, a problem if carried too far. Participating in support groups with people who share a similar experience can be a solution. It is healing to laugh and to cry with others who also awaken every morning at 5 a.m. or who forget the way to work. Recently I spent a week-end with friends who had just had a still-born child. They had decided to attend a gathering of old friends, in spite of their grief, and were very open in sharing what had happened with those present. During the week-end, they cried, they laughed, they danced, they held another baby who had been born at nearly the same time as theirs. Their openness and their acceptance and consideration of those attending the gathering made it possible for all to participate in the healing of their sorrow. This seems to me an ideal way to process grief, though it does take special people and a special awareness.

Grieving people often have recurring dreams of the deceased, and significant grief work can be accomplished in this way. Forgiveness can occur; relationships can be altered; anger, fear, and love can be expressed. A great deal can be learned about the progress of the grief work by questioning the bereaved about the content of dreams.

Grieving people seem to alternate between trying to re-establish contact with the deceased and to separate from the relationship. Often, both activities are pursued with real passion. One day the bereaved person may be putting pictures of the deceased all over the house, wearing a favorite shirt, carrying objects that were meaningful to him. The next day the pictures may all be down, and the bereaved may not even want to mention their loved one's name. In this way, the process of gradual separation takes place.

Emotional Expressions of Grief

Worden lists the following emotions as the most common in grief response: numbness, guilt and self-reproach, sadness, anger, anxiety, loneliness, fatigue, helplessness, shock, yearning, emancipation and relief (1982, pp. 20–22).

Initially, it is very common for the bereaved person to be nearly without feelings; generally, the more massive the shock, the longer it is before feelings return. Even though my father's death was not a great shock, I experienced something of this delayed response. Since he had been ill for some time, we had been able to prepare for the death. At the memorial service, my brothers and sisters and I sang the old canon that for years we had sung as a family for grace, and we rejoiced in his memory, and felt complete in our grieving. Much to my surprise, four months later, during a meditation retreat, I found myself in the woods, sobbing my heart out over my father.

Very often people marvel at the composure of the bereaved at a funeral; they may be very relieved that they are "taking it so well." However, it may be weeks or months before the bereaved even begin to grasp the reality of the changes in their lives, and at that point feelings may be nearly overwhelming. Unfortunately, by that time, they may not receive the support they need because, based on their earlier composure, friends and family have assumed that they have somehow finished with grieving.

Closely aligned with this initial numbness are the physical symptoms of shock. Especially when the death is unexpected or violent, the grieving person may experience dizziness, cold chills and hot sweats, adrenaline rushes, diarrhea, and convulsive shaking. This is especially intense in the first few hours after the death is discovered, but may recur later when a memory is evoked.

Guilt can be a big factor in the grief process, particularly if the relationship with the deceased was troubled, or if the death was by suicide. But in every grieving process, when guilt is felt it is often more intense than would seem reasonable. The impression I have gained in working with grieving clients is that there is a very strong need to regain power over the world at a time when the world seems very much out of control. For example, accepting the blame for not taking someone to the hospital in time to prevent a death at least lets the grieving person feel as if he or she were in control of fate. It is very difficult for some people to accept that life and death may in fact really be out of their control.

Sadness, yearning, and loneliness are the feelings that we more commonly associate with loss of a loved one so they generally do not come as a surprise to a grieving person. Perhaps only the intensity of the feelings is unexpected.

Anxiety and helplessness are closely related to one another and are usually a source of bewilderment for the grieving person. Normally competent people find themselves suddenly fearful of all sorts of things and unable to handle the everyday problems of life. Shortly after my fiancé was killed, the roof on my house developed a leak, and water was actually running down the wall inside the dining room. I had previously restored that house, doing much of the work myself and had never faced a problem that I could not solve. However, when the roof started leaking this time, it terrified me. Months went by before I finally had the roof fixed; the water continued to run down the dining room wall, and I felt incapable of fixing it. It is a humbling and sometimes confusing experience to find oneself so stripped of normal capabilities.

Another emotion that is difficult for the grieving person to deal with is anger. While it doesn't seem to make sense to be angry after a death—unless there is an obvious culprit such as a drunken driver or a murderer—grieving people often experience a great deal of anger: anger at life, anger at God, anger at fate, anger at their own impotence. Unfortunately, it is the rare person who can identify this anger and express it appropriately. It is generally directed at others—a hospital or doctor who is believed to have caused the death, or the person at the cleaners who lost the laundry—or at oneself to surface later in physical symptoms.

Finally, grieving people often experience emancipation and relief after a death. Especially if the dying period has been long and painful, the survivors may welcome a chance finally to resume their lives. This is sometimes a source of guilt for the grieving person who may not think that such positive feelings should be part of the grieving period, yet these feelings can be used to great benefit for recovery from the grief.

Grief Following Violent Death

Most of the research that has been done on grief has used older widows and widowers as the subjects of study. For this reason, relatively little information is available on the nature of the grief process when death has occurred due to violence. In 1981, murder was the tenth leading cause of death in the United States (Federal Bureau of Investigation, as quoted in Rynearson, 1984). Under any circumstances, losing a loved one is difficult enough, but when the event is due to murder, there are some additional psychological problems which present themselves. Dr. Edward Rynearson of the Mason Clinic in Seattle has conducted a study of family members of victims of homicide who had also lost family members due to non-homicidal death. It was their unanimous observation that the psychological processing of homicide was accompanied by reactions that differed from the previously experienced forms of bereavement.

Rynearson makes the observation that in the case of murder, death is violent and transgressive. He observed that all family members of homicide victims noted the presence of intrusive, repetitive images of the homicide. Since none of them had actually witnessed the murder, these images drew from the reports of witnesses, the police, or their own imaginations. Because of these recurring, intrusive images, which often also filled dream life, the subjects' concentration and thought sequencing were disrupted daily or weekly for a period of six to eighteen months. All subjects reported a pervasive fear that lasted in most cases six to eight months. For a few of the subjects, the fear never subsided:

> Compulsive behaviors of self-protection were so intense during the first year of bereavement that the subjects' usual range of territorial and affiliative behaviors was constricted; unfamiliar surroundings were circumvented, home became a protected fortress, strangers were avoided, and there was a compulsive need for the proximity and tangible assurance of the safety of remaining family members. . . . All subjects noted anger directed toward the murderer . . . and all subjects noted behaviors directed toward retribution. (Rynearson, 1984, p. 1453)

Family members of suicide victims also report recurring images of the victim's death, increased feelings of guilt, and occasional feelings of being drawn toward committing the same act themselves. The reasoning seems to go as follows: if my family produced one person who committed suicide, perhaps it will produce another. As one of my clients wrote after the suicide of her sister:

> Once it has been done within the same constellation, within the same family, as close as the sister's psyche (scrambled eggs in bed), it is possible for me. Next. A conceivable route, a possible way. The little sister looks to see what the big sister points out, with admiration. Am I supposed to admire this? And suppose that it is an answer? I am caught by conflicting answers.

At the same time as the bereaved is working to separate from the deceased, there is also a strong tendency to identify with the deceased. This represents a particular problem in the case of homicide and suicide because the survivor has an internalized identification with someone who has suffered a very violent act. Encouraging the process of separation—seeing oneself as different from the deceased and not controlled by the same fate—is especially important in these cases.

Spiritual Aspects of Grieving

Because bereavement brings up many life and death issues, the mourning period can be a profound time. The bereaved person's whole system is working overtime to heal the shock of the death, and the grieving may be remembered as one of the times of being most in touch with the essence of life and of Self, even for people who have had no previous spiritual awareness at all. The bereaved person readily perceives certain profound truths during the grieving process.

At the same time, because the mourning person may be in a terrible argument with God and with life, he or she may alternate between moments of sublime union and moments of deep doubt and anger. If the death has been shocking or seemingly unjustified, the grieving person may be in the process of questioning his or her most basic beliefs. Following the untimely death of his wife, C. S. Lewis wrote:

> Not that I am (I think) in much danger of ceasing to believe in God. The real danger is of coming to believe such dreadful things about Him. The conclusion I dread is not, "So there's no God after all," but "So this is what God's really like. Deceive yourself no longer." (1961, p. 5)

For Lewis, as for many bereaved people, making peace again with God is part of the grief process. Psychosynthesis is ideally suited to dealing with these spiritual aspects of grieving because its conceptual framework already acknowledges Spirit and suggests ways to work with it. To dialogue with the Self when one is greatly at odds with and distrustful of it opens a door to the radiance of the Self which may overcome pain and assist in healing wounds.

Stages and Tasks of Grieving

Several writers have divided the aspects of grieving into stages. Bowlby describes the stages thusly (1980, p. 85):

Phase 1—numbing that usually lasts from a few hours to a week and may be interrupted by outbursts of extremely intense distress and/or anger.

Phase 2—yearning and searching for the lost figure, lasting some months and sometimes for years.

Phase 3—disorganization and despair.

Phase 4—greater or lesser degree of reorganization.

Parkes (1972, p. 7) also divides grieving into stages, and calls them numbness, pining, depression, and recovery.

Freud (1917, p. 244) talks about the "work" of mourning. The objective is to recognize gradually the reality of a death that has occurred and to withdraw one's attachment to the deceased.

An understanding of the phases one is likely to pass through in the mourning process is helpful as long as one does not get caught in the belief that phases must be experienced in a precise order. Many people seem to be in several phases simultaneously. The explanation I use in psychosynthesis work is that each of the subpersonalities must pass through all of the phases, and each may have a different rate in doing so.

It is also helpful to know that grief work, except in the very early stages, does not go on all the time. The bereaved person may have hours or days of intense grieving interspersed with relatively normal times. It is important to remember that people grieve in different ways, and what is normal for one should not be expected from another.

A balance is required in grief work between moving too slowly and moving too quickly. In the early stages after a death, the whole system may shut down because there is simply too much to take in all at once. There may be a reluctance to open up to the material again because earlier it was so overwhelming. Yet without opening to the grief, it cannot be successfully processed.

In his work on grief counselling and grief therapy, Worden (1982, pp. 11–16) presents a slightly different view of the phases of grieving. He affords the grieving person a far more active role by addressing what he calls the "tasks" of grieving. I find this approach, in which the Will can assist in the healing, to be very helpful. According to Worden, the tasks are as follows:

Task 1—to accept the reality of the loss. The searching behavior mentioned earlier is part of this task. The bereaved person must leave no stone unturned until he or she is completely convinced that the loved one is truly gone. Only then can he or she begin the next task.

Task 2—to experience the pain of grief. Parkes (1972) suggests that anything that allows the person to avoid or suppress the pain of grieving can be expected to prolong the course of mourning. He questions the appropriateness of using drugs for this reason. Worden notes, "There may be a subtle interplay between society and the mourner which makes the completion of Task 2 more difficult. Society may be uncomfortable with the mourner's feelings and hence may give the subtle message, 'You don't need to grieve.'

This interferes with the mourner's own defenses, leading to denial of the need to grieve" (1982, p. 13). Bowlby comments, "Sooner or later, some of those who avoid all conscious grieving break down—usually with some form of depression" (1980, p. 158). This is most likely to occur on the anniversary of a death that has not been mourned, or at the time of another loss, even if of a relatively minor kind, or upon reaching the age of a parent who has died.

I suggest an addition to Worden's Task 2—namely, healing and transforming the wound. I think it is important not only to express and experience the pain of grief, but also to acknowledge that in that very experience an alchemical process can occur which transforms the pain and makes us deeper and more insightful as human beings. The negation of Task 2 is not to feel; experiencing the pain of loss enables one to move on to the next task.

Task 3—to adjust to an environment in which the deceased is missing. This may involve learning new skills and taking on new roles. In many cases, this may open up a whole new world of possibilities for the bereaved so that even though the task may be frightening it offers great rewards.

Task 4—to withdraw emotional energy and re-invest it in another relationship. At the right time, it is necessary to move on to new relationships. Resistance may occur, either because it appears to indicate infidelity to the one who has died, or because there may be fear of entering something which could lead to a similar loss. Some people realize years later that they lost a certain ability to love after the death of a loved one. The successful completion of Task 4 lies in opening again to the full depth of love.

The Role of Friends and Therapists

> The person who is most valued [at the time of bereavement] is not the one who expresses the most sympathy but the person who "sticks around," quietly gets on with day-to-day household tasks and makes few demands on the bereaved. Such a person must be prepared to accept without reproach the tendency of the bereaved person to pour out feelings of anguish and anger, some of which may be directed against the helper. In fact, it may be necessary for the helper to indicate to the bereaved that he or she expects such feelings to emerge and that there is no need for them to be "bottled up." The helper should not "pluck at the heartstrings" of the bereaved until breakdown occurs any more than he or she should connive with the bereaved in endless attempts to avoid the grief work. Both probing and "jollying along" are unhelpful. The bereaved person has a painful and difficult task to perform which cannot be avoided and cannot be rushed. True help consists in recognizing this fact and in helping the bereaved person to arrange things in whatever way is necessary to set him or her free for the task of grieving. (Parkes, 1972, p. 161)

Friends can help most by understanding the nature of the grief process the bereaved is undergoing and by supporting it. This is most possible for those who have dealt with their own grief issues.

Principles of Grief Counselling

Worden (1982, pp. 39–48) has offered some very helpful principles for working with grieving clients. In the following section, I would like to adapt these principles for the use of the psychosynthesis practitioner. The principles stated are Worden's; the techniques suggested to implement each principle are my own, based in Psychosynthesis.

Principle 1—Help the survivor to actualize the loss. When the loss seems too overwhelming to comprehend or when it doesn't even seem that it happened, the counsellor can serve as a reality check, affirming that the death has in fact occurred. And when the grieving person is overwhelmed with the actuality of the loss, the counsellor can provide a sense of perspective: yes, there has been a loss, but it is not the only factor in the bereaved person's life. In order to integrate the reality of the loss that has occurred, the subpersonality which best grasps the reality can explain to the other subpersonalities what has happened. The others can then express the sense of unbelief. In the ensuing dialogue, the more protective subpersonalities can be encouraged to allow the fearful subpersonalities to experience sorrow.

When the pain of the sorrow is too great, the practitioner can use disidentification exercises in order to draw back from the pain: "I am experiencing pain, but I am not that pain." On the other hand, when the client has lost a sense of the reality of the event, the practitioner can help by asking such questions as, "Tell me when it happened?" or "Who was present at the last moments?" A bit of gentle questioning is usually all that is needed to allow the bereaved person to begin to talk about the experience. There is always a balance between moving too fast and moving too slow in actualizing the loss. The grieving person has his or her own inner rhythm which dictates how fast the work can be done.

Principle 2—Help the survivor to identify and express feelings. Because of the perceived necessities of living, the grieving person may bury feelings so much that they are difficult to access, even in a counselling session. Gentle non-verbal techniques, such as drawing, listening to music, singing, and lying on one's back, are often able to dislodge the expression of feeling. Sometimes the grieving person just needs some time and a safe space in which to cry. Sometimes levels of rage are felt which can astonish and frighten the individual. To help clients express rage, the technique which I use (for which I would like to credit Elisabeth Kubler-Ross) involves destroying a telephone book with a rubber hose. Among my clients, the record for the number of telephone books destroyed in a single session is held by a grieving woman who succeeded in totally disintegrating three large telephone books in less than an hour. Rage must be given a voice and an expression if the client is to move through the grief.

Principle 3—Assist the survivor in living without the deceased. This may mean assisting clients with very practical problems, such as exploring the possibility of living in less expensive accommodation, overcoming the fears around looking for a job, and making decisions as a single parent for the first time. Because the bereaved person may have a great number of practical tasks to accomplish at once, and because he or she may feel less capable than ever at performing these tasks, he or she may need assistance in thinking problems through and deciding on a plan of action. As the grieving person begins to perform new tasks, old subpersonalities also die and must be mourned; new ones are being born and must be nurtured and welcomed. A client who lost her husband had difficulty in welcoming a new more independent version of herself because, after over 40 years of marriage, she had developed an apparent disdain for self-reliant women. So as one part of her enjoyed new-found strengths, another part blamed herself for growing "unfeminine."

Principle 4—Facilitate emotional withdrawal from the deceased. This can be done through talking about lost loved ones, and on occasion dialoguing with them in another chair. This must be handled with sensitivity because the bereaved will alternate between needing to remember the deceased, needing to complete the relationship, and needing to move on to other relationships. The counsellor must respect the current phase, and know that its complement will present itself in time.

Principle 5—Provide time to grieve. This may mean suggesting that the grieving person take time off work, drop some responsibilities, or go back to a familiar and comforting place. Leading the client in a guided imagery exercise along a path which goes "back home" may give some clues as to where the grieving person is most likely to receive comfort.

Principle 6—Interpret "normal" behavior. After a significant loss, many people have the sense they are going crazy. It is reassuring to clients to know that their symptoms, while uncomfortable, are at least normal for grief process. Helping clients to construct an ideal model for their grief process allows them to choose to participate in the process rather than to be bounced around by what appears to be craziness.

Principle 7—Allow for individual differences. All people do not grieve in the same way. Encourage the client to validate his or her own experience regardless of what others may be saying or experiencing.

Principle 8—Provide continuing support. Even though clients may terminate therapy, or move on to other issues in their lives, from time to time the grief will surface again. Very often the grieving person will have a recurrence of symptoms around the three-month, one-year, and two-year anniversary of the death, and around other significant times, such as birthdays, wedding anniversaries, holidays, and so on. When a client is experiencing a renewal of symptoms, the counsellor should ask if the date is significant.

Principle 9—Examine defences and coping styles. Since coping styles such as substance abuse, overwork, overeating, or denial will be heightened after loss, this is a good time to examine their effectiveness. The counsellor should also encourage positive coping techniques such as meditation. Clients have a unique opportunity to observe how their customary practices serve them in a time of stress.

The Psychosynthesis Context

What is of even more importance than techniques is the framework in which the therapeutic work is done. Psychosynthesis offers a unique approach which acknowledges the spiritual qualities of the client. For its practitioners, the Self, that spark of Divine Essence, is always at work, no matter how bleak the situation may appear. This means that they know that they are not alone in providing relief. Because inside each grieving person there exists a core of being which knows, therapeutically, the right thing to do, the work of the practitioner is to support grieving people by honoring what is true for them and by acknowledging that their feelings, beliefs, and intuitions are probably more accurate at this time in their lives than they have ever been. It is my experience that grieving people are more likely than other kinds of clients to have a strong sense of what is needed for healing, and so the work of the practitioner is to validate these feelings. The grieving person's own sense of what to do may often fly in the face of what society says is correct or what friends and family advise. But my belief, culled from Psychosynthesis, is that the healing force within each person is to be recognized and supported.

As psychosynthesists, we are also uniquely able to validate the spiritual experiences that the grieving person may be having. In the grief experience, there is often a re-arranging of priorities, a sense of new values emerging, and in many cases a sense of being in touch with profound spiritual energy. It is of great value for the practitioner to "normalize" these occurrences, especially for clients who have no prior experience of such things. The psychosynthesis practitioner who has developed a spiritual discipline can at once support and encourage the spiritual insights that occur in a time of grief, and can serve as a reality check when the bereaved person becomes "ungrounded" and needs to deal with the more mundane parts of the grieving task.

At the same time, one of the traps the psychosynthesis practitioner needs to be aware of in working with grieving clients concerns the subject of spirituality. In working with clients who are having profound spiritual insights with great regularity, psychosynthesists, because of their general inclination and the historical tendency of their discipline, may be tempted to collude with them in spending too much time on spiritual issues as a way of avoiding the terribly painful therapeutic work that eventually must be done. The clues are usually there when the client needs to move into other arenas. The alert practitioner who is comfortable with dealing with difficult issues will be able to read them.

The greatest gift that the practitioner can give to sorrowing clients is to both fully share their burden, their loss, and their horror and to maintain contact with Spirit, to help them discover that in the darkest moments healing is present. It has been my experience, in both my work and in my personal process, that unearthing buried griefs can bring new freedom to the soul, new depth to the experience of life, and a greatly expanded ability to love. Recognizing the symptoms of grief, and understanding the nature of the tasks to be completed, can facilitate the healing and transformative potential in the grieving process. As psychosynthesis practitioners and as human beings, we have much to gain from embracing the grief that comes to us.

I would not have chosen for my fiancé to die, but I am grateful for the transformation that has occurred in me as a result of his death. My priorities are different now, and my understanding of life extends deeper. As I write these words, I am preparing to marry, and my primary challenge is to open my heart wide enough to accept the joy that is now mine. All of Life is a gift, if we choose to see it that way, and experiences of loss are sometimes the most profound teachers.

References

Bowlby, J. (1980). *Attachment and loss: Loss, sadness and depression*. New York: Basic Books.

Freud, S. (1917). *Mourning and melancholia* (Vol. 14). Standard Edition.

Kalish, R. (1985). *Death, grief and caring relationships*. Monterey, California: Brooks/Cole Publishing Company.

Lewis, C. S. (1961). *A grief observed*. New York: Seabury Press.

Lindemann, E. (1979). *Beyond grief: Studies in crisis intervention*. Northvale, NJ: Aronson.

Parkes, C. (1972). *Bereavement: Studies in adult grief*. New York: International Universities Press.

Rafael, B. (1982). *The anatomy of bereavement*. New York: Basic Books.

Rynearson, E. (1984). Bereavement after homicide: A descriptive study. *American Journal of Psychiatry*, **141** (11).

Steiner, R. (1930). *Between death and rebirth*. London: Rudolf Steiner Press.

Tatelbaum, J. (1980). *The courage to grieve*. New York: Harper & Row.

Worden, J. M. (1982). *Grief counselling and grief therapy: A handbook for the mental health practitioner*. New York: Springer.

Psychosynthesis and Integrative Marital and Family Therapy

Sheldon Z. Kramer

Roberto Assagioli (1973) in his book *The Act of Will* outlined a program of research on the will and its applications. This program of research was known as the Will Project. Although Assagioli wanted Psychosynthesis to go beyond the individual sphere to include both interpersonal and social relationships, many psychosynthesis concepts and technical procedures have been applied only to individuals. A number of psychosynthesis institutes have focussed on group dynamics, but there is still a paucity of psychosynthesis literature and work on couples and the family group. It is the purpose of this article to help bridge some of the basic psychosynthesis concepts and techniques to a family context.

Psychosynthesis is a name for a natural process of personal growth. The psychosynthesis perspective views growth as a natural tendency in each of us to harmonize our various aspects at higher levels of organization. It is considered a process whereby each individual who chooses to participate in evolution can co-operate with living matter to perfect itself. Psychosynthesis aims at facilitating one's natural processes to come in alignment with one's purpose.

Psychosynthesis, like other forms of humanistic psychotherapy, has often viewed growth as an individual experience. Many psychosynthesis practices focus on developing spirituality, which, traditionally, has been viewed as a task that is undertaken alone. Thus meditators go off to retreats and have limited contact with others in order to further delve into their mind-body process. However, it is my opinion that Psychosynthesis, in order to be a complete theory, needs to include the possibility of growth within an interpersonal model. In fact, inner work can be better realized for certain individuals when working within an interpersonal context.

Many people who search for growth and spirituality have been hurt interpersonally and it is not by accident that they choose growth experiences that involve separation from others. Consequently, many folks have made a "pseudo-individuation"; yet they are not able to withstand intimate encounters, especially with their current most significant relationships and with their family of origin.

Interpersonal and family relationslips can increase or hinder one's spiritual growth. We enhance our growth when we choose to be with others who have similar goals and who allow us the necessary time to be alone as well as gently confront us on the qualities that we need to strengthen. Our intimates can help us become aware of identifications that distance us from our personal "centres." Further, we can practise expressing our higher qualities to those who are most important in our lives and work with them in removing the blocks that stagnate our innermost energies. The most powerful openings within the self can come from trusting another human being. If this basic trust is lost, relationships can inhibit spiritual development.

Subpersonalities

Psychosynthesis is based on the fundamental psychological principle that we are dominated by that which we become identified with. Alternatively, "we can dominate and control everything from which we disidentify" (Assagioli, 1965). Tied in with the concept of identification is the idea that each individual is made up of many identifications or subpersonalities. It is the word "I" that gives us the illusion we are always the same person.

The main concept connected with subpersonalities is that we express different aspects of ourselves at different times. The aspects that we are expressing now may not be the same ones that were there one hour ago, or we play different roles in different circumstances. Sometimes we get so lost or identified with a subpersonality (or role) that we mistake one aspect of ourselves for the whole. Rigid identifications occur within certain social contexts. Different situations call out in each of us well-defined reactions and responses. From this point of view, subpersonalities can be easily activated by environmental circumstances. It is often the task in psychosynthesis to become more aware of the situations in the environment which "hook" us into reactive, predictable patterns. Thus, a subpersonality is a synthesis of traits, complexes, and other psychological elements that are embedded in a social context. In exploring subpersonalities from the perspective of an individual growth model, it becomes apparent that many conflicts are related to unfinished business with one's parents.

Family Dynamics and Object Relations

In order to understand how subpersonalities are formed, it is helpful to study familial transactional processes. Frank (1957), expounding on the idea of transactional fields, said that "we think in terms of circular, reciprocal relations . . . [in] which the component members of the field participate and thereby create the field of the whole, which in turn regulates the patterns through the individual's activities." Ackerman (1956), an early pioneer in family therapy, presented a conceptual model of interlocking pathologies in the familial context. Ackerman was concerned with looking at the interchange of unconscious processes which occurs between family members in an interpersonal context. From this point of view, any single member's behavior can represent the distortion of boundaries between individuals within the family. Framo (1970) also discussed the concept of interlocking pathologies. "Departing from the conventional, simplistic view of symptoms . . . [as] stemming from a central illness," Framo's (1970) view was that "symptoms are formed, selected, faked, exchanged, maintained and reduced as a function of the relationship context in which they are naturally embedded." He stressed the need for an integrative model that focussed on the relationship between the intrapsychic and the transactional. According to Framo, "the creative leap of the family systems theory was [in] recognizing the interlocking, multipersonal motivational system whereby family members collusively carry psychic functions for each other."

In Psychosynthesis, subpersonalities can be thought of as intrapsychic patterns and/or types of behavior which have been learned in terms of what significant others (i.e., parents) expected or demanded of us. Over time, these expectations can lead us to identify with what is being reflected back to us. Many times, according to Framo (1970), an "irrational role assignment" is the cause of symptom production. He also states that the "implicit and explicit irrational assignment of roles in the family reflects unconscious attempts by parents to master, enact or externalize their intrapsychic conflicts about these powerful human needs derived from experiences in their family of origin."

To understand fully the process of irrational role assignment, it is necessary to focus on the work of Henry V. Dicks (1967) which describes Kline's and Fairbaren's object relations model and integrates their concepts in a theory of marital pathology. Fairbaren's position is that unresolved love-hate feelings toward parental figures (primary objects) become internalized in the young child. The child resorts to an internal mechanism called "splitting"—he "splits" his parents to fit a *good* and *bad* image in order to deal with the dissatisfaction of not being able to receive instant gratification. In the child's psyche, he preserves the good parent image and controls the bad, frustrating parent image.

According to object relations theory, the child also resorts to splitting the bad parent into an exciting, a rejecting, and an ideal object. The exciting object is the seductive parent who excites the child but doesn't gratify. The rejecting object is the parent who actively denies satisfaction. The ideal object is the parent who is stripped of all negative attributes—a new idealized image which is projected onto the real parents since the child must feel some stability.

The three object splits, according to Fairbaren, have a parallel effect on the ego. The exciting object responds to the libidinal ego: this ego craves closeness to the parent. If this split occurs early in one's development, it can result in an ego that remains very infantile. Because of the unmet dependency needs, the libidinal ego can withdraw and not show its vulnerability.

The rejecting object relates and reacts to the identification of the split-off anti-libidinal ego. The rejecting object is also viewed as a severe, sadistic super ego which persecutes the anti-libidinal ego. The internalization of the rejecting object results in the anti-libidinal ego becoming fearful and guilty.

The other ego split corresponds to the idealized parents after the disturbed aspects of both objects in the ego have been split off and repressed.

Tyson and Tyson (1982) discuss the ego ideal as composed of subparts including ideal object representations based on early impressions of parents who are perceived as perfect, admired, and omnipotent. Another subpart of the ego is the ideal child representation; this representation is the parents' image of the "model child" or person. In addition, there are ideal self-representations. The ideal self contains aspects of loved, admired, or feared objects, the "good" or "desirable" child, as reflected by others, and ideal states that the self has previously experienced in reality or in fantasy.

The splits within the internal object world are closely related to Assagioli's concept of subpersonalities. For example, the good representations could be called the "Nurturer," "Protector," the "Loving One," the "Encourager." Good self-representations could be manifested as the "Fulfilled One," "Worthy One," and the "Open One."

The exciting object, a split of the rejecting object, could be labelled in the psychosynthesis framework as the "Seductive One" or the "Exhibitionist." The exciting object representation, as stated previously, is a seductive parental imago that does not gratify the child. Corresponding self-representations could be related to subpersonalities that could be called the "Deprived One," the "Sad Child," the "Empty One," and so on.

The rejecting object could represent the "Critic," the "Sadist," and so on. The self-representations corresponding to the rejecting object could be labelled the "Frightened Child," the "Guilty One," the "Suffering One."

The ideal object and the self-representations are reflective of formations of subpersonalities that could include themes such as the "Perfect One," the "Ideal One," the "Guru," the "Mystical One," the "Devotee," the "Worshipper," the "Dependent One."

In order to understand further subpersonality formation from an object relations standpoint, it is best to look at how the young child deals with the behavior of parents who are interpreted as rejecting, deserting, or persecuting. The child, unable to give up the external object, handles his intense frustration by introjecting the loved-hated object. This introjected or psychological representation is at the heart of subpersonality formation. Good objects are retained while bad objects are split off and remain as unconscious "internal sabboteurs" (Framo, 1970). The earlier in life splitting occurs and the more suffering one has had in the interpersonal sphere, the more dependent one will be on an inner object world. The consequence of this state of affairs is that interpersonal relationships are distorted to meet preconceived psychological representations directly related to childhood disappointments and frustrations and split-off self and object representations. Others are forced to change in relationship to preconceived internal role models.

Framo (1970), widening Fairbaren's object relations theory to include dynamics within the family, stated, "the various children in the family come to represent the valued or feared expectations of the parents, based on parental introjects; sometimes the roles of the children are chosen for them even before they are born." This process, as stated previously, has been referred to as "irrational role assignment" or "projective transference distortion." These preconceived role assignments help parents deal with their inner object world, especially negative representations which have been split off from consciousness. In addition, they help parents preserve good representations as well as remain loyal, in reality, to one's family of origin. The fixed roles that are assigned in a family are parallel to the subpersonality identity formations which help crystallize our preconceived ideas of who we are. In fact, family members tend to label one another to help reinforce projections. For example, there are "black sheep," "bad seeds," "saviors," "good children," and so on.

Goals of Family Psychosynthesis Therapy

In individual psychosynthesis, the goal of growth is to help the subpersonalities come into harmony with each other. Suffering is related to identification with or attachment to subpersonality formations. From this point of view, the rigidity of our identifications results in narrowed perceptions that govern our reality and limit our inner freedom to choose alternative methods of thinking, feeling, perceiving, and acting. The goal of individual psychosynthesis is to help individuals become aware of their subpersonality identifications, disidentify from narrow perceptions, and expand one's Self to include a variety of different functions and qualities.

This process is attained by developing within oneself an "impartial centre" (the "I") which observes one's subpersonalities as well as one's overall mind-body functions. The "I" is a neutral aspect of the Self in that it can be objective when observing one's Self. In addition, the "I" has channels to the "higher aspects" of consciousness which reflect spiritual values and virtues such as love, forgiveness, patience, persistence, tolerance, and courage.

Family psychosynthesis can be conceived as having similar goals. Recently, there has been interest in research in the area of what constitutes a "normal family." Olson, Sprenkle, and Russell (1979) discussed a typology of family and marital systems derived from a model which looked at two dimensions of family functioning: (1) cohesion which was defined by the bonding of family members and (2) adaptability which was defined by the ability of the family and its members to change with the normal developmental processes in the life cycle. The cohesion dimension was measured on a continuum, from disengaged families to those who were overinvolved or enmeshed. The adaptability dimension was also viewed on a continuum, from families who were rigid in terms of the rules governing their interactions to those who were chaotic. Research showed that healthier families function in the mid-ranges of cohesion and adaptability, that is, such families have both a separate and interpersonal style and a set of rules and roles which appropriately reflects developmental needs of family members. From this point of view, functioning within narrow extremes represents a rigid way of being in an interpersonal context. Rigid styles can be compared to overall themes within the family that correspond to subpersonalities. For example, in enmeshed families, each member can help maintain the other's position by rigidly identifying with particular roles. The mother may be the Protector of the father who is the Frightened One, and the child plays out the Sacrificer who does not grow in order to preserve her "needy" parents. All of these roles help to maintain the members' overinvolvement with one another and serve the needs of the family to retain the status quo, a position due to underlying conflicts usually occurring in the marital dyad. Rigid patterns in interaction are reinforced in order to preserve family cohesiveness and to protect the family from disharmony and dissolution.

The overall goal of family psychosynthesis is to help individual members become aware of and eventually disidentify from the rigid roles they are playing in their families. In this situation, the therapist needs to "unbalance" the family's status quo by helping each member see his or her contribution to reinforcing the family's narrow group identity. In order to reach this goal, it is important for the therapist to facilitate the realization of whatever purpose each member may have and the transformation of the family's collective perception of reality. Usually, individual and family purposes are "higher qualities," such as humility, understanding, respect, love, compassion, and forgiveness, which are trying to emerge from the "supra-unconscious." These qualities reflect positive energies that can help both individual members and the family to grow as a whole.

Phases of Family Psychosynthesis Therapy

In the individual process of psychosynthesis, a main part of the work involves the harmonization of the subpersonalities, a process which includes (1) recognition, (2) acceptance, (3) co-ordination, (4) integration, and (5) synthesis.

The first two phases, recognition and acceptance, involve becoming dis-identified from a variety of subpersonality configurations and coming to a realization of how each one thinks, feels, acts. The third phase, co-ordination, involves helping the subpersonalities become aware of their wants and needs in relation to the other parts. By means of internal dialogue or gestalt procedures, one is able to achieve more clarity on what each aspect needs in order to help balance an underlying conflictual state. The fourth phase, integration, involves respecting the different wants and needs within oneself and finding ways in which seemingly conflicting aspects can be reconciled to form new, more inclusive identity formations. Finally, synthesis concerns the personality as a whole and focusses on achieving congruency between the subpersonality world and the interpersonal sphere.

The model presented in the remainder of the article also involves five phases of treatment. Though these phases often follow in sequence, they overlap at times in the treatment. The first stage involves being able to define the family structure and interactive process. The second stage involves clarifying the rules that are governing the family system. The third stage, which often occurs after the identified patient (usually a child) has been de-triangulated from the marital conflict, involves a more intense intra-psychic exploration that focusses on subpersonality identifications and how spouses tend to project disowned aspects of themselves onto one another and their children. The fourth phase of family psychosynthesis therapy involves actual work with each spouse's family of origin. The fifth phase, that of family coherence, involves aligning the whole family system to the higher values and qualities that are congruent with their spiritual nature.

1. Structural/Interactive Phase—The main goal in this phase is to form a rapport with each family member. This involves listening to each member's perception of the presenting problem as well as the overall changes that they feel need to occur in the family. Some techniques utilized during this phase are to focus attention away from the identified patient and to respect the hierarchy in the family constellation. It is usually best to begin with the parents in the family system and then go on to the sibling subsystem.

In talking with each family member, tracking procedures are utilized which aim at feedback through active listening. It is important to establish empathy when listening and to reflect back to each member their concerns. One can track content either by summarizing thoughts (i.e., "It sounds like you said . . .) or by following affect, that is, by picking up on the feeling and reflecting back to the speaker what you heard (i.e., "It sounds like you feel . . .). During this phase, it is good to ask questions which get at complementary, transactional roles in the here and now and which give you a sense of how the family system works. For example, you can ask the wife what her husband does when she hollers at her children. In this way, you will be better able to understand the patterns that repeat themselves in the family system.

In the first phase of family therapy, it is important to get family members to "transact" in the here and now. Salvador Minuchin (1974) called this process "enactment," which literally means to put into action. In individual psychosynthesis, you pick aspects of the Self that are in conflict and through guided imagery or gestalt work invite these aspects to talk to one another. In family therapy, you might ask two members, who represent two aspects of the family's subpersonalities, to transact. (Through the rapport established in the beginning, you have found out that these two members are having difficulty with one another.) At this point in therapy, it is useful to try to develop competence in family members who are acting weak; therefore, it is good to select transactions between the person who has been defined as incompetent and the other member with whom he or she is having difficulty. You will need to watch keenly the interactional sequences of behavior, both overt and covert, and it is useful to focus on breaking down the structure of the interactions: for example, you could start to analyze how many words a person says, who says the most words, and who speaks the loudest. It is also important to watch the responses of other members to the enactment and to see how they either enhance or prevent a dyad from functioning.

The steps to achieve the enactment thus include defining a goal (a content that would be defined as a problem), focussing on interactions between family members, especially those who are most frustrated with each other, setting up these transactions, via directives, and then disengaging from the encounter. For example, as a directive, you can say to a family member, "Talk to him, do it now" or "It may be silly to do this, but I want you to talk to each other about this, it's important that you get it straight." As the therapist, you can show disengagement by putting your head down or moving your chair back, thus facilitating a direct dialogue between family members.

As you watch family members interact with one another, you can start to study the rigid sequences of behavior and how these are organized around psychological symptoms. You can make the family more aware of these patterns by reflecting back "process observations," or those aspects of the interactions which are more covert. For example, a process observation could be, "When you speak, she withdraws." Then the transaction could be pointed in a new direction. For example, you could say to a husband, "I see you are being very helpful to your wife; however, she needs to learn to talk with you directly." By helping family members develop a theme around their interactions, you can help them listen to one another's wants and needs and co-ordinate their positions in the family so that they can organize themselves in a more harmonious fashion.

Another technique utilized in the first phase of family therapy is "reframing," which is defined as the restructuring of the family's sense of reality in order to broaden their perspectives. Reframing challenges the family's perceptions of reality. Just as subpersonalities have lower and higher qualities, so do transactional symptoms in a family. The therapist's task is to help translate "a negative symptom" into a positive quality that is trying to be developed not only by a symptomatic family member but also by the family system as a whole. For example, a delinquent boy can be viewed as incompetent because he always gets caught and does not know how to think or to plan things. One can first shift the problem to his immaturity and incompetence in dealing with other situations, like making appropriate friends, and then move on to how learning to think and to plan things can be a sign of developing higher qualities, such as patience, which parents can help their child to develop. This can transform a negative energy flow into a more productive, positive one.

Another method of changing negative qualities to positive ones is "relabelling" the problem. For example, the child who is seen as unmotivated can be reframed as unknowledgeable about certain areas in life, which helps point to a new direction in therapy. Someone who has anorexic symptoms can be viewed as oppositional, as stubborn, and as wanting to establish her own autonomy, which is the higher quality that is needed within the family.

Another method is "spreading" the problem to include other members. For example, a mother says, "My son won't listen to me, he's just got a bad attitude." This can be reframed as, "You haven't found a way to get your son to listen to you" or "You haven't found a way to get your son to respect you." Therefore, the energy focussed on the son who is "bad" is expanded to include the mother who must find a way to get her son to respect her. Respect, then, is the higher quality to work on in the transactional plane.

2. Communications Phase—A major goal in family therapy is individuation, which is strengthened as members form better boundaries between one another. During this phase, an elaboration of the first, members gain more knowledge about the rules of interaction in their family.

One technique to help people become more individuated is to state the rule that no one can talk on behalf of anyone else or that no one can talk about any person who is not in the present session. Another technique is to separate the overinvolved dyad either physically in the room or by seeing each person separately.

During the communications phase, as well as during other phases of family psychosynthesis therapy, many resistances start to appear when family members are encouraged to dialogue with each other. Resistances, from a transactional standpoint, are buffers that help each family member as well as the family as a whole remain in a homeostatic position. There are many techniques that can be utilized, especially from a psychosynthesis perspective, to help overcome resistances within the family system. For example, when you set up a dyadic interaction and individuals try to talk about a conflict that seems to be unresolved, you can ask one or both of them to go to another chair. Observing the interaction from this new position, they may be able to see what needs to happen in order for them to hear one another better and to resolve conflicts. If you are trying to build one parent's power in the family because he or she has not assumed hierarchical authority, it may be best to work with that parent and help him or her disidentify from a submissive role by observing the interactions from a third chair. Many times, the parent can see the need to become more of an authority in order to help their child develop in a variety of different ways.

Sometimes people become so narrow in their perceptions that they have no motivation to work. If this occurs, a psychosynthesis technique evoking various aspects of their Will can be utilized. For example, you can ask a mother and child who are at an impass in their interaction why it would be important for them to change. You can help them develop an ideal image of what their relationship could be. You can ask what benefits they see in the resolution of their conflict and how it would help the family as a whole. When you start focussing on an ideal model for a relationship and thereby evoke the Will, you tap a great deal of positive energy which can help neutralize negative affects or resistances.

Another technique which is useful for working through resistances was stated previously: you can utilize other members in the family to act as the observing "I" to help an overinvolved dyad co-ordinate their needs and wants. For example, a father who is peripheral to the system can act as a coach, helping an overinvolved mother distance herself from a child. In this way, the father acts as the observing "I" which results in re-aligning his own relationship with his wife so that it is more supportive and collaborative and in disengaging the child from potential or ongoing marital conflicts.

Another technique in the work with resistance is to teach family members to meditate on images of Wise Old Persons or to let symbols come spontaneously to consciousness which suggest what needs to occur if the family is to work together more harmoniously. Through meditation, certain themes emerge that point to a direction that is needed to work with a resistance. Many of these help realign the purpose of the work in the family as well as reinforce the Will of each member to continue to engage in their work.

Through engaging in transactional work with those who are most significantly related to us, we can help ourselves and others realize more harmonious relationships. We can co-ordinate our wants and needs by listening to each other and respecting each other's position. At times, we can learn how to compromise with our own subpersonalities, giving each part time, for example, to express itself. Through interacting with others, we can also compromise and do what the other wants to do for periods of time. Time sharing can help create a more balanced relationship in which both parties feel like they are in a win-win situation.

Sometimes integration can occur within dyadic interactions. For example, spouses with different interests or qualities can help each other work on aspects that they thought could never be included within themselves. The overreactive, hysterical wife can take on more of her husband's analytic abilities. In reverse, the husband can be helped to develop more spontaneous reactions within himself. In helping each other work on less developed qualities, they can help each other feel more whole, not only within themselves but also in their relationship. Many times, members of the dyad have interests which appear to be polar-opposites and produce marital conflict. For example, a practical businessman who is concerned with making a living can be contrasted with a wife who believes in spontaneous creativity. But they can respect these differences as helping their relationship if they integrate them in an enterprise that includes both aspects such as a "creative business enterprise."

3. Dynamic/Object Relations Phase—The third stage focusses on the marital dyad, particularly on the details of each parent's family of origin.

During this phase, you can encourage the parents to look at how their particular roles in the family were formed. Discussions can focus on how each of the parents learned how to parent through identifying with aspects of their own parents. You can break up a child's strong negative feelings toward his or her parents if you can teach him or her to view them as "victims" of their own childhood. This kind of understanding can help bond children and parents.

If some discussion can occur around the influence of the family of origin on the parents and their parenting of their children, the seeds for later phases of therapy that focus on working with the marital dyad can be planted. During the Structural/Interactive and Communications phases of therapy, you can help improve the identified patient's (child's) functioning; in fact, the child can become less symptomatic, at which point people often stop therapy. However, if you have planted the seeds for looking at the early role models of parents in relation to their family of origin, you can help the marital couple begin to explore in greater depth their own relationship and the interactions which may be causing family stress.

During the later stage of this phase, a more detailed exploration can be pursued of how conflicts in the marital relationship are repetitions of what went on between each spouse and their respective parents. Many times, even when communication improves, there can still be a tendency to distort others according to introjected figures from the past. The need to fit one's spouse with preconceived ideas is directly related to subpersonalities and internalized parental images. Role playing and gestalt procedures as well as other standard psychosynthesis techniques for individual work can help each spouse see how and why he or she is distorting the other. Usually, this has to do with unfinished business with one's family of origin. Another way of looking at the need to repeat in the present one's interactions with one's parents is to view it as an act of loyalty. Some adults are emotionally cut off from their family of origin while others are overinvolved and avoid conflict by not asserting their own needs. Conflicts that belong in the family of origin are split off and played out in marital interactions; one stays loyal to his or her family by not dealing directly with them. During this phase of the family therapy, the therapist helps clarify how parental imagoes contribute to marital stress which can help break up rigid ways of perceiving one's spouse.

4. Family of Origin Phase—Much of this process reflects the work of James L. Framo (for further reference see Framo, 1982). This phase of therapy, however, especially when working with the couple, may not be implemented. Many people have already achieved progress in their therapy and do not want to move into a more in-depth level of work. This wish needs to be respected, although it is advisable to discuss with family members the work that may need to be done at a later time.

For those couples who see the need for continued work, especially because they still have a proclivity to distort each other based on early parental imagoes, working directly with each spouse's family of origin is highly desirable. This stage of work really begins in the Dynamic/Object Relations phase. During this phase, when you have both spouses in the room, you encourage each one to bring in their family of origin to help them rework ongoing dysfunctional patterns. Each spouse helps the other form an agenda for their separate family of origin sessions. When the agenda has been worked out, it is the task of the therapist to help each spouse bring their family of origin into therapy. Because many family members live out of town, this work is usually done over a weekend, on a Friday night for two hours and then on Saturday morning for two hours. It is best to do this work with a heterosexual co-therapy team to facilitate transference phenomena.

The role of the therapist in the session is as a facilitator of dialogue; the goal of the sessions is to help people clarify unresolved misunderstandings and, most important, heal psychic wounds that have been with each family member through the life cycle so far. The major intervention of the therapist during this time is to help family members hear each one another's perceptions and feelings. It is important for each member to empathize with the other's position in order for there to be an understanding of why things occurred in the past and/or what is maintaining them in the present.

It is often helpful to engage the adult son or daughter in dialogue with their parents about their parents' parenting. In other words, many adults have not been told what it was like for their parents to be children and how they learned to be who they are. If there can be an open dialogue about these issues, empathetic impulses can come into play. When adult children feel empathy for their parents, they can start to perceive them not only as their parents but also as victims of those who parented them—something already done, in part, with the children in the nuclear family.

Adult children have often remarked how sad they were when they thought about how rough it was when their parents were being raised by their parents. Being able to see their parents as children can help them form a link that wasn't there previously. If true empathy occurs between family members, a greater sense of connection occurs in the transactional field. Many times, empathy can produce higher qualities, including love and compassion for one's parents. If this occurs, the next phase of family of origin therapy can be implemented.

Forgiving one's parents as well as oneself for misunderstandings or misdeeds in the past and in the present can have tremendous benefits. As one clarifies distortions, empathizes with other family members, allows more love to be expressed, and eventually lets forgiveness occur, one changes the nature of the parental imagoes. In other words, as the relationship with one's parents in the here and now changes, the introjects also go through changes. One's perceptions of significant others as well as other individuals in general can be transformed.

5. Family Coherence/Transformation Phase—The fifth and last phase of family psychosynthesis occurs when individual family members can reorganize their own needs and simultaneously complement the needs of the family system as a whole. In this state, balance is achieved. A new coherence has occurred in the family whereby the highest qualities in one's psyche can be experienced on a transactional level. Thus, family members fully express higher qualities which further transforms negative emotions and mental representations. The expression of higher qualities, such as love and forgiveness, can be reached through interpersonal dialogue, resulting in a family which is a beautiful, powerful, and creative unit of spiritual life.

Family systems can continue to achieve coherence by utilizing some practical procedures. For example, once a week, family members might meet together and express their higher qualities to one another. Parents might express positive feelings about each child and what they appreciate about him or her. Children might also express gratitude toward their parents. The family might also discuss if members feel that they are co-operating with one another on a daily basis and if a change is needed so that everyone experiences more harmony.

Another method of promulgating family coherence is through the whole family meditating together. Everyone might focus on a quality that the whole family needs. Or each member might allow a symbol to emerge of a quality he or she needs to complement the family. These inner experiences could be discussed.

During family meetings, individual and collective goals can be discussed and further attention can be placed on how an individual, with family support, can realize them. This kind of discussion can help build up the Will of individuals and the family as a whole, especially if specific plans are drawn up along with concrete actions to implement them.

Summary and Conclusions

I have focussed in this article on the integration of psychosynthesis concepts within those of general systems theory and family therapy. Five different phases of family therapy have been described. The article has also focussed on the healing that can be realized across generations when both sides are open to understanding what has led to the interpersonal imbalance. Through empathy, love, and forgiveness, the deepest part of our psyches can be liberated. We can experience growth at an individual, interpersonal, and spiritual level.

I have tried to demonstrate that the psychosynthesis paradigm can be extended to a transactional framework and that individual psychosynthesis work is not the only way to help integrate and harmonize the Inner Self. Many times our external relationships reflect our inner world and by working with the external relationships that are most significant to us, mainly our familial relationships, we can transform our inner world as well as ground inner transformations in our daily interactions.

References

Ackerman, N., & Behrens, M. (1956). A study of family diagnosis. *American Journal of Orthopsychiatry*, **26**, 66–78.

Assagioli, R. (1965). *Psychosynthesis: A manual of principles and techniques*. New York: Viking Press.

Assagioli, R. (1973). *The act of will*. Maryland: Penguin.

Dicks, H. (1967). *Marital tensions*. New York: Basic Books.

Framo, J. L. (1970). Symptoms from a family transactional viewpoint. In N. W. Ackerman, J. Lieb, & J. Pearce (Eds.), *Family therapy in transaction*. Boston: Little-Brown.

Framo, J. L. (1976). Family of origin as a therapeutic resource for adults in marital and family therapy: You can and should go home again. *Family Process*, 15(2), 193–210.

Framo, J. L. (1982). Exploration in marital and family therapy. In *Selected Papers of James L. Framo, Ph.D*. New York: Springer.

Frank, L. (1957). Research for what. *Journal of Social Issues* (Supplemental Series), **10**.

Minuchin, S. (1974). *Families and family therapy*. Cambridge, MA: Harvard University Press.

Minuchin, S., & Fishman, C. (1981). *Family therapy techniques*. Cambridge, MA: Harvard University Press.

Minuchin, S., Rosman, B. L., & Baker, L. (1978). *Psychosomatic families: Anorexia nervosa in context*. Cambridge, MA: Harvard University Press.

Olson, D. H., Sprenkle, D. H., & Russell, C. (1979). Circumplex model of marital and family systems: Cohesion and adaptability dimensions, family types and clinical applications. *Family Process*, **18**, 3–28.

Satir, V. (1967). *Conjoint family therapy: A guide to theory and technique*. Palo Alto, CA: Science and Behavior Books.

Synthesis: The realization of the Self. (1975). *What is Psychosynthesis?*, **1**(2). (Redwood City, CA: Synthesis Press).

Tyson, R. L., & Tyson, P. (1982). A case of pseudo-narcissistic psychopathology: A re-examination of the developmental role of the superego. *International Journal of Psychoanalysis*, **63**.

Vargiu, J. (1974). Subpersonalities. *Synthesis: The Realization of the Self*, **1**(1). (Redwood City, CA: Synthesis Press).

Religion

Subpersonalities and Prayer: Psychosynthesis and Spiritual Direction

Jane Vennard

The perspective of Psychosynthesis calls people into wholeness. The experience of wholeness is validated as is the experience of diversity. We are all one and we are all many. The spiritual journey is the movement from wholeness through diversity into wholeness and back into diversity, an evercontinuing spiral. This journey includes the already and the not yet.

Psychosynthesis is useful in many ways for those seeking spiritual direction: it emphasizes the use of the Will in the act of discernment, the claiming of one's own authority, the use of dream images to guide and/or make clear the unfolding journey, the discovery of patterns which block loving relationships, the discovery of our full richness to bring into ministry, the healing of old wounds that block our movement into a more complete life. The work of Psychosynthesis is spiritual work for it always holds God's loving power as a guiding force in one's life. Psychosynthesis does not exclude the power of past experiences (personal, familial, societal) in shaping behavior, but infuses these experiences with meaning by viewing them through a transpersonal lens.

In this article, I focus on one small aspect of Psychosynthesis and spiritual direction: working with subpersonalities to uncover, develop, and deepen prayer. Because spiritual direction is always done from the understanding that God, not the individual and not the director, is guiding the process of growth and unfoldment, prayer is at the heart of spiritual direction. The recognition and acceptance of subpersonalities that both block and enhance prayer helps a person to respond to the call and the guidance of God in her or his life.

Subpersonalities and Prayer

At the age of 35, I wanted to learn how to meditate. I felt called to the discipline and the peace and energy that people reported who were involved in meditation. But I could not do it. I would set a time to begin, and the time would go by. In group meditations, I would close my eyes and then begin to feel extremely anxious. During one long exercise, I left the room for the intensity caused me to panic.

The invitation to begin meditation came in my study of Psychosynthesis. This transpersonal psychology described a perspective which granted to

112

the human person a spiritual aspect that was as influential in the ongoing development process as one's drives, needs, and past experiences. I was finding Psychosynthesis to be intellectually and emotionally powerful in my life, but I could not move into the spiritual realm. During a session with my guide, I found the nature of my resistance.

In guided imagery, I was directed into a meadow to relax and to await the coming of the part of me, the subpersonality, that was getting in the way of meditation. In my imagination, I sat in the meadow, waiting and waiting, inviting that part to come forth. I was aware that there was a presence in the woods at the edge of the meadow. I could catch a glimpse of movement, but I could not see who it was. Then very slowly a figure began to emerge. She was about 20 years old and dressed in a gossamer gown, long and flowing. She seemed very afraid, and I reassured her, telling her I truly wanted to get to know her. She came toward me, and came to rest in front of me. She told me that her name was Esmeralda, and that she was the part of me I had left in Europe after the experience at the Ecumenical Work Camp that I had attended in Holland when I was 19. Memories of that summer flooded over me: the excitement of the many other young people from different nations and different faiths, the hard work of brick laying, the taste of Dutch chocolate melting on my tongue, the Bible reading, the singing, the prayers, and the worship. And then suddenly I was in Paris watching a man being run over by a speeding taxi and killed instantly before my eyes. Esmeralda's emergence triggered the experience that was blocking my meditation.

In talking subsequently with my guide, I relived the memories and realized that the joy of the camp and the horror of random death could not be contained in the theology I was working with at that time. Five weeks of camp had heightened my experience of a loving and all-powerful God who cared about each and every one of us. In my 19-year-old mind and heart, I could not hold both experiences. I was alone and terrified; the experience of darkness was all the more overwhelming after the experience of light. The pain was too great, and to protect myself from encountering that pain again, I closed down my religious and spiritual experiences, for I knew I could not protect myself from death. Esmeralda, the spiritual part of me, who had the will and awareness for meditation and prayer, had been left in Europe at the age of 19.

When I knew which subpersonality had been blocking my spiritual development, I could begin the process of education. I helped Esmeralda slowly grow up as I discovered a theology that could hold both the light and the dark. I could experiment with different forms of prayer and meditation, and integrate the spiritual into my life. All my resistance to prayer was not gone, and I have had periods of difficulty along the way. But a major hurdle had been overcome and the joys and struggles of the spiritual life opened out before me.

Subpersonalities that Block Progress

Since that time, in my work of counselling, teaching, and providing spiritual direction, I have witnessed other people discovering subpersonalities that have been blocking their prayer life. One 40-year-old man worked with an

11-year-old boy named Rodney. Rodney was terrified of God. "The Devil was easy," he said in one session, "God was the one to fear." This man's early religious training was so filled with a frightening and judgmental God that he closed God off in adolescence and had no desire to re-open the relationship. "Who would want to talk to a God like that?" he said.

"I am not worthy," a young woman said to me in a class. "How can I take myself to God? I don't expect Him to listen to me. I am so unworthy of even asking for His attention. I feel totally cut off from any of God's love or guidance. And being unable to pray makes me feel even more unworthy." This woman was not reporting a subpersonality; she was totally identified with a part of herself that was invisible, unknown, and unworthy.

Another woman reported an overachieving subpersonality that kept telling her she wasn't doing it right. "No matter how long I sat, no matter how beautiful my words, no matter how peaceful my heart, my prayer would be interrupted with the doubts of whether I was doing it as well as others, whether I was truly pleasing God. My mind held a great desire to know more and more about prayer, but all the time I was being pulled away from the experience of prayer."

Still another man talked about the part of himself that was committed to social action and ending injustice in the world. Every time he began a regular prayer experience, this other part berated him, "How can you just sit there when there is so much to be done. Prayer will take you out of this world. This is the world that needs you. If you get too involved with spiritual things you will lose your power and force in the world."

All of these subpersonalities were an aspect of personality, a part of the whole. Some were developed in the past, some in adult years, but each one served to interrupt the prayer life of the people involved. By recognizing "who" was causing the problem, each person was able to begin working with that part that pulled them away from their relationship with God, and move more deeply into the life of the spirit.

Subpersonalities and Prayer Styles

Just as our subpersonalities can block prayer, they can be great helpers and friends in prayer, if we allow them to pray in ways that are most comfortable and nourishing to them. Every subpersonality has access to God, and because of the different nature of the many subpersonalities, prayer can be experienced in many different ways.

Occasionally a subpersonality will decide that he or she is the one who really knows about prayer, and so will try to make the other subpersonalities conform to a particular form or routine: "To pray correctly I have to set aside a full 30 minutes, first do my stretching activities, then quiet my mind with the use of my breathing, then I read a section of Scripture and reflect on its meaning in my life. This is followed by the cards on which I have written the names of people I wish to hold before God in my prayers. I then pray for myself, asking forgiveness and giving thanks." The person who reported this form of prayer to me also reported that her prayers were happening less often and that they were dry and routine and "just another thing to be done in the day." When I suggested that there might be other ways to engage God in her life, she was surprised, excited, and doubtful. This woman's prayer life was being controlled by a subpersonality most likely developed through her religious training.

When we honor the many different forms and styles of prayer and trust that all are acceptable to the God with whom we pray, much creativity is released. The following descriptions are subpersonality reports of experiences of prayer. I have gathered these over the years with clients and students, and use them with permission:

River Rat connects with God in Nature. She is happiest in the wilderness where she can take off her clothes and drink in God's world with every inch of her being—the touch and the taste, the smells and sounds as well as the visual beauty that surrounds her.

The musician in me praises God with my music. When I sing out, when I write music, when I direct women's voices into harmony. I am singing, singing, singing for the glory of God.

One night when I was in distress over my mother—her health, her emotional anxiety, and our relationship—I was finding my prayers unhelpful, agitating, in fact. But then I realized I needed to pray as a daughter, and I needed to pray to a Mother of God. When I shifted my position and made specific my image of God, release, hope, and consolation began to flow through me.

Every year I make a retreat for seven days. I don't think I could get through my life without that time. The Mystic in me is so happy, and although it gets some attention during the year, only in brief moments. During that week I fully identify with Mary Ann, as I call her, and let all my other subpersonalities rest. They are as happy as Mary Ann, for they know that when I return to my busy life, the energy and love and peace that Mary Ann feels will be shared with them. Mary Ann is able to teach the others what she has learned.

I truly feel the presence of God when I serve regularly at St. Anthony's kitchen. Standing behind the tables ladling out the stew, watching all manner of folk pass before me, I am humbled and I see in each and every face the person of Jesus and hear his words: "As you do for the least of them, so you do unto me."

I was overcome with awe as my newborn infant was placed in my wife's arms. Witness to a miracle of creation. And now, as the realities of parenting are constantly before us, I still, at moments, simply stop, and the same awe overcomes me as I look at my child. To be a parent is to be constantly reminded of God.

Speedy is on the move. She laughs and clowns and wears the most comfortable clothes no matter how she looks. She is learning to juggle, and I feel as I laugh and juggle and drop the balls and laugh some more that God is laughing with me for Speedy knows that God loves to laugh even if I forget it.

Every morning when I put on my running clothes, stretch out my muscles, tighten the shoelaces, I feel as if I am preparing to run toward my God. For as I run, I feel within my breath and my body the glory of living. My running is a prayer of thanksgiving for health and movement and energy all contained in this body I have been given. And I pray that I may use this body and this energy to further serve the God of creation.

Summer is a new subpersonality I am developing. She is quietly and comfortably in relation with God. Her spirituality infuses her being. All my other subpersonalities have a frantic quality about them. They may talk to God, but usually only in their own self interests. Summer recognizes the needs of all and trusts that those needs will be met. Her task in prayer is to listen, just listen and then share what she hears. It is amazing to me, after so many years of praying and asking and asking and praying and getting no answer. Now that Summer is praying, and praying simply by opening her heart, she is hearing. Some of my subpersonalities are a little doubtful, for Summer is so new. But many recognize her gift, for as she is more and more in charge they realize she uses love to guide herself and them, and in the light of her love, the love that comes from God, they are more accepting, less frantic, and more willing to cooperate.

Implications for Spiritual Direction

Working with subpersonalities through the stages of recognition, acceptance, co-ordination, and integration is an integral part of spiritual direction. When subpersonality work is centred around prayer, movement can be experienced within the whole personality; a reaching toward God, a deepening of the relationship with God, and the experience of God in one's life.

The descriptions of the subpersonalities that block prayer as well as the ones who have their own preference for prayer are examples of the first stage of subpersonality work—recognition. Each subpersonality is recognized, named, and explored to find out what the needs and wants are, what the gifts are, and how the subpersonality thinks and feels about life in general, and prayer specifically. The next stage is acceptance. Each one of these subpersonalities needs to be accepted as a valuable part of the whole personality. There may be blocked or distorted behavior, but each subpersonality needs to be heard and welcomed. Often when a subpersonality is discovered, another subpersonality will emerge to reject it. This rejecting subpersonality may be the judgmental type as in the case of the woman whose subpersonality felt she was not worthy to be with God; this part of herself berated her for being spineless, and although seemingly committed to building her up, was not listening to the real pain of the Worthless One.

Often a judgment will be issued from subpersonalities that believe another form of prayer is wrong or inferior. The Disciplined Mystic might say to Speedy, "That's not prayer! You're having too much fun!" Or a priestly subpersonality might tell River Rat, "For shame! Cover yourself! Who do you think you are, cavorting like a pagan?" Or Summer might be told by the Organized Doer, "All that peace and tranquillity will make you lazy. On your feet, girl, there is much to be done."

In order to develop an acceptance of all the parts of the personality, the process of disidentification needs to occur. When the conflict has been recognized and named, and fully explored through imagery or gestalt chair work, the person can be invited to move to a third place where he or she is no longer identified either with the subpersonalities or with the conflict. The individual stands outside, in a place where he or she can see, hear, and bring understanding and acceptance to both parts. This third place is another subpersonality, one with a wider view that can see more, accept more deeply, and aid in both the healing of wounded subpersonalities and the mediating of the conflict between them.

From the third position, co-ordination becomes possible. With co-ordination comes the decision to share time, so that both the Disciplined Mystic and Speedy, for example, would have time to pray in their own ways, neither one insisting that there was only one way. The subpersonality that sees and values both positions can also encourage integration by helping the subpersonalities learn from one another. The idea is *not* for the two to become one, but rather to share some of the qualities unique to each so that in this case Speedy might become more disciplined in her playful prayer, and the Disciplined Mystic might begin to lighten up his prayer life and approach it with a more playful heart.

I have worked with clients in whose personality this third place, this loving, caring subpersonality, is readily available. In other clients, this part is not fully developed and needs to be evoked and loved into being. The subpersonality Summer is an example of one of the latter. In all the work Dorothy had done, she had recognized her many subpersonalities. All were vivid and well-formed, but narrow and self-interested. They were rich and exciting and brought her great diversity and gifts, but not one of them was willing to serve the whole personality in a loving and caring way. When she disidentified from any conflict, she stepped directly into another subpersonality that would keep the conflict going, or she would step into a judging subpersonality that would defeat her with such words as "Aren't you ever going to get this together?!" In guided imagery, she called to an unknown part of herself, a part that could help her in her frenzied life. Summer appeared. The ongoing work with Dorothy is to help her get closer to Summer, to trust her, to bring her into her life. Because Summer carries and plays the flute, Dorothy uses her breathing to remind her of Summer's existence. She also uses the words of Summer: "I am spiritually content. I deserve God's love." Dorothy told me in our last session that Summer was real to her, but it was as if she was sitting next to her. Dorothy could not yet become Summer and trust that her qualities were her own.

I believe that God calls each and every one of us to wholeness. We move toward wholeness as we learn about our diversity, for we are One and we are Many. We are Whole and we are Broken. We are Divine and we are Human. Spiritual direction is a response to that call toward wholeness, and prayer is at the heart of the process. By intentionally working with the subpersonalities, particularly with their varied experience of God and their individual relationships to God, clients can discover their internal riches which they can then bring to their relationship with God. This relationship with God through prayer allows for more riches within the personality to be revealed and explored, enriching the full life which is being led. When subpersonalities are taken seriously and their fears and wants and needs and gifts and hopes listened to, the whole personality can move toward God, toward others, and toward all of life with more intention, with more awareness, with more joy, and ultimately with more love.

A Theology of Blessing:
A Psychology of Growth

Joan C. Borton

Psychosynthesis does not aim or attempt to give a metaphysical or theological explanation of the great Mystery—it leads to the door, but stops there.
ROBERTO ASSAGIOLI (1978)

Growing up as a rebellious preacher's kid, with parents and grandparents who were teachers, ministers, and missionaries, I had a strong sense of my roots in the Christian tradition. Choosing to study religion and biblical studies in college, I explored theology and various paths to "the great Mystery." Having sworn never to marry a minister, I met a deeply seeking man who became a minister and, contrary to my sworn oath, I chose to become his wife.

As I look back, I see myself as an intense and searching soul, whose sense of oneness with creation brought her closest to that door of Mystery. A major block to that path was my wanting to control, my lack of trust. My psychosynthesis training enabled me to let go and trust the unfolding process of each person and all creation. I then began to open myself to the Mystery at the heart of my own tradition. I was drawn in a new way to the one called Jesus the Christ and to the way he was with people. Jesus did not use jargon when he talked with people, nor did he present a belief system. He engaged them at a level which asked for their trust. His trust was in their potential for wholeness or holiness. I responded to this Jesus who challenged people to trust, who spoke to the image of God in each person and called it forth. I wanted to learn more of him.

So I began, with gratitude to Roberto Assagioli and his conception of the human being, on a journey which led me to my spiritual home. The following article is both an expression of that gratitude and an attempt to share from the Christian tradition my discoveries on the way.

During my training I discovered the work of Meister Eckhart, a 13th-century spiritual theologian. I found myself making connections between his words and my understanding and experience of Psychosynthesis. The process of bridging the two became very exciting to me when I encountered a contemporary theologian, Matthew Fox, who was interpreting Eckhart for our time. This led me to recover for myself the spiritual tradition within Christianity known as Creation-Centred Spirituality. This theology of blessing offered an articulation of my religious experience which expanded the

118

richness of my tradition and deepened my willingness as a counsellor to engage in trust with people on their life journeys.

At a time when the Church's voice is often exclusive and is used to define someone as either "in" or "out," I find Eckhart's understanding of spiritual paths expansive and inclusive. In an age of personal and planetary threat to life, Creation-Centred Spirituality speaks of Justice and Compassion as the fulfillment of the Hebrew tradition and of the Christian gospel. It is my purpose to present the four paths of Creation Spirituality in a way that connects with the personal-spiritual growth work of Psychosynthesis. I intend to illustrate this theology of blessing with some of the principles and techniques of Roberto Assagioli's psychology of growth toward wholeness.

Meister Eckhart and the Hidden Treasure

Meister Eckhart was a Dominican preacher and teacher whose holistic spiritual vision challenged the established church. His politics were also questionable for he involved himself as spiritual director with a community of lay women who worked with the poor but were not accepted by the church as nuns. They were early feminists, and so was he. Eckhart viewed all persons as "royal persons," which was an affront to the class structure of the time. He was condemned after his death by church authorities (Fox, 1980), but his sermons and writings have continued to be influential.

Mystics within the Catholic church such as Hildegard de Bengen and Julian of Norwich drew on Eckhart's spirituality. The Protestant reformer Martin Luther and the father of Quakerism George Fox were also influenced by his thought. Carl Jung was touched by this Dominican, as were D. T. Suzuki and Thomas Merton who both saw Zen in his writings. The breadth of Eckhart's influence and his particular relevance for our time challenged a contemporary Dominican, Matthew Fox, to translate his sermons and present them with commentary in *Breakthrough: Meister Eckhart's Creation Spirituality in New Translation*. In 1985, Fox published *Original Blessing, A Primer in Creation Spirituality*, which thematically reclaims this tradition within the setting of 20th-century Christianity.

The starting place for Eckhart's spiritual journey is one's created nature, which he calls "the treasure." His model for the spiritual traveller is the artist:

> If a skilled artist made an image in wood or stone, he or she does not place that image within the wood but chisels away the pieces that have hidden and covered it up. . . . Then what lay underneath shone forth. This is the treasure that lay hidden in the soil, as our Lord says in the Gospel [Matthew 13:44]. (Fox, 1980, p. 412)

Psychosynthesis views the traveller as beginning the journey also by discovering that treasure which is uniquely his or her created nature. This is the beginning of healing, a moving toward wholeness. As with the process of psychosynthesis, Eckhart sees this movement not as a linear progression but as a spiral motion of four different paths that lead into and return to each other as we become more fully co-creators of our lives with God.

Matthew Fox (1983) has named these paths: Befriending Creation, Befriending Darkness, Befriending Creativity, and Befriending New Creation.

Path 1—Befriending Creation

Vincent Van Gogh's painting *Starry Night* expresses in greens, golds, and blues the pulsating vibrancy of the cosmos, the aliveness of creation. The Hebrews had a word for the energy that Van Gogh expresses: *dabhar*, the creative energy of God. It is this energy that is celebrated in the psalms of the Hebrew scriptures:

> Oh Lord how manifold are thy works!
> In Wisdom thou hast made them all;
> the earth is full of thy creatures.   (Psalm 104:24)

The two creation stories in Genesis proclaim through the language and context of the Middle East the sense of God or *Yahweh* as Creator and Giver of Life. That Life is the *dabhar,* shared with all creation, and blessed by Yahweh, "And he saw that it was good" (Gen. 102:4a). Thus the original state of creation was good and the Creator was one who blessed all forms of life.

In the first creation story, written in the ninth century, the author's imagery expresses the loving quality of this "Lord God" *(Elohim)* who wants to create a human being. "So the Lord God took the dust of the earth and blew into it and *adam,*" meaning all humanity, male or female (Kenik, 1979, p. 50), "became a living being" (Gen. 2:46). Matter, from which all creation was made, was enlivened by spirit and the creative energy of God was shared. The Yahwist whose creation story comes from the tenth century also expresses the *dabhar* enacted through the spoken word. "And God said . . . let there be light . . . let us make *adam* in our image" (Gen. 1). That spoken word in Hebrew is *dabhar;* it involves action. The word has the power to create (Fox, 1983, pp. 35–41).

The same word is used in the Gospel of John in reference to Christ: "In the beginning was the Word, and the Word was with God and the Word was God" (John 1:1). Creation-Centred Spirituality is a theology of creation and incarnation. The incarnation of that creative energy of God in the person of Jesus is an embodiment of God's intention for all people to realize their fullness and divinity: "I have come that you may have Life and have it in abundance" (John 10:10). This abundance was expressed by the writers of the creation stories. The Garden of Eden was a place of fullness and of blessing. "It was good" and it was enough for all creation. Wanting more than enough led to the separation of man and woman from the Creator and other creatures (Gen. 3).

This experience of separation from the Oneness that is the inheritance of humanity and from one's own true nature is often what brings a person to counselling, even though he or she may present specific problems as the initial reason. The relationship between spiritual growth and personal growth is one of interconnection. Psychosynthesis counselling recognizes this. The healing work of discovering our created nature is a form of "befriending creation," beginning with one's self. This takes place over time and is experienced in some of the following ways:

• **Touching** those transpersonal qualities, intimations of the Garden of Eden, that each of us longs to experience in a fuller way: love, courage, joy, patience, hope.

• **Holding** those qualities as affirmations for the journey while we disidentify (Crampton, 1977, pp. 22–27) from the roles and personae we have created in order to discover the "self" beneath that build-up.

• **Working** with the various subpersonalities (Brown, 1983, pp. 29–34) that have blocked the expression of the *dabhar* (God's creative energy) in us; experiencing growing communication between what has appeared to be opposing inner forces.

• **Finding** the gold hidden in our most frightened parts.

• **Embracing,** as Carl Rogers observed, "the richness and complexity, with nothing hidden and nothing feared in oneself—this is the common desire in those who seemed to show much movement in therapy" (Rogers, 1984, p. 14.).

The process of befriending creation can start on a very personal level. This part of the spiritual journey is where travellers begin the life-long process of claiming the abundance of the Garden of Eden and their own state of original blessing. They begin to own that creative energy of God within themselves, and all creation is enough. For enough *is* abundance. To realize that on a personal level, a spiritual level, and a planetary level is the prophetic call to us as a species as we approach the 21st century.

Path 2—Befriending Darkness

The spiritual heritage of Christian mystics encompasses two basic approaches. The first tradition emphasizes visions, light, images, and positive affective experiences as the way to come to know God. The second tradition is based in silence as the place of meeting God. The traveller engages in a process of emptying, which Eckhart speaks of as the second spiritual path. It involves a willingness to be open to the darkness, which is experienced in silence as a letting go of words, images, thoughts, and affections. It is a way of entering into nothingness, a trusting of empty space. The movement is one of sinking, letting go, resting or emptying. It involves a deep level of trust.

> We become a pure nothing by an unknowing
> knowledge which is
> emptiness
> and solitude
> and desert
> and darkness
> and remaining still. (Fox, 1982, p. 48)

This movement in therapy is very crucial. As therapists and counsellors, we need to be willing to be there with another person in the emptiness, to be present at a time when he or she experiences not knowing and to let be what is (Fox, 1982, p. 48). This means that we too must have allowed ourselves to go into the darkness. This experience can be frightening. It is essential to be able to trust even when we are in darkness or to let someone else do the befriending when we do not have it in ourselves to trust.

Matthew Fox makes an important distinction regarding this part of the journey. On the one hand, there is a sinking or emptying motion in spiritual life that we can choose to follow. On the other hand, there is the experience of *being* emptied when circumstances outside ourselves such as loss, sexual abuse, catastrophe, or illness bring darkness and pain. When this happens, we cannot decide whether or not we want to go along with it; it is just there. Thus there is a qualitative difference between emptying and being emptied.

When I was on my back for a long period of time, working hard to heal myself, I finally recognized that the healing was taking place in the spaces between my efforts, in the empty spaces. I had to have trust that by letting go and letting be I could choose to empty myself of my effort. I could not choose whether or not I had pain. I was being emptied by the pain, and that emptying was the gift of this period of darkness for me:

> God does not ask anything else of you
> except
>   that you let yourself go
>   and let God
>   be God
>   in you. (Fox, 1982, p. 52)

During this time, I read *Breakthrough*, Eckhart's sermons edited by Matthew Fox, and found I was helped by the process of being emptied by pain. The Japanese poet Kenji Miyazawa suggests that we can embrace pain and burn it as fuel for our journey. Fox, who also suffered from back pain, explored this further:

> We pick up our pain as we would a bundle of sticks for a fireplace. We necessarily embrace these sticks as we move across the room to the fireplace. Then we thrust them into the fire, getting rid of them, letting go of them. Finally we are warmed and delighted by their sacrificial gift to us in a form of fire and heat and warmth and energy. This is the manner in which we can and indeed must deal with our pain. First comes the embrace, the allowing of pain to be pain. Next comes the journey with the pain, then the letting go but in a deliberate manner into a fire, into a cauldron where the pain's energy will serve us. And finally comes the benefit we do indeed derive from having burned the fuel. Pain is meant to give us energy. (Fox, 1983, pp. 142–143)

We deal with pain as counsellors. Much of our work is helping young people to embrace their pain rather than denying it, pushing it away, or running from its reality. *Focussing* (Gendlin, 1981) is one way of strengthening a client's will while dealing with a painful thing. He or she might be asked, "Can you be with this [painful thing] as if it were a hurt child? Can you put your arm around it?" (Campbell, 1985, pp. 124–125). Gestalt methods, expressive exercises, imagery, and subpersonality dialogue are various ways of befriending the darkness. One begins to embrace the painful part and to walk with it until one can let it go, releasing its energy. This journey with a painful part of ourselves can be a long and sometimes desperate process. Yet in the depth of emptiness, we can experience the compassionate heart of God, for there is communion with God who also suffers with the darkness.

"Christ on the Cross" painted by Georges Roualt speaks in deep reds of the process of Jesus emptying himself in order to allow pain to be pain (Philippians, 2:5–9). The crucifixion is, for me, Jesus' willingness to go with the pain of human history and to trust in God in the midst of darkness and not knowing. This is a powerful image which can help us during our own experiences of darkness, and also enable us to be there in dark times for other people.

Eckhart said that our souls grow by subtraction, not by addition (Fox, 1982, p. 45). To trust this process while experiencing nothingness is the challenge of the second path. This experience brings us back in a spiral motion to the first path. For our willingness to go to the place of nothingness brings us to the beginning of creation; it is out of darkness that light is created. According to Matthew Fox, the relationship between the first and second paths causes a dialectic from which creative energy comes forth.

Path 3—Befriending Creativity

The third path emerges as the place of the birthing of human imagination. Being "created in the image of God" means that we, too, are image makers. In expressing the *dabhar* in ourselves, we become co-creators with God.

The colorful collages of Henri Matisse are my icons for this path. In the middle of World War II, this Frenchman felt that he had to make a statement for joy. In his later years as an invalid, he did most of his work from his bed, drawing sketches on the walls and ceiling of his room by attaching charcoal to a bamboo pole. His assistants would then cut out the vibrant shapes, which would become a mural or a stained glass window. The creative spirit of this image maker has inspired many travellers.

The creative potential of this path holds awesome power. Eckhart reminds us, "We are heirs of this fearful creative power of God" (Fox, 1983, p. 182). In similar vein, Dag Hammerskjold asks, "Do we create or do we destroy?" (Fox, 1983, p. 178). The possibility for birthing and blessing is ours as co-creators with God. The other side of that wondrous inheritance is the power to destroy all that has been created. Both Eckhart and Assagioli were deeply aware of this potential and thus emphasized the importance of *response*-ability.

The Artist, for Eckhart, is that part of ourselves which expresses our deepest self. And it is the Will, for Assagioli, that motivates the expression of the Self in the world. Trusting our images is central to this process of expression, birthing, or creating the Self. Discernment is crucial at this level of trusting. As Fox said, we must decide which images we are going to ride. This involves discipline. For Assagioli, working with images is involved in techniques for developing our will. This is a training process. In both Creation-Centred Spirituality and Psychosynthesis, willing and imagination go hand in hand.

The same elements are present in the Genesis story. Man and woman were created in the image of God—with the potential to be creators themselves, using their imagination. In their freedom within the Garden, they had the choice to accept its abundance or to seek more and "be like God" (Gen. 3:5). How do we develop our creative potential (the power of our imagination) and at the same time be responsible stewards of the resources that are entrusted to us by God (the enhanced will)?

Assagioli's work with the Will is fascinating on a theoretical level as he explores the relationship between image and action in his Psychological Laws (Assagioli, 1973, pp. 51–65). More important, he translates this into very helpful exercises for the training of the Will. I often find myself returning to use the Stages of the Will (1965, pp. 125–143) for clarity in my own decision-making. I use a process of willing with clients as a tangible way to make changes on a behavioral level. Each step in the process can be valuable in itself. The total process of movement from "purpose" to "directing the action" is empowering. Assagioli places this exercise in personal willing within the greater context of Love—Transpersonal and Universal Will. Like the self-expression of Matisse, this phase of the journey is associated by Assagioli with joy. He concludes *The Act of Will* with the words of Evelyn Underhill:

> The enhanced will, made over to the interests of the Transcendent, receives new worlds to conquer, new strengths to match its exalted destiny. But the heart, too, here enters on a new order, begins to live upon high levels of joy: that is, the sea of delight, the stream of divine influences. (1973, pp. 201–202)

This enhanced will, this conscious expression of the *dabhar*, connects us with the Transcendent. On the path of befriending creativity, we participate in the resurrection energy of Christ. With a sense of this potential, we are led to the fourth path which leads us, in the words of Underhill, toward a "new order."

Path 4—Befriending New Creation

Our creativity must be directed by compassion. This quality must guide us in all our decisions on the path of new creation. Yet as we travel, we find that the experience of each previous path is included. As we seek a just world order based on our knowledge of planetary interdependence (Path 4), we call on the birthing of the *dabhar* in all people (Path 3), which is generated by facing the darkness of possible nuclear destruction (Path 2); this experience of the darkness results from our great love and our sense of oneness with all creation (Path 1).

Deep passion for justice is expressed by Eckhart in his understanding of compassion:

> Whatever God does, the first outburst is always compassion. (Fox, 1983, p. 277)

> Compassion means justice and compassion is just to the extent that it gives to each person what is his or hers. (p. 103)

For Assagioli, the process of synthesis and expanding awareness is expressed by a commitment to "the psychosynthesis of Humanity", a realizing of interdependence, solidarity, and co-operation (Horowitz, 1984).

Eckhart sees that our vocation, what we are called forth to do with who we are in the world, is to turn the blessing that we are back into the process of creation. This movement makes available more of the creative energy of God in the Universe. It is Matthew Fox's view that all of us are potential prophets, that our task is interference and awakening for the purpose of transformation, that we should ask ourselves, "How is my work interfering with injustice? How am I planting seeds of harmony in the cosmic world?" (1983, p. 261). On this fourth path, we must trust in our prophetic vocations, not in our own ability to figure this out, but in the grace of the Holy Spirit which is available for all of us to appropriate. As Jesus met each person in his or her uniqueness, so, too, the Holy Spirit leads each of us to our unique expression of this vocation.

When I gaze at the photograph of our planet taken from the moon, I see rich blues and greens wreathed in white swirling clouds. I see that small fragile whole against the backdrop of deep, dark space. I no longer see separate land formations, continents, East or West. I see the earth in its entirety. I recognize the interdependence of all its parts and feel a longing to tend and care for this creation in its wholeness.

As we experience the life and death nature of our interdependence on this planet, we need to know that justice is "erotic," that it is intimate, passionate, and involved (Fox, 1983, pp. 286–305). When Jesus said, "I have come that you have life and have it in abundance" (John 10:10), his commitment was to become involved with all of creation.

When as a psychosynthesis counsellor I am with one person who expresses despair over an inability to experience the creative life of God, or when as a Christian lay person I see the outrage of a people who may never know abundance, I confront my vocation. I feel called to draw on the creative energy of God, the *dabhar*, to care for this created world and its inhabitants in the ways that I am able so that others may experience the abundance that has been created for all of us.

References

Assagioli, R. (1973). *The act of will*. New York: Penguin.

Assagioli, R. (1978). *Psychosynthesis: A collection of basic writings*. New York: Penguin.

Brown, M. Y. (1983). *The unfolding Self: Psychosynthesis and Counseling*. Los Angeles: Psychosynthesis Press.

Crampton, M. (1977). *Psychosynthesis: Some key aspects of theory and practice*. Montreal: Canadian Institution of Psychosynthesis.

Campbell, P.A., & McMahon, E. (1985). *Bio-spirituality: Focusing as a way to grow*. Chicago: Loyola University Press.

Fox, M. (1980). *Breakthrough: Meister Eckhart's Creation-Centered Spirituality in new translation*. New York: Doubleday.

Fox, M. (1982). *Meditation with Meister Eckhart*. Santa Fe: Bear & Company.

Fox, M. (1983). *Original blessing: A primer in Creation Spirituality*. Sante Fe: Bear & Company.

Gendlin, E. T. (1981). *Focusing*. New York: Bantam.

Horowitz, M. (1984). Psychosynthesis and world order. In J. Weiser & T. Yeomans (Eds.), *Psychosynthesis in the helping professions: Now and for the future*. Toronto: Department of Applied Psychology, Ontario Institute for Studies in Education.

Kenik, H. (1979). Toward a biblical basis for Creation Theology. In M. Fox (Ed.), *Western spirtuality: Historical roots, ecumenical routes*. Notre Dame: Fides Claretian.

Rogers, C. R. (1984). *A therapist's view of personal goals*. Wallingford, PA: John Spencer.

House Church: A Spiritual Group Growth Experience

Elinor Berke

House Church is a group spiritual retreat set up each June at the Chicago Theological Seminary. We use a series of psychosynthesis exercises to help participants increase their awareness, confront their stuck places, and move on to feel a sense of choice and empowerment in their lives. This process frees up the super-unconscious energies to strengthen the life of the Soul, which can then express itself in the work of the world.

Figure 1

The egg diagram provides the framework for the week's work.

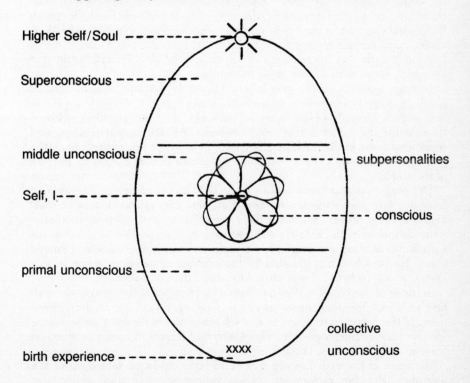

All our work takes place within the framework provided by the egg diagram (see Figure 1). We work with all the parts: conscious and unconscious, birth and childhood trauma, early patterns, subpersonalities, ego and observer, mind, body, and emotions, the various areas of the unconscious, dreams, and the aspirations of the highest self. We are careful to include the shadow side. Indeed, it turns out that this is where most of our work is done. Reaching toward spiritual energies stirs up unresolved issues from the past as well as automatic patterns of behavior that are no longer useful and need to be replaced.

The name House Church was used by the early Pauline churches which met in homes of dedicated believers. The name is appropriate for our group in that it describes a religious commitment which is grounded in both an immediate individual experience and a supportive, caring group. Such a commitment is religious in the true sense of the Latin *religiare*, which means to bind together: at House Church, we bind ourselves to one another and we create the context within which we bind together the parts of ourselves, healing ourselves and each other into wholeness.

Dr. Philip Anderson, Professor of Pastoral Theology at Chicago Theological Seminary, originally developed House Church in 1968 using gestalt methodology. When I began working with him in 1976, I introduced the concepts of Psychosynthesis as a context for gestalt, body, and early childhood work. Since then, our vision has evolved together to the point where the entire framework for House Church comes out of Psychosynthesis. The strong spiritual orientation of Psychosynthesis, its methods for dealing with the primal energies of the lower unconscious, and its emphasis on the Will, choice, and empowerment fit well with the House Church objectives of helping people live increasingly from their central core and using that energy in some form of service in the world.

It is not unusual for the people who choose to enrol to be experiencing blockage or pain somewhere in their lives. For some, the pain is severe. A few attend through curiosity or as partners of those enrolled, without thought for the benefits they might receive. All are engaged in spiritual seeking of some kind. Each person comes in at his or her own place on the journey, and almost all complete some significant personal steps by the end of the week.

Dr. Anderson and I run House Church at the seminary as a week-long intensive group for experienced ministers, seminary students, church staff, and interested others. We meet daily from 9 a.m. until 10 p.m. in a large room furnished with cushions and low-back rest seats. We take our meals together in another building. Most people stay in seminary housing for the week. House Church is planned for the number of people that can fit in a house, about 16 to 20. Some attend for more than one year.

Because of our belief in the transformative energies of the group, we work first to form a spiritual community that is caring, accepting, healing. Since many of the participants know us or each other and since most are so ready, "community" happens quickly. Those who find it hard to trust may focus on trust as their main area of work for the week.

We work in the ever-present Now with body, feelings, imagination. We use music, drawing, movement, sensory awareness, meditation, and journal writing, integrating imagery, healing, and spirituality. We provide experiences and images which people can use to confront and integrate parts of themselves. We teach and use communication skills to keep our community open and receptive to the input and feelings of all. We use this focussed community energy to help people move into their life blocks and pain, and then if possible, beyond. We assume that individuals will tap into the collective energy, enabling them to go further on their personal journeys than they would have been able to do alone.

As the week unfolds, participants experience a transformation of negative energies, or an enlargement of their viewpoint which is experienced as transformative. Individuals are in charge of how they use their time and how far they will go. There is no way to know what will happen or what we as guides or as group will be called upon to do. As I enter the week-long retreat, I have the feeling of engaging in a great adventure.

People usually do their work around issues: Presence, Trust, Belonging, Responsibility, Anger, Regret, Sadness, Fear, Helplessness, Dependence. These come up the first evening and remain a topic throughout the week. The meditation exercises and the Four Pictures are also structured to bring up issues. Everyone in the group works privately on whatever each person selects as his or her issue. Some of these issues are Taking Risks, Self-Worth, Fear of Other's Judgments, Meeting Family Standards, Being Vulnerable, Doing it Right, Asking for What You Want, Being a Victim, Making Decisions, Holding On, Letting Go, Losses, Guilt, Grief, Forgiveness, Owning One's Wisdom, Repression of the Sublime.

We do not provide participants with a theory before they experience something; rather, we provide the opportunity for experience and then let them theorize and theologize about it. I think you will better understand what we do and how it works if I take you with me through the week. I will focus on one participant, Peter, as an example of the kind of growth that can occur.

Sunday—Building the Caring Community

We gather as a group on Sunday evening. Phil and I begin immediately with warm-up exercises to help create a trusting atmosphere and accelerate the process of getting to know each other. Both of us take part in all these exercises, and share whatever thoughts and feelings seem appropriate. We do our best to model openness, trust, egalitarianism, and caring at whatever level is real to us in this moment. Psychosynthesis exercises are also introduced. The following are the trust exercises we employ.

1. **Shuttling**—This exercise is designed to help us acknowledge our past history, then let go of it, and become fully present here.

> Close your eyes and pay attention to your breathing for a moment. Now allow yourself to return home or wherever you came from. See if there is anything you need to finish there. Is there something you need to say to someone? Imagine yourself saying it. Then bring yourself back to this room and look around, making eye contact with several people here. Now go back again and finish up anything you didn't get to do before. Come back here and make eye contact again.

Here are some of the experiences participants have shared:

> I went to see my mother in the hospital. I never was able to get there today. I told her I was sorry. She said that's OK and she hopes I learn a lot this week. I think I'll call her tomorrow morning.

> I went home to see my family. I hated to leave them to come here, but they were all watching TV anyhow and didn't need me so I am glad to be here.

> I went home to see my wife. She was angry when I left, but I had to leave. When I went back I kissed her, and she said she wished she was going too. Maybe she'll come next year.

> I was amazed at what I did. I've never been to Chicago before. I sat on the roof of the seminary so I could see the lay-out of the land. Now I feel more comfortable being here.

2. Learning Names and Facts—We are beginning to learn one another's names, to find some commonalities and connection points, to participate in the process of sharing. We are beginning to establish a community in which we have a place.

> Going around the circle, please repeat: "I am _____ from _____. Something I want you to know about me is _____."

People tell each other about their children, pets, relatives, homes, jobs, hobbies, and so on.

3. Will You Help Me in My Becoming?—This exercise has to do with acknowledging our mutual value as individuals and as a community. We are all part of this process. It is important for us to begin to feel what we can do for each other, to be able to ask for the help we need, and to make some kind of commitment to be present for one another.

> Each member makes, and the group repeats, a simple ritual saying:
> "I am _____ (repeat your name as you want to be known in this group)."
> "I am _____ (make a feeling statement)" "Will you help me in my becoming?"

Many times, I have been moved to tears upon hearing a group of people say they were willing to help me grow enough to get through the rough times. It is here that we begin to acknowledge that although we may feel independent, we need one another and are, in reality, interdependent. We are important to one another. We have much to give and to receive from each other.

4. Sentence Completions—We cannot feel close to a group unless we feel close to the people in it. We need intense one-to-one contact if we are to have data on which to make our trust decisions. And each time we make the decision to trust the individual in front of us and proceed on that trust and find that nothing bad has happened, we come closer to trusting the whole group. For most people, this happens after a half dozen encounters.

> Pick someone you do not know to be your partner. Decide who will go first. Each complete the sentence: "When I am scared I _____." You have about two minutes to share. Then take time to process how you felt sharing an

intimate feeling with a stranger. When you are finished, tell each other goodbye in some way.
Example: By the time we finished talking we weren't strangers any more. I
felt close to him and hated to leave. I wanted to continue to talk and hear
more about him. We are a lot alike.

Pick a new partner, someone you do not know. Each complete this sentence,
taking about two minutes: "When I am hurt I _____." Process your feelings
about what happened. Tell each other goodbye.
Example: I don't usually let anyone know I am hurt. I cover it up with anger
or something. I felt very close to her after we had cried together and didn't
want to get a new partner.

Pick another partner you do not know. Each continue the following statement:
"I never sang for my father _____." Complete the processing.
Example: It was hard to share stuff about my family, and my regrets about
my relationship with my father. My relationship with my mother is not that
great either. Now that I've said it, I feel better, especially after learning I'm
not the only one with parent problems.

Find a new partner. One person is to make a fist, the other person is to try
and get that person to open their fist. Do this non-verbally. After both have
had a turn, process what happened and say how you felt. When you have
finished, say goodbye to this partner.
Example: I hate being confronted by a fist. At first fear rose and I wanted to
fight back, but then I decided there wasn't anything to be afraid of so I just
sat there until it opened.
Even when I used all my strength and got her hand open, the minute I let
go she closed it tighter than ever and I couldn't make her open it, I felt
helpless.
I figured right away I wasn't strong enough to do it by force. I had to find a
way to make him want to open his hand, so I just massaged it tenderly, and
it opened to me.

5. Trust Walk—This exercise is intended to reinforce growing feelings of
interdependence and responsibility for one another. The point is to allow
ourselves to be dependent on another to do for us what we cannot do alone,
to be reliable for others, and to take the risk of trusting.

Number off: No. 1's form a circle at the centre of the room with eyes closed.
No. 2's choose a partner. You may go anywhere in the building or out into the
enclosed garden. If you are the leader, you are to both guard your partner
from harm and provide him with experiences involving all his senses except
sight. After about ten to fifteen minutes, switch roles. We will notify you (if
you are not too far away to hear) when to switch. Do this all non-verbally. In
pairs, process your experience, then come back into the circle and we will all
process together.

The lamps shining on the arches of the cloisters, the moonlight on the
flagstones, the flowers of the garth—all these contribute to a "high" of
spiritual beauty. Those with eyes open can see the devoted attention given
to the "blind" members. In processing what has happened, some like leading, some like being led. Some prefer choosing a partner, some like being
chosen, some fear they will not be chosen. Some like being responsible for
another person, some are afraid of the awesome responsibility. Some are

fearful and tense with their eyes closed. Some like giving over responsibility for themselves to someone else. All get something from the exercise. Sometimes the pairs remain special buddies all week.

As the evening draws to a close, one last exercise is presented.

6. Homework/The Four Pictures—Within the context of the group which has formed, we now begin to focus on our individual problems and stories. Phil and I assign the task of the Four Pictures, a psychosynthesis exercise, involving four questions:

(1) What is my life/my world now?
(2) How would I like my world to be?
(3) What blocks me from having that?
(4) What do I need to overcome the block? (see Figure 2)

Participants are given large sheets of newsprint and a selection of crayons, craypas, or magic markers. We suggest that they select medium colors, those that elicit some emotional response, and those that seem fun. Then we suggest that after getting into bed, they relax and breathe deeply, think of the questions, allow images to emerge, and sleep on them. In the morning, they should ask themselves the questions again. As the images emerge, the idea is to capture them on the paper. We try to encourage people to draw rather than to merely use letters. Artistic ability is irrelevant, and simple geometric shapes or stick figures are fine. We suggest that they use whatever symbolism presents itself, that there is no right or wrong imagery or answer to the questions, that they try to remove self-judgment and take what comes to mind, activating both sides of the brain.

Figure 2

my life/world now	my life/world as I would like it to be
what blocks me?	what would it take to remove the block?

Monday—Telling Our Stories

We begin each day with a meditation or psychosynthesis visualization exercise. The purpose of these is to contact deepening areas of the personality so that issues needing to be encountered can emerge. Only toward the end of the week do we use exercises focussing on the Self/Soul.

Today is our first experience with visualization and some of you are unsure if

> you know how to image, so we practise. Close your eyes and let yourself breathe for a moment. Imagine a white screen. Now imagine a red circle on the screen. Move the circle around. Change it to green. Change it back to red. Make it a ball. Let it bounce. Divide it in half. Make two balls. What happens now?

Once in a while, a person has trouble seeing the image but can hear it or feel it. They are encouraged to do the imagery using their dominant mode but to allow their images to come, even if they are foggy or half-formed. Soon they will become more proficient in visual imagery. Others may have to learn to allow feelings or sounds to accompany their images.

Images are the instruments by which we know the world. They determine our attitudes and possibilities. If we can't imagine doing something, we won't be able to do it. Images are also our contact with the unconscious, a meeting of left and right brain. We can act on our images using our will, make choices, change negative images to empowering ones. We can also tap into the collective unconscious.

Monday Meditation—This is a guided imagery exercise in response to the question, "Where is my place in the world?" This exercise also asks the unspoken question, "What is my place in this group?" The person's previous experiences with belonging and having/not having a place are experienced here. Ministers, because they move so often, are often in the position of having to provide a sense of belonging to others while they are struggling to find it themselves.

> Close your eyes and relax. Breathe.
> See the earth spinning in space, a beautiful blue ball in the darkness. Gradually allow yourself to come nearer and nearer until the earth becomes larger and larger, until you can see the green and brown continents and the blue water. Come nearer and nearer until you can see countries as the earth spins, and nearer and nearer until you can see cities and countryside, until you can see streets, trees, animals, people. Now ask yourself as the earth passes in front of you, "Where is my place?" and without forcing, just allow the image to present itself to you. You will clearly see your place on the earth. You may see more than one.

The participants take a few moments to write and draw their experience. Then we take some time for those who want to share their experience. Here are some examples:

> I saw that I had more than one place. My home in Ohio where I saw my family and waved to them, and here at seminary where I am now. My body chooses to be here but my heart is in Ohio. I nearly cried.

> Flying low over the trees, suddenly I was in the war again. I felt everything very intensely, the beauty and the horror. I was very frightened. In war there is no place, only a sense of polarity, of us/them. I must get them or they will get us. We did horrible things to human beings in the name of peace. I don't know if I can forgive myself. This is what brought me to seminary.

To be a person is to have a story to tell. We understand our present situation more fully as we acknowledge our past. We feel more grounded in our being as we re-experience our history, as we embody it, even if it is painful. But there seems no purpose in the telling without sympathetic listeners, without witnesses to our experience. For so many of us, there were not witnesses to our inner childhood experience, only to the outer events. We have tried to tell our story and been told, "No it wasn't like that, you couldn't have felt that." And so this experience remains unacknowledged, undigested, unusable for our own growth. And then we doubt our perceptions and ourselves. Indeed some of us internalize the criticism and become judgmental of ourselves and others instead. For others the disparity between inner and outer experience is so great that they are filled with self-doubt.

After the meditation, the drawings assigned the night before (The Four Pictures) are completed. Since people put so much of themselves into the pictures, they are very vulnerable to criticism. Others want to be helpful but are not sure how. A little instruction is much appreciated and facilitates the process. We suggest that the pictures be received in the following way:

Listen without judgment, without labelling. Simply receive the other's interpretation of their world. Don't invent your own story about the other.
Be fully present and listen carefully to what is said and what is unsaid. Ask questions for clarification.
Accept that this is the other's existence. We do not rescue the other by protecting ourselves from feeling our own pain around his or her issues.
Create a safe space for emerging. We should offer ways for people to work with their world, to experiment, to rethink, to translate early experience.

Group Offerings—Everybody lays out their picture, tells their current story, and then the group makes offerings to them. Phil and I are in charge of making our own offerings as well as monitoring the group offerings so that they help the person take the next step on his or her particular spiritual journey. Offerings come from what is shown in the pictures and from what is revealed in the telling of the story. They may explore the possibility of dialogue between parts of a conflict or a new way to experience something through acting out the pictures or the story. Offerings may also explore embodiment ("Where in your body do you experience this?"), presence and acceptance, regression (going back in time to an earlier unresolved era) and working to "own" something that's being asked for in the fourth picture. Peter's experience at House Church provides an example of the kinds of offerings participants receive.

Peter is a hard-working young minister of Scandinavian descent serving his first church. Confiding to the group, "one of my patterns has been to hang back," he went on to present his Four Pictures:

(1) *My life/world now* shows us and our brand new baby in front of our little church with the congregation over to one side, smiling but also intruding. I feel a lot of pressure from them.
(2) *My life/world as I would like it* shows us in front of a much larger church in California. The sun is shining. We are with my relatives. I am playing with my nephews. It feels wonderful to imagine being here.
(3) *What blocks me?*—the church settlement process is so slow. And money is a bigger problem now that we have the baby.
(4) *What could overcome the block?* shows a moving van, "just doing it," not talking about it, just moving. But I can't do it.

Noticing there were no emotions in Peter's story, Phil suggested he play out the first picture to get more contact with his feelings about what was happening. Peter asked specific people in the group to play his wife, his baby son, and his church. Everyone positioned themselves according to Peter's directions:

I am sitting as if I am in Merville, near my church, with my wife Helen and my new son Bruce. Helen is leaning on me, holding Bruce. I feel stuck, and the longer I sit, the more stuck I feel. Finally, I can't go on any longer. I tell Helen how awful it is for me. I feel some relief when she listens.

The "church" is peering over us, making it difficult to communicate. They are putting pressure on my shoulders that feels like the real thing. Oh, how I hate being in this situation. Yet I can't let go. I need the closeness of Helen and the church. These are the most treasured experiences in my life. I can't give them up even if it's painful sometimes. But I can't stay here either. Staying feels so stuck. I feel the tug of wanting to be in California. Being with my extended family, with their kids, is an experience I crave. It means more than simply physically moving to California. To be with kids is to be energized, alive. It means letting my kid out from inside. Letting the kid play means aliveness and spontaneity, experiencing the joyfulness of life. To be with the kids is to be unstuck.

Phil next offered Peter the experience of the pull of the old situation and that of the new one. Half the group lined up on each side of Peter and pulled in opposite directions on his arms. He endured this for a seemingly endless time, to everyone's discomfort. But this was Peter's world they were witnessing, so they did their best to help him experience it fully. Later Peter wrote in his journal:

The tug of war gets me in touch with my power to decide. I can choose to have spontaneity and creativity in my life regardless of where I choose to live. But I have to find a new way to have them, with more sharing and less leaning on.

I feel intensely lonely. Loneliness is a real theme for me now. Part of that is the pastoral role, friend of everyone and friend of no one. Part of it is the rural church, where tradition reigns supreme. I can't go any further. I can't resolve this right away, I need more time. I do feel my power to choose and I will be able to do that when I am ready.

This was as far as Peter could go right now. It was not up to us to decide how far he was ready to go.

Our work with the Four Pictures continues Monday afternoon and evening, people volunteering to enter this process as they become ready to do so.

Tuesday—Working With Subpersonalities

The concept of subpersonalities and the psychosynthesis diagram are introduced. I indicate that each subpersonality constructs a reality, has a particular worldview, which it maintains by use of selective filters. I emphasize that they are all valuable and have strengths, but can't run things or the person will be in trouble. It is important to know there are many "people" inside, sharing one skin.

Tuesday Meditation—As well as being able to identify some of their subpersonalities, it is important for people to be able to disidentify from them and to understand and strengthen the Observer. The following meditation, or guided fantasy of the personality, is suggested:

> You are walking in a meadow. You can feel the grasses brushing against your legs, and you smell them as you walk. The sun is warm on your back, and you can feel a soft breeze on your face. You can hear the swish of the grasses and some birdcalls from the distant woods. As you continue to walk, you see a house off to one side, and you begin to walk in that direction. As you come near, you can hear sounds, the door opens, and something emerges. Describe it to yourself. Ask it what it wants and listen for the answer. Ask it why it wants that. Ask what it needs. Ask it why it needs that. Allow the dialogue to continue if there is more to say. How does this being see the world? If this were the only point of view, what would be missing?
>
> The door of the house opens again and another being emerges. Describe it to yourself. Now ask it what it wants and listen for the answer. Ask it why it wants that. Ask it what it needs. Ask it why it needs that. Allow the dialogue to continue if there is more to say. How does this being see the world? If this were the only point of view, what would be missing? Can the two beings talk to one another? Can they interact?

This is what Peter shared with the group:

> My house was an old neglected wooden house with paint peeling off the side and a loose screen door opening and shutting with the breeze. As the House, I felt used up and deserted. I took care of others but no one has taken care of me. The feeling was of utter loneliness, very painful.
>
> A collie dog came out of the house. As Peter, I rolled around with him and played. When I asked the collie what he wanted, he answered, "I am lonely and I want someone to live with me, to pet me, and play with me."

Loneliness emerged again as Peter's issue. He came to the awareness that he was the one keeping himself lonely by trying to present himself as very strong and capable, both with his wife and in his work at the church. He never allowed himself to complain about feeling overburdened. As a man, he felt he had to handle situations by himself, giving up more and more of his recreational time.

After the meditation, I draw the egg diagram on the blackboard and explain where we have been working so far. After answering questions raised by the diagram, I suggest we begin work again on the Four Pictures, using the images and symbols that people bring. All of the work is about synthesis, about connection in some way, with parts of the Self, with body and feelings, with other individuals, with the group. Throughout the presentations we stress experiencing, rather than mere telling. Why is experiencing so important? Because it is more than cognitive and must be done by the whole person. It provides a new image, sometimes a new self-image. It helps us see how we can go toward the problem areas of growth and avoid getting stuck in our usual negative and helpless attitudes. By fully accepting these areas, they become positives. For example, one participant, concerned with being selfish, found that when her selfishness was lived, it served a boundary purpose for her, allowing her to say no and to be more self-nurturing. For some people, this kind of experience can be a breakthrough which they may have to go back and stabilize in individual therapy. At the retreat, we merely want an anchoring of the experience in symbol or body. Making contact with each person from the new perspective can serve this purpose.

By now, through extended interactions and sharing, through fantasy exercises and imagery work, through our regard for each other and our work with one another, everything we do has come to have a spiritual quality. We are beginning to feel nourished by that energy. Yet we are careful to include our shadow side in our work.

Disidentification Exercise—On Tuesday afternoon, before continuing the process of working with the Four Pictures, we do a disidentification exercise as a way to introduce the Observer:

I am not my body, I have a body.
I am not my emotions, I have emotions.
I am not my mind, I have a mind.
I am a centre of pure being, an observer, centred and contentless.

This is a place which is calm and constant throughout our lives. It takes practice to move out of the various feelings and subpersonalities into this space and it is important to be able to centre oneself here.

Wednesday—Focus on the Wounded Child

One of the things we have in common is the Wounded Child. Each of us has been wounded as children, some so severely it colors our perception of the world and all our intimate relationships. It is very important for each of us to assess the degree of our wounding and to begin the process of healing.

The Wounded Child I—Encountering the Wounded Child is a painful business and requires all the support that can be mustered. Doing this as a group is often the easiest way to begin:

1. Get comfortable, breathe, relax.
2. Begin going backward through your life looking for your Wounded Child.
3. When you get back far enough you will see him or her there. Now see the wounds even though they might be invisible to ordinary eyes. Don't flinch from seeing them. It's important for you to know them. Take your time. Whenever it seems too painful, back up. See them with a telescope if necessary.
4. Make contact with the child, very gently, in some way that feels appropriate. The child may only allow a touch, perhaps only letting you sit next to him or her. Even if you want eye contact, the hurt may be too great to allow it. Be patient.
5. Begin to talk about what happened. The child may have to depend on you to put words to the experience if it was too powerful or the child was too young when it happened.
6. Listen to the experience of the child. Some of what we do not take seriously as adults is very wounding for children. If your child says it is a wound accept it and don't minimize it. Talk as much as is necessary for the child to know that you get it. If no dialogue happens, accept that too, and just sit quietly with your feelings of love focussed on the child.
7. Now take the child away from the hurtful environment to a place that is special to you, a beautiful place. Share the meaning of the place with the child. Talk again about the hurt from this special place.
8. Find a gift there, something for both of you. Talk about what this gift means.

9. Say goodbye, or, if necessary, bring the child back to the room with you.
10. What is the next immediate step for healing?

We have all been wounded. Wounds help us to be compassionate, connect us to others. *Blessure* in French means wound: we are wounded and blessed. Ninety percent of personal work comes from childhood wounds, and some of the deepest therapeutic blocks come from this pain. The child also holds the key to the most spiritual qualities. After the exercise, at first the group is very quiet. They sit without looking at each other. Some sob softly, some merely have wet eyes. After making their own notes, they begin to share a variety of images. Here is what Peter shared with our group:

> I see a forlorn child, sitting alone on a curb, but the child will not allow any contact yet. I still get that awful isolated feeling. I never knew where it came from. I'm glad I know now. It won't be so devastating anymore.

The Wounded Child II—We go more deeply into this exercise at the beginning of the afternoon. Seeing who wounds the child's wounder increases our understanding of how wounding takes place and prepares us to be forgiving:

1. Get comfortable, breathe, relax.
2. Find your child again.
3. Observe the child. Any changes since your last visit? Note them to yourself, perhaps to the child if it seems appropriate.
4. Make contact with the child in an easy comfortable way.
5. Listen to anything the child needs to say right now.
6. Together go to the crystal ball.
7. Look in to see who or what wounded the child. Mother? Father? Friends? Relatives? Teachers? School?
8. Use x-ray vision to see what's behind the figure in the crystal ball. What or who wounds the wounder?
9. See both the child and the wounder/abuser.
10. Can they talk to each other? Can you talk to them?

Again, in silence, the group sits, each person contemplating what they have seen and what it means in their life. Some weep quietly. Soon they want to share experiences with each other, knowing how beneficial this sharing has been for each of them. From Peter:

> In the crystal ball is my father, sort of speaking like God, faking it like the professor in the Wizard of Oz. "Why don't you just talk to me, father, rather than acting like you have all the power and authority?" His answer came, "I don't know how to relate to you on that level." Behind him was his dead father. My father's father died when he was only four and suddenly he was the "man of the house." He has been faking authority ever since. He must have been really scared when he went through some of the episodes I remember growing up. I feel a lot better about him now seeing this.

The Wounded Child III—There are other aspects of the Wounded Child to examine. Sometimes the wounding is circular. Very often, the Wounded Child and the Wounder are locked into tormenting each other. It's as if a child has a string tied to a gorilla's toe and keeps pulling on it, constantly enraging the gorilla but feeling abused when the gorilla retaliates, as if he has no part in what happened. Sometimes each contains parts of the other that the other needs:

1. Get comfortable, breathe, relax.
2. Go back and find your child again.
3. Observe the child and the wounder. Any changes since your last visit? Note them to yourself, perhaps to the child later, if it seems appropriate. Are they linked in a circle of torment?
4. Make contact with the child.
5. Listen to anything the child needs to say right now.
6. Can they let go? Free each other? Forgive each other? Can you help them?
7. Can each reclaim their lost parts?
8. Can they transform the situation?
9. Rewrite a painful childhood episode from this new perspective.

In silence, the group sits and writes, each person contemplating his or her life as newly seen and how it makes well-known facts take on a different meaning. Some eyes are moist. Soon participants want to share experiences with each other again. One woman found that the exercise "released some of the tremendous hostility I've had for my father, his public reprimands, spankings, etc. I see how I provoked him by not obeying and thus not proving him a good father. Seeing all this and now being able to see his pain as well, I can let go of my anger and begin to forgive him for the humiliation I experienced as a child. In this letting go I begin to reconnect with lost parts of myself."

Phil and I teach some elements of family dynamics and then we divide into two groups to begin leadership training. Here present and future ministers and church leaders can begin to try out their skills as facilitators on each other. A church can never have too many loving arms. Phil supervises one group and I take the other. In these small groups, the work begun earlier with the Four Pictures and the Wounded Child is moved along.

Thursday—Opening Up to Superconscious Energies

The morning meditation helps to open up new areas. It is a guided fantasy that makes visible the hidden fears in people's lives. After they begin to face these fears, talk about them, integrate them, there is an opportunity for a greater opening of the superconscious. We pursue this in the form of a guided fantasy around a wisdom figure.

Guided Fantasy—Part I

1. Get comfortable, breathe, relax.
2. Go back to the meadow and find yourself walking again. Over on one side is a woods. You are near the woods. It is cloudy. The woods are very dark.
3. You begin to have a sense of foreboding, all senses alert. After a bit, you hear some sounds and, suddenly, something scary comes out of the woods. Your skin prickles, your scalp and chest feel tight, and your breathing is shallow. Take care for your safety but don't leave. After experiencing the fear and possible danger, create a safe place for yourself right there.
4. Describe to yourself what emerged from the woods. How are you feeling?
5. Dialogue with the scary being if you can. What does it want? What does it need? Why?
6. Be the scary being. Deliberately imagine living in this symbolic world, and experience it as deeply as possible.
7. Come back into yourself. Do something nice for the scary being. What part

of you is scary? How does the scary being look to you now?
8. Walk again in the meadow. The scary being may come with you or it may stay behind in the woods.

I ask about the fears first. People look around at one another, checking out whether it is safe to be this vulnerable. Some fears are personal, some are professional. When we all admit we have fears it makes it easier to really look at our own fears and to share them with others. This is the beginning of integration. That is what Peter reported:

> Something frightening is coming out of the woods. It is a group of people who threaten me professionally, people who attack me as a minister. I feel like leaving, like going to a part of the country far away from these people, to where I have relatives who love me. But what if these critical people are right, what if I fail there near my relatives?

The fear of being criticized is what drives Peter to work night and day, give up his free time and family time, and then feel burned out. He is amazed to find all this. He had no idea he was feeling so threatened.

As the fears are examined and accepted as parts of ourselves, they lose their power. Many people report that they stopped being afraid because the monsters shrank when they were fed or petted or thanked. We can go ahead now and open ourselves to the superconscious energies within and around us.

Guided Fantasy—Part II

1. Focus on your breathing until it is even again and you are relaxed.
2. Straight ahead is a mountain. You will be making a trip to the top.
3. See if the being that emerged from the woods will go up the mountain with you. Get up the mountain any way you can.
4. At the top you see a shrine, or temple, or cave of some kind. Nearby you find a wisdom figure who looks at you very kindly. Describe it to yourself.
5. Ask it a question and listen for the answer. The answer may be plain or cryptic. Receive it and meditate on it.
6. Introduce the scary being or any other beings that accompanied you. They may have questions to ask. Listen to the answer given. Give your thanks.
7. The wisdom figure has a gift for you. Describe it. Receive it with thanks.
8. When you are ready, come down from the mountain and back to this room.
9. Think about how what happened might relate to your present life situation.

There is much response to this exercise in the group. For many of the women, a goddess appears. Others find an old man or old woman. For some, the wisdom figure is Jesus. The gifts are many and varied. One woman said, "I ride up the mountain on my wild horse. It is a lot of work to get to the top. I couldn't have done it without the strength of the horse and I tell him so and thank him. He whinnies with pleasure, sets me gently down. Strength doesn't have to mean cruelty or insensitivity. For most of my life I have been taken advantage of by strong and ruthless people, especially men. I have been afraid to be strong myself. Now I see it is essential." Peter experienced the following:

> I go up the mountain to the widsom figure, a wise old man. I ask, "Why don't I take action on what I already know?" He answers, "You are not centred."

I ask, "Do you think I am running away from some of the craziness in my parish?"

He answers, "Somewhat. But perhaps you are simply getting bored with that situation. Maybe it's time to move on to a new challenge." And he offers me the gift of Centredness. I receive it gratefully, feel it inside me. Now moving on seems absurdly easy.

The energy of the Soul is loving, caring, nourishing, and reinforces Will. We have been working toward the release of these energies all week.

The remainder of Thursday morning and the entire afternoon are spent in the small groups. Participants take turns being counsellor and being counselled under the supervision of Phil and myself, working further with images from the drawings and from the fantasies and bringing up other issues that may be important to people.

We teach that as guides it is important to live our own lives as therapeutically as possible, to be honest in our relationships, to stay open through some form of meditation to the Higher Self, and to feel open communication with our various subpersonalities. With the Observer, for example, one should ask, Where am I listening from? What part of me? My head? My guts? A subpersonality? What does this part need or want? How can I be a path for the larger energies of the universe? What is my body saying? What does this stir up in me? My body is a sensitive instrument. I listen to it as carefully as I can. Sometimes I have work of my own to do before I can be present to others. It is important that I make the time to do this so my problems and concerns don't color the therapeutic work.

Phil and I are also questioned about how we run House Church. Here are some of our replies that readers may find helpful:

1. Leadership—It is best to have two leaders, one of each sex, if they can work well together. People generally feel better represented and understood by a leader of their same sex; they also like the opportunity to work on issues they have with the opposite sex. Both Phil and I have run House Church retreats alone, but prefer working with another leader. When two are working together, it is important for them to stay very tuned in to each other as well as to the group. Each must monitor the work of the other so they do not get in each other's way, but rather can facilitate each other in the desired direction. They may have to meet together before and after sessions to tune in to each other more finely. Leaders should address to the best of their ability any complaints from group members, during or after group hours, without becoming defensive.

2. Meals and Lodging—It is best for the group to stay together and eat together, whether the retreat is a week or a weekend. This minimizes outside concerns and allows people to build trust and to focus more deeply on their interior concerns. Sometimes we hire a cook for the group. This doesn't mean everyone *must* eat together, simply that the opportunity is there. Sometimes participants feel the necessity to withdraw and spend the mealtime alone thinking or writing.

3. Program—The selection and the order of the exercises have been determined from long experience with the problems of ministers and seminary students. It may be that for a different group the selection and order would be different. It takes experience with a specific population to know what their issues might be, though general human issues would be the same for any group.

After dinner on Thursday, we begin to explore how to bring what we have been doing into the church. At House Church, we are attempting to train the enablers, the facilitators, to help liberate the church by first liberating themselves. Through the transformation of our own pain into compassion, we can see more deeply into our own hearts and into the hearts of others. There we find goodness and love, but also fear. We learn to be cautious in dealing with people who are afraid. Yet we also need to learn to have respect for our own fears and the fears of others. Eventually, when we learn to trust, love drives out fear. We also ask at House Church, what is beyond personal growth? What can we do to make a difference in the world? One woman wrote, "The first thing that must be done is make individual and personal changes. These inner personal changes have an effect on the outer structures. But this is more difficult and discouraging than one first imagines. To make changes in my thinking is not enough. I must face my inner demons. Also I can't change all alone. Patterns are between people." A man expressed his concern with our approach, "I have heard it said that the well-off or comfortable preach an ethic of love; the poor and oppressed proclaim an ethic of justice. Both are found in the Scriptures. There has to be a way to bring them together. Sometimes I feel suspicious of House Church with its roots in psychotherapy which was born of the elite. Is it merely a tool to keep the comfortable from feeling the guilt of their social responsibility?"

After long, intense discussion, the evening ends with a party—music, food, and dance help to release the tensions of the week.

Friday—The Need for Closing

We want to make the most of this day, yet not neglect our need for closing and completion. Letting go of a good experience, saying goodbye, is always hard to do. Yet without completion, we are left hanging on, not able to use what we have learned in other parts of our lives.

Guided Fantasy—The morning meditation is a guided fantasy to help us discover our interior Wise Person, what our purpose on earth might be, and what we need to learn. This puts a different perspective on relationships and the trials of living. It makes love and forgiveness easier.

> Get comfortable, breathe, relax. Go backward quickly through your life through childhood, birth, before birth, to an enormous place of Light. Experience the light. A wise being is in the centre of the light. Dialogue with this wise being about your coming mission to earth. You are being sent to a specific family. The wise being is telling you about your parents-to-be, what you are to teach them, what qualities you will need, what obstacles you will meet as you try to do this, what learnings you will receive. What is my mission in this life? What am I being sent to earth to learn? To teach? What does the earth require from me now? What is my next step?

As we stay with the imagery, feelings surface. The shut-eyed faces are serious, some pained. From Peter:

> I was sent to learn and to teach people to be more open in difficult situations. Nothing could be more closed than the family I grew up in, but that is how they made their own pain. Now that I am learning openness I would like to help them. I am looking forward to living closer to them. I already feel I am living closer to myself.

Next we take up the question of the theological implications of House Church. What does the House Church experience tell us about God? About ethics? About grace and forgiveness? About being saved? About responsibility? About revelation and transformation? Some share what they have experienced of these things during the week:

> The theme of forgiveness both to self and others is tied to the grace of God. Learning to let go of hurts and to be gentle with oneself is a great step forward.

> Loving is *being* as openly and honestly as I can—and not expecting another person to do all of the giving. Loving is trusting and sharing with others. As we become quiet and peaceful and calm with one another, we may experience the serenity and the awesomeness of our relationship to the whole of the cosmos. In quietness shared, in stillness, in ritual, we may sense the Whole and become One with it together. I believe that this is what a loving and worshipful community offers.

The final segment is offered by Phil, a simple communion of bread and wine. He says that for these to be of use to us we have to transform them— we have to chew the bread, we have to drink the wine, as we chew up and drink in our experiences in House Church and in life. Thus we transform suffering and pain into strength and compassion. It was Jesus the Jew who said, "This is my body, take and eat." Phil explains that this means: "Accept my offerings. Let me be of use to you." We feed each other the bread as acknowledgment of our interdependence.

We sit quietly and experience the group energy, let images flow of support, permission, caring, love, acceptance. We imagine putting them in a pocket or a box that we can take with us. We are going back into the world—what does the world require of us? Certainly to be honest and true to ourselves and our values, and to care about human beings and our environment as best we can. One woman summed up what she learned at House Church: "Be aware of the Wounded Child in your congregations, the tender places. In the child within is the key to the most spiritual qualities."

House Church encourages the Wounded Child to play again, to love again, to laugh, to trust again, to embrace brothers and sisters. We believe this is the essence of being the church or the healing community, the community of witnesses.

House Church is an experience of intense contact, with parts of oneself, with others, present and absent. This contact makes change and growth possible. Peter, who I chose to follow throughout the week, not because his presentation was unusual but because it was so ordinary and unpretentious, made slow and steady changes all week. His greatest change came when he returned home. He was able to establish a more open relationship with his wife and church and is feeling more relaxed and happy than he has in years. He wants his wife to attend the next House Church. The work goes on.

Throughout the week, participants work with their own issues, even when they are helping others work through theirs. For instance, taking part in a group member's re-enactment of her childhood pain, the man who played her stern father discovered the unloving part of himself. Each person is in charge of what they give and what they take. We get as much as we are willing and able to reach for, as much as we are able to take in. There is always more to do.

Some people have called their House Church experience a rebirth, meaning that although nothing in their external situation has necessarily changed, they experience their life situation very differently and are able to respond creatively, to trust more, to make changes inside. This is the supportive community we each want, from which we can go out to fight for peace and justice and come home to be nurtured. This is where we are renewed and healed. This is where we can express our deepest fears, our deepest selves, and still feel accepted, where we feel belonging, our sense of "home."

Health Care

Who Heals the Healer?

Mary Marcus

Too often we don't realize the healing potential within. Nursing is particularly in need of such realization. A nurse myself, I find that our profession is unable to meet our own need for healing. Among 20 nurses I recently interviewed, one said, "When I feel a need to be given to myself, I have to go to work. No matter how I feel inside, I have to give out, no matter what, because they need me more . . . but I need to be given to. I need someone to give back to me, and I'm forced to give back to them." This expresses the dilemma in nursing: who heals the healer?

Nurses often find that the reasons for which they entered nursing are no longer valid for their remaining in the profession. The nurse quoted above also said, "I went into a humanitarian profession and now I feel I'm in a business. The key for me in nursing was touch. I really enjoyed being able to touch the patient." The close connection with patients that drew her to nursing had been severed by the administrative aspect of the job.

Why are we as nurses unable to meet our needs? I would like to examine our role model as nurses to answer this question. This examination, as part of my own growth process, focusses on women; I am unable to assess its relevance for men.

The Role Model—Mom-Nurse

The central conflict in nursing, that of caring for others while needing care oneself, has its roots in the mother-child relationship that is re-created in the nurse-patient relationship. For the patient, illness and disease re-create the child's dependency on the mother, and the patient's child-like dependency causes the nurse to act out the role of all-giving, nurturing mother. Illness legitimizes the regressive behavior of the patient; it demands all-giving nurturance—what I call being "perfect Mom"—from the nurse.

Because the nurse-patient relationship replicates the mother-child bond, any unresolved issues, distortions, misconceptions, or societal and cultural pressures concerning mothering will surface, as with transference-counter-transference in therapy. The nurse herself, the patient, the relative, the hospital administrator, the physician all have specific, and frequently conflicting, ideas about how Mom-Nurse should act. Caring for people is commendable, but when caring gets in the way of personal growth, it becomes detrimental to the care-giver. It is my belief that the distorted image of perfect Mom prevents nurses from self-nurturing.

As an example, let us say a nurse goes to administration and asks for a raise. The hospital administrator is likely to look at her, as representing Mom, and say, "You should be grateful to meet the needs of sick patients.

What do you need more money for?" The thought behind this is: would Mom ask for money to do what is natural and necessary—namely meeting the needs of her children? Jean Baker Miller (1976) puts it this way:

> Subordinates [women] are assigned to generally less valued tasks. It is interesting to note that these tasks usually involve providing bodily needs and comforts. . . . Women are encouraged to do two things [by the dominant men]. First, they are diverted from exploring and expressing their needs. Secondly, women are encouraged to transform their own needs. This often means that they fail automatically, and without perceiving it, to recognize their own needs as such. They come to see their needs as if they were identical to those of others—usually men or children. (p. 22)

Thus, when we ignore our own need for healing, we are not only acting upon our own expectations as nurses but also upon the expectations of a patriarchal society. Dorothy Dinnerstein (1977) writes:

> What we have worked out is a masquerade in which generation after generation of childishly self-important men, on the one hand, and childishly play-acting women, on the other, solemnly recreate a child's idea of what adult life must be like. (p. 87)

What is the result of perpetuating the myth of the perfect Mom we want to remember from our childhood? Carol Gilligan (1982) writes that the result is "a silencing [of her own voice] enforced by the wish not to hurt others but also the fear that, in speaking, her voice will not be heard" (p. 55). We become trapped in a self-defeating pattern of trying to maintain the image of perfect Mom. Because this image of perfection is impossible to attain, frustration and distorted behavior are unavoidable. In the next section, I examine six subpersonalities which typify the distorted behavior commonly seen in the nursing profession. Each of these subpersonalities, when out of control, blocks personal growth and healing.

Patterns of Distorted Behavior

1. **Martyr Subpersonality**—The Martyr usually denies her own needs, which feeds into a belief that she doesn't deserve to have her needs met. A feeling of poor self-worth comes from self-denial. In one nurse's words, "Some days I don't feel very well physically and I have to bend over to crank up the bed and if they vomit I have to clean it up. So, I say to myself I have to do it. I'm here, I have to get through it. I have to be strong . . . the work has to be done."

As nurses, we neglect our own physical needs, believing that by meeting the needs of others we are meeting our own. This idea may have come out of a time in childhood, when, in order to get love or approval from a parent, we met the needs of the parent, by doing tasks around the house, for example. Approval was withheld when we didn't fulfill parental expectation. In short, we were rewarded for giving to our parents, and our sacrificing behavior won us love. But over the years, self-sacrifice becomes distorted. The distorted behavior doesn't work any more, yet we still continue with it. In 1848, Elizabeth Cady Stanton wrote, "The thing that most retards and militates against women's self-development is self-sacrifice" (quoted in Gilligan, 1982, p. 129).

2. Critic—"Sometimes I might put myself out while another nurse wouldn't even consider doing that, so I get down on a lot of people I work with." The Critic is another variation on the perfect Mom theme: no one is as good on the job as I am. The critic subpersonality gives us a feeling of control over the other's life, which is especially appealing when we have little control over our own lives. Further, if we can fault another nurse on the job, no one will notice how we are functioning.

This pattern of behavior may have originated in childhood when we were rewarded for excelling in school. As years pass and we are no longer able to excel, we denigrate others to maintain our feelings of superiority. This subpersonality got us love from our parents, and, even though it isn't working now, we continue with it. A shift is needed from critical superiority to self-respect. As with the growth from self-sacrifice to self-development, this subpersonality needs to be transformed in order to be productive.

3. Needy Child—In looking at the Needy Child, an interview I conducted with a nurse who admitted to being burned out was particularly revealing. She buried her Needy Child when she came to work. She simply left her needy side at home. What is that side? "I hate to admit it, but the warm, soft side of me. There is a whole side of me that people I work with don't know. My close friends know, but my associates and co-workers do not." By blocking this vulnerable side, she decreases her effectiveness on the job. "I took care of an AIDS patient the other day. His needs were so . . . uh . . . I mean he had such deep psychological needs. He was so afraid, and I couldn't meet· those needs. I left the hospital so depressed. I can't tell you how depressed I was. I was beyond despair, it was terrible. I couldn't touch him . . . I felt responsible and guilty . . . I should have been able to support him more . . . he was dying."

But how can we support others when our own needs to be nurtured are not being met? The nurse's Needy Child is unfulfilled, yet she feels responsible for another's Needy Child. A nun in the same no-win position writes, "I felt I was defaulting on a promise to God" (Curb, 1985, p. xxi).

The nurse may have learned to hide her emotions as a child; her parents respected her strength. Now, her method of survival causes despair. In order to disidentify from this subpersonality, she must attain self-reliance rather than self-suppression. Self-reliance can only be achieved when the Needy Child is nurtured.

4. Rebel—"I have a difficult time with administration; I don't easily follow orders. I find it difficult doing so. Working with old women has never been my forté . . . . There are a few people I work with who are condescending to me, but not intimidating. I'm not intimidated by anybody. I don't allow myself to be. I fight back." This subpersonality rebels against the perfect Mom model, but the rebellion is itself a distortion of Mom. And, as this nurse says, "It makes for a worse environment."

Because she is young and inexperienced, she needs help from the other nurses, yet she alienates those who could help her. Her strategy is to tough it out. Her philosophy: "Basically, human nature is selfish. We care about ourselves regardless. I don't think anybody is completely humanitarian." In spite of the tough talk, she admits, "People scare me. I still stutter when I'm nervous." When given an assignment that was beyond her skills, she admits, "I didn't know what to do, I was a nervous wreck." Thus, acting as the Rebel doesn't get her what she needs—help from the "old women" nurses. Nonetheless, with each crisis, she continues to rebel, reinforcing the subpersonality. A more centred behavior pattern would be assertive rather than rebellious.

Peer support among women is one way of disidentifying from the Rebel. Jessie Bernard (1981) writes: "Every woman valued her standing within the women's circle because, at some time in her life, she might need their support. . . . The women who had the most influence on village affairs were those who worked through the women's community" (p. 44). In describing Western migration in the last century, Bernard states: "There can be little doubt that for a good many women, East, West, North and South, the 'Bonds of womanhood' were supportive and the resulting sisterhood a real, genuine basis for building their lives" (p. 102).

The rebel subpersonality leads to alienation from other women, the loss of peer support, and the inability to offer and receive help. Throughout the nursing profession, bonding and support are lacking. Jean Baker Miller (1976) writes, "Women will not advance except by joining together in cooperative action. . . . No one can undertake this formidable task alone. Therapy, even if we knew how to do it in some perfect way—which we do not—is not enough" (p. 95). In childhood, being tough may have won parental respect; as adults and as nurses, the Rebel divorces us from the help and support of others.

5. Saint—One nurse influenced by the Saint says, "I'm a very religious person and I believe there is life after death, so when you die there is hope on the other side. On the other hand, if you die without Christ, you have no hope and that's the end for you." The Saint subpersonality relies on the outward appearance of sainthood rather than inner meaning.

In nursing, the Saint generally sees spirituality as something out there in the stratosphere, not something integrated into the practice of our work. In addition, the Saint feels superior to those others who have spiritual needs. Both our nursing past and our individual pasts encourage us to become Saints. The roots of nursing are religious: nuns were among the first nursing practitioners. Many nurses today were raised as Catholics; in childhood, female saints were held up as adult role models (another variation of perfect Mom). However, a number of nurses distance themselves from their religious past. A former nun describes her divorce from the church:

> My spiritual growth has been solidly linked with the process of being me. I am no longer aligned with the Catholic Church even though I claim being raised in its traditions. It leaves me no room to profess my full identity. I will no longer put myself in the position of being judged. There has been too much agony to come to where I am. And this pain has formed my philosophy, one which is growing and changing and simplifying. . . . I have felt deep sadness watching my ideals dissolve. Even so, no disappointment, no heart-hurts over relationships begun and ended, can ever match the pain of not being me, of believing I was sick and guilty, of feeling so split from myself. (McLarson, 1985, pp. 122–123)

The nurse acting as a Saint states, "I think I have a fair share of compassion for people's needs. I have a concern for people who are not feeling well and are needy . . . but apart from judging other nurses, I think I'm a hell of a lot more than they realize I am, because I bring a lot more to the position." Thus, as the Saint, we live up to the external ideals of our nursing past, yet inwardly resent those ideals; we are also trapped by feelings of superiority to other care-givers. As children, the Saint got us recognition from the nuns in school and A's on our papers. We are now left with another impossible role model. To disidentify, we must attain awareness.

6. Fixer—In the extreme, this subpersonality has the nurse fighting the odds against death. As one nurse says, "You [as a nurse] are going to fight death. It's my biggest enemy. You know someone is dying before your eyes, and there is nothing you can do about it. It's like fighting the clock . . . you get so angry and think, my God, why can't I move faster? And you get frantic." Taking on responsibility for someone else's life is exactly where the Fixer lands us: somehow we can control an inevitable natural process, or Mom can fix all.

I recently learned that many people in the healing professions are eldest children, and hence have a heightened sense of responsibility. Perhaps the Fixer originated when, as children, we were rewarded for being dependable. Reliability, when extreme, leads to the Fixer—with the impossible goal of preventing death. As Fixers, we are constantly frustrated, and the energy that could be used for growth is diverted into an unattainable goal. A centred behavior pattern would allow us to see equally our abilities and our limitations.

In Summation

As nurses we are not getting the nurture and the support we need. This is because we try to live up to perfect Mom. To support this frustrating, impossible ideal, certain subpersonalities are formed. These subpersonalities prevent the formation of genuine coping skills that could allow us to nurture ourselves. As long as these patterns are continued, we are bound to repeat the self-defeating behavior.

Naomi Remen (1984) states, "We are all in search of healing from the moment we are born. People hope to find healing in the Doctor's office. Actually, of course, they bring it with them" (p. 84). It's the healing potential within us all. How do we unlock our potential? To quote from Dr. Remen:

> What we do is create conditions that foster wholeness, that make the manifestations of wholeness more possible. We do this with our skills, our questions, with our attitudes, and most important with our love . . . our wholeness exists in us now. It can be evoked. And we have all experienced this. There are certain situations in which we have experienced greater love, greater compassion, more wisdom, and more healing than we are experiencing at the moment. (p. 85)

Alice Walker (1982) in *The Color Purple* writes about one such moment:

> [Shug say] one day when I was sitting quiet and feeling like a motherless child, which I was, it come to me: that feeling of being a part of everything, not

separate at all. I knew that if I cut a tree, my arm would bleed. And I laughed and I cried, and I run all around the house. I knew just what it was. In fact, when it happen, you can't miss it. (p. 203)

Locked into self-defeating patterns, we can miss the moments of connection.

By disidentifying from perfect Mom, by supplanting this ideal with activities that support feelings of nurture and self-worth, we can lessen the hold of the Mom's image. By encouraging each other, much like the pioneer women of our past, by helping each other in support groups, the self-defeating cycle can be broken. William Schofield writes, "In the 20th century, there is a general absence of the kind of friendship that could readily provide the relationship required for therapeutic conversation" (Bernard, 1981, p. 104). Let's bring those friendships back!

Other conditions that foster wholeness are indulging our aesthetic tastes, taking courses, going on walks in the country, getting involved in sports, and getting in touch with the spiritual or the transpersonal, whatever we consider that to be. When we free ourselves from expectations that our job is responsible for self-development, we will rely on ourselves, and our future and the future of nursing will be happier and healthier.

References

Bernard, J. (1981). *The female world*. New York: Macmillan.

Curb, R. (1985). What is a lesbian nun? In R. Curb & N. Manahan (Eds.), *Lesbian nuns: Breaking the silence* (pp. xix-xxxii). Tallahassee, FL: Naiad.

Dinnerstein, D. (1977.) *The mermaid and the minotaur*. New York: Harper & Row.

Gilligan, C. (1982). *In a different voice*. Cambridge: Harvard University Press.

McLarson, J. E. (1985). Dissolving my masculine ego. In R. Curb & N. Manahan (Eds.), *Lesbian nuns: Breaking the silence* (pp. 117–123). Tallahassee, FL: Naiad.

Miller, J. B. (1976). *Toward a new psychology of women*. Boston: Beacon.

Remen, N. (1984). Imagery and the search for healing. In J. Weiser & T. Yeomans (Eds.), *Psychosynthesis in the helping professions: Now and for the future*. Toronto: Department of Applied Psychology, The Ontario Institute for Studies in Education.

Walker, A. (1982). *The color purple*. New York: Washington Square Press.

Psychosynthesis: A Conceptual Framework for Holistic Medicine

Robert A. Anderson

The last two decades in Western society have seen the development of aspects of medical care which do not conform to the conventional model. This trend, involving a number of concepts which I shall enumerate shortly, seems to be gaining some momentum as judged by the content of published scientific and medical data, pronouncements of traditional bodies of evaluation for various diseases, and the proliferation of "holistic" or "wellness" centres which emphasize disease prevention and health promotion.

A very practical consideration, that of cost containment, has also played a role in focussing attention on the role of holistic medicine. The enormous cost of highly technical procedures to salvage a brief bit of time for patients in the twilight of their earthly lives boggles the mind. Last year, the cost approximated 11 percent of the gross national product in the United States. The figure for 1985 exceeded 380 billion dollars. The cost of care for terminal illness is estimated to consume 20 to 35 percent of all sickness care financial outlays.

The major premises of holistic medicine include the following:

- encouraging the client (or patient or consumer) to accept significant responsibility for his or her life style and decision making;
- developing a collegial relationship between the healer and client;
- recognizing life style as a significant determinant of both morbidity and mortality;
- moving toward a "whole" view of the client/patient, including the effects of the interaction of physical, mental, and emotional aspects of the personality on each other and the transformative effect of the Transpersonal Self on all levels of energy and experience;
- recognizing that sickness may frequently be a teacher;
- allowing the dying process to occur as an expected phenomenon as free of fear as possible;
- emphasizing the sometimes tenuous but quintessential connections to life's meaning and purpose;
- focussing on Love and Will as essential personal, interpersonal, and global qualities.

The conventional relationship between the physician and the patient in Western culture in the last 40 years has been that of parent/child;

152

top dog/underdog; dispenser/receiver; knowledgeable/uninformed. This relationship, of course, is now decidedly altered, though many established health practitioners find great difficulty accepting with comfort, much less enthusiasm, the decisions, questions, and suggestions put forward by the assertive consumer. Others, having come to the new relationship, in one way or other, actually find it a relief. Not to have to be alone in making the hard decisions regarding treatment, procedures, and prognoses, not to have to face the demand of being "right" 100 percent of the time, is a potentially healing element for the healer.

The burden of doing things *to* consumers bears its own stress sooner or later; the adaptive mechanisms include withdrawal and non-involvement, opting for an extremely authoritarian stance, repressing the emotions which accompany the development of a relationship, or taking a dehumanizing stance toward the patient who becomes the "case" or the "gall bladder in Room 532."

In investigating the utilitarian considerations of different models, I must say at the outset that the data are far from in. Yet the conclusions I am able to reach are not without extensive research evidence; the impact on cost-containment, longevity, and more appropriate use of the system, while not "proven" in the narrow scientific sense of the term, is quite plainly written in the experiences of many people. Yet if wellness or holistic medicine is to be embraced, it must be based on a valid theory and an understandable model, and grounded solidly in the experience of both its enthusiasts and its detractors. Psychosynthesis, because of its integral, unifying, and global aspects, is an ideal model.

A Human Function Model

At the personality level, human beings may be viewed, in many aspects, like computers, taking in data, processing them, and coming to some integration of output in the form of emotional experience and behavior. The input may be viewed as having three components: perceptions of the external world, perceptions of the inner physical world, and perceptions of recall. These perceptions may be wholly conscious or not. (See Figure 1.)

We need to recognize that perceptions are influenced by numerous factors, including attitudes and the level of tension within the system. It is the clear experience of all observers that two individuals who have been exposed to the same visual or auditory phenomenon experience widely disparate perceptions. Health practitioners commonly encounter differing perceptions of pain in patients undergoing precisely the same procedure or experiencing the same illness.

At the outset, it is important to note that beings of higher intelligence do not respond to reality, but to their perceptions of reality. The two are not always the same. It is possible, roughly, to equate tension with the *quantity* of our perceptions. Experiments show that intelligent animals possess an "inhibitory" nervous system which inhibits input beyond a comfortable level of tension (Hernandez-Peon, Scherrer, & Jouvet, 1956). Studies also support selectivity in inhibition by a set of neurological parameters which closely conform to what psychologists call attitudes (Rosenthal & Jacoben, 1968).

Figure 1/A Model of Human Functioning

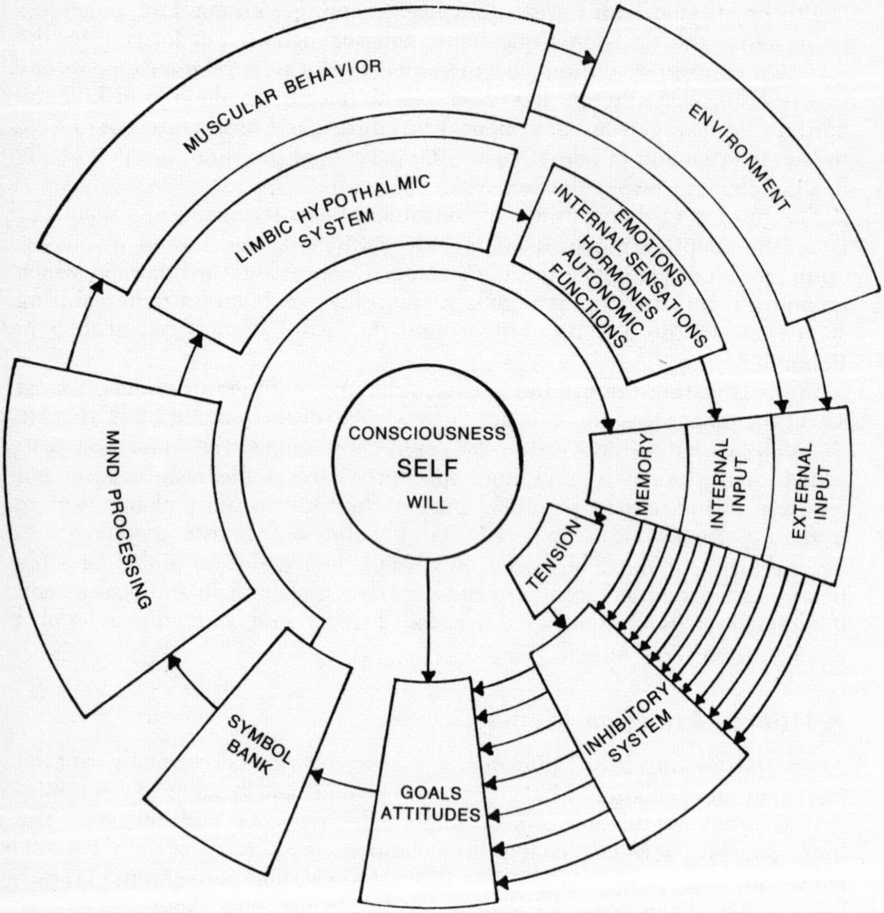

CONSCIOUSNESS
SELF
WILL

MUSCULAR BEHAVIOR

ENVIRONMENT

LIMBIC HYPOTHALMIC SYSTEM

EMOTIONS
INTERNAL SENSATIONS
HORMONES
AUTONOMIC
FUNCTIONS

MIND PROCESSING

MEMORY

INTERNAL INPUT

EXTERNAL INPUT

TENSION

INHIBITORY SYSTEM

SYMBOL BANK

GOALS ATTITUDES

Adapted from R. A. Anderson, "A Functional Model of Man," Stress Power! How to Turn Tension Into Energy, Human Sciences Press, New York, 1978, p. 104.

We can say that attitudes control the *quality* of our perceptions. Positive attitudes tend to be linked to the perception of positive characteristics in ourselves, others, and situations; negative attitudes tend to be linked to negative perceptions.

If our responses, then, depend on our perceptions, and our attitudes tend to shape our perceptions as either positive or negative, it is very important to become intimately familiar with "attitude psychology" and investigate what may appear to be optimum attitudes and what may appear to be distorted attitudes and their effects on health, sickness, survival, and costs (of all kinds) to society.

Attitudes are mind-sets. We have all come across the small sign behind the desk that reads, "The answer is no!" "My mind is already made up. Don't confuse me with the facts." Persons truly espousing this stance have fixed their attitudes, and give notice that they are determined not to change them. Yet we know that attitudes do change. They do not rapidly change as do emotions, but they do change. They change as a result of experience, insights, observations, and psychic phenomena. My attitude about mental telepathy, for example, changed when I had the experience of picking up a telephone receiver and immediately being aware of a mental picture of the home of the caller before speaking into the mouthpiece. A generically negative attitude of a man regarding women changes when he has a positive experience with an individual woman. Our attitude about mathematics may change when we have an "aha" insight regarding the theory of numbers.

Negative attitudes may be grouped around the prototypical attitude of hostility. Hostility tends to lead to negative emotional experiences of excessive anger, sadness, and fear-anxiety; to negative physiological and biochemical events at the physical level; and to negative behavior directed at oneself or others. The finger has been pointed at hostility as the pathological element in the syndrome of "Type A Behavior." In fact, it is probably more accurate to refer to this cluster of psychological characteristics as Type A Attitudes rather than Type A Behavior.

What evidence do we have that attitudes significantly alter the course of sickness, or influence longevity? The scientific evidence clusters around recent studies in which significant-sized groups of persons were followed for 20 to 25 years after completing the MMPI (Minnesota Multiphasic Personality Inventory) within which was constructed a special hostility scale. A group of medical students were given this specialized MMPI and divided into low-hostility and high-hostility cohorts. Followed for 25 years as physicians, the mortality rate of the high-hostility group was 6.6-fold greater than the low-hostility group. The incidence rate of acute coronary artery events (heart attacks) was 4.4-fold higher in the high-hostility cohort (Shekelle, et al., 1983). Similar results have been reported in studies of longshoremen (Williams, et al., 1980), indicating that both morbidity (illness) and mortality (foreshortened longevity) are significantly influenced in an adverse way by the negative attitude of hostility.

The evidence for the beneficial effects of positive attitudes is less clear at this point. Positive religious attitudes have been correlated with increased longevity. Norman Cousins is convinced that creativity, faith, and love contribute strongly to the experience of healing and engaging life-giving perceptions (1979). A life orientation of hardiness, recently shown in studies to be correlated with being able to live with high stress and little illness, seems to involve positive attitudes (Kobasa, 1979).

Conventional medicine provides no guidance regarding the importance of positive or negative attitudes in the genesis of sickness and disease, or in the promotion of health or wellness. Even Preventive Medicine, as a specialty area of expertise in American medicine, does not embrace these concepts of psycho-social medicine, much less the transpersonal aspects. Likewise, most conventional psychological schools or techniques do not mention attitudes as important in the diagnostic or therapeutic milieu. Psychosynthesis, on the other hand, offers appropriate thought forms for conceptualizing, understanding, utilizing, and teaching the emphasis of attitudes in diagnostic and therapeutic schemata.

The presence of unconditional positive regard as the prototypical positive attitude has been mentioned by many. Love is emphasized by Assagioli, as a quintessential characteristic of the Higher Self, and as having several differing aspects. The model above depends heavily on the concepts of Psychosynthesis. Holistic medicine looks at attitudes, beliefs, emotions, physical being, mental/intellectual function, spiritual life, and the social, natural, and cosmic environment as essential ingredients in the balance of life/death, health/sickness, and the evolution of individuals and society.

The Human Function model has characteristics of feedback. Behavior and interaction with the environment are outputs from the system and, in turn, become inputs as we become aware of them. While internal sensations, emotional experience, and autonomic nervous system function can be considered outputs, their feedback is also input for further processing within the system. Recall (memory) is continuously available as supplied data, chiefly from the middle unconscious, but from the superconscious and lower unconscious as well. Much of the recall function may be conscious, but much more is probably unconscious.

The two entry points for changes in this feedback mechanism are from the environment and from the inner/personal self. I maintain that one of the most important functions of the will of the self is to set in place and maintain attitudes. The will has seldom been mentioned as an important factor in the theories or function of conventional psychiatry and infrequently mentioned in modern psychology until the past two decades. Psychosynthesis, through its emphasis on the will, provides a second important factor in conceptualizing a new model that embraces the ideas of Wellness Medicine.

Parameters of Holistic Medicine

Collegiality—Holistic medicine emphasizes the collegial nature of therapy, counselling, and medical care. It is becoming less and less common for the physician, or therapist, to tell the patient/client what to do or what medicine to take. Decisions are frequently made jointly. The health practitioner makes suggestions or acts as a guide to help interpret the experience, thinking, or plans and goals of the patient/client. This is done in a spirit of positive regard for the client. Disagreements can be faced in the spirit of good will. Frank (1975) has pointed out that the most significant determinant of outcomes in therapeutic situations is the quality of the relationship which develops between therapist and client. My interpretation would be that the more positive the qualities present happen to be, the better the therapeutic outcome is likely to be. The participation of the client in the decision-making process has been helpful in changing the image of health practitioners as gods on pedestals holding the choices of life and death over the patient.

Certainly Psychosynthesis lays heavy emphasis on personal responsibility for choices at the physical, emotional, mental, and transpersonal levels of experience. Indeed, it not only provides convenient substance for a model of holistic medicine, but also it has probably provided impetus for its very development.

Holism—Psychosynthesis is integral. Levels of experience and energy clustered around the body, emotions, mind, personal and Higher Self emphasize the point. Holistic medicine is integral. The only comprehensively based medical organization dealing with this area, the American Holistic Medical Association, states, "Holistic medicine encompasses all safe modalities of diagnosis and treatment, including drugs and surgery, and includes the consideration of mental, emotional, physical, spiritual, and environmental aspects of the patient, and emphasizes the personal responsibility of the patient in promoting health." The first act of the President of this organization at its founding meeting in 1978 was to lead the assembled physicians in Assagioli's disidentification exercise.

Openness—Assagioli emphasized many times that Psychosynthesis was not static, but an approach to therapy and to life which would embrace kindred concepts as it grew. The same could be said of holistic medicine. New techniques, insofar as they are understood to be safe, and prudently practised, can be embraced by holistic medicine more readily than by many conventional medical disciplines which experience a certain amount of inertia in taking on new concepts. The creative quality of Psychosynthesis and its contact with the collective creative unconscious in meditation enable new ideas and concepts to surface. This same approach to creativity by practitioners of holistic medicine has engendered an openness to innovative approaches in sickness treatment, disease prevention, and wellness promotion. A technique or approach is accepted when it bodes reasonable evidence of success, even though final scientific proof in the strictest sense is not yet demonstrated. At the same time, experts have written that only 15 percent of what allopathic medical practitioners do meets criteria of proof in the strictest scientific sense. In addition, there is always direction from the age-old medical principle, "Do no harm."

Emphasis on Growth—Psychosynthesis may be viewed as a growth psychology. Emphasis is placed on the evolution of the human person toward a personal and transpersonal synthesis of body, mind, emotions, and spirit. Holistic medicine emphasizes both the disease aspects and the sickness-prevention/wellness-promotion aspects of human experience. Interestingly enough, because of the tremendous cost of the highly technical and generally dehumanizing therapies of conventional medicine, there are economic pressures on the profession to simplify medical approaches and search for cost-effective prevention and health promotion. The ideal cost-effective model of holistic medicine turns out to be a model which most people in Western society would choose: a model which promotes a meaningful life, of whatever length, filled with one's share of joy, creativity, and wellness that when one's time to leave this earth arrives, is terminated quickly, without significant disability. A motto of my office practice is, "Our purpose is to help you die quickly as late as possible."

Psychosynthesis incorporates certain concepts about dying, including the naturalness of the process, the acceptability of the process, and the importance of completing certain tasks in one's relationships as the time of dying approaches. Conventional medicine emphasizes the prolongation of life at very significant cost. Part of this emphasis may be misplaced, since many persons, especially the elderly and those in scarcely controllable pain, have already chosen and prefer to die. Philosophically, holistic medicine can accommodate these situations more easily, permitting a humanitarian and dignified approach to the patient and the family regarding the dying process as an acceptable and natural process.

Change—Sickness implies change; chronic illness implies continuing change, nearly always involving deterioration, that is, movement toward a less functional state. Preventive medicine implies preparation for maintaining the status quo and, during certain periods, slowing the deterioration process. Health promotion implies movement toward greater functionality. Again, looking at these three models—interventive care, preventive care, and health promotion—few criteria for understanding the process exist (see Figure 2). Psychosynthesis embodies the philosophy of the evolution of a whole being toward balance, creativity, joy, service to humanity, and self-actualization. It is for this reason that Psychosynthesis provides a model for the principle of change in holistic medical concepts.

Figure 2/Models of Sickness/Health Care

Interventive Care	Preventive Care	Whole Care Health Promotion
Asymptomatic healthy origins.	Asymptomatic healthy origins.	Asymptomatic healthy origins.
Early chemical changes, decrease in performance testing.	Reform/cessation of self-destructive habits: smoking, overeating, drug/alcohol overuse, abuse.	Adoption of healthy lifestyle habits: exercise, meditation-relaxation, optimal nutrition, positive beliefs/attitudes, imagery and mind-body effect.
Signs of lack of vigor.		
Symptoms of lack of vigor.	Early detection with history, physical, and lab evidence of treatable disease and degenerative processes.	
Premature onset of disability for normal activities; high incidence of diseases.		High-level wellness: energy and vitality, manageable tension, satisfaction and joy, challenge and productivity.
Health crises; surgical and medical interventions; marked disabilities.	Maintenance: Immunizations, seat belts, exercise, dietary restrictions.	
Heroic surgical and mechanical-technical interventions.	Slow onset of disability for normal activities.	Self-actualization: creativity, learning from life experiences, service to humanity, integration of spiritual dimension.
Premature death.	Reduced period of severe disability and surgical-medical interventions.	High adaptation to disabilities.
	Death.	Death as a part of life.

Change is usually not accomplished without the use of the will. The contributions made both by Assagioli in understanding the nature of the will and by writers in various psychosynthesis fields in understanding its various applications have been essential to practitioners of holistic medicine. The will is back in fashion; the skilful will and the application of will through imagery are a unique combination of ideas deriving from Psychosynthesis that are widely applied in holistic fields.

Emotions—The inclusion of emotions in the spectrum of important medical data to be considered by the health practitioner is not conventional. "Psychogenic overlay" is the term commonly used to relegate emotional symptoms or data to a position inferior to physical and laboratory data. Emotions, however, which are accompanied by (or perhaps representative of) certain biochemical changes deserve equal consideration. Many times a patient will be in chemical balance, as ascertained by the laboratory, yet do poorly and even die because of unconsidered emotional factors. A fearful patient, compared to a confident patient, does poorly facing surgical or medical procedures. The recent revelation of the effect of catecholamines (adrenalin and related chemicals) deserves careful attention. The breakdown products of the catecholamines contribute to the load of free radicals in the body. Excesses of free radicals contribute significantly to degeneration and to the aging process. Psychosynthesis gives full recognition to the emotions, derived from Assagioli's description of their importance: "Emotions tend to and demand to be expressed."

The self-destructive habits of substance use and abuse, improper eating, failure to use due care and caution, and smoking have a strong basis in the emotional sphere. These alone account for the vast majority of premature deaths in Western society. Holistic Medicine addresses the whole person, including the consideration of all these life-style factors in sickness and health, and the contributing emotional factors from which they stem.

Psychosynthesis, emphasizing the three aspects of personality and the transpersonal dimension, is an inclusive model for formulating concepts of the whole person.

Global Implications

Holistic medicine includes careful scrutiny of the environment. It considers the array of assaults of the physical environment on living species. Incredible numbers of heavy metals, petrochemical derivatives, wave-form energies including ionizing radiation (x-ray and nuclear), dusts (asbestos and silicon from coal), side-effects of drugs (prescribed and non-prescribed), and smoke toxify and sensitize the environment for humans and other living species. In the consumer economy, ecological disasters are threatened, including loss of forests, habitats, soils, and exhaustion of finite reserves of minerals, to say nothing of the increasingly problematic disposal problems of the throw-away society.

Psychosynthesis speaks to the synthesis of persons, groups, and nations. It is, in short, a universal concept which has no bounds, and is not attached to narrow sectarian interests. As such, it accepts the ideas of environmental medicine and global concerns more easily.

William Osler, a prominent physician at the turn of the century, is widely quoted as having said, "It is far more important to know what kind of patient has a disease than to know what kind of disease a patient has." Conventional medicine has tended to treat symptoms and diseases; holistic medicine is prone to treat persons and causes. Consider the following example as a final illustration of my premise that Psychosynthesis provides the best working model to date for the concepts and practice of holistic medicine.

A woman in her fifties developed intractable diarrhea. Instead of treating her symptomatically, attempts were made to determine an organic cause for her problem. No such evidence was forthcoming after numerous tests and examinations. Attention was paid to her apparent anger. After persistent rejection of this idea by the patient for several months, continued loving contact won out, and ultimately a most vexing issue between herself and her sisters surrounding the death of their mother was recognized. The patient ultimately agreed to be led through a forgiveness exercise, and the diarrhea ceased permanently the day she completed the exercise. Concepts regarding love and human relationships which have been incorporated as essential by holistic practitioners find an ideal working model in Psychosynthesis.

Healing and the Transpersonal Dimension

It may come as news to some physicians and surgeons that they have never healed a patient. A significant portion of the population, whether overtly religious or not, recognizes that healing depends on numerous factors, known and unknown, and may include spiritual beliefs and dependence on a higher power. The scientific evidence for the importance of beliefs is the wealth of placebo studies now published in the medical literature. Beliefs have the capability of changing physiology and biochemistry. To be aware of, to influence, and to cultivate and refine beliefs is part of the healing process. The vast complexity of the human frame with its one-quadrillion cells, each operating 5,500 enzyme systems all at the same time, suggests that even the hard sciences possess a tiny degree of knowledge with respect to the whole. The understanding of disease processes themselves, the possibility of "creating our own reality," and how we may have knowingly or inadvertently contributed to a sickness may hold the key to our own healing. In my experience, being aligned with an awareness of a purpose in living, and having intentions of carrying out that purpose in specific goals and projects, contributes greatly to the healing climate. Transpersonal Psychosynthesis may speak much more decisively in the healing process than any deliberate balancing of biochemistry.

All physicians know numerous patients who have survived for years in what appeared to be very precarious health by having a purpose and a determination to serve. One patient I recall, 70 years of age, has volunteered at a local hospital four half-days each week, having contributed over 14,000 hours of time in the last decade. She has had three episodes of heart and vascular problems, each of which had the potential to take her life. Lying in a hospital bed, sustained by tubes and wires for several days, her question always was, "When can I go back to work?" How important it is to be aligned with the Higher Self to fully release the powers of healing of the whole being to fulfill a chosen purpose.

The energy sustaining the holistic medical movement derives from the power of concepts whose time has come. Psychosynthesis is among the most integral of those concepts. It is, indeed, an ideal model for evolving holistic medicine.

References

Cousins, N. (1979). *Anatomy of an illness*. New York: Norton.

Frank, J. D. (1975). Mind-body relationships in illness and healing. *Journal of the International Academy of Preventive Medicine*, 2(3), 46–59.

Hernandez-Peon, R., Scherrer, H., & Jouvet, M. (1956). Modification of electric activity in cochlear nucleus during 'attention' in unanesthetized cats. *Science*, 123, 331–332.

Kobasa, S. (1979, January). Stressful life events, personality and health: An inquiry into hardiness. *Journal of Personality and Social Psychology*, 27(1), 1–4.

Rosenthal, R., Jacobsen, L. F. (1968, April). Teacher expectations for the disadvantaged. *Scientific American*, 19–23.

Shekelle, R. B., et al. (1983, May). Hostility, risk of coronary heart disease and mortality. *Psychosomatic Medicine*, 45(2), 109–114.

Williams, R., et al. (1980, November). Type A behavior, hostility, and coronary atherosclerosis. *Psychosomatic Medicine*, 42(6), 539–549.

Education

The Inner Classroom: Teaching with Guided Imagery

Jack Canfield

Guided imagery is a very powerful psychological tool which can be used to achieve a wide variety of educational objectives: enhance self-esteem, expand awareness, facilitate psychological growth and integration, evoke inner wisdom, increase empathy, expand creativity, increase memory, facilitate optimal performance, evoke a more positive attitude, and accelerate the learning of subject matter. In this article, I will share with you what I have learned from 15 years of exploring the application of guided imagery to the classroom.

Introducing Imagery

The first step is introducing guided imagery to your students. For most of them it will be something new, something that does not fit their experience of what school is about. There are a number of effective methods for making this transition. I have found that the most effective approach is a combination of giving them a clear rationale for its use plus a few really engaging imagery experiences right at the beginning.

I usually start by asking my students how many of them remember what they dreamed last night. Usually about a third do. I inform them that everybody dreams at least three dreams every night but we often don't remember them. We then discuss dreams, nightmares, recurring dreams, why we dream, and daydreams. I ask them where they think dreams come from. We generally then have a free-wheeling discussion based on their *experience*.

After a while I introduce them to the idea that their brain has two different sides, which, while they work together, seem to do different things better than each other. In school we use the left side more for things like reading, writing, and math. The left side seems to do most of the sequential, rational, linear, and logical work. The right side, on the other hand, is more oriented toward creativity, feelings, intuition, art, and holistic understanding. The right side is usually neglected in education. It doesn't get enough of a workout and therefore makes the entire brain less effective. By working with guided imagery, they will get to exercise the right side of their brain. I tell them that this will make them smarter, help them tap into their creativity, and discover aspects of themselves that they may have never known were there before. I tell them that they can use imagery to increase their memory, answer questions they have, increase their performance in

164

athletics, get rid of headaches, and many other things. Finally, I tell them that learning to use imagery is as important a skill as reading, writing, spelling, and mathematics.

As you might imagine, many kids are uncomfortable at first about closing their eyes for a long period of time. What I usually do is to make a game out of it. It goes something like this:

> See if you can close your eyes and open them again so fast that someone looking at you would not know you had done it. . . .[1] What do we call that? Right, a blink. Now see if you can close them long enough to know you've had them closed. Then open them again . . . O.K., now close your eyes and see if you can see a red dot or a red ball. Once you've seen it, then open your eyes again. Take as much time as you need . . . O.K., now close your eyes again and see if you can see a large blue circle. Take as long as you need and once you've seen it, open your eyes again . . . now close your eyes again and try to see a yellow triangle; as soon as you've seen it, open your eyes.

Some kids will find these introductory exercises very easy. Some will find them more difficult, seeing the shape but not the color and vice-versa. A few may not see anything at all. It is important to tell them not to worry about not seeing anything yet. They will. It is simply a matter of time and practice. I continue, after each exercise, to ask the class if there was anyone who didn't see anything. The number gets smaller with each exercise. I have never worked with anyone who didn't eventually begin to see images.

The next thing I do is ask them to close their eyes just long enough to see an animal. When all the eyes are opened again, I ask them to share what they saw. We talk about all the different animals, what they looked like, and why everyone got different animals. Next I ask them to close their eyes again and watch that same animal as if they were watching a movie and simply notice what the animal is doing. The kids report all sorts of interesting scenarios. By now, they are getting hooked on the process and I can begin to move to the next step.

For people who are having trouble imagining, I ask them to visualize their front door or some other tangible object they see every day. It is much easier for people to visualize things they see a lot than to visualize things which are abstract or things they have never seen before. The next step is to introduce a more powerful and engaging imagery experience. My two favorite ones follow below.

The Skyscraper Fantasy—This exercise is designed to demonstrate to your students just how much power the images they hold in their minds have over their experiences in the world. There is an important psychological law which comes into effect here. That law, simply stated is: All images or mental pictures tend to produce the physical conditions and reactions which correspond to them. Every image or picture which we hold in our mind will create a physical reaction in our body and will thereby affect our experience and our behavior. Let's demonstrate that principle with the following exercise.

Ask your students to sit up straight in their chairs and close their eyes. Ask them to take a few deep breaths and relax. After a few seconds elapse, take them on the following guided fantasy:

Imagine you are standing in the middle of a small terrace on top of the tallest skyscraper in the entire world. Also imagine that this terrace has no railing . . . As you are standing there, look down at your feet and notice what the terrace is made out of. Are you standing on marble, tile, concrete, asphalt, wood, stone, or what? . . . Notice what the weather is like. Is it warm or cold, sunny, or overcast? . . . What noises can you hear? Maybe there are some pigeons or other birds up there. Maybe you can hear a helicopter flying by or the street noises below . . . Now, I'd like you to walk to the edge of the terrace and look down at the street far, far below . . . (pause) . . . As you are doing that, notice what you are feeling in your body and choose to remember whatever it is . . . Now, I would like you to slowly walk or crawl back to the centre of the terrace . . . When you have reached the middle of the terrace, I'd like you to open your eyes and come back into the room at your own pace. Take as much time as you need to make that transition. There is no hurry.

Once the students have all opened their eyes, ask them to share with you and the class what they experienced in their bodies as they walked to the edge of the terrace. Tell them that you are not interested in what they saw or heard, but what they felt in their bodies.

Almost all of the students will report some physical reaction. Possibilities include increased rate of heart beat, sweaty palms, shallow breathing, constriction around the chest, dizziness, nausea, a hollow feeling in their stomach, shakiness, a tightening of the legs, and clenching of fists. I have even had some students who have opened their eyes in the middle of the experience because the images were so scary.

Some students will start to tell you what they saw or will say things like, "I couldn't walk to the edge; I had to crawl." Just politely cut them off and say something like, "That's neat, but what I'm more interested in now is what you were feeling in your body during the experience." Some students will say, "I felt scared," or "I felt excited." Ask them, "Where in your body did you experience the fear?" or "What did you experience physically that you are calling excitement?" They will usually respond with something like, "I felt a tightness in my stomach," or "I felt tingling all through my body."

After a few minutes of this sharing, ask them to consider the following questions: "Where was your body really?" (Here in the room, sitting on your chair.) "So what was your body responding to?" (The image you created in your head.) "Who created the image?" (The students did. All you, the teacher, did was to say the words: they created the images!) "So, who created the experience you had in your body?" (You did! And, what's more important, we do this all the time.) "Can anyone think of other examples of images you create that produce physical reactions in your body?" (Examples would be butterflies before a football game, muscle tension when you think of your boyfriend with another girl, physical excitement when you think of somewhere you are going to go, a hollow feeling when you imagine being rejected, salivating when you think of eating a lemon—you can actually have them do this one—and so on.)

The Apple Fantasy—This fantasy experience is a lot of fun and acts as a subtle diagnostic test to see how well students can control their imagery. We need to learn to control our imagery so that we do not become the victims of our imagination, but rather the masters of this aspect of our mind:

Again, I'd like you to close your eyes and let your body find a relaxed position . . . Take a few deep breaths and with each breath allow yourself to become more and more deeply relaxed . . . Now take whichever hand you normally eat with and hold it out in front of you as if you were holding an apple in it. Notice, what color is the apple? Is it red, yellow, green, or multicolored? . . . Notice what kind of apple it is. Is it a Macintosh, a red delicious, or golden delicious, or maybe it's an organic apple with little scars on it . . . Now, notice the temperature of the apple. Is the apple cold, like it just came out of the refrigerator, or is it hot, like it's been sitting in the sun? . . . See if you can feel the weight of the apple in you hand . . . Lift the apple up to your nose and see if you can smell it. What does it smell like?

Now, I'd like you to keep imagining the apple, open your eyes, and, without talking, trade apples with someone near you. Use both hands, just as if you had real apples . . . Now, close your eyes again and look at the apple you received in the trade . . . What does this apple look like? What color is it? What shape? What kind? . . . Notice how you feel toward this apple . . . Do you have any judgment about it? Is it a better apple or worse apple than the one you gave away? . . . Look at it from all different angles. Turn it upside down . . . Look at the stem; is it there, or is it broken off?

Now, open your eyes again, and once more, without talking, trade apples so that you get your original apple back . . . When you've got your own apple back, close your eyes again . . . Make sure it's the same apple, that they didn't cheat you or dent it or take a bite out of it . . . Notice how you feel having your own apple back . . . Now, still keeping your eyes closed, I'd like you to stop imagining the apple . . . (pause) . . . okay. Whenever you're ready, just open your eyes and come back into the room.

After the students have completed this imagery experience, ask them the following questions:

- Did any of you have any trouble in stopping imagining the apple? Raise your hands . . . Does anyone want to share what happened?
- How many of you preferred *your* apple, somehow felt more comfortable with it?
- How many of you felt that the apple you gave away was better than the apple you received in the trade?

I then tell the students to consider the following ideas: We become attached to our images of ourselves, other people, and how the world is. We only had the image of the apple for a minute or two and many of us had trouble making it disappear. This is what we do with our self-image. I may have an image of myself as a klutz or an awkward person. Even when the data begins to change, I may still cling to the old image because it is comfortable and familiar. Many students have self-images of being an A, B, or C student. Just like the skyscraper image, these images control us unless we learn to control them.

Classroom Atmosphere

After the basic idea of imagery has been introduced, there are some general guidelines to follow that will facilitate the best results.

1. Creating a Safe Space—When students are participating in a guided imagery experience, they are in an altered state of consciousness. Their brain wave activity is slowed down. They are highly relaxed. It is therefore advisable to minimize potential distractions. If your classroom is prone to a lot of interruptions, place a sign on the door which says "Do Not Disturb," "Concentration Training," or "Testing." If necessary, assign different students on a rotating basis to be door guards to intercept any potential disturbances outside of the door. If you have the ability to turn off your intercom, do that also, or alert the office to hold back all messages for the next 15 minutes. Do not start a guided imagery experience right before the bell is about to ring. A school bell can be extremely jarring to the nervous system in the middle of a guided imagery experience.

2. Lighting—It is easier to visualize in a room where the lights have been dimmed and/or the shades drawn. Be careful, however, not to totally darken a room. This can frighten some people. So, keep at least a night-light on or a candle lit.

3. White Noise—If your classroom is in a noisy area, you can use what is called "white noise" to block most of it out. White noise is some constant sound like that produced by a fan, air conditioner, or electric motor. This is especially helpful in urban settings. Soft, relaxing music can also be used or a recording of natural sounds like the seashore or the rain.

4. Timing—It is best to avoid conducting imagery experiences immediately following a meal or late at night. The usual result of ignoring this guideline is that most of your students will fall asleep. I should also point out here that it is okay for someone to fall asleep during a guided imagery session. It simply means they needed sleep more than they needed awareness at that point in time. Snoring, however, is disruptive, so I instruct my students to gently reach out and nudge someone who has started to snore. This usually stops it. Sleeping can usually be avoided by periods of active physical exercise before the imagery experiences.

5. Positions—There are three positions which seem to work best for guided imagery. The first is lying down in a comfortable position. My experience is that the position you normally wake up in is the best one. This works best in a carpeted classroom. The next position is called the taxi driver position. It is done sitting up, hands relaxed on the thighs, and the head tilted slightly forward, like a cabbie asleep at the wheel. The third position is done sitting at a desk with the head resting on the arms which are folded on the desk.

I have found that the following rules contribute to effective guided imagery sessions:
  1. Students are to keep their eyes closed. You will find, however, one or two students in a hundred who actually visualize better with their eyes open. For them it is okay to have their eyes open. It is advisable for people with contact lenses to take them out if the imagery session is going to be a long one.
  2. No talking during the imagery experiences. This disturbs others. Also, no touching others unless they are snoring.

3. It's okay to fall asleep; it is not okay to snore.

4. It's okay to go on your own trip. Often the unconscious mind will take over and the students will find that they imagined something entirely different from the images described in the instructions. This is generally okay because the unconscious will often create its own priorities. There are, however, times when we are practising control over our images. In these cases, we would encourage concentrated effort. In other, more open-ended experiences, it does not make any difference. In these cases, it is best to trust the natural process of the unconscious mind.

5. Raise your hand if you need assistance. Occasionally a student will have a scary image. They need to know that you will be there to comfort them if they do.

6. Students may go on a *detour fantasy* to a favorite place if they find the imagery becomes scary or evokes uncomfortable feelings. Students should practise detour fantasies ahead of time.

7. If students ever find themselves stuck or blocked, they can send to *central control* for whatever they need to get unstuck—a magic ring, a ladder, a magic wand, a space car, wings, an elevator, a companion, a guide or whatever would be helpful. They are to know that whatever they need is immediately available from central control by wishing it or by snapping their fingers.

8. Do not compare, judge, or analyze other people's images.

9. There is no pressure to share verbally afterwards—just an "invitation."

10. If there is an interruption from the loudspeaker, just pretend it is like a TV commercial. Remember the information if it is personally relevant; forget it if it isn't.

Relaxation

It is useful to start each guided imagery with a brief period of relaxation. There are many types of relaxation exercises. I shall describe a few of them here and then refer you to several books which contain a great deal more. The first three, Breath Awareness, Breath Imagery, and Breath Control, are breathing exercises.

1. Breath Awareness:—Now that you have your eyes closed, simply become aware of your breathing. Notice how your stomach and chest rise and expand as you inhale and contract and fall as you exhale. Just concentrate on the rising and falling sensation, over and over again, like the waves of the ocean rolling gently in and out at the beach . . . now place your awareness at the top of your nose. Notice the feeling of coolness as you inhale and the feeling of warmth as you exhale . . . now place your awareness on the place where your breath stops coming in and starts going out, on the transition from inhaling to exhaling. Notice what happens there. What do you feel?

2. Breath Imagery:—Imagine breathing in a beautiful white light. Imagine that with each breath you take, your whole body is beginning to fill up with this radiant white light. After several breaths, you can begin to feel your body becoming bathed in a warm (cool) glow. You can feel yourself growing very calm. This white light is dissolving any tension, anxiety, fear, doubt, worry, or negativity that you may have been experiencing in your mind or your body. Just continue to imagine breathing in this wonderful, soothing, relaxing white light. You can feel yourself growing more and more relaxed with each breath.

3. Breath Control:—Close your eyes and become aware of your breathing. In a moment, we are all going to begin to breathe together. We are going to inhale for the count of four, hold our breath for the count of two, exhale for the count of four, and hold our breath out for the count of two. We will then repeat that pattern for a minute or two. Okay, let's begin. Inhale, two, three, four. Hold, two. Exhale, two, three, four. Hold, two. Inhale, two, three, four. Etc. Be sure not to count too fast or too slow. Practise beforehand.

The next two exercises are Stretching and Progressive Relaxation:

4. Stretching:—There are a number of stretching exercises which range from simple exercises like bending over to touch one's toes, to more complicated yoga postures. The simplest ones are *slowly* bending over to touch the toes, slowly rotating the neck, stretching the arms overhead, and bending over to the side. There are numerous books available on yoga exercises for adults and children which can be used successfully in the classroom. They are listed in the resource guide at the end of this article.

5. Progressive Relaxation:—Get into a comfortable position and relax. Start by tensing all your muscles in your feet as tight as you can. Keep them tight and notice the tension. Then relax them. Now tighten the muscles in your calves as tight as you can. Keep them tight. Now relax them. Now tighten the muscles in your hips and buttocks. Keep them tight. Then relax them . . . (continue this process with the lower back, stomach, chest and upper back, hands, arms, shoulders, neck, and face). This process can also be done in a wavelike fashion. Start by tightening the feet, then calves, thighs, hips, stomach, chest, back, hands, arms, shoulders, neck, and face. Then starting with the feet again, relax each part of the body in the same order. It is like a wave of tension washing over the body and then a wave of relaxation. Once kids learn to do it, they can relax themselves very quickly with this method.

There are numerous other methods of relaxation. They include autogenic training, meditation, sensory awareness, chanting, biofeedback, Feldenkrais, massage, movement, and polarity awareness. See the resource guide at the end of this article.

Sometimes our students need to be awakened and enlivened rather than relaxed. There are also numerous activities to accomplish this. They include running, jumping, dancing, bioenergetics, calisthenics, and new games. By far, the most fun are the new games, which are creative, non-competitive play experiences. I have listed several sources of new games in the resource guide.

Part of the art of being a master teacher is knowing when to use a relaxation technique and when to use an energizer. Trust your own intuition and ask your students for feedback, too.

Induction Techniques

Once the students have been appropriately relaxed or energized, it is time to begin the actual imagery experience. The first step is called the induction. This is simply the transition phase from regular consciousness to the imagery state. There are basically two techniques for this—deepening images and music.

Deepening images are images which are designed to deepen the state of consciousness of the students. They are simply relaxing and repetitive images which include visualizing the waves on a lake growing calmer and calmer until the lake is as smooth as glass, visualizing clouds drifing slowly by, visualizing sand falling from the top half to the bottom half of an hourglass, or boats drifting slowly by on a river or lake.

Music can be used in two ways. You can use relaxing classical, oriental, or New Age music to deepen the relaxation state, or you can use instrumental or vocal music to create a certain mood or theme for the imagery.

Music for relaxation includes calm, classical pieces, Japanese koto music, certain Indian ragas, flute and harp music, and some of the electronic and New Age compositions by such people as Steve Halpern, Iasos, and Ron Dexter. (For a fairly complete guide, order *A Guide to Tapes and Records to Accompany Relaxation and Guided Imagery* by Jack Canfield from the National Humanistic Education Center, 110 Spring Street, Saratoga Springs, New York, 12866.)

Music that I have used to create a certain emotional mood or effect includes "Theme from Rocky" (courage), "Ali's Theme" (caring and love), "You've Got a Friend" by Carly Simon (during an imagery experience exploring friendship), Greek music (during a visit to ancient Athens), and "The Ultimate Seashore," a record from the Environment Series (for a visit to an island). All of these records are also catalogued in the Guide to Records and Tapes mentioned above.

The Main Imagery Experience

Further on in this article, I will describe several classroom applications of guided imagery and give you detailed scripts which you can use. At this point I want to discuss some of the general principles that you will need to be aware of in creating and guiding imagery experiences.

Use all of the senses in an imagery experience—visual, auditory, kinesthetic, olfactory, and taste. This will allow all students, no matter what their dominant perceptual system may be, to relate deeply to the imagery. Referring to all the sensory systems will also heighten and sharpen the imagery experience for everybody. The tendency for most people when they are just beginning to use imagery is to only use words like "Imagine you see . . . ". This is very limiting. Let me give you some examples of how to incorporate the other systems. Suppose you were guiding a fantasy trip through a meadow. It might sound like this:

Imagine you are walking through a beautiful meadow on a warm summer day. The sky is blue, the sun is shining a bright golden yellow, and you can see one or two small, fluffy, white clouds (visual) . . . As you walk along, you become aware of how free you feel in your body. There is nowhere to go, nothing to do, and no right or wrong way to do it. Maybe you even run, skip, or turn a somersault or two. Notice how your body feels (kinesthetic) . . . As you walk along, you can feel the warmth of the sun on your face and arms; however, there is a slight breeze so that you do not become uncomfortably hot (kinesthetic) . . . As you look off to your left, you see the edge of a forest. You can hear birds singing there and the sound of a babbling brook (auditory) . . . As you continue to walk along through the meadow, you notice that it is filled with beautifully colored wildflowers. Stay a moment and smell their beautiful fragrance (olfactory) . . . As you continue to walk through the meadow, you notice a very special flower, different from all the others. You stop, reach down, and touch the flower, noticing how soft and delicate its petals are (kinesthetic) . . . As you are looking at this flower, feeling its petals, and smelling its special fragrance, you realize that you, too, are special, just like this flower. You are one in a million. There has never been another person on earth exactly like you and there never will be. How do you feel, knowing you are so special? (mental insight, emotional response) . . . As you stand up to say goodbye to your special flower friend, you see a beautifully gift-wrapped box nearby. It has been left for you by a fairy that lives in the nearby forest. It contains a gift to help you remember how special you are. Go over to it and pick it up. How much does it weigh? (kinesthetic) . . . Now carefully open the box and see what is inside . . . Look at the gift carefully from all sides (visual), pick it up, and feel it (kinethetic), and see if it makes any sounds (auditory) . . . You may keep this gift forever to help you always remember how special you are . . . In a minute, I am going to ask you to return to the room, gently open your eyes, and draw a picture of your gift. Before we do that, just notice what sounds you can hear inside and outside of the room right now (auditory) . . . Good. Now just gently stretch your body a little bit and feel what that feels like (kinesthetic) . . . and, then, when you're ready, just open your eyes and look around the room for a minute (visual) . . . Welcome back.

So, as you can see from the above example, you can integrate all of the various sensory systems into the imagery experience. We could also have integrated taste by adding something like, "Off to one side, you see an apple tree. As you approach it, your eyes are drawn to one apple in particular that you can easily reach. Let yourself reach up, take the apple, and bring it up to your face. How does it smell? What does it look like? Now let yourself take a bite out of the apple. What does it taste like?" or "You notice that it tastes a little sour." You can also add dimensions of temperature, texture, weight, hardness, softness, and so on. The more richly you create the images, the richer the experience will be for the students.

There are two ways of presenting these sensory experiences. One I call directive and the other non-directive. A directive instruction tells the student what to experience—what sounds to hear, what smells to smell, what feelings to feel. The non-directive approach asks the student what she hears, smells, feels, and sees. An example of a directive instruction would be, "As you are walking through the forest, you can hear the birds singing and the wind blowing through the leaves." A non-directive instruction would be,

"What sounds do you hear as you are walking through the forest?" You may also combine the two approaches. For example, "As you are walking through the forest you can hear many sounds. Perhaps there are some birds singing back and forth to each other, maybe the sounds of animals scampering away as you approach. What other sounds do you hear?" My experience is that for most imagery trips some mixture of the two works best.

Changing perspectives heightens the imagery. Let's say you ask your students to close their eyes and let an image or symbol appear that represents a quality of courage. After they begin to see the image (perhaps a heart, a sword, a lion, or a warrior), ask them to look at it right up close, to thoroughly examine it. Then ask them to step away from it and view it from a distance—with more perspective. Look at it from above and below. Go inside it and look at it from the inside. Also listen to it, smell it, touch it, feel it, taste it. This process will heighten imagery that is vague or fuzzy. It will also add new dimensions of insight to the meaning of the symbol and its relationship to the student's life.

Whenever you take a student *up* in an imagery experience (via stairs, escalators, elevators, clouds, magic carpets, ski-lifts, airplanes, rockets, climbing, a giant bird or butterfly, a balloon, magic), you will be encouraging the student to move into a higher level of consciousness which is generally associated with emotional and spiritual upliftment, inspiration, creativity, insight, healing, transmutation, transcendence, inner widsom, the transpersonal, and alignment with the higher qualities of love, joy, courage, perseverance, justice, peace, tranquillity, harmony, integration, and synthesis. On the other hand, taking a student *down* (via stairs, elevators, escalators, submarines, diving gear, magic turtles and fish, into caves, tunnels, and below the sea) will likely take the student down into the lower unconscious part of the mind, which is associated with negative emotions, the past, repressed traumatic experiences, unresolved conflicts, repressed aspects of the personality, darkness, monsters, and fear. It is therefore a good idea to avoid taking students below the ground unless you have a clear psychological purpose and are adequately trained in psychodynamic techniques of counselling such as gestalt, transactional analysis, psychosynthesis, or neurolinguistic programming.

This doesn't mean to *never* go down. For instance, if you have been studying in a science class how rabbits live or have been reading *Watership Down* in an English literature class, you may want to take your students on a guided imagery trip through a rabbit warren. However, if you do, be very directive rather than non-directive, provide a source of light in your description so they can safely see, be sure to remind your students of their detour fantasy before you begin the imagery experience, and remind them about using a magic wand or suggest that they surround themselves with light. Afterwards, make sure that you ask them if any of them had a bad trip, had a negative experience, got in touch with anything scary, or would like to help in sorting anything out.

Any time you leave ground level in a fantasy journey, *always return to ground level* before you ask the students to open their eyes and return to the classroom. If you don't, you may find that some of your students will seem "spaced out," ungrounded, not quite all present, or overly euphoric if you elevated them, or tired, sluggish, or depressed if you took them underground or underwater.

When working with students who have apparent physical handicaps such as blindness or loss of limbs, you will need to adapt consciously some of your verbal instructions. For example, with blind students don't use words like *see* or *visualize*. Instead use words like *imagine, sense, pretend, feel* and the other auditory, kinesthetic, olfactory, and taste words suggested earlier. With paraplegic and quadriplegic students, use images such as elevators, ski-lifts, flying, floating, magic clouds, magic carpets, and driving to replace climbing a mountain or walking along a road.

Voice and pacing should be relaxed, calm, rhythmic, regular, and slow— but not so slow that your students wander or fall asleep. The best delivery will be developed over time with practice and feedback. When developing your timing for a specific guided imagery script, practise by speaking into a tape recorder. Afterwards, close your eyes and play the tape back to yourself and see how the images, voice, and pacing work for you. Are the images rich enough? Do you use enough different sensory modalities? Is the pace so fast that you don't have time to develop an image before the next instruction is given? Is the pace so slow that you get bored, wander, or start creating your own images? Is the voice tone so dead, unanimated, or hypnotic that you begin to nod off or fall asleep? Is the voice too high or grating? Do you need to add or eliminate anything? You can also practise on a friend, your spouse, or your own children. Also, and probably most important, ask your students for feedback. Remember, you do not have to be perfect the first time you do it. Guiding imagery sessions is an art, and like any other art, it takes time to become a master. I have been using guided imagery for 15 years and I am still learning more about it every year.

Most noise distractions can be "incorporated" into the imagery experience. If a loud plane flies by overhead, just say ". . . and imagine you hear a loud plane flying by overhead." This will work for most interruptions of sounds. Another method for dealing with predictable sounds is to tell the students that each time they hear the sounds, their imagery will grow deeper and more clear. For instance, "Every time you hear the lawn mower come by the window, just let the sounds carry you deeper into the land of courage. Each time you hear the sounds it is a signal to your unconscious mind to make the images stronger and clearer."

Coming Out

After the imagery experience is completed, you need to bring the students back to normal waking consciousness. There are basically two methods for doing this. One I call *organic* and the other *numeric*. You can experiment with both ways of doing it. I prefer the organic method for imagery sessions that are especially deep or long. Some people will need more time than others to make the transition and this method allows for that.

The organic method would sound like this: "In just a minute, and there's no hurry, taking as long as you need, just honoring your own internal rhythm, perhaps on one of your exhalations, just gently open your eyes and bring your visual awareness back into the room. There is no hurry; just take as much time as you need." It is important when you do this to wait until all eyes are open before proceeding onto the next stage. If there are one or two students who seem to be taking an inordinately long time to return, you can say something like, "O.K., is everybody back? I'd like to move on now." That will usually get everybody to open their eyes in a few seconds.

The numeric method looks like this: "In just a moment I am going to count from 1 to 10. When I reach the number 5, I'd like you to join me in counting out loud. When we reach 10, I'd like you to return to the room fully alert and awake, rested from the experience and remembering everything that you have experienced . . . 1 . . . 2 . . . 3 . . . 4 . . . 5 . . . everybody counting out loud with me now . . . 6 . . . 7 . . . 8 . . . 9 . . . 10. Eyes open, fully alert and awake, feeling refreshed and rested . . . Welcome back." This method, as you can see, is more directive and uses more suggestion, "You will feel alert and awake, refreshed and rested, and you will remember everything you have experienced."

Another aspect of the coming out stage is what I call *anchoring*, which is the process of recalling or returning to a visual, auditory, or kinesthetic cue which has been previously established. This can greatly aid the transitional process. I use three types of anchors—external, physical, and imaginal.

External anchors can be visual or auditory. For the visual anchor, I ask students to gaze around the room until they find an object that attracts them. I then ask them to continue to look at that object and to study it carefully. I let this continue for about 30 seconds. Then I ask them to close their eyes and I proceed as usual with a relaxation exercise and the imagery experience that I have planned. At the end of the experience, after the students have opened their eyes, I ask them to once again find the same object and study it carefully. This helps refocus their awareness back into physical reality.

I use music as an auditory anchor. You can use the same piece of music at the beginning and the end of an imagery experience. This provides an auditory bridge into and out of the imaginal state of consciousness.

Physical anchors are any physical sensation that you can have the students focus upon, such as the rise and fall of their stomach and chest as they breathe in and out or the sensation of their back against the floor or the back of their chair. You can use physical anchors at the beginning and at the end or you may introduce them at the end simply to ground the student's awareness back into his or her body. I have used all of the following anchors with great success—taking a deep breath, feeling your stomach rise and fall as you breathe in and out, listening to the sound of your inhalation and exhalation, rubbing your hands together, wiggling your fingers and/or toes, rubbing the soles of your feet together, stretching your arms and legs, feeling yourself in your body, feeling your back against the chair, and feeling your feet on the floor.

Imaginal anchors are images that you establish in the beginning of the experience and return to at the end. These imaginal anchors provide an artful transition and sense of closure to any imagery experience that you create. For example, let us say that you begin an imagery experience by asking the students to imagine they are in school and they get up and walk out of the school and find a magic carpet waiting for them in the playground.

They take a ride to a special land and have some sort of adventure there . . . At the end, have them get back on the magic carpet, return to the playground, walk back into the school, into the classroom, and back into their own seat. This is a use of an imaginal anchor. Other examples are a trip on a cloud, a plane ride, a boat ride, riding a school bus, and walking out of and back into the school. Whenever you take the students up (a mountain, stairs, an elevator, etc.), first have them look down at the ground beneath their feet and see what is there. Is it carpet, grass, dirt, rocks, cement, asphalt, a wood floor, or what? When they come back down, have them look down at what they are standing on again and look at it once more. This acts as an anchor for the normal plane of waking consciousness.

Paula Klimek and Hans Poulsen, two colleagues of mine, have designed the most creative sequence of anchors I have ever seen. They call it "The Magic Island Sequence." They design a room to look like the deck of a sailing ship, complete with ropes and sails. To get into the room, each student walks over a gang plank and is greeted by the captain of the ship. Once they set sail, they hear the Sailboat/Country Stream record, one side of which is an actual recording of the sounds of a sailing ship. The students are also treated to cider, grape juice, cheese and crackers. Along the way, they all sing "Ship-a-Sailing," a song which Hans has written and recorded on *The Wonderful Family Singalong Songbook*.

As they approach the magic island, on which they will take several imagery trips—on the beach, at the waterfall, and at the mountain top—they begin to see slides of a south sea island projected upon the wall. As they leave the island, the sequence is repeated in reverse. They re-enter the boat, hear the sailing sounds, see the slides in reverse order, eat more cheese and crackers, drink more cider and grape juice, sing "Ship-a-Sailing," and disembark over the gang plank. It is quite a thrilling and fun experience and one that is artful and complete in its design.

Grounding and Processing

After the students have returned to normal waking consciousness, there needs to be some form of "grounding" or processing of the imagery experience. Like dreams, imaginal experiences have a tendency to be lost from memory if they are not quickly recorded or acted upon in some fashion. We have all had the experience of unsuccessfully trying to remember a dream that we experienced so vividly only an hour earlier. It is the same with imagery.

There are numerous forms for grounding an imagery experience. They include drawing the image or images you saw, writing about it in a journal, writing a poem about it, discussing your experience with a partner (or in a small group or with the whole class), acting it out with other members of the class, making what you saw (a statue, a mask, embroidery, etc.), and creating an affirmation for whatever message you received.

I like to use a combination of drawing, writing, and discussion for most imagery experiences. I first have the students draw what they saw (5 minutes), write about it (5 minutes), and then share their picture and discuss their experience with a partner or in a group of three (5 minutes). This seems to be a very effective combination for grounding. It involves all three of the perceptual systems—visual, auditory, and kinesthetic. It also gives the student a visual and mental record of the event as well as an opportunity to share the experience and hear from one or two others.

It is possible to create more elaborate and integrative forms of grounding such as the radiant body and mandala processes which Paula Klimek and I have written about in our paper "Discovering Your Radiant and Creative Self: A Transpersonal Arts Approach to Expressing One's Potential" (National Humanistic Education Center, 110 Spring Street, Saratoga Springs, NY 12866); it is also contained in my book *Self-Esteem in the Classroom: A Curriculum Guide*.

When discussing or processing the students' images (what they saw, heard, felt, and otherwise experienced), there are several guidelines that are useful to follow:

1. Don't interpret. Let students discover their own meanings for their symbols and images. Based upon their unique experiences, a symbol may mean different things to different people. Also it is important to let the students learn that they have their own answers. Students in America have been overtrained to look outside of themselves for the answers to their questions.

2. Don't judge people's images. Students may come up with bizarre, weird, negative, sexual, violent, unexplainable, discontinuous, or otherwise confusing or unusual images. The unconscious mind will sometimes take over and attempt to bring unresolved psychological material to the surface of one's consciousness. It is important not to judge whatever comes up as bad or unacceptable. Judging will only create lying, non-participation and possible withdrawal.

3. Don't grade any guided imagery experience.

4. Don't allow students to get into comparing their images. Obviously, they can share them with each other. However, comparing them as better or worse can be a negative experience. Some people may have beautiful, cosmic, three-dimensional, superscope, color images. That is fine. Tell them both that it doesn't make any difference. You get what you get and it will change from time to time. People image differently.

5. If students don't understand what the imagery means, tell them not to worry about it. Some of the methods they can use to extract more meaning from their images and symbols are to imagine having a dialogue with a particular image or symbol and asking it what it means or why it is there or what it is trying to tell them. They can also just go back and observe the imagery at greater length, for the symbol or image may start or continue to change and move. Often a theme will emerge from the flow of images. They can also reflect or meditate upon an image. Also, the process of grounding it—writing, drawing, and talking about it—will elicit greater clarity of meaning.

There are several process questions that are helpful in getting students to talk about their images. These are:

- What did you see?
- What did you feel?

- What did you think?
- What did you do?
- What did the imagery mean to you?
- What did you learn from it?
- How can you use what you learned?

If the imagery session was focussing upon some aspect of personal awareness or growth, it is important to encourage the students to act on any new insights they may have received. It is helpful to use questions such as, "How can you use what you have learned in your everyday life, in this class, at home, or with your friend? What would you say or do differently now that you know that? Are you willing to choose that? What would you have to give up? What support do you need? How can you get it?" It is also helpful to have the students set action goals that are measurable and that have deadlines.

Let us turn now to some of the different uses for guided imagery and some scripts of imagery sessions that you can use with your students.

Imagery for Self-Awareness

In one sense all guided imagery leads to greater self-awareness but the two that follow, The Motorcycle fantasy and the Rosebush fantasy, are especially useful as a type of diagnostic instrument to assess how one really "sees" oneself.

> Imagine that you are a motorcycle . . . What kind and color are you? . . . How old are you . . . Where are you kept when you are not being ridden? . . . What kind of condition are you in? . . . What do you sound like when you start up? . . . Do you start up easily or with difficulty? . . . Imagine you start up and you are driving along a road . . . What is the road like? . . . How is the traffic? . . . How fast are you going? . . . Now imagine that you have a rider. Look back and see who it is . . . Now have a dialogue with this person. Just carry on a conversation with each other . . . (long pause) . . . Now let yourself go anywhere you'd really like to be. Once you get there, just stop and park yourself . . . Let yourself enjoy being there for awhile . . . Whenever you are ready, I'd like you to gently open your eyes and return to the room.

After you have done this exercise, ask your students to find a partner and describe themselves as the motorcycle, starting each sentence with, "I am . . .". This will give them a lot of insight into themselves. I have had students realize that they don't like how they are being taken care of, that they are not self-starters, that they are afraid of being run over by other people, and that they have a feeling of being driven too hard by someone in their life. The images are indeed a metaphor for their lives.

This next guided fantasy has a similar purpose and is taken from John Stevens' book *Awareness* (New York: Bantam Books, 1973).

> I'd like you to imagine you are a rosebush. Become a rosebush and just discover what it is like to be this rosebush . . . Just let your fantasy develop on its own and see what you can discover about being a rosebush . . . What kind of rosebush are you? . . . Where are you growing? . . . What are your roots like? . . . and what kind of ground are you rooted in? . . . See if you can feel your roots going down into the ground . . . What are your stems and branches

like? . . . Discover all the details of being this rosebush . . . How do you feel as this rosebush? . . . What are your surroundings like? . . . What is your life like as this rosebush? . . . What do you experience, and what happens to you as the seasons change? . . . Continue to discover even more details about your existence as this rosebush, how you feel about your life, and what happens to you. Let your fantasy continue for awhile . . .

In a little while, I'm going to ask you to open your eyes and return to the class and express your experience of being a rosebush. I want you to tell it in first-person present tense, as if it were happening now. For instance, "I am a wild rose, growing on a steep hillside, in very rocky soil. I feel very strong and good in the sunshine, and little birds make their nests in my thick vines" or whatever your experience of being a rosebush is. O.K., whenever you feel ready, open your eyes, find a partner and express your experience of being a rosebush.

Imagery for Self-Esteem and Learning

Most students have been programmed by their past educational experiences to believe that learning has to be difficult, boring, or even painful. It certainly is not supposed to be easy and fun! But if you will look back on your own life, you can no doubt remember times when you enjoyed learning something new—something that was fun, challenging, self-satisfying, perhaps even exhilarating. Maybe it was learning to swim, water ski, or ride a surf board, or learning to fish, cook, or do macrame. No matter how young or old your students may be, they have all experienced moments of positive learning.

There is a psychological law which states we can create any desired feeling state simply by vividly re-creating in our imagination any prior event in which we experienced that same feeling. As teachers, we can use this psychological phenomenon to our benefit. We know that our students will learn better in a state of relaxed anticipation of a positive event. The desired mental state is, "We are about to learn something new and we know that learning can be easy and fun . . . so let's go!" You can evoke this state by using the following exercise, which I first learned from Jolene Somsky, who is a very creative elementary school teacher in Sioux City, Iowa.

The Positive Learning Recall—Ask the students to get into a comfortable position and to gently close their eyes. Ask them to concentrate on their breathing for a moment . . . to focus on the rising and falling of their chests as they breathe in and out. After a brief moment of relaxation, ask them to imagine the following:

> Imagine you are walking through a spring meadow . . . You can feel a light breeze against your face and the warmth against your back . . . You can hear the birds singing nearby and you can hear the buzzing of honey bees in the air . . . You feel comfortable and relaxed. Only peace and harmony is here . . . You're enjoying the flowers that are here, taking in their beautiful colors and smelling their wondrous fragrance . . . In the meadow there is a special flower that is different. It is special and unique . . . You find it. You're going over to it. You observe its petals and smell its fragrance. This flower is truly unique in all the world . . . You are this flower. Find a way to become this flower . . . You are special, unique, very caring, great and powerful . . .

Everyone in the room is like this. You feel very good now and very relaxed
. . . (longer pause) . . . Now go to a time when learning was fun for you,
perhaps when you were a little child—learning to tie your shoelaces, camping
with friends, or learning to fish or cook—maybe it was later, but find a time
when learning was easy and fun for you . . . (longer pause) . . . When you
have that time, raise your hand . . . (wait until all or almost all of the hands
are up) . . . You can put your hands down. Now, become aware of who you
were with . . . What did you feel in your feet . . . stomach . . . hands . . .
and face? Let that good feeling spread through your whole body and let it
spread through the whole room . . . (longer pause) . . . In a moment we're
going to open our eyes and everybody will be coming back into the room with
that very special feeling that they are unique in all the world and that learning
can be easy and fun. Will you open your eyes now and return to the room
relaxed and alert?

When the students have returned, they are ready to begin whatever lesson
you have prepared.

Beverly Galyean, the former Director of the Confluent Language Project
in the Los Angeles City schools, developed a similar guided imagery experience which she used to help students in an inner city high school Spanish
class to reduce negative behaviors such as lateness, disruptions, and put-
downs and to increase positive behaviors such as affirmative communication
with other students and oral and written participation in learning activities.
The activity was used daily during the first 5 to 7 minutes of class for a
period of three months. The results were highly positive. Students exhibited
increased attentiveness, increased involvement with the lessons being
taught, an increase in the number of supportive interactions among the
students themselves, and an increase in the number of supportive responses
to the teacher. Here is the Perfect Student exercise:

Close your eyes for a few minutes and relax. Take a deep breath. As you
breathe in, imagine yourself taking in all the most beautiful, wholesome, helpful, and good energy around you. As you breathe out, see yourself breathing
forth any tension, worry, doubt, or negativity you might be feeling. (pause)
Take another breath, breathing in the good around you. This time, as you
breathe out, feel yourself floating away . . . floating gently away from this
room. (pause) Float away now to a place where you really like to be. This is
a favorite place where you feel really good. Go there now . . . gently . . .
floating to your place . . . (pause) When you get there, just enjoy being there
. . . (pause) Now, while at this place, look into the sky and see the sun . . .
warm . . . brilliant. Ask the sun to descend upon you making you feel very
warm . . . comfortable . . . secure. Notice how the sun warms but doesn't
burn. The sun seems very friendly today . . . (pause) Now, call the sun to
enter your body through the top of your head. See how it lightens you . . .
makes you feel weightless. Gradually, it descends through your head . . .
releasing all tension from your eyes . . . jaws . . . neck . . . shoulders. Then
it quietly descends through your shoulders . . . arms . . . chest . . . stomach
. . . hands . . . thighs . . . legs . . . and feet. Notice how light you feel.
Experience the good that is you . . . (pause) Now see yourself as absolutely
perfect . . . capable of achieving anything you want. You have all the ability
to succeed. See yourself as perfect. (pause) What do you look like as perfect?
How are you behaving? How do others think of you? . . . (pause) See yourself
as absolutely perfect. Now see yourself as perfect in this class. You have all
the knowledge . . . all the ability to be a perfect student. It's up to you. What

do you look like as a perfect student? What are you doing in the class? How are others responding to you? (pause) Now, take a moment to say some things to yourself to remind yourself that you are, indeed, perfect, and that you can be perfect any time you wish. Repeat to yourself: I am a perfect person . . . (pause) I am a perfect student. (pause) The others are here to help me continue to be perfect . . . (pause) I am here to help myself continue to be perfect . . . (pause) Say this to yourself three times . . . (pause) Now, take the sun that has descended through you and slowly draw it back up through your body . . . leaving you with a feeling of lightness and brightness. Send the sun back into the sky and feel your body so light . . . so gentle . . . so cared for . . . (pause) Take a deep slow breath . . . hold it at the top . . . and slowly let the air out and feel yourself floating back to us here in the room . . . (pause) Open your eyes and enjoy the deep feeling of relaxation.

Imagery and Remedial Reading

Dr. Gerald Jampolsky, Director of the Center for Attitudinal Healing in Tiburon, California, has successfully developed and implemented a guided visualization for remedial readers at the elementary level. The seven-step process is as follows:

Let your body find a comfortable position either lying down or sitting up. Let yourself begin to take long, slow, deep breaths and just let yourself become more relaxed with each breath. There is nowhere to go and nothing to do except become more and more relaxed with each breath that you take . . . Let yourself open and close your eyes until you become comfortable with having them closed . . . Notice that with each breath that you take that you become more and more relaxed . . .

Now, imagine entering an elevator on the first floor of a building. As you look up above the door, you can see the number 1 is lit up. After the door closes, the elevator begins to ascend one floor at a time. You can see the numbers above the door changing from 1 to 2 to 3 and so forth . . . You can feel yourself becoming more relaxed as the elevator ascends . . . more relaxed as each floor goes by . . . until you are finally at the tenth floor . . .

Now, imagine that you reach up to the top of your head and you find a long zipper that runs from the front of your head to the back of your head. Go ahead and unzip the zipper and gently remove your brain and place it on the ground in front of you . . . Now, imagine you have a hose in your hand and begin to wash out your brain with the hose . . . Get rid of all the dirt and grime in your brain . . . Wash out all the old painful memories of having difficulty with learning to read . . . Wash out all of the old ideas that are in your brain that interfere with your reading. Wash out all the ideas and phrases like, "I can't." "It's too hard." "I'll never be able to do this." "I'll try." "If only . . . " and "But . . . " These words and phrases only create negative pictures in your mind that will make the past repeat itself. As you wash your brain out, you are replacing these words with, "I can." "It is easy." "Reading is simple and fun." "I like to read." "I am successful at everything I do." You are washing away your old negative belief system about your ability to read. You are replacing it with a new one that will help you to read easily and quickly. You will be surprised and delighted to see how easily you can read now that you have washed away these old ideas from your brain . . . You will be pleased with yourself and very proud . . .

Now, very gently reach down and pick up your clean brain. Notice how white and clean it is now. All the negative thoughts and memories have been washed away . . . Now, very gently place it back in your head and zip the zipper closed again . . . Very good . . .

Now, imagine that you are sitting at your desk at school . . . Think of your most favorite subject in the whole world, the thing you most like and are the most interested in. Now, imagine that you are writing a small book about that subject . . . Think of all the things that you would say in such a book . . . Realize how easy it is for you to write the book. You know all the words that you need to know and you know how to spell them correctly. You are really enjoying writing this book. It is fun and exciting . . .

Now, imagine that you are reading the book you have just written. You can read all the words easily because they are all words which you wrote earlier . . . Imagine that you are reading the book out loud so that you can hear each word. Listen to how your voice sounds . . . You are able to read each word fluently and easily . . . See yourself flipping the page over as you go onto the next page. Notice how the pages feel in your hand . . . They are very smooth and crisp . . . Also notice how the cover feels. It is stiffer than the pages . . . You feel very confident and joyful as you read because you know that you can recognize, pronounce and understand all of the words without any problem . . . You can feel a big smile come onto your face as you continue to read.

Now, imagine that you are sitting in front of a big motion picture screen. On the screen you see a movie of yourself reading a book. You can see that you are reading with pleasure and ease because there is a big smile on your face. You are reading successfully, fluently, and without effort. All of the words come very easily to you. Just watch and listen as you see yourself reading out loud with ease . . . (long pause) . . . Now, imagine that there is a door right in the middle of the motion picture screen. Let yourself stand up, open the door, and walk right into the movie and climb right into your own body on the screen . . . You are now that person who reads successfully, without effort, and with a big smile on your face . . .

Now, take this picture of yourself reading with ease and put that picture in your blood cells. Just imagine every cell of blood as it pumps through your heart being filled with the picture of your reading with a big smile on your face . . . Now, see all of these blood cells going to all the organs and your skin . . . You have become one with the picture of yourself reading well . . .

Now, imagine yourself entering the elevator ŏn the tenth floor again. See the door close and look up at the numbers above the door. You see them changing from 10 to 9 to 8 to 7 to 6 to 5 to 4 to 3 to 2 to 1. As you reach the first floor, you see the elevator door open and you step out into the lobby . . . Now, focus on the rise and fall of your chest and stomach as you breathe in and out . . . Feel your feet on the floor and your back against the back of the chair.

When you are ready, taking as much time as you need, for there is no hurry, just begin to bring your awareness back into the room and open your eyes when you feel like it.

After the students returned to normal waking consciousness, Dr. Jampolsky had each student record the same guided experience on a cassette tape in his or her own voice. They were then instructed to play the tape and do the visualization experience for five to ten minutes at night before going to sleep, and in the morning for five to ten minutes before coming to school. The parents of the children were encouraged not to be involved in the childrens' reading program and not to try to get them to read. The teachers were encouraged to develop positive mental pictures of the children reading more fluently and pleasurably, to feel a lightness and fluidity in their relationship with the children, and to stop all critical statements.

The results of this experiment were that during this one-month period students in the experimental group showed an average increase in their reading skill of one and one-half years as compared to an average increase of one month for the control group. There was also a tremendous increase in the experimental group's self-esteem. The parents reported that they felt much closer to their children, that they were less tense and driven. The teachers not only reported a difference in the children in this project, but they also reported that they felt more relaxed and less tense with all their students. They all reported more energy at the end of the day. The students were retested one year later and, compared to the control group, were continuing to make excellent progress.

Imagery and Inner Wisdom

To me, the most interesting use of guided imagery is the evocation of the wisdom that lies deep within each of us. The most exciting experience I ever had with this grew out of a discussion of the television show *Kung Fu* with a group of sixth graders. We were discussing how it was that Cain always knew the right thing to do in any situation no matter how difficult or hopeless it may have appeared. They told me that each time he was in an emergency situation, he could close his eyes and flash back to a time when his teacher had told him something very wise and important. I asked them what this was called. One girl said, "It was like meditation." I agreed and said that it was. I then asked them what kind of teacher Cain talked to. Was he like their sixth grade teacher? They all agreed that he was a different kind of teacher, somehow special, wiser, and more trustworthy. They all agreed they would like to have a teacher like that.

I then asked the kids if they would like to have a wise old teacher whom they could consult for advice in times of pressure and confusion. They all said yes they would, but they weren't sure where they'd find one. Most of them decided they'd have to go to China or Japan or India. I asked them where David Cain went when he needed help. They finally realized that he had closed his eyes and gone inside himself. At this point, I suggested that we all try that and see if we could find a Wise Old Teacher inside our minds who could share his or her wisdom with us. They excitedly agreed to try. Here is what I asked them to visualize:

> Close your eyes, take a few deep breaths to relax. I want you to imagine that it is a pleasant day and you are walking in a friendly foreign land, a place where you've never been before. What does it look like there? . . . Can you feel the ground underneath your feet? Look down and see what you're walking on. What does it look like? What sounds do you hear? What smells are you aware of? . . . Off in the distance to your left, you see a very tall mountain. What does it look like? . . . As you look at the mountain, you begin to feel drawn toward it. As you approach the foot of the mountain, you see a path going up the side of the mountain. It is an easy path with no obstacles or difficult places and you begin to walk up this path toward the top of the

mountain . . . As you reach the half-way point, you stop and look back and see that you have come a long way up the mountain. You can see very far in all directions . . . Then you turn around again and continue up the mountain. . . . Eventually you begin to reach the top . . . When you get to the top you notice a temple—a very special building. As you approach it, you can feel the solemnity and sacredness of this place. You decide to go inside, but before you do, you carefully remove your shoes and place them beside the doorway . . . Once inside, you notice thousands of candles burning, creating a great light inside. At the far end of the room, you see a very kind and wise old person. As you approach this person, you see a very loving smile and bright, happy eyes. As you get closer, you realize that there is a question about life—your life in particular or life in general—that you want to ask this wise old person. When you are ready to ask, ask your question and let him or her respond. If at first you don't understand the answer, ask for more clarity. Have as long a conversation as you need to understand the answer. (Long pause—about one minute) . . . O.K., now, realizing that you can always come back to this place and ask your wise old teacher any question you have about anything, say goodbye for now and begin to leave the temple . . . Once outside, remember to put your shoes back on and begin to come back down the mountain . . . As you're coming down the mountain, feel the warmth of the sun on your skin and feel the ground beneath your feet as you walk . . . When you reach the bottom, look down again and see the ground beneath your feet. What does it look like? How does it feel? . . . Okay, when you're ready, and taking as much time as you need, take a few deep breaths again, open your eyes and come back to the class.

I gave them about a minute to get back and then I asked them to share their experiences. It was incredible listening to them. They had been given wisdom as old as time, things like: "If you're nice to people, people will be nice to you." "You can only be happy if you decide to be happy." "Things would be easier if you didn't try so hard." One girl had asked the wise old woman the question, "What is the meaning of life?" She said that her wise old woman didn't say anything, but held up a mirror to her. I asked her if she understood what that meant. She said, "Yes, it means to me that life is what I choose to make it." That's an amazingly sophisticated insight for a sixth grader.

Another boy said that he did not see a wise old man or woman but that he had felt "a nice strangeness." I asked him what he meant. He said it was a strange feeling—one he had never felt before—and yet it was very nice. When I asked him what was nice about it, he said that he felt relaxed—"like no hassles."

Everybody was very eager to do it again. And everybody also agreed that there were very few times that they didn't feel hassled and uptight. It's very difficult for students to learn, let alone be creative, when they're uptight. It is necessary to be relaxed for the unconscious mind to work. (That is why so many inspirations and solutions to problems come in the morning, right after waking up from a relaxed and calm sleep.)

The Life Purpose Fantasy—Paula Klimek developed this guided imagery session. We have used it with kids in the sixth grade and with adults. It is a very powerful experience which can help students become aware of their essential nature, their highest potential, their unique gift to the world, and their life purpose. Especially as kids enter adolescence, they often become confused and are usually unable to get clear answers from their parents or their teachers about many basic questions of life, such as Who am I? What difference does my life make? and What do I really want to do? My experience has been that when those core questions are addressed from within and when students experience recognition and affirmation of their essence, their core self, and their inner wisdom, remarkable transformations occur.

Before conducting this guided fantasy, you will need to conduct a class discussion of what is meant by the term *life purpose*. Just have the class brainstorm on what the concept means to them. After you are satisfied that they have an adequate understanding of the concept, ask them to find a comfortable position, close their eyes, and relax. Then you can begin the session.

> We are about to review your life. As you begin to experience yourself going backwards in time, begin by thinking about this day. Go back to when you woke up this morning . . . What have you done all day? . . . Now, look back at the past week . . . the past month . . . the past year . . . Review the significant events of this time . . . What did you look like? . . . Who were you with? . . . Where have you been? . . . If you get caught up in any particular event or find yourself being judgmental, just allow yourself to let that go. Allow your life to pass by as if you were watching a movie . . . Now, go back to your previous grade . . . To your elementary grades . . . To the primary grades . . . To the time you first entered school . . . To being a young child . . . A 2-year old . . . a baby . . . to the time of your birth and the time you were in your mother's womb . . . And now go back to the time before your conception. You are about to meet a special guide, your own special guide. A guide whom you may ask what the purpose of your life is . . . Meet this guide and pose your question . . . Feel your guide's unconditional love and strength and beauty . . . Let whatever happens happen . . . communicate with your guide in whatever way possible. (pause) As you continue to listen to your guide, the guide hands you a beautifully wrapped box. The guide tells you that it contains a gift to represent your purpose, your essence, your unique gifts, your genius . . . Open the box and see what is inside . . . Now it is time to begin your journey back. Say farewell to your guide knowing you may visit your guide at any time . . . Begin to make your journey back bringing with you both your life purpose and the gift from your experience. Make your journey through time, through your birth, your infancy, your childhood, and finally to the present moment in this room . . . When you are ready, open your eyes, remain silent and draw and write about your experience. We will share our journey after a few minutes.

The responses from the students to an exercise such as this are usually quite profound and moving. Subsequent drawings of the experience have included rainbows, the sun, the light, contact with another being, mountains, meadows, flowers, birds, and animals. The students' writings have been poetic, creative, beautifully simplistic, and yet full and rich, as in the following response: "When I met my guide and asked my question, he gave me a great big smile and held my hands. It was like he was saying it's real neat. Try it. It's a great thing to be a person. He gave me a sense of wanting to be just by holding my hands. My guide seemed like a real nice person, the kind people would like to know. When we were holding hands I thought, 'Wow, I hope everyone's like this.' When I was leaving, I looked back. It seemed as though he was saying, 'It's O.K., go ahead,' just by looking at me. We met in a place full of nothingness."

Imagery for Empathy

Guided imagery can be used to increase empathy. It allows the student to enter into the experience of another, to literally walk a mile in their shoes. It can be used to increase empathy for pets, other students, parents, someone you are afraid of, a student you are having a problem with, a person of another race, nationality, or even another time in history.

One class that I worked with had a tendency to treat the class gerbil much too roughly without the proper concern for the gerbil's comfort and safety. Rather than a lecture, which would turn the students off, I asked them to close their eyes and participate in the following guided fantasy:

> Imagine you are a gerbil in a cage in a fourth grade classroom. How does it feel to be in a cage all day long? How does it feel to be totally dependent on others for food, water, and adequate warmth and love? . . . Imagine that it is early in the morning and you are simply sitting around and relaxing. All of a sudden the fluorescent lights switch on and you run to the side of the cage to see what is happening. It is the teacher. She comes in and sits down at her desk. Several minutes later you hear a lot of noise and you look up again. A whole bunch of people are running into the classroom pushing and shoving and shouting loudly . . . Several of them approach your cage. You see these two big hands reaching down and grabbing you. Then you hear a loud shout and two other hands reach out for you. They seem to be fighting over you. Your skin hurts as they pull you in two different directions at the same time. All of a sudden you find yourself falling. You land on the hard cement. How does that feel? . . . You quickly run and hide under the radiator. But now there are all these big hands reaching in to get you . . . etc.

Imagery and Subject Matter

A number of researchers have now shown that imagery can be used to accelerate the learning of subject matter. The students learn the material more quickly and retain the material over a longer period of time. Studies have shown that with each additional psychological function that is utilized in a lesson—body, mind, emotions, imagination, and intellect—there is a geometric progression in the rate and retention of learning.

I will give you a few examples below. The possibilities are endless.

The Bee Dance—Suppose you are teaching science and the subject for the day is how bees communicate with each other. You are planning to show a film on the bee dance, which German scientist Karl von Frisch discovered and studied. Before discussing the bee dance or showing the film, you take the students on a guided fantasy.

> Imagine you are a bee. You are flying along over fields and through valleys looking desperately for flowers that are in blossom. There has been a drought recently and flowers and blooms have been hard to find . . . Finally you spot a field of color. You fly down closer. You are very excited by your discovery. You fly back to the hive where you live and find that most of the bees are

there . . . Without talking—since bees can't talk—how do you communicate to the rest of the bees where the flowers are located? . . . O.K., in a minute, when you are ready, come back to the room with your eyes open and we'll each share how we did it.

After the students have had a chance to share, show them the film. They are much more curious now than they would have been otherwise. After the film has been shown, repeat the guided fantasy and this time have them imagine doing a dance to communicate the location of the flowers to their fellow bees. To heighten the experience, once the students have their eyes open again, have them actually get up and do a bee dance similar to the one they just did in their fantasy. You have now engaged three functions—the intellect, the imagination, and the physical. They will definitely remember the material.

Electronics—Here is an example of how to use guided imagery in an electronics course:

> Imagine you are an electron . . . What does it feel like to be such an incredibly small piece of negatively charged matter? . . . Imagine as you are moving along through space that you encounter two very large coils of wire. Notice how large the coils are . . . As you get closer and closer, you begin to realize that there is a huge and rapidly changing force field around the coils . . . As you enter this force field, you can feel the effects of it . . . Next, imagine that you are entering the wire of the coil . . . You see thousands of other electrons moving within the coil. How are these electrons affected by the rapidly changing force field?

You could continue this experience by telling the students that another coil of equal size and strength has come toward them, that the two fields begin to interact, that the interactions become very violent as the coils come closer to each other, and so forth. Again, you could follow this up with a movement exercise.

Spelling—There are several imagery techniques I have used with helping children to spell better. I will share two of them with you here, The Magic Carpet and The Magic Blackboard. These are both methods for dealing with misspelled words.

> Imagine you are standing on a sandy beach. You can hear the sound of the waves rolling rhythmically onto the beach. You can see the blue sky, the bright sun, and lots of seagulls flying overhead. The sun feels warm upon your skin . . . All of a sudden, you look up and see a flying carpet flying toward you. It lands on the beach and you get on . . . Very gently it takes off and flies you across the ocean to a very special island—the island of words . . . As you begin to land, you notice the word *judgment* (j-u-d-g-m-e-n-t) waiting for you on the beach . . . Each of its letters is a bright blue, like a neon sign. One by one the letters flash on and off (j-u-d-g-m-e-n-t) . . . As you look down at your feet, you see a box that has been carefully wrapped. Inside the box is a gift from the word *judgment* to help you remember to spell it correctly in the future. Open the box and see what is inside it . . . Thank *judgment* for the gift and get back onto your magic carpet . . . As you wave goodbye to *judgment* on the beach, your magic carpet begins to fly and take you back home . . . Pretty soon, you are back again and ready to open your eyes.

When the students have returned, have them open their eyes, write the word *judgment* in large blue letters on the top of a piece of paper and then draw the gift they were given underneath. This could then be added to a folder or book of spelling words, which could be reviewed later for reinforcement.

Every student can be taught that they have a magic blackboard inside of their head. This blackboard can be used for math, spelling, remembering dates and other facts, and for writing down affirmations. Here's how it could be used for spelling.

> Visualize your magic blackboard. On it see the word *judgment* misspelled as "jujment." Visualize your own hand reaching out and placing a big X through the misspelled word . . . Now, take your magic eraser and erase it . . . Now, again with your own hand, reach out and write the correct spelling, j-u-d-g-m-e-n-t . . . Now, look at what you have spelled . . . Imagine now that the blackboard becomes framed by a beautiful and brilliant white light . . . Once again, visualize yourself spelling the word correctly j-u-d-g-m-e-n-t . . . When you are ready, open your eyes and write the word *judgment* three times on a piece of paper.

Mathematics—I learned this one from Robert Rose, an elementary school teacher in San Bernardino, California.

> Imagine you have a whole lot of numbers with decimal points that need to be added together. Visualize each decimal point as a glowing bead which flashes on and off like a Christmas tree light. Visualize all the beads hanging down in a straight line as if they were suspended on a string. All the colored beads should always be in a straight line. You may need to help put them in their places. Then when all the numbers are lined up, you can add them . . . Remember this every time you have numbers with decimals in them.

You can also use the Magic Board technique for math tables, formulas, and so on. Another technique is to have the students imagine they are floating in a balloon above a beach. From the balloon, they watch as people draw math tables (i.e., 2 × 2 = 4) in the sand with a large stick.

Social Studies and English—Social studies and English are probably the two easiest subjects in which to utilize guided imagery. You can have the students take visual trips to ancient times and places (Egypt, Greece, Rome, Colonial America, and feudal England), visualize being a great figure from history (Benjamin Franklin, Napoleon, Lincoln, Joan of Arc, St. Francis, Martin Luther King), visualize participating in a process you want them to understand and remember (coming through Ellis Island for immigration, working in a meat packing house in the Chicago stockyards for unionization, being a dust bowl migrant for *The Grapes of Wrath*, etc.), and visualize how they might have acted if they were in a particular situation (a slave in the old South, a soldier called to war in one of Shakespeare's plays or a novel, a juror in the Scope's trial and so on).

Final Thoughts

So as you can see, there are innumerable possibilities for the use of guided imagery in teaching and counselling. I hope you will attempt some of the suggestions that I have presented here. If you do, you will embark upon a new and adventurous journey in your teaching. You can expect some profound changes to occur in your classroom. At the very least, you will have regular periods of silence in your classroom, and in these days of stress and burnout, that's a nice thing to look forward to.

Note

1. Whenever three dots appear in the guided imagery exercises, they indicate a pause of about 5 seconds. Whenever a longer pause of about 15 seconds is appropriate, I have written the word "pause" in parentheses. Editors' note: Readers will notice that ellipses points are used conventionally in the other articles to indicate material that is left out.

Resources

There is a quickly growing field of literature on imagery and education. I will list here books, organizations, and people that have been most helpful to me. Good luck with your future quest.

1. Books on Guided Imagery

Bagley, M. T., & Hess, K. (1982). *200 ways of using imagery in the classroom*. Woodcliff Lake, NJ: New Dimensions of the '80s Publishers.

Canfield, J. (1986). *Self-esteem in the classroom: A curriculum guide*. Pacific Palisades, CA: Self-Esteem Seminars. (Write to Self-Esteem Seminars, 17156 Palisades Circle, Pacific Palisades, CA 90272, and ask them for their catalogue describing the curriculum and other educational materials for teachers.)

DeMille, R. (1973). *Put your mother on the ceiling. Children's imagination games*. New York: Viking Compass.

Eberle, R. R. (1971). *SCAMPER: Games for imagination and development*. Buffalo, NY: DOK Publishers (771 East Delevan Ave., Buffalo, NY 14215).

Galyean, B. C. (1983). *Mind sight: learning through imagery*. Long Beach, CA: Centre for Integrative Learning. (Available through Zephyr Press, 430 South Essex Lane, Tuscon, AZ 85711. Ask Zephyr to send you their catalogue which is full of books for teachers to help students reach their full potential).

Harmin, M., & Sax, S. (1977). *A peaceable classroom: Activities to calm and free student energies*. Minneapolis, MN: Winston Press.

Hendricks, G., & Wills, R. (1975). *The centering book*. Englewood Cliffs, NJ: Prentice-Hall.

Hendricks, G., & Wills, R. (1977). *The second centering book*. Englewood Cliffs, NJ: Prentice-Hall.

Hills, C., & Rozman, D. (1978). *Exploring inner space*. Boulder Creek, CA: University of the Trees Press (P.O. Box 644, Boulder Creek, CA).

Murdock, M. (1988). *Spinning inward: Using guided imagery with children*. Berkeley, CA: Shamballa Press.

Rapkin, M. (n.d.). *The power of pretend*. Available from Maurice Rapkin, 10480 Santa Monica Blvd., Los Angeles, CA 90025.

Rozman, D. (1975). *Meditating with children*. Boulder Creek, CA: University of the Trees Press.

Rozman, D. (1976). *Meditation for children*. Millbrae, CA: Celestial Arts.

Samuels, M., & Samuels, N. (1975). *Seeing with the mind's eye: The history, techniques and uses of visualization*. New York: Random House/Bookworks.

Vitale, B. M. (1982). *Unicorns are real: A right-brained approach to learning*. Rolling Hills Estates, CA: Jalmar Press. (Write to B. L. Winch at Jalmar Press, 45 Hitching Post Drive, Building 2, Rolling Hills Estates, CA 90274, and ask for their educational catalogue. They have a complete line of books on enhancing self-esteem, fostering creativity, and unleashing human potential in the classroom.)

2. General Books on Imagery

Gawain, S. (n.d.). *Creative visualization*. Berkeley, CA: Whatever Publishing (P.O. Box 3073).

Lorrayne, H., & Lucas, J. (1974). *The memory book*. New York: Ballantine Books.

Nichols, R. E. (1978). *Picture yourself a winner*. Lakemont, GA: CSA Press.

Sherman, H. (1978). *How to picture what you want*. New York: Fawcett Goldmedal.

For those of you who wish to pursue guided imagery in real depth, you may wish to subscribe to *The Journal of Mental Imagery*, Brandon House, P.O. Box 240, Bronx, NY 10471.

3. Books on Relaxation

Davis, M., Eshelman, E. R., & McKay, M. (1980). *The relaxation and stress reduction workbook*. Richmond, CA: Harbinger Publications (624 43rd Street, Richmond, CA 94805).

Mason, L. J. (1980). *Guide to stress reduction*. Culver City, CA: Peace Press (3828 Willat Ave., Culver City, CA 90230).

Walker, C. E. (1975). *Learn to relax*. Englewood Cliffs, NJ: Prentice-Hall.

White, J., & Fadiman, J. (Eds.). (1976). *Relax*. New York: Dell.

4. Books on Energizers

Fleugelman, A. (Ed.). (1976). *The new games book*. Garden City: Doubleday/Dolphin.

Ichazo, O. (1976). *Arica psychocalisthenics*. New York: Simon & Schuster.

Weinstein, M., & Goodman, J. (1980). *Playfair*. San Luis Obispo, CA: Impact Publishers.

Self-Care

Conscious Fathering:
A Personal Journey

John E. Franklin

In the fall of 1978, I went to California to enter graduate school, and I left behind a 3-year-old daughter in Pennsylvania. The intensity of the ensuing separation and loss had a tremendous influence on me, both personally and professionally. Attempting to come to terms with my role as a father has been challenging. The process of being a conscious father has been an important part of the journey toward my core self. It has also inspired me to guide others who have chosen fathering as an area for personal growth.

During the years of my training, I dreamed of becoming a professional healer—in private practice—doing my part to save humanity. I had an intense drive to heal the world. This "New Age neurosis" demanded most of my time and energy. I was also in a committed relationship with a woman which required daily work and attention—a prerequisite for the "conscious couple" of the '80s. Yet, at the same time, the father inside of me felt deeply wounded, alone, and in great need. I had a daughter living 3,000 miles away. I saw her a few weeks in the summer during which I mostly entertained, haunted by a deep sense of guilt.

Like a hidden splinter, the undeveloped father in me became a major source of discomfort. The loss of a satisfying relationship with my child did not feel like a necessary sacrifice I had to make along the spiritual path. I decided that one possibility would be to use my situation as an opportunity to develop a well-integrated personality that would have room for all the various aspects of myself, including the father. This new role could be more sensitive and responsive to my deeper needs, both as a father and as a healer. I knew from my psychosynthesis training that this possibility existed and could even be happening without my conscious awareness. I decided to test this hypothesis and take responsibility for my healing. First, I needed to deal with the wounds of the inner father that were crying out for help and attention.

I began by searching my inner file on the topic of "fathering." I found two pieces related to the subject. One said, "Our Father who art in heaven. . . ." The other was, "Yours was never there—no information provided." I realized that what was missing was all the stuff in between. And since I had basically no idea of how to be a full-time father, and had even less of an inkling of how to be a long-distance father, I decided that this was a good place to begin.

As my thinking progressed, I began to see my role as father, and more specifically fathering, as a microcosm in which the search for meaning and

192

purpose could unfold. My first step was to explore the meaning of the term itself and to discriminate what I knew from what I didn't.

In redefining the concept of what it means to be a father, I realized that it was not a static "thing" I became when my baby was born. Fathering is more of an action verb. It reminds me of the story of the *Velveteen Rabbit* who becomes "real" with time and love. Real fathers are also soft and gentle yet resilient and durable. I know there is something special about grandfathers. They seem to do it with ease, enjoyment, and patience. But, I wondered, do I have to wait that long? Can I be more "real" now?

Someone once said, "Fathers are a biological necessity but a sociological mistake." Perhaps they are a necessary evil, like taxes and dandruff. In many ways, the father in our society has been misunderstood. He has been a forgotten commodity relegated to an inferior place in the emotional realm of the family system.

Although I am not sure how to be a "real father," my best answer is that fathering has no point of arrival. It is more of an ongoing process. It is more active than passive—like peace. Peace is more than just the absence of war. Peace must be created intentionally with effort, skill, and focussed attention. We have to have a degree of inner freedom to be at peace. Peace implies vigilance, responsiveness, and purposeful direction. Like fathering, peace is something that unless developed and expressed with consciousness, intention, and focussed attention, can by virtue of its absence victimize us as well as our children, their children, and so on.

It is interesting to note that fathering is receiving a lot of attention today. To me, this collective interest around the changing role of the father represents much more than the impulse to do better than our own fathers. It represents an ideal coming further into reality. There are deeper implications to this process of conscious fathering that involve human relations, relatedness, and an acknowledgment of the importance of the family unit as an essential building block of a peaceful world.

It seems apparent that our work in fathering is not to re-invent the wheel. There have always been nurturing/caring fathers. Yet there is a great need to *affirm* the role of the nurturing male parent as a role in which the father can learn to find fulfilment, meaning, purpose, and a deep sense of connection with his family and also with himself. In this respect, fathering is an arena for personal growth, an opportunity to develop new qualities, expand preconceived boundaries, and blend intrapsychic polarities into new levels of integration that can release new energies into the personality.

It is also an opportunity to experience transcendence. No, it is not a panacea, not a short-cut to meditation and spiritual discipline. But if you talk to enough fathers who attended the births of their children, you begin to realize they all sound like mystics or saints. Maybe attendance at the birth should be mandatory for all fathers. Maybe this is an alternative to years of spiritual discipline. It's not, but it is deeply satisfying and helps men open their hearts.

Fathering is a context in which men can add new dimensions and qualities to their lives. Some fathers find it safe to express traditionally feminine qualities—qualities that in our culture often get repressed or projected onto women. Other men find that fathering is more than being a man with good mothering skills. Researchers who study paternal deprivation say that male nurturance is a viable, necessary, healing energy that the world—especially children—needs more of. Robert Bly (1986) refers to a male mode of feeling that is unique to a man's experience and psyche. Arthur Coleman (1981) calls the archetype that expresses this particular quality of energy the "Earth Father" and says it has been around for thousands of years although it has been lost in our culture. This new, more inclusive role of the father, a product of the integration of traditional values, attitudes, and behavior with the more caring, nurturing aspects, is the goal of conscious fathering. Affirming this new role, along with the ideal models that are emerging, is one of the most crucial issues in fathering today.

Fathering is a complex organic concept that is continually changing. It is not an obligation, a job, or a chore one faces at the end of a long day. Nor is it a perpetually smiling face, a grinning male parent "blissed-out" by changing diapers. On the one hand, the traditional father, struggling to earn a living, often pushes away the job inherent in active parenting. On the other hand, the New Age father, although in touch with the joy and excitement of being a father, pushes away the conflict, pain, and struggle necessary in being a conscious, whole father. Both are equally trapped in a static role identity.

Fathering, as we are redefining it today, is a process filled with possibilities, difficulties, and adjustments. It is an open system with peaks and valleys that could try a god. Conscious fathering is an art and a skill that involves a fundamental shift in how we view our roles, our relationships, and ultimately ourselves. It requires the courage to look at our strengths and weaknesses and to choose healthier patterns than those that have kept us trapped in the past. Fathering involves the struggle inherent in any creative effort toward more satisfying and fulfilling relationships. Becoming a father requires taking risks that can move us into deeper levels of intimacy. In taking those risks, we bring more love and caring into our homes, our community, and the world.

An adaptation of Assagioli's (1981) egg diagram can serve as a map of the territory the first-time father covers as he moves from confusion to the willful art of fathering. Conscious fathering can be seen as a journey into each region of the psyche in order to understand and eventually work through the issues, dynamics, and patterns that qualify and condition the role of the father. As each level of the unconscious is explored and brought into the field of awareness, the father has the opportunity to act on the beliefs, feelings, and behaviors that influence and determine his role at any given time. Each level is issue-specific, that is the lower unconscious contains the blueprint of the integrative role and the ideal father image that acts both as a guiding principle and as a reservoir of superconscious qualities.

In order to deal honestly and openly with the tasks and issues inherent in each region of the psyche, a father must bring the material into the field of awareness. To do this, he must be willing to confront the unconscious issues that create pain, guilt, and inertia when left unresolved. As Ferrucci (1982) reminds us in *What We May Be*, psychological friction can result through both the repression of the lower unconscious material and also the suppression of the superconscious qualities and energies that want to come into the personality but are blocked.

Looking more closely at the lower unconscious of the father's psyche, a major issue emerges. Feelings, beliefs, expectations, images, and reactions from the father's past relationship with his own father lie deep in the lower unconscious. These intrapsychic wounds, commonly referred to as "burrs under the saddle," tend to have an effect on the substance, structure, and quality of one's fathering role. Therefore it is not unusual to see prenatal fathers in psychotherapy working through issues that emerge regarding their own fathers, and confronting their fears of repeating their fathers' negative behaviors and patterns with their own children.

Another issue found in the lower unconscious is one of grief. Robert Bly deals with the process of bringing to awareness the deep grief men carry in relation to their fathers. Bly's work is important and useful for many young men today who tend to turn away from pain and conflict and then lose courage and withdraw from their relationships and families. These men are wounded by distant fathers at an early age and develop defence mechanisms to protect them from commitment and intimacy. Bly says that in order for healing to occur, the father needs to explore the depths of his psyche to find the grief—the loss and the despair—of separation. Through the experience of deep grief, the healing process begins and the man can move toward expanded awareness, new possibilities, and the release of creative energy.

Once the past and lower unconscious is explored, the journey into fathering continues with increased awareness. The middle unconscious can be explored with the focus being the integration of the traditional role of providing and protecting (learned from our fathers) with the nurturing care-giving role. The process of integrating the two is not without conflict, struggle, and effort. Often these two roles are seen as opposites that require an either/or response. However, if value can be seen in both and if what is essential and useful can be consciously differentiated from what is outdated or harmful the possibility of integration becomes easier. The new father learns how to psychologically distil the qualities and behaviors of his father that worked for him when he was a child, and add to them other sensitive, nurturing qualities to fill out a more integrative fathering role for himself. This process is facilitated by the father's courage to forfeit the comfort of being like his own father and to develop new styles and behaviors in line with his values as a nurturer.

As the integrative process continues, the influence of the higher unconscious is felt in the life of the father. New qualities become available to him in times of greatest need. It is as if one's inner father, found in the region of the higher unconscious, guides and organizes the practical fathering role and eventually becomes a source of wisdom. The implied goal of this part of the conscious fathering journey is to evoke and build the inner ideal father and to become receptive to the corresponding qualities that lead toward greater levels of responsibility, commitment, and purpose. The process of fathering helps a man develop his intuition as he opens to new ways of being a parent. Without appropriate outer models in our culture, the conscious father can first imagine and then build in substance a personalized role that is unique to him. Since energy follows thought, visualizing practical solutions to the daily balance of parenting one's children and working in the world paves the way for the outer implementation.

In a small yet significant way, conscious fathering, like conscious mothering, is a creative expression of love in action, motivated by goodwill, and working toward peaceful relations within the individual and community. Conscious fathering is a true contribution to the healing and well-being of our earth.

I have learned a great deal about myself and others from being a father. My greatest awareness is that as fathers or mothers, we are innately sensitive, caring, and basically fragile creatures. These qualities, when developed and valued, can help us feel connected, loved, and loving with our children, our partners, and ourselves.

Currently, I am no longer a long-distance father. My oldest daughter is now 3 hours rather than 3,000 miles away. However, I am still challenged to maintain a relationship over distance, and being a father challenges me to keep trying, to keep reaching out, and to trust the power of my nurturing. I am learning how to sustain relationships and in doing so have a deeper appreciation for the beauty and mystery in life.

References

Assagioli, R. (1981). *The act of will*. New York: Penguin.

Bly, R. (1986, July/August). *The Common Boundary, 4*(4).

Coleman, A. (1981). *Earth father sky father*. Englewood Cliffs, NJ: Prentice-Hall.

Ferrucci, P. (1982). *What we may be*. Los Angeles: Tarcher.

Psychosynthesis and Gay Sexuality

Michael Gigante

I have many different identifications.

I am a psychosynthesist. I was trained at San Francisco's Psychosynthesis Institute and I am now the Director of the Psychosynthesis Center of New Hampshire. Psychosynthesis is my life's work.

I am a rural New Englander. I heat my house with wood; I wear flannel, denim, chamois, and down. I cross-country ski, ice skate, and hike. I do all the things we rural New Englanders are supposed to do. I feel like a New Englander.

I am an Italian-American. I was raised in an Italian neighborhood in New York City within the context of a huge extended family. I was 14 years old before I discovered that antipasto, lasagna, and connoli were not part of the traditional American Thanksgiving dinner. I still feel like an Italian, even though I no longer live among Italians, speak the language, or have that mega-family nearby.

I have many identifications. But there is one I want to focus on now. And that identification is of being a gay man.

I am Gay in that my sexual partners and lovers are men. I was also Gay when my sexual partners and lovers were women. I was Gay before I had sexual partners. I was Gay before I was aware of sexuality. I have always been Gay. Even as a child, I could sense I was different. I could feel it. I didn't have a name for it, yet I had this identification.

My gay and lesbian clients and friends today attest to the same fact. We all knew we were Gay long before we knew what the word meant. We could *feel* it. We became identified with this feeling, and sometime between early adolescence and our mid-twenties, we discovered the terminology, and identified with that. But we were always Gay, as we were always Italian, or Jewish, or Black, or male.

Personal Testimony

My gay identity is one which I did not choose. I came into the world this way. If I chose to come in this way, I am not aware of that choice just as I am not aware of the choice to come in as an Italian in New York City in 1949. The choice I am aware of making is the choice to *express* my gay sexuality. As I choose to express my Italian identity by continuing to eat lasagna on Thanksgiving, I choose to express my gay sexuality by exchanging love, affection, and sexual union with other men. I did not choose to be

Gay, as I did not choose to be Italian. I do, however, choose to express each in ways suitable to me.

Growing up Italian in an Italian neighborhood was not difficult for me. The times I ventured out beyond the boundaries of our little ghetto, and returned home with new words swimming around my head like "WOP," "Guinnea," and "Dago," I went home to a family and to a world filled with WOPs, Guinneas, and Dagoes who comforted me, supported me, and reassured me that it was others' envy, jealousy, and the like that inspired those insults.

Growing up Gay in a world that admires macho men and dependent women is another story. Who could I turn to when the epithets were "faggot," "fairy," "Mary," or "queer"? There was no comfort, no support, and no reassurance at these times. I felt ashamed, and very much alone. For I was sure that I was the only person in the whole world for whom these insults were true. So I vowed never to let this identity be shown to the world. I had to keep it "in the closet" so no one would find out. I had to suppress and repress the hurt, the pain, the anger, and the fear of disclosure. Although I wasn't "straight," I felt I had to appear straight. David McReynolds, a long-time leader in the peace movement and a national staffer of the War Resisters League, wrote an article entitled "The Right Not To Lie" in *Fellowship* magazine (the magazine of the Fellowship of Reconciliation). He wrote:

> The problem is that society does not realize how many homosexuals there are, because we have learned the value of invisibility in order to survive. As blacks, to survive, gave the appearance of accepting Jim Crow, and as women, to survive, gave the appearance of welcoming male domination, the homosexual, to survive, learned to vanish. (1985, p. 7)

That's exactly what I did. I vanished for 15 years. The disguise worked well. No one knew, no one even suspected. And while my body was busy loving women, my emotions were off on a journey loving men. On rare occasions, before I turned 30, certain "invisible" men, with secret façades and fantasies of their own, broke through my invisibility, and we engaged in a clandestine union that brought some pleasure, but much guilt and shame to us both.

From my early teens through my twenties, I learned that hiding was my ticket for avoiding humiliation and ridicule; for avoiding the discovery of this perceived darkness that existed within the depths of my soul. I tried to change it. I made several sincere attempts to alter my sexual orientation from Gay to Straight by using a variety of techniques including behavior modification, meditation, prayer, denial, and spiritual discipline. All failed. My final prayer after more than ten years of such futile actions was: "Please help me to understand, accept, and live contentedly with this accursed affliction."

Then I met Ellen. I fell in love with Ellen immediately, and loved her in a way I had never loved any woman or man before. I shared with her, for the first time in my life, the secret of my soul. And to my shock, she loved me anyway. At least to Ellen I was still lovable despite my perceived severely handicapping condition. She supported me in my search for understanding and self-acceptance. Around the same time that I had met Ellen,

I also discovered Psychosynthesis through the *Synthesis* journals given to me by a friend. I was amazed to find a psychology that was so positive and so accepting. Within a year, I had moved to California to study Psychosynthesis at Synthesis Graduate School for the Study of Man.

San Francisco was a wonderful place to learn about Psychosynthesis and, as it turned out, to learn about my gay sexuality as well. At that time, an estimated 20 percent of the city's population was gay. One in five! What a find!

With the support of my psychosynthesis friends (all of whom were non-gay), my guide (a non-gay and sensitive man), and the gay friends and lovers I made there, I made great strides in learning to accept and love myself for who I was. Three years later, I was able to return to New England a very different person from the person I had been when I left.

And yet there is still a struggle. Vestiges of an old, negative self-image still remain, still plead with me to hide. Why, after so many years of therapy, with such skilled and supportive guides, should this be so? The excerpt quoted below from *Christopher Street* magazine sheds some light on what I am up against in my struggle for self-acceptance:

> Some twenty years of organized campaigning for the social rights of homosexual men and women have brought the merest handfuls of concessions from the merest handfuls of American localities. Many of our gains have proven fragile and easily reversed. There is still no nationwide appreciation for the gay community, nor sympathy for it, nor even much tolerance toward it. Gays still have absolutely no legal protection from discrimination outside 15 counties and 8 of the 50 states. Astonishingly, open homosexuals across our nation still have no right to work or shelter. Their children may be taken from them. They still receive no protection from public ridicule, severe harassment, and humiliation. Of the nation's major outgroups, homosexuals are still the blackest untouchables. (Kirk, p. 33)

Gay as the Modern Nigger

Here are some statistics from the American Civil Liberties Union regarding the civil rights of gay people in the United States. (Unless otherwise indicated, the information can be found in Boggan, 1983.)

• At the time of this writing, 28 states and the District of Columbia still have laws on the books explicitly illegalizing homosexual behavior between consenting adults. Only 22 states have decriminalized private, consensual adult homosexual acts. And out of these, only a handful ensure gay people equal opportunity under the law.

• In most situations, private employers may lawfully discriminate against employees solely on the basis of sexual preference. Though federal legislation now protects women, racial minorities, and most other groups, Gays are exempt from this protection.

• Gay people have been denied, or have had revoked, occupational licenses (and thus have been denied the right to practise their occupation) on the grounds that their "sexual orientation or activities are indicative of a degenerate moral character." It is interesting to note that if William Shakespeare,

Michelangelo, Tchaikovsky, or Tennessee Williams were alive today, they would not be permitted to teach English, art, music, or drama, respectively, in most American public schools (Kirk, p. 41).

● Since the late 1940s, authorities in the federal government have adhered to policies excluding Gays from important jobs in the federal government by denying them security clearances.

● Approximately 1,700 people are forced to leave employment in the American military each year because of their homosexual orientation. Although the discrimination against Gays in the armed forces is blatant and inexcusable, one can't help but fantasize about the possibilities for peace should all American men suddenly turn Gay!

● Known gay men and women are routinely denied visas or entrance into the United States. This practice was upheld by the Supreme Court in 1967. Interestingly, gay people are also denied visas and immigration into many other countries from the U.S. So, we can't get in, and we can't get out. And, if a gay person enters the U.S. unknown, he or she can later be deported by the Department of Immigration and Naturalization on the grounds of "homosexual conduct." An individual can be denied American citizenship on these same grounds.

● Several states, including California and more recently Oklahoma, have attempted to enact laws authorizing immediate dismissal of any school teachers involved in "private homosexual activity." Fortunately, both bills were defeated.

● Gay people may legally be denied the rental of an apartment or the purchase of a house solely on the basis of their sexual orientation everywhere in the U.S. except in California, Wisconsin, and a few municipalities. Civil Rights Acts have been passed in 1866, 1870, and 1964 prohibiting housing discrimination on the basis of race, color, religion, national origin, or sex. Since 1975, Congress has had a bill before it that would extend equal rights in housing to gay people as well, but has so far failed to act on this bill. And passage in the near future seems slim.

● Gay people may be denied mortgages on the basis of sexual orientation alone, and are often ineligible for public housing as well, because preference is usually given to traditional family units.

● No state now recognizes gay marriages. Thus, benefits, rights, and privileges of people who commit themselves to such relationships are denied to gay people, including advantages in paying income, gift and estate taxes; advantages in inheritance; advantages in ownership of property and businesses; etc.

● Custody and visitation rights may be denied to a gay parent after a divorce solely on the basis of his or her sexual orientation.

● Adoption and foster care of children by gay adults has recently become outlawed in several states, and a similar bill has just been passed in my home state of New Hampshire. In Massachusetts, a child was recently removed from his home because the foster parents were both gay men. (I wonder if anyone considered the wishes of that child, or of the needs of the many children currently awaiting good homes, when this type of legislation was being acted upon.)

● "In New York City, the Catholic Church and the Salvation Army receive public funds for some of their programs and are required by law to hire without regard for race, creed, or color. When Mayor Koch tried to extend these civil rights to homosexuals by executive order, Cardinal O'Connor went into court, with support from the Salvation Army and the Orthodox Jews, protesting that being forced to hire homosexuals violated deep Catholic beliefs. Hiring atheists was one thing—but not Gays! Temporarily, the Cardinal has won. Until the law is changed he will not be hiring homosexuals" (McReynolds, 1985, p. 7). When I first read of this action, I wrote a letter to the local chapter of the Salvation Army in response to their annual fund drive, to which I had been contributing previously. I expressed my indignation over their action, and informed them that I would no longer contribute money to their organization. I never received a response, though appeals for money still come addressed to me at my home.

● "In Boston, the *Christian Science Monitor* won the right in court to fire a staff member who was a lesbian and had refused to undergo a church-ordered 'healing'" (McReynolds, 1985, p. 7).

● "In Providence, Rhode Island, Bishop Louis Gelineau, in urging defeat of a bill guaranteeing homosexuals the right to equal treatment in employment, housing, and security credit, said that while he deplored the brutal beatings to which homosexuals are often subject, the fact remained that '. . . homosexual acts are contrary to God's command and contrary to his purpose in creating sex. To give support to this proposed legislation may easily be interpreted as supporting the homosexual lifestyle'" (McReynolds, 1985 p. 7).

● In the spring of 1983, while flipping through the television stations of my TV set, I stopped long enough at one commercial station to hear a talk between several Fundamentalist "Christian" ministers about the "homosexual problem." They advocated that we should "smite dead" all of the homosexuals of this country.

● When "Houston's mayor had added protection of gay government employees to the city's anti-discrimination ordinance, angry opponents mounted a public referendum in January 1985 that forced withdrawal of such protection by a stunning vote margin of four to one" (Kirk, p. 36). Similarly, gay rights bills have been repealed in Miami, Eugene, Wichita, and St. Paul.

● And across America, public opinion polls show overwhelming opposition to state support for gay rights *of any kind* (Kirk, p. 34).

And the list of condoned acts of bigotry and prejudice by government and by private and religious bodies goes on and on. These acts were created by the attitudes and values of the general public, and are then communicated to gay people growing up within the culture. There is no other group left in the United States today that is treated with such flagrant disrespect.

Can you imagine what all this accepted bigotry does to the self-esteem of the gay person growing up under its influence? Imagine what the anti-gay attitudes, epithets, and violence do to the self-image of one who, through no choice of his or her own, identifies with being Gay. If you take this little imagery exercise to its extreme, you may find yourself in a place where I have been, and where so many of my gay and lesbian clients are when they first consult me: in the depths of self-hatred.

Gay Self-Hatred

This is not to say that all gay people have experienced the depths of self-hatred, nor that all self-hatred is motivated by being Gay. However, there is a pattern running through the experience of my gay clients, friends, and acquaintances which is too strong to deny or gloss over. It is the experience of feeling like society's trash, like a less than human subspecies; the experience of feeling feared and hated by humanity and damned by God; the experience of realizing that by the very nature of one's identity one can be turned out of housing, refused employment, fired from a job, disowned by one's family, and turned away from church.

First, I want to emphasize that my gay and lesbian clients who experience this self-hatred feel that they have been Gay all their lives, that they did not have a choice in deciding their orientation. Second, it is important to stress that although life is difficult for them, not one, when pressed for a decision, wants to change his or her orientation. (Admittedly, I have neither the desire nor the capability to change a client's sexual orientation.) And third, the gay person willing to explore beneath the self-hatred often finds a message of purpose, of goodness, and of perfection in the very fact of Gayness. From images of the Wise Old Being, from Jesus, from the sun, comes the message of needing to be both a student and a teacher, of needing to *learn* some important lessons and needing to *teach* some important lessons by virtue of being a gay person in an ostracizing society. Many sense that their gay sexuality is a choice of the incarnating soul (or some other higher being) for specific purposes.

Each year, 10 to 15 percent of my clients are gay or lesbians and present their issues (and the underlying self-hatred) often with great pain. Although each individual is unique, there are several scenarios common to these clients:

1. The Need for Self-Love—The gay man or woman has reached a point in life where he or she is tired of hiding, and feels the need for self-love despite what he or she has learned to be "true" about gayness. Often these folks have worked for years trying to change it, cover it up, deny it, or overcompensate for it. Now, often with exasperation and pain, they are willing to try accepting it.

Much like myself many years before, these people are filled with guilt, shame, and self-disgust when entering therapy. They often feel backed into a corner: they can't change who they are, and yet they're afraid of accepting and giving expression to who they are. Psychosynthesis, by being so accepting and non-judgmental, allows acceptance to form gradually and develop within the gay client. This is a process which takes time. By allowing clients to experience fully the feelings and beliefs around the issue, and by holding them with respect, Psychosynthesis enables them to move toward the self-acceptance and self-love so badly needed in their lives.

2. Vacillation Between "Coming Out" and "Staying Hidden"—Married men or women feel that they are no longer willing to suppress their gay identity, or are no longer able to maintain the charade. (Some have been married longer than 20 years before their initial session with me.) Often believing that a steady, committed, heterosexual relationship would "fix it," they had gotten married only to discover that frustration and self-hatred build over the years rather than diminish. Discovering another gay person in a similar predicament, these folks frequently find themselves with a gay lover as well as a heterosexual spouse: "Something dead, or dormant in me came alive when I met [my lover], and now I don't know what to do!" Guilt, fear of the loss of their spouse and children, and fear of society's rejection bring these individuals into crisis, and then into therapy.

These people seem to need a period of vacillation (which could go on for anywhere from a few weeks to years) between "knowing" they need to "come out" to their families, and "knowing" they need to stay hidden. From session to session, they may bounce back and forth between the two. They will commonly drop out of therapy for a period of time. This period of vacillation seems to function as a time for the personality to re-organize itself, where changing images of the self, of the world, or of God are explored and experimented with. This exploration takes place naturally and unconsciously. Psychosynthesis guidance can bring it to consciousness, thus facilitating the process.

3. Being Thrust Out of the Closet—An intense panic reaction, most usually in gay men, occurs when a clandestine, supposedly anonymous sexual encounter at a rest area, bath house, bar, or public toilet threatens to "thrust open the closet door," exposing the gay man's sexual pursuits and orientation in public. This can happen by being "seen" in one of these areas by a colleague, friend, or neighbor; by being arrested by an undercover police officer; or by being blackmailed (rare). It is common for gay men who are still in the closet to frequent special gathering places for anonymous sex as the only outlet available to them. Generally speaking, as the client comes to accept his sexuality more fully, he can enjoy more fulfilling sexual relationships, and the need to frequent these areas begins to wane.

Being thrust out of the closet can be an excruciating experience, frequently accompanied by anxiety, fear, anger, panic, depression, and feelings of suicide. These individuals may be dealing with legal battles, loss of job, loss of family, loss of friends, in addition to the unexpected and unwanted experience of facing their gay identity. They often feel lost, overwhelmed, and painfully alone. Psychosynthesis can help by allowing these individuals to feel fully each emotion as it arises, and then to find that place of me-ness, that central identity (the "I"), which transcends the judgments and pre-judices of society.

4. Religious Conflict—Conflict increases, often to a "breaking point," in a gay person between his or her homosexual urges and his or her religious beliefs. Often these people will seek the counsel of a priest or minister and have biblical scripture quoted to them, reinforcing the message they've received all their lives anyway: "You're bad!" As a therapist, I've been told, "He [the minister] told me I should give myself to Jesus, and turn away from Satan, and Jesus will change me. Well I tried that—for years—and it didn't work!" The guilt, the shame, the self-blame, the anger, and the pain seem greatest in individuals who espouse a religious belief system (usually fundamentalist) that condemns their sexuality. They are truly tormented because on a deep level they know who they are (i.e., Gay) and believe, on some level, that God rejects them for it. They can hide from family, friends, employers, and society—but they know they cannot hide from God and from the eternal damnation awaiting them. Ultimately, these people need to hear from a "higher" source (e.g., Jesus) who, most often, can provide the necessary love and peace.

Psychosynthesis can help the gay client at this point. By experiencing and moving through their difficult emotions, they can find the "Jesus" within who is non-judgmental, loving, and totally accepting of their urges. From this often arises the experience of "I am good" which over time grows stronger than the belief of "I am bad."

5. AIDS Anxiety—Lately "AIDS Anxiety" is striking fear in the hearts of gay men. The fear of getting AIDS is very real, and thus needs to be respected and addressed. This is best done through education. AIDS is a disease of "what one does," and not of "who one is." Its spread has been a function of certain *practices*, not a function of *identity*. Changing sexual behaviors and adopting safer sexual practices is the best antidote to AIDS Anxiety. Problems arise, however, when the gay man confuses sexuality with intimacy. One can achieve deep intimacy and sexual union with another human being without engaging in sexual practices that are potentially dangerous. As a guide, I try to help the client make this distinction clear. Specific sexual practices must change, but sexual expression and intimacy need not be affected, and can even be enhanced as a result of working through this anxiety.

Having accepted the anxiety as valid, the individual's typical next step is to find ways of preventing fear from interfering with the enjoyment of sexuality. Education in safer sexual practices often leads to increased communication between sexual partners, a decision to work on a monogamous relationship, a decision to spend time deepening friendships in place of spending time in clandestine unions, and increased awareness of one's own sensuality which must be appreciated in new ways since the old ways have become dangerous and thus fear evoking.

6. Self as Sexual Object—I have seen gay clients, again usually men, who have little or no appreciation for themselves other than as sexual objects. As they age, their self-esteem crashes along with the waning of their perceived sexual attractiveness. These men obviously need to look a little deeper into their souls for their sense of self-appreciation.

Subpersonality work is very useful here. The subpersonality that is expressed through physical attractiveness has received so much attention over the years that other subpersonalities have been ignored (e.g., subpersonalities that express themselves through artistic creation, intellectual inquiry, education, etc.). Through the subpersonality work of Psychosynthesis, these subpersonalities can be recognized, developed, and harmonized, thus shifting the individual's self-image from his physical being to other parts of himself, thus elevating self-esteem.

7. Creating Role Models—And, finally, there are no real role models because most of our gay predecessors and forefathers were closeted. So, as more and more of us "come out," we are in the process of creating a more visible and viable subculture. However, this process causes much confusion, regrets over past decisions, and pain over perceived failures. It also leads to negative reactions from a non-gay and hostile society. There is no answer to this aspect of the struggle other than to pick ourselves up, brush ourselves off, and try again. We can do this by supporting visibility, solidarity, brother/sisterhood, and mutual respect.

At the same time, there are role models emerging throughout the culture for gay people to emulate. These models are being developed by gay individuals who have felt deeply the pain of exposure, the anger of rejection, and the fear of vulnerability and have come to realize that this pain, this anger, and this fear are far less debilitating than the constriction, the self-deprecation, the incessant insecurity, and the continuous frustration of maintaining the façade and remaining closeted. They have recognized that this gay orientation is a part of who they are, and is one, and only one, aspect of their identity. They are *not* gay physicians, gay artists, gay construction workers, gay therapists; they are physicians, artists, construction workers, and therapists who also happen to be Gay. They don't make a point of advertising themselves as Gay, just as they don't make a point of advertising themselves as Polish, or male, or physically handicapped. But they do not hide from their gayness, just as they do not hide from their Polishness, maleness, or handicapping condition. They accept themselves for who they are, and respect their various identities, including their sexual orientation.

They may join with another in a visible monogamous relationship, thus emulating the "marriages" of the non-gay world. Or they may choose to maintain this part of their lives in an atmosphere of exploration and experimentation. Either way, they are examining the rightness of a lifestyle that suits them, accepting and respecting who they are, regardless of who they believe society says they should be.

Achieving Self-Acceptance

To get to this level of self-acceptance is not easy given the conditions of modern society. It often requires much support: support from family, friends, therapists, a gay community, or a non-gay but understanding and supportive network of people. These support systems are crucial. Once in place, however, the journey is much less tedious, much more hopeful, and, most important, possible in a way that has not yet been possible in modern Western culture.

There are many factors affecting the gay individual's self-esteem and hence ability to achieve self-respect and self-acceptance. One main factor is society's willingness to accept the gay individual and to drop the barriers that separate it from the gay subculture. This has been difficult for society to do primarily because as a culture we have been almost totally invisible. This invisibility has caused myths, stereotypes, and misconceptions to flourish; and the information to counter these misconceptions has not been readily available. The resulting prejudices have allowed gay people to become the "bogey man" lodging in the bedroom closet of a culture that has repressed its sexuality and fears its own basic impulses. These fears and repressed energies are projected onto that monster in the closet. Only by thrusting open the closet door and exposing the dark, ominous shadow for what it is will those misconceptions, myths, and prejudices subside.

When I first entered psychosynthesis therapy while living in San Francisco, I can remember feeling excruciatingly pained at the very idea of even mentioning to my guide that I was Gay. I was filled with disgust and hatred for this part of myself. But the psychosynthetic process, loving and gentle as it is, encouraged me to enter the depths of this self-hatred—to experience, really and fully, the pain of it; to explore and learn to express and cherish other parts of myself that were being overshadowed by this perceived darkness; to find the Wise Old Being, the Light within, the power and love existing in my own superconscious. It was this process, slow and agonizing at times, light and joyful at others, that allowed me to come to accept and to love myself for who I was—not just *despite* my gay sexuality, but also *because* of it. And it was through this process that I have been allowed the freedom to increase gradually my visibility.

Gays and Psychosynthesis

I often wonder as I look around the psychosynthesis community why there isn't a proportionately greater number of gay and lesbian psychosynthesists. When I look at the general population, I see approximately 10 percent who are Gay; when I look at the community of practising therapists, I see 10 percent who are Gay; when I look at the physicians, lawyers, businesspersons, laborers in my midst, I see approximately 10 percent who are Gay. Ten to fifteen percent of my clients are Gay. Yet when I look to the psychosynthesis community I see only myself. I have only once had face-to-face contact with another gay psychosynthesist. Why is that? Might there be something in the attitudes and beliefs, perhaps some unconscious prejudice or fear, that has successfully kept the proportion of Gays and Lesbians low? Perhaps. I'm not sure.

I do know that personally I have never felt any direct or indirect expression of bigotry from any psychosynthesist I have yet met. But I have also seen a tremendous importance placed on marriage and family. When entering a marriage or having a child, people receive a kind of support and adulation that I will never receive given the choices I have made regarding my orientation. So, in this way, I have felt excluded—perhaps even a little ostracized. And perhaps this is exclusively my issue.

It appears evident to me that much of the bigotry against Gays stems from a concept held by the general public that gay men (in particular) represent unbridled sexual expressiveness and uncontrollable sexual desire. Perhaps this stereotype stems from the general public's fear of its own sexuality, and its own life of the impulses—a fear that is projected onto Gays:

> Homosexuality is vulgar to the mainstream for still another reason. Although they've loosened up considerably in recent years, Americans retain a prissy Victorianism about the naughtiness of sex. And to most heterosexuals, homosexuality is all about sex and nothing but; *not* love or romance. It is about wanton promiscuity, not fidelity and bonding. It cannot lead to marriage and family, so it is dirty and profane. And to top things off, gay sex reveals its own sinfulness because it is furtive. (Kirk, p. 36)

Now, quite noticeably absent from psychosynthesis literature is research on sexuality—any sexuality. We write about health, community, world affairs, therapeutic process, self-care, religion, organizational development, and education. Yet we do not write about sex. Are we all celibate? Have we all transcended our sexuality? Have we all successfully moved beyond our hang-ups and difficulties of the sexual arena? Why aren't we thinking, studying, writing, and sharing about sex?

Maybe it's because as a community we too have a dis-ease with our instinctual life. Maybe we too feel the stresses around our sexual impulses. And maybe it's because of these difficulties that we haven't produced any contribution to the sexual literature. And maybe this too is why Gays haven't been flocking into psychosynthesis training programs at a rate that reflects their numbers in the population. Gay people have become so sensitized to the sexual hang-ups of our culture—hang-ups that become convoluted and express themselves as bigotry, oppression, and violence. Maybe they see that sexuality is unchartered territory within Psychosynthesis, and stay away. It's something to consider.

Perhaps we psychosynthesists have prematurely attempted to transcend our sexuality. Perhaps by placing so much emphasis on elevating our sexual energies into "higher" centres, we have ignored the creative potential, the playfulness, and the joy that are there for us when sexual energy is expressed naturally. I believe that as a community we have much to learn by exploring this area further. Those of us who work with clients are often faced with their sexual issues and concerns. We need to share this work with each other—how it affects us as therapists and, more personally, as sexual beings. We need to come to a better understanding of sexual energy—a powerful force in each of us—and the myriad of ways this energy expresses itself in our lives. Perhaps we've been hiding from our sexuality, and perhaps that needs to change.

Conclusion

Since I began writing this article, I have been asked by many friends, both gay and non-gay, "Why?" "What do you hope to accomplish by doing this?" I feel that there have been several reasons. First, it has felt cleansing to clarify my thoughts and to express my feelings. And maybe this has been my main purpose. And second, I felt that I wanted to make a statement for myself to gay people, to non-gay people, and to the psychosynthesis community.

To the Gay Community—There are fears on both sides of the line that separates the gay community from mainstream society. There are the very real fears of Gays regarding the loss of jobs, of friends, of family, and of housing; fears of ostracism, of humiliation, and of violence. But there are also very real fears on the other side. We represent the destruction, real or imagined, of many things society holds dear: continuation of the family and propagation of children, suppression of the impulses and of instinctual life, predictable order and organization, clearly defined sex role behavioral patterns, and conformity.

In our struggle for the rights, privileges, and most of all the respect we deserve as members of this human family, we need to recognize, acknowledge, and respect the fears existing on the other side of the line. Only through respect will the line vanish. We can succumb to the bigotry, hatred, fear, and intolerance that surround us, or we can develop our self-love, self-respect, and pride, thus rendering fear of homosexuality and of gay people powerless. We can do this by increasing our visibility and our solidarity in the face of homophobia. By dealing with each other with respect, we can affect the homophobic attitudes themselves.

To the Non-Gay World—Homophobia affects and damages everyone, both gay and non-gay. It creates artificial boundaries between people; it sets up walls that prevent one from seeing the worth, value, and humanity of another; it prevents or destroys one's capacity to love. Homophobia, as with any form of chauvinism, also creates objects for our projections. It allows us to disown our issues, and then project them onto others—in this case, gay people. This robs us of our ability to acknowledge, accept, and subsequently deal with our "shadows," thus interfering with our potential for growth.

To the Psychosynthesis Community—Gay people do exist, and we exist in vast numbers worldwide. *Because* of our unique experience as outcasts in a homophobic and heterosexist world, we can contribute much to the evolution of Psychosynthesis. We have a unique perspective, and this perspective needs to be shared. But first, we must attract gay people into our community. To do so may require a more honest and deeper exploration of our own sexuality and, perhaps, of our prejudices as well. Given that approximately 10 percent of the population are coming in with this orientation, it seems safe to assume that 10 percent of the babies from our current psychosynthesis baby boom are also coming in Gay. We can help them greatly by engaging in these kinds of explorations.

So as I challenge the gay community to become more visible and to explore the self-love that exists naturally within each individual, and as I challenge the non-gay world to let go of its projections, its hate, and its fear, I also challenge the psychosynthesis community to explore its dis-ease around its instinctual life and to bring its sexuality out of the closet. It is only through honest exploration that we will come to understand the powerful energy within each of us and then be able to help ourselves and others toward greater sexual fulfillment.

Finally I want to say that I value my sexuality: not just to channel energy into "higher" forms of expression, but also as an experience in and of itself.

It is an experience of play, of deep communion and communication, of bonding, of sensuality, of stress management, of cathartic release, of recreation, and of joy. And beyond this, I value my *gay* sexuality: through the kinds of struggles that I have waged, it has taught me compassion, tolerance, and self-respect and a definition of man-ness that fits who I am, not who society thinks I'm supposed to be.

In response to the TV evangelist who admonished, "Don't blame God for making you gay," I say, "That's right. I don't want to *blame* God for making us Gay, I want us to *thank* God for making us Gay."

References

Boggan, Haft, Rupp, & Stoddard. (1983). *The rights of gay people: An American Civil Liberties Handbook*. New York: Bantam.

Kirk, M. K., & Pill, E. Waging peace. *Christopher Street*, **95**.

McReynolds, D. (1985, December). The right not to lie. *Fellowship*, **51**(2).

Toward Our Heroic Self: New Images of Women

Cherie Martin Franklin

When I was very small, I kept a little box filled with a collection of what to me were precious things—pale yellow canary feathers, translucent seashells, pieces of quartz. Still today, I find myself amassing a pile of "little things" in one corner of my desk—a sanddollar, peacock and bluejay feathers, smooth pebbles, a slice of agate—things of natural beauty that strike a chord in me, close to the core of who I am.

As a child, my collection was not something I talked about, shared with anyone, or really let myself value—it was just something I quietly kept. In recent years, however, I have noticed that if I follow the call of the things that draw me, they lead me closer to something essential and real in myself; like the bread crumbs Hansel and Gretel dropped on the path, they show the way home.

Our culture tends to gobble these things up. It invites us *not* to listen to our heart's song, or let our natural inclinations lead us, trust ourselves, or own our real power, especially our power as women.

But the need for that in us which is good and strong and can be trusted is very much evident in our world today. The earth is teetering on the edge of technological overload, ecological imbalance, social disease, and nuclear disaster. Many people spend ten hours a day or more away from their homes and their children doing things they don't enjoy or want to do. Countries are at war, marriages don't last, and teenagers are committing suicide. We live in a world where each sunrise sees the corpses of 50,000 starved children (Steindl-Rast, 1985, p. 95).

Recently, in my neighborhood, a young woman dressed in combat boots and army fatigues walked into the local shopping mall at 4:00 on a weekday afternoon and gunned down a 2-year-old boy and an elderly man and shot eight other people. It is disturbing enough to hear every night on the evening news about men murdering men, abducting children, and raping women, but when a *woman* opens fire on innocent strangers in an all-American shopping mall for no apparent reason—what is going on? A woman has the capacity to give birth and nourish life from her own body. How far from her own source can she be to take a human life? How out of balance is a culture in which this can happen?

Many women in our society are depressed and anxious because their lives are not turning out as they expected them to. Some experience this so deeply that they begin to doubt their own sanity or contemplate suicide. I have heard many women say they feel like "strangers in a strange land"; that what they find inside themselves doesn't fit with what everyone around them is saying and doing. We live in exile from our inner subjective experience. And our culture perpetuates this alienation.

The stories and role models that condition us as women feel inauthentic—the prince and the "happily ever after" never seem to arrive. Our literature is filled with stories about men, but offers very few about women and what they feel and think and how they relate to and value themselves and each other. The stories are about how they attract and fight over men, compete with each other, devalue themselves. If the hero has 1,000 faces, the heroine has less than a dozen.

That is why it seems so important that we are thinking anew what it means to be a woman. We are in fact being called to this task both individually and collectively—called to revalue and reclaim that which is natural, beautiful, and powerful in ourselves as life givers and life protectors. The world needs feminine energy to get back in balance. In Lynn Andrews' words, "Both men and women must re-educate their femaleness. It is the woman in all of us that needs to be healed and reborn" (1984, p. 3).

Old Images of Women

The stories and traditions of our Western culture are worth naming because they shape our actions and expectations of ourselves. Who did we grow up with?

There is Sleeping Beauty, waiting passively for her expected other who will make her life meaningful and fulfilling, waiting for the kiss that will awaken her. There is Snow White, the good and passive victim of fate and her wicked stepmother. There is Goldilocks, looking for her right place in the family, but not finding it. There is Cinderella, waiting to be rescued from her chores by the prince with whom she will live happily ever after.

The messages of these stories are be passive, be the desirable object, be romantically vulnerable and wait, live for others, look outside for approval and direction. In our wedding rituals we play out these same themes. In the traditional wedding, the bride is hidden from the groom beforehand. She is *given* away by her father. The ring is *placed* on her finger. She is carried over the doorstep and then whisked off to some secret honeymoon spot. Her participation is, again, passive. In our culture, woman "sees herself as someone that things will happen to, not as one who will make them happen. She has no conception of 'autonomy' as a life-goal; she seeks only the state of 'belonging'" (Kolbenchlag, 1979, p. 15).

On the other hand, there are the negative myths and images of Eve, temptress of Adam, of Pandora, keeper of the box of all the evils in the world, and of the wicked, scheming witches of the fairytales. In these stories, whatever power women do have is portrayed as dark and dangerous, the seducer of men.

We live in a society that thinks dualistically—men/women, white/black, light/dark, spirit/matter, masculine/feminine, good/bad. And women are identified in this schema primarily with the dark, the weak, the subordinate, with everything separate from the good, the real, the intrinsically meaningful. It is subtly agreed that men's work is more important than women's work—constructing buildings, making things happen in the world, and creating corporations are more important than taking care of children, cooking food, tending gardens. Spirit is made more important than matter. Man is more important than and entitled to sovereignty over animals and the earth. Thinking is better than feeling, the mental is valued over the physical. The answers are assumed to be outside ourselves or in the masculine rational mind rather than inside ourselves in our capacity for intuitive, non-linear knowing. At the same time, the qualities that are valued in men are seen in women as threatening—like assertiveness, boldness, and (God forbid!) loud forceful action.

What do we learn growing up female in such a world? We learn to be soft and secondary; to be beautiful, not with our *natural* beauty, but with corrections from the outside such as make-up that hides our faces and clothes that render us useless (like high heels). What do we learn about our bodies? TV advertisements for health spas entice us to train our bodies, not for joy or health or sense of purpose, but in order to catch men on the beach in the summer. We are conditioned to think of ourselves as worthless, and we learn to let someone else make decisions for us. We learn to give our power away by the fistfuls.

So many women I see in my practice feel compelled to be busy all the time proving their goodness or worth. One reports that she cannot go shopping for herself without buying something for her children, husband, or mother first. And if she does buy something for herself, it must be cheap or on sale. Another woman is a slave to her list of tasks, and as soon as it is accomplished she is busy making a new list of things to be washed, fixed, bought, transported, or refinished. The list, of course, rarely includes anything self-nurturing, self-generated, or self-affirming.

We are always trying to fix ourselves to be more loving or more attentive to others, and to push our own feelings even further into the background. We end up having no idea what we ourselves want or need. When asked where we'd like to go to eat we say, "Wherever you want" or "I don't care." We acquiesce. We have acquired the "habit of deference."

John Enright uses the analogy of the trained falcon to illustrate living under the illusion of powerlessness. The falcon, after making a strike, always returns its prey to the master and then gratefully accepts a small strip of flesh from the kill as a reward. The bird has been trained to be dependent, to the point that it has forgotten its freedom and its ability to take care of itself. The source of food has come to be associated only with the master. When we become dependent, we forget that we are our own source.

> Think for a moment of the images of women that you grew up with, the messages you heard about women, what you learned about power from your mother. What image of self—the person others expected you to be—did you develop in response?

In psychosynthesis terms, this is the subpersonality we developed and identified with as a way of gaining approval and love. And in order to have the freedom to make choices about or change the beliefs, habits, and behavior of this persona, we must first be able to see it, name it, and disidentify from it. If we can see and name the images that have shaped us, we can see that they are not all of who we are.

But what happens to all the suffocated talents and capacities that don't fit with this self-image? They often find their way to the surface in such excesses as hyperactivity, overworking, overcleaning the house, shopping, being superorganized, overeating, depression, insomnia, and alcoholism. Many women today are haunted by fears of being left alone, or of doing new things. Some escape into sleep and soap operas, living a comatose, Barbie-doll life, cut off from the "real" world. As Jane Fonda put it when she was doing the movie *Barbarella*, her life was "like pasteurized cheese."

Awakening

1. **Feeling Our Pain**—The first step out of the illusion is to feel our real pain. We must abolish the false stories we've told ourselves to cover it up. We must peek out from behind the mask of who we're trying to be and face what else has been kept in exile in ourselves and in the world.

I remember a time in my own life when I couldn't relate to the evening news. I would stare at the television screen and not really see the images. All I would see was a blur of snow. One day I realized this was happening and I broke through to the horror of what was coming at me every night over the kitchen counter. I wrote this about it: "I am part of the earth. / My baby is every mother's child. / We really are one family on one planet with one Life. / Anything that happens around the globe is part of me . . . I am beginning . . . to feel it in the marrow of these bones . . . / What I didn't have words for or what They told me wasn't my concern has cracked . . . / And I am flooded with the truth—there's so much pain in the world, and it doesn't belong to "Them" anymore." Margaret Atwood describes this waking-up process in a line, "Feeling was beginning to seep back into me, I tingled like a foot that's been asleep" (cited in Christ, 1980, p. 46).

This awakening is the beginning of real responsibility. We don't *take* responsibility, we grow response-able, that is, we re-open our senses to see and feel and respond to needs within ourselves and in our world. We break out of the confines of a limiting self-concept tailored to please others, and begin to get in touch with and listen to our own *inner authority*. And we begin to learn what it is we value enough and believe in enough to do something about.

2. **Recognizing the Self-Hater**—What gets in the way of our doing this naturally and effortlessly?—that voice we think is so particular to us, that mocking, self-deprecating critic, the one telling us beforehand, "You can't do that, you're going to screw up, you better hold back, you better hide, you better stay safe." And after the fact, "There you go again, see what you did? I told you not to try. You better not risk exposing yourself again or they'll find out you're a fake." Sound familiar? I call this the self-hater. The women I work with all find it in their way at some point. Each has her own name for it—"my demon," "the monkey on my back," "the blob," "Mr. Right," "the taskmaster," "the judge," "the voices," "the steel trap." Whatever its name, it is controlling, seems overwhelming in its power, and is often masculine.

How can you find out what you really need and want and believe when there is constant noise inside your head? As long as the running commentary is allowed to go on unchecked, everything that hints of confirming the same message becomes fuel for the self-hater's fire. The genuine mistakes we make or the constructive feedback we receive from the world are not perceived as learning experiences but as tangible proof that the self-hating voice is right. This leads to an insidious, undetected kind of psychic lynching.

3. Breaking Through—What can we do about the self-hater? Is this who we are? A limited self and an all-powerful, demeaning controller? What is the path leading deeper to something real, essential, and authentic?

The breakthrough happens in all of us, often spontaneously. But we need to be awake to it, to witness it, to recognize the authentic experience when it appears, to take hold of it long enough to *name* it and claim it as our own. Often it comes when our pain gets bad enough and there is nothing we can do but let go. And then we find that behind that awful dark void we expect at the bottom lies not the nothingness we've feared but a solid bedrock, a core, a self: our original starting point.

Such an experience can come through crisis, illness, or a death (a time when many people disidentify spontaneously from a major subpersonality and have direct access to their will). When I was young, I saw my mother have this experience. My little brother and sister were chasing each other around the neighbor's pool, and my brother ran into the door of the bath-house and put his whole arm through the glass window, ripping it open from elbow to armpit. He and my sister came running hysterically down the hill to my mother. When she saw what had happened, there was an instant of shock on her face, and, then, before our eyes, this gentle, meek, supportive woman, so good at putting herself last, grew large, steady, and calm. Her presence reached out to embrace us, our panic, the trauma, my brother's pain. She took him inside, wrapped a dishtowel firmly around his arm, called the ambulance, held him quietly in her arms, and spoke to us in low reassuring tones that instantly diffused our fear.

It was the most powerful and immediate transformation I have ever seen in a person. When her child was in danger, she broke through her normal level of functioning and her lightweight, in-the-background way of being to a solid, wise presence that could hold and support whatever happened. It was like the layers of her learned way of thinking of herself and acting in the world—as wife and mother and culturally acceptable female—fell away revealing a powerful, capable woman whom we hardly ever saw.

> Take a moment to remember an experience that demanded more from you than you thought you had, a time when you felt stretched beyond your limits and found the resources you needed to get through. What fears or imagined limits in yourself did you go beyond? What strength or quality did that experience call forth in you? How would your life be different if you lived from that more of the time?

Sometimes we break through to our deeper self through transcendent or peak experiences in which, for a moment, our personal awareness expands and we experience our (transpersonal) connectedness to the larger whole.

This can happen when lying on the ground looking up at the stars on a clear night, or watching the waves for hours on end and realizing that the ocean is always there, or connecting with a wild animal, in silence, eye-to-eye. These are moments of what Brother David Steindl-Rast (1984) calls "limitless belonging, moments of universal communion . . . our own mystic moments." At such times, we are in touch with the wisdom in it all, the way all things seem to have their right place in a larger plan, just as we have our right place, our purpose, our unique and particular reason for being.

What happens to these experiences? As powerful as they are, how can they just drop into the background of our everyday comings and goings and be forgotten? Although at the time we think we will never forget, invariably we do. Our path is one of *remembering* what it all means, who we really are, and why we're here, *and then forgetting* again. Brother David says, "What counts is not the frequency or intensity of mystic experiences, but the influence we allow them to have on our life" (Steindl-Rast, 1984).

Not remembering our deeper awarenesses is a problem common to all human beings, but especially to women because we have so few stories, models, or guides to remind us of what we know.

4. Reclaiming Our Own Authority: The Inner Warrior—Before we can give expression to what is authentic and powerful in ourselves, we must honor it enough to claim and protect it. We must come to the realization that there is something in ourselves that is intrinsically valuable and worth speaking out for, taking a stand on, and, if necessary, worth fighting for.

We have grown up valuing, nurturing, and protecting everything but ourselves. As women, we have a wonderful "hurt no one" ethic. The only problem is that it does not include us! So we become the dutiful person, the false persona, busy dismantling rather than creating a conscious sense of self, and in the process *overlooking* our own inner gift waiting to be delivered. Madonna Kolbenchlag says, "Sin is not the revolt against authority or pride, but the failure to fight against injustice, the desertion of the creative human task" (1979, p. 181).

Turning the tide takes incredible individual courage. It takes, as Margaret Atwood says, "this above all, to refuse to be a victim. To give up the belief that I am powerless" (cited in Christ, 1980, p. 49). When we fail to say "no" when we need to, or set limits that are in line with our real values, we play the part of the victim, we desert our "creative human task." But, as Angie Arrien (1984) points out, behind every victim lies an Inner Warrior—the one who is willing to take a stand against the self-hater, willing to hold fast to her truth in the face of fear, willing to pick up her sword to protect life.

In the image of *woman* as warrior, the traditional meaning of the term as referring to one carrying guns, dropping bombs, and destroying life is transformed. For how can a woman, who is, by definition, life giving and life sustaining, kill another human being? Stand firm, yes; fight for justice and human decency, yes; but degrade or take human life, no.

The most original meaning of the word *warrior* is to honor and respect oneself in order to honor and respect another. And the root meaning of the word *respect* is the willingness to look again (Arrien, 1984). When we are willing to look again at ourselves, we see through and disidentify from the old stereotypes and false assumptions about ourselves as women, and begin to take responsibility for our true strengths and limitations—to honor and respect ourselves.

5. Facing Our Fear—But as Anne Yeomans states in her article "Self Care During Dark Times," "We often fear our best parts even more than our worst . . . there is a terror that can be known in relationship to one's own wisdom, one's own power, one's own joy, one's capacity for healing and health" (1984, pp. 73–74). In venturing beyond our familiar and comfortable self-images, we inevitably encounter such fear.

Our self-hater tells us to turn back, to stay safe, to recoil from the fearful unknown. But by not facing our fear, we capitulate and thereby feed the self-hater. By not facing our fear, we let it control us. In our culture, men are taught to deny fear and women are taught to let it control them. In the words of Native American medicine woman Agnes Whistling Elk, "The greatest danger, if you have not walked with your fear and made it your ally, is that you will have no purpose and no direction and your power will be homeless and transient. It will destroy you" (Andrews, 1984, p. 131). The witches have a saying, "Where there's fear, there's power" (Starhawk, 1982a, p. 47). Go toward the fear and the power will be there. We must do the thing we are most afraid to do.

When you face your fear, you go through to the other side of it. You take your own territory back from the self-hater and make it your own again. You return to the homeland of your authentic self. And from then on you have some place to come back to. From then on, you can start believing in yourself—you can begin to love yourself.

What this means is that we must stop looking to some external authority who knows better than we do to show us the way. We must stop fighting the battle "out there" and bring it back inside. We must do battle with our own outdated beliefs about ourselves, our doubts, our fears and resentments. We must *introject war* and change our own inner landscape. Sam Keen calls this process "endarkenment." It can be done in many ways— through therapy, a wilderness experience, a relationship, a discipline, like the martial arts, or political action. But the process is an ongoing one and must be confronted many times on many levels.

In introjecting war, we take responsibility for the defence budget inside ourselves. How much of our own energy goes into defending ourselves against attack? Into attacking others? How much goes into blaming and finding justification for our actions? How much psychic violence are we doing to ourselves and others? What is our emotional ecology like? Are we dumping toxic wastes? Polluting our thought streams with negative images and illusions?

This is the work of our inner warrior—to reclaim our own territory. If everyone on earth did this, there would be no more war because there would be no more enemy "out there." The enemy would be called back to the centre, reclaimed, made sacred again. The inner warrior is the difference between what the world would make of us and what we would make of ourselves.

New Images

What *would* we make of ourselves as women? We become what we imagine, positive or negative. What images would we put in the place of the old? This is the new frontier for women—to find and create new models of our ideal selves as women.

I have chosen the word *heroic* for these new images because it carries the energy of all the real-life women of our history who were, in their own way, heroines. Heroic does not refer to an abstraction, like courage, commitment, or power, but to a real person who *embodies* courage and puts it into action for some good in the world. Heroism is, by definition, *lived*.

Many of the myths and legends of our past contain stories of active, powerful, and wise women and women-goddesses. These long-lost images of goddesses and heroines are "our potential shapers of identity" (Spretnak, 1982, p. 89) once we reclaim them. And as we uncover our true heritage and history as women, we unearth some very different versions of familiar myths. The helpless Cinderella we know today, for example, came down to us from Hera's great-great-great grandmother—The Goddess who was all-powerful, life-giving, and universally worshipped in pre-patriarchal societies as the One Goddess, The Great Mother.

Power in goddess-centred cultures was seen not as power over but as power from within, power as connectedness with all life. It was the power of the female to create and sustain life, and it was this power that was given "worth-ship" (an earlier form of the word *worship*). The female's power was not greater than but inclusive of the male because it was the female who brought together the various elements of life in her ability not only to give birth but also to give birth to her opposite, the male child.

Research indicates that woman was the focus of human life and spirituality for millenia:

> Women's natural abilities to create life and food, plus their menstrual coordination with the cyles of the moon were regarded as evidence of their intimate relationship with the mysteries of the universe. Thus women were revered as shamans, healers, priestesses and oracles. (Iglehart, 1983, pp. 10–11)

In the goddess-centred cultures of Old Europe (circa 4500 B.C.), spirituality was an integral part of everyday life, and there were altars and shrines everywhere. Divinities and their worldly representatives were essentially female. These cultures revered the earth, produced sophisticated art, had no fortifications or weapons, and appear to have lived in peace for 1,000 years (Iglehart, 1983, p. 85). There were no separate structures for rulers. Everyone lived and ruled together. Neither women nor men exercised oppressive power over one another, animals, or the earth.

What is our power as women today? The word *power* itself has almost become a dirty word in our culture by virtue of how it has been used. But *power* comes from the Latin *podere* meaning "to be able." It is the power that comes from within—the power we see in a seed, in the growth of a child, in expressing our own creativity and vision, the power I saw in my mother that day my brother got hurt, the power we know through giving birth, the power of chopping wood, building a fire, shovelling snow, planting a garden, digging in the dirt, holding our children, riding a horse. It is the power of our connectedness as women—to the mother earth, to our own bodies, to our babies, to our ability to heal, and to create. It is the power of all the qualities we are naturally good at as women—nurturing, supporting, and sustaining. As Jean Baker Miller (1976) says, these qualities are not the ones that win success in our world as it is, but they may be the ones needed to make the world better.

What images of heroines do we have today? Gloria Steinem talks about her heroine of the forties, Wonder Woman:

No longer did I have to pretend to like the pow and crunch style of Captain Marvel or the Green Hornet. No longer did I have nightmares after reading ghoulish comics filled with torture and mayhem. Here was a heroic person who might conquer with force, but only a force tempered by love and justice. Wonder Woman was beautiful, brave and explicitly out to change a world torn by hatred and war. She had a heroic mission. (in Spretnak, 1982, pp. 115–116)

In the 1980s, my young daughter likes Supergirl and She-Ra, Princess of Power, both of whom wield power and confront the forces of evil in order to protect life. In Chinese history, there is the Black Butterfly who was a waitress in her father's inn by day and a masked bandit by night who robbed the rich to feed the poor (Beh, 1982, p. 123). Going back even further, there are the Greek goddesses described beautifully by Jean Shinoda Bolen in *The Goddesses in Every Woman:* Artemis, Hestia, Hera, Demeter, Persephone, and Aphrodite.

We also have Joan of Arc, who disobeyed her father's wishes, put on men's clothing and armor, and led her troops into the front lines of battle to save France. The image of Joan of Arc, burned at the stake and later canonized St. Joan, has come to symbolize the courage of one willing to risk everything for her convictions.

We have Antigone, who defied the law of the land and the authority of her uncle, Creon, and, knowing she would die for her act, buried her brother's body. Antigone says, "I will not be moderate. What a person can do, she ought to do." The program notes of Jean Anouihl's production (People's Light and Theatre Company, 1984) comment: "Although we weep for Antigone's sacrifice of life and love, we would feel cheated if she had given in. For Antigone's nobility of spirit speaks to some part of each of us where the hero[ine] slumbers, where we desire to do what is right because it is right, and to stand fast in our 'no' when to do otherwise will diminish us."

Who is this part of us? She is all that we aspire to. She is all those strengths we keep forgetting we have. She is the deep self in silence.

My heroine often takes the form of a native American Indian I've named Running Brook. She runs silently barefoot through the woods, spotting deer and fox, sensing the rhythms of the earth, in touch with her natural wisdom. She is a vision of the Mother, in Barbara Hill Rigney's words: "almost witch-like, with her long hair and wearing her magically powerful leather jacket, the mother feeds wild birds from her hand, charms a bear, and is in tune with the seasons" (Starhawk, 1982a, p. 27). This image grounds me, gets me out of my head, brings a sense of freedom, and counter-acts that rigid, self-battering part of me. Running Brook is outwardly directed and connected, not self-focussed. She trusts herself.

Recently I was running along the bridle path in our woods, envisioning myself as Running Brook on a mission to protect my child, fetch medicine from another village, warn my people of impending danger. As I ran, I began to feel like her, long legs flowing effortlessly, purposefully against the soft earth, my senses keen to the wildlife around me, when all of a sudden I found myself entangled in cob webs. They were strung everywhere across the path from the night before, and I had flies and spiders in my hair, on my face, arms, and legs. I was annoyed, jolted out of my imagery, and, it seemed, prevented from going any further. I stopped and stood there— caught in the webs. Just as I was about to turn around and go back the way I had come, I noticed another response going on inside. I found myself looking around for a creative solution to the challenge, as Running Brook would have. (After all, she was on a mission; lives depended on her.) I got a stick and set off again swishing it both high and low to clear the path. Then I discovered a more effective strategy. By holding the stick up vertically in front of me, I could hit the webs no matter what height they were. By the time I reached the end of the path, I was flying downhill with long, bold strides, feeling purposeful and victorious, holding the stick at the hilt like a great sword. The power of my image had enabled me to move through my conditioned reaction of recoiling from conflict and to bring to the obstacle in my path energy, know-how, and a willingness to see the conflict through.

Evoking an image of your heroic self is a powerful tool for developing desired qualities. As Assagioli said, "Images or mental pictures and ideas tend to awaken emotions and feelings and to produce the physical conditions and external acts that correspond to them" (1974, pp. 51–53). And we can use these forces skilfully "to build in ourselves what we choose to have" (Assagioli, 1974, p. 51). This is the basis for the psychosynthesis techniques of the Ideal Model, Evoking and Developing Desired Qualities, and Acting "As If."

It is important to name your inner heroine, to envision her, and to express her in action. If you don't act from your best, it will slip forgotten into your private fantasies of what could be but remains unborn. This is not a one-time thing. It is choice after choice, like putting one foot in front of the other. It is an ongoing act of will to get centred, to maintain integrity, to stave off the voices of doubt and fear. It is your choice not to allow your boss or your husband or your own self-hater to demean you or someone you love. It is your choice not to vent your frustration and anger on your children but instead to be response-able to your own real needs. It is your choice not to be stopped by the old messages of your doubting self but instead to feed your positive, heroic possibilities. This takes a commitment to stand firm with what Starhawk calls "raging love against all that would diminish the unspeakable beauty of the world" (Starhawk, 1982a, p. 44).

And it takes action. Even when you don't feel like it, it takes acting "as if" there was something worth protecting, worth fighting for in yourself and in others. When I was little, I was struck by the idea of treating everyone like Jesus because one would never know when a person might be Jesus in disguise. As women, we need to honor that sense of the Holy Presence, the Goddess in ourselves, right here, right now.

Keep the light of your best self burning. Look for images that speak to you, think about women you admire—Florence Nightingale, Katharine Hepburn, Liv Ullman, Winnie Mandella. Cut out their pictures, read their biographies. Find clothes that feel like your choice, not just what's in or what's appropriate. Lynn Andrews (1984) talks about making an act of power or an act of beauty in the world to make tangible what is powerful and beautiful within. The self perishes without articulation. Paint it, draw it, write an article or a book. Find out what you believe in and commit yourself to a cause, feed a starving child in Ethiopia, visit an elderly woman in a nursing home, wash vegetables as though it mattered.

And make it concrete. As Starhawk says, we must learn to "think-in-things, to experience concretely as well as to think abstractly" (Starhawk, 1982a, p. 27). We do this as children, but in our culture abstract reasoning is valued over concrete experience. Abstractions can be very useful, but they tend to disconnect us from our deeper feelings and from our bodies. "The concrete reveals the unseen" (Starhawk, 1982a, p. 28). When we collect the things that embody strength for us, we learn something about our real power. In my workshops, women spend time alone outdoors with nature, sitting on the ground, searching for some natural object that represents what is powerful and essential in themselves—a stone, a piece of wood, water, flowers. This one object reveals more than hours of intellectualizing.

So, if it is more strength you need, think of it as the trunk of a tree; if it is courage, know it as fire. And express it in your own body. Throughout the ages, the body has been referred to as one's temple, a precious vehicle of awakening. The spine, in particular, has been identified as the seat of power. Thus women who "back away" from their power end up with back problems.

By virtue of the fact that we have a body, our power is always *embodied* power. As Rollo May says, we "cannot escape in some way or other literally 'taking a stand'" (1969, p. 238). In the martial arts, the physical stance is the starting place and the resting place: a place of balance from which the fighter can move out and recover, ready for anything. The stance of the Samurai is like the stance of our inner warrior. We can be knocked off centre by our emotions, self-doubts, and fears, but we can recover to a place of balance within (the Witness, the "I," or Objective Observer). To do this requires self-discipline—making of the self a disciple.

Some form of *physical* discipline is wonderfully empowering because when you get out there every day and run or swim or ride, you are not only training your body, but you are also training your ability to believe in yourself. No matter what else, you can begin by holding your head up and your back straight. You can act as if you know what you want and where you are going. You can hold yourself large and stand for what you value. You can disallow humiliation of yourself, your children, other women. The world needs us. She is crying out for our courage and our love, our strength, and our intuitive wisdom. There is a reason we are here. There is a balance to be restored.

I run with my dog through the woods. The spring air is moist and spun through with the scent of green. I feel the blood pounding in my veins. Behind the trees, the sun is a warm blaze. "And I am not, we are not separate from any of it. We are of the world and of each other, and the power that is in us is a great, if not invincible power. It can be hurt, but it can heal, it can be destroyed, but it can also renew. And it is morning. And there is still time to choose" (Starhawk 1982b, p. 183).

References

Andrews, L. V. (1984). *Flight of the seventh moon*. San Francisco: Harper & Row.

Arrien, A. (1984). *Myths and symbols of integration* [audio cassette]. San Francisco: Arrien Tapes.

Assagioli, R. (1974). *The act of will*. New York: Penguin.

Beh, S. H. (1982). Growing up with legends of the Chinese swordswomen. In C. Spretnak (Ed.), *The politics of women's spirituality*. New York: Anchor Books.

Christ, C. (1980). *Diving deep and surfacing*. Boston: Beacon Press.

Iglehart, H. (1983). *Womanspirit: A guide to women's wisdom*. San Francisco: Harper & Row.

Kolbenchlag, M. (1979). *Kiss sleeping beauty goodbye*. New York: Bantam Books.

Lindbergh, A. M. (1948). *The wave of the future: A confession of faith*. New York: Harcourt, Brace and Company.

May, R. (1969). *Love and will*. New York: Dell Publishing.

Miller, J. B. (1976). *Toward a new psychology of women*. Boston: Beacon Press.

People's Light and Theatre Company. (1984). *Jean Anouilh's production of Antigone* [program notes of play]. Malvern, PA.

Spretnak, C. (Ed.). (1982). *The politics of women's spirituality*. New York: Anchor Books.

Starhawk. (1982a). *Dreaming the dark: Magic, sex and politics*. Boston: Beacon Press.

Starhawk. (1982b). Consciousness, politics, and magic. In C. Spretnak (Ed.), *The politics of women's spirituality*. New York: Anchor Books.

Steindl-Rast, D.F.K. (1984). *Gratefulness: The heart of prayer*. New York: Paulist Press.

Steindl-Rast, D.F.K. (1985, Spring). The price of wholeness. *Parabola, 10*, 95.

Yeomans, A. (1984). Self-care during dark times. In J. Weiser and T. Yeomans (Eds.), *Psychosynthesis in the helping professions: Now and for the future*. Toronto: Department of Applied Psychology, Ontario Institute for Studies in Education.

Theory

Psychoanalytic Psychotherapy Through the Lens of Psychosynthesis

Maria T. Miliora

In this article, I present what I have found to be the areas of coherence and discrimination in Psychoanalytic Psychotherapy[1] and Psychosynthesis. The article is intended as an introduction to what I believe is the deep integrative richness that exists, in potential, between these two models. My discovery of the potential for integration evolved for me from the juxtaposition of my training. I had completed my training in Psychosynthesis shortly before beginning an institute training program in Psychoanalytic Psychotherapy. When colleagues asked me how I integrated the two schools, I would react with some puzzlement because I had no apparent difficulty holding a psychosynthesis conceptual framework while doing psychoanalytic psychotherapy. As I worked with people in therapy I experienced the coherence between the two schools intuitively. Only at a conscious level was I aware of their attitudinal and semantic differences.

I believe that each school can benefit from the experience and expertise of the other. Within the context of Assagioli's egg diagram, the psychoanalytic school has evolved an impressive body of material on early development and object relations theory[2] and a methodology for exploring the unconscious, sometimes called the "lower unconscious" in psychosynthesis terminology. Psychosynthesis, on the other hand, has an effective methodology for exploring the superconscious and provides validity to the spiritual drive intrinsic to our nature, to the experiences of higher consciousness, and to the concept of the Self.

The focus of Psychoanalytic Psychotherapy is the unconscious mind. Its methods, in the ideal, are non-intrusive and are aimed at allowing clients to experience a therapeutic environment that is safe enough for regression to occur. In this environment, the energy of repressed, often painful, unconscious content can be uncovered, released, and dealt with consciously, thus letting clients achieve a measure of freedom from its domination. The psychoanalytic therapist doesn't try to make things happen, to fix things for clients, or to make clients fit some image of what they should be and how they should get there. Characteristically, the therapeutic stance is neutral, curious, empathic, and non-directive.

Assagioli recognized that the first step of the process of Self-realization is "thorough knowledge of one's personality." He wrote:

We have recognized that in order really to know ourselves it is not enough to make an inventory of the elements that form our conscious being. An extensive exploration of the vast regions of our unconscious must also be undertaken. We have first to penetrate courageously into the pit of our lower unconscious in order to discover the dark forces that ensnare and menace us—the "phantasms," the ancestral or childish images that obsess or silently dominate us, the fears that paralyze us, the conflicts that waste our energies. It is possible to do this by the use of the methods of psychoanalysis. (1971, p. 21)

More recently, Friedman has cited the value of psychoanalytic insights to Psychosynthesis in his attempt "to build a bridge between the schools" (1984, p. 31).

Yeomans has acknowledged the value of exploring the unconscious. Within his scheme of the dimensions of psychosynthesis—the personal, transpersonal, and spiritual—he places the exploration of the unconscious in the transpersonal dimension (1985, p. 3). He makes the point that after some personal work is done (personal psychosynthesis), deeper identifications may emerge which he terms, "pansystemic" (1986). He considers these identifications to have their origin in early object relations and to be more powerful in their effect on the personality than subpersonalities. According to Yeomans, "Work here deals with the earliest childhood trauma and identity formation" (1985, p. 3).

Exploration of the unconscious can lead to a transformation of the structure of the personality and to a reduction of the rigidity and control exerted by pansystemic identifications. This allows for the integration of unconscious content into the personality and thus healing and growth. From a psychoanalytic perspective, pansystemic identifications can be conceptualized as constituents of the underlying character structure of the person which may emerge clearly only after considerable time in therapy. It can be said that psychoanalytic methodology facilitates the emergence of these unconscious identifications and thus enables the personality to disidentify from them and to release their energy. This helps the person achieve greater maturity and self-expression and, ultimately, clearer access to the Self. Within this dimension of therapeutic work, then, the methods of Psychoanalytic Psychotherapy can be appreciated and valued as means for preparing the ground for spiritual work and thus for releasing the energies of the Self. This methodology, then, can be utilized to support the goal of Psychosynthesis.

Psychoanalytic Methodology

The methodology of Psychoanalytic Psychotherapy derives from a fundamental belief in the unconscious. The psychoanalytic therapist is guided by this belief. It is assumed from the first meeting that clients bring with them all of their life experience, much of which is repressed in the unconscious and some of which is conflictual. It is further assumed that clients' reactions to the therapist are colored by this experience; in other words, they enter therapy with their own reality. In referring to the therapeutic setting, Langs (1976) uses the terms, "framework" or "frame," and describes this as the reality perceived by the client.

It is believed that the client's reality induces intrapsychic activity as he or she adapts to the therapeutic setting. This adaptive context (i.e., what the client perceives about the therapist and the surroundings) stirs unconscious material in the form of fantasies, memories, thoughts, and feelings. Much of this is outside the client's conscious awareness. The psychoanalytic therapist maintains an awareness of this phenomenon—that is, the transference—and works with the client so as not to interfere with it and indeed to encourage its development. Thus, characteristically, a psychoanalytic therapist will not answer clients' questions, particularly those concerning the therapist, in order to encourage fantasies. As Rutan states, "to the degree that [clients] 'know', it is more difficult for them to fantasize" (1984, p. 120). Alternatively, the therapist explores the meaning behind questions and associations and listens to the client's manifest content, with an ear attuned to the latent, or unconscious, content. When appropriate, the therapist helps to bring this unconscious material to the client's conscious awareness.

Also characteristic of the psychoanalytic therapist is a neutral and a reactive rather than an initiative stance (Rutan, 1984, p. 119). Thus, the therapist waits for the client to begin sessions, in general is non-directive, and often sits in silence. This allows the client to move to deeper levels and evokes associations and fantasies. Fantasies, associations, and dreams are explored with clients to uncover their latent content. Like transference, they are considered windows to the unconscious and their analysis and understanding contribute significantly to psychoanalytic psychotherapy. The psychoanalytic therapist also pays attention to his or her own experience while sitting with clients and to feelings that arise outside sessions. These emotional reactions evoked by clients—counter-transference—are considered important diagnostic tools.

At the beginning of a psychoanalytic psychotherapy, the therapist (1) sets the frame, (2) works to form an alliance, (3) gathers information in order to make a dynamic formulation, and (4) pays attention to transference and counter-transference. Alternatively, a psychosynthetic therapist characteristically (1) assesses a client's identifications, including the system of subpersonalities and the relationship among them, (2) assesses the client's capacity for disidentification and how free the Will is, (3) pays attention to practising presence and using the intuition, and (4) evolves a plan for the psychosynthesis which includes hypothesis, direction, and strategy (Yeomans, 1984). In the sections that follow, these elements as well as working with dreams and fantasies are explained in greater detail.

Setting the Frame and Creating a Holding Environment—An essential element of the initial stage of a psychoanalytic therapy is setting the frame, the context within which the therapy will be conducted. In psychoanalytic practice, it is considered important to set a frame that is consistent so that clients will experience a clearly bounded field within which they will, in time, feel safe enough to regress and explore unconscious content. In addition to those aspects of the frame created by the client's perceptions, the physical environment, and the personality of the therapist, several concrete elements of the frame are discussed and negotiated. These include the time and frequency of sessions, the fee, the cancellation policy, and other items which are within the norms of psychotherapeutic practice. Also included are the client's treatment goals which are made explicit and agreed to by client and therapist. During the course of the therapy, frame issues arise repeatedly (e.g., a change in the fee or the hour, a missed appointment, lateness). Every such change or "break" in the frame, ideally, should be processed with the client so that the implications are understood.

Analogous to the frame is Winnicott's concept of the "holding environment" (1965, p. 43) which is derived from the idea that it is important to provide a child with a reliable, consistent, and regular "home" environment in order to foster his or her optimal development. This concept is adapted to the therapeutic context where it is assumed that many clients have suffered from inconsistency in their early object relations. Consequently, an ideal therapeutic relationship, one which promotes positive development, is also a corrective emotional experience in that it provides clients with what was lacking in their earlier home environments. It is believed that this consistency can help clients internalize those aspects of the therapeutic interaction which they need for their development.

Building an Alliance—From the outset, the psychoanalytic therapist is conscious of the need to begin building an alliance with the client, wherever he or she is, so that they may work together therapeutically. Clients come into therapy with some level of distress, anxieties about the process, and hopes of feeling better, perhaps of finding a "cure." In the ideal, they encounter a therapist who is non-judgmental, listens attentively, and is empathic and curious. Negotiating frame issues and discussing the goals of therapy are early elements of the alliance-building process which, in effect, grows out of the transference.

Sometimes clients experience some symptomatic relief early in therapy deriving from a feeling of gratification that the therapist is paying attention to them and apparently cares about them. This first type of alliance, in which there is some trust in the relationship, is sometimes termed the "narcissistic alliance." Assagioli noted that psychoanalysis does not include work at the middle level of the unconscious or with the more conscious aspects of the personality (1971, pp. 22, 68). Although this was probably true earlier in this century, today psychoanalytic psychotherapy does include work at this level, and with some clients much of the early alliance-building stage is so constituted.

In long-term therapy, there seems to occur a stage at which clients realize that deeper work can be done, that this work will be difficult, that there will be no "cure" by the therapist. At this stage, clients face a choice about continuing the process. If the therapy does continue, the client and therapist enter what is called the "therapeutic or working alliance." Adler, deriving his use of these terms from the earlier literature, defines this alliance as one "between the analysing ego of the analyst and the patient's reasonable ego. It involves mutuality, collaboration, and the mature aspects of two individuals working together to understand something and to resolve a problem" (1980, pp. 547–548). In this phase of therapy, clients can hear interpretations with less defensiveness and more readily acknowledge resistances and blocks. The length of time needed to enter into this stage of the relationship depends on the capacity of clients to observe themselves and the type of transference that has developed.

Using Yeomans's perspective of the three dimensions of the process of psychosynthesis; the transition from the narcissistic to the therapeutic alliance seemingly corresponds to a shift from work at the personal or conscious level to work at the transpersonal or deep level. In psychosynthesis language, work at the personal level, which probably focussed on subpersonality work, development of the personal will, and expansion of the personal self, led to some alleviations of the original symptoms. After this, clients face the issue of whether to go more deeply into the roots of the identifications that they experience as limiting their freedom—that is, whether to explore unconscious content and open themselves to the superconscious.

Dynamic Formulation—The function of a dynamic formulation is to enable the therapist to have some understanding of how a client's present experience, including problems, defences, and ways of relating to the therapist, relate to his or her past. The formulation is a working hypothesis and is continually expanded and refined throughout the course of therapy as additional material and understanding emerge.

In arriving at a formulation, the therapist adopts a developmental perspective and considers the tasks and potential problem areas associated with developmental milestones (e.g., separation-individuation, oedipal). The therapist then makes a tentative assessment of how well the individual has managed these periods (Blanck & Blanck, 1974). There are several developmental schema that can be applied to gain this perspective, including those of Freud, Erikson, Piaget, and Mahler. Essentially the therapist views the client against the developmental backdrop and asks what may have happened to hinder optimal development and what strategies have been created by the client to enable him or her to cope. In other words, the therapist considers both the strengths and the limitations presented by the person. Given some understanding of the major developmental periods and what may have hindered optimal development, it is assumed that the developmental tasks corresponding to that period need to be accomplished during the course of the therapy.

In sum, the purpose of a dynamic formulation is to correlate the how's and why's of an individual's functioning with his or her developmental history. With this understanding, the therapist undertakes the therapy with a hypothesis of what needs to happen developmentally and behaviorally during its course.

This psychodynamic assessment is comparable to the evolution of a therapeutic plan in Psychosynthesis which includes a hypothesis, direction, and strategy. In such a formulation, psychosynthetic therapists characteristically include an assessment of superconscious potentials and patterns. Psychoanalytic therapists who have access to a greater body of conceptual material on early development and object relations will formulate the case more intensively at this level, but they will limit the assessment to this level. Ideally, an integration of the two approaches will achieve a fuller assessment.

Transference—Transference is essentially an unconscious process defined as the client's biased experience of the therapist. It may include wishes, feelings, fantasies, and drives which are derived from and are a repetition of earlier experiences with significant others in childhood. Greenson (1965) emphasizes that for a reaction to be considered a transference it must have the following two characteristics: (1) it must be a repetition of the past and (2) it must be inappropriate to the present. Within the psychoanalytic school, there is also the broader conceptualization that transference is simply the client's experience of his or her relationship to the therapist. From this perspective, transference is always present. Further, some theorists have referred to "transference-like phenomena" and "archaic transferences" that develop in the treatment of pre-oedipal personality disorders (Chessick, 1985, pp. 101, 110). These are distinguished from transference in the classical sense in that they are not repressed strivings from childhood but, rather, "regressions to normal developmental positions" (p. 125).

Within the psychoanalytic model, considerable attention is given to transference, encouraging it, working within it, and analyzing it. The psychoanalytic therapist listens for the metaphorical message of the transference and, when appropriate, brings it directly into the session.

In the following example, a female client is speaking about distancing herself from female friends, saying that if she lets them get too close, they'll abandon her. I intervened:

Therapist: Are you distancing yourself from me?

Client: Yes.

Therapist: What's your concern?

Client: If I get too close, either you'll leave me or I'll leave you.

The analysis of the transference is used to deduce information about a person's early object relations. In the case cited above, the client's fear about my deserting her if she gets too close to me probably derives from her experience with her mother, a relationship in which closeness could have meant abandonment. This kind of issue suggests that a developmental problem occurred during the first two years of her life, the period when, developmentally, a child takes the first steps toward physically separating from the primary care-giver.

Transference is a window to the unconscious. The psychoanalytic therapist works with an appreciation of its occurrence within the relationship and an awareness of its value in uncovering repressed unconscious content. Bringing the transference message explicitly into the room deepens the relationship, that is, it intensifies presence. This in turn promotes the healing field within which clients can experience greater ease in working therapeutically and in giving expression to painful affect. Interpreting the transference with those clients who have good insight enables them to realize consciously what was previously unconscious.

In the following example, a therapy group has just terminated with the two therapists (one male, one female) who have led the group for two years. At the first meeting of the group with me as the new leader, Member 1 spoke about two of her friends who had hated their babies:

Member 2: I can't believe there are mothers who hate their babies.

Member 3: That really shocks me.

Member 4: What do you mean? There are mothers who kill their babies.

Therapist: The group is wondering if this mother [referring to myself] is going to love her children.

Member 1: I'm tired of this. I don't want to go through this with another mother.

In this exchange, by interpreting what I believed was the metaphorical message of the transference, Member 1 was able to give direct expression to the anger she felt around losing her previous mother (the former female therapist) and needing to begin again with me.

Within Psychosynthesis, a therapist would characteristically work with a client who was transferring so as to encourage the client to disidentify and take responsibility for the transference. The aim is to strengthen the "I" or Observer and to encourage a mature relationship between therapist and client. Further, a psychosynthetic therapist who uses active techniques such as subpersonality work and dialogic imagery discourages the development of transference in the classical sense (Friedman, 1984).

In attempting to integrate these seemingly disparate approaches to transference, it is perhaps key to consider using transference in a discriminatory fashion according to clients' developmental level, ego strength, and capacity for disidentification. An assessment can then be made as to how the transference can best be used to promote a person's growth. Those clients with a relatively cohesive observing ego, whose principal issues suggest an oedipal level of development, can perhaps make effective use of disidentification and thus best use the transference to expand their self-knowledge and awareness. On the other hand, for those clients with a limited capacity for self-observation, with a fragmented sense of self, and/or whose material suggests a pre-oedipal level of development, disidentification may not only be fruitless, but it may also be contra-indicated. In such cases, a positive therapeutic experience may only be effected if the transference develops fully, allowing the client to use the therapeutic relationship as a reparative growth experience. Utilizing active techniques in such cases may interfere with what needs to happen for that person in the way of "unfinished business" from the past. In my view, only when such clients have achieved enough structural growth to profit from active techniques are such techniques as disidentification appropriate.

Counter-Transference—Historically, counter-transference was thought of as the feelings of the therapist that interfered with effective communication between therapist and client (Wolstein, 1964). This definition gave the phenomenon a negative connotation. More recently, the definition has undergone a shift and is now thought of simply as any feelings aroused in the therapist by the client (Rutan, 1984). Now cast in a more positive light, counter-transference is considered a valuable source of information about the client. A simple example of this is to consider that if the therapist finds the interaction with a client to be consistently unpleasant, it is reasonable to assume that the client affects others in a similar way. Knowing this, the therapist is in a good position to analyze and understand the client's interactional problems. In this sense, the therapist can be thought of as an instrument in the therapeutic process:

> A male client attributes to himself only feminine qualities and is split off from competitiveness, anger, and assertiveness. He avoids working a normal job or going to school and spends much of his time reading psychic books, doing yoga, and walking in the woods. Nevertheless, he often speaks about his concern that he is "flitting his life away" and having no life direction. At times, I felt frustrated and had the impulse to tell him that he should stop "flitting about" and enter the cultural mainstream.

In a consultation, my counter-transference was interpreted as the client's projecting his split-off aggressive feelings onto me. In my gaining awareness of this dynamic, I no longer felt frustrated and I was more able to help him own his projections.

Another example of counter-transference, one in which my unconscious feelings limited my capacity to work therapeutically, involved a client in a therapy group who reported that she had just learned that she might have cancer. For the rest of the session, I said nothing about that to her and was unaware of feelings. When I processed the session the next day, I became aware of my intense anxiety about cancer. I worked through these feelings and at the next session I was able to communicate empathically with the client.

Dreams, Fantasies, Images—Among Freud's earliest and most significant work was his analysis of the importance of dreams in exploring the unconscious (1901). Within the psychoanalytic model, dreams are considered a regressive phenomenon and thus as providing information about repressed memories and some ego functions, including the capacity for observation (Greenson, 1969). When a therapeutic alliance has been established, a psychoanalytic therapist will use dream interpretation to provide clients with an understanding of the interrelationship between their past and present. Psychoanalytic dream interpretation derives from a conceptualization of the processes involved in dreaming, including symbolization, and from the therapist's intimate knowledge of the client's historical past and current circumstances (Altman, 1969).

A psychoanalytic therapist characteristically listens without comment to the manifest content of dreams reported by clients and then explores with them, through their associations, the emotional content and the latent meaning. Fantasies and images are explored similarly. Consider the transference dream reported by a client at the last session before my vacation. The manifest content included images of being chased by someone who wanted to hurt her and not finding safety in a place she had previously thought of as a refuge.

Therapist: How do you understand the dream?

Client: Everyone lets me down, I can't trust anyone.

Therapist: Like me, letting you down by going on vacation.

Client: You have a right to go on vacation.

Therapist: That's coming from your head. How do you feel about it?

Client: I'm going to miss you. By the end of the week, I'll be tearing my hair out.

In this exchange, the client gave expression to feelings about me that had been preconscious and thereby expanded her capacity for self-expression.

Unlike the more limited psychoanalytic conceptualization of dreams as windows to the lower unconscious, within Psychosynthesis dreams are conceptualized as providing access to all levels of the unconscious, including the superconscious and the collective unconscious. Thus, from a psychosynthetic perspective, dreams are considered to provide information not only about the past, but also about the future. In this latter capacity, dreams can serve as opportunities for rehearsing future events and for providing us with guidance and predictions about our next steps. In working with dreams, a psychosynthetic therapist might utilize techniques of the active imagination, for example, identification or dialogue with a dream figure, and actively work with the emotional charge contained in the dream and its symbols.

Clinical Case

The clinical material presented below illustrates a case in which psychoanalytic methodology was utilized to enable the client to explore unconscious content.[3] The application of this methodology notwithstanding, the case can also be viewed from a psychosynthesis perspective that includes subpersonalities, the process of disidentification, development of the will, and the principle of Inner Wisdom. The case illustrates that if Psychosynthesis is viewed from the perspective of principles guiding human life rather than a set of techniques, its universality will apply regardless of the methodology and conceptual basis that is used in psychotherapy.

The clinical material, the case of "Jen," is presented from the first to the fortieth session. Viewed in this way, the themes of emotional deprivation and abuse can be seen as recurrent, but as moving progressively to deeper levels of content and affect.

My therapeutic stance with Jen has been consonant with the psychoanalytic model described above. She has almost always been on time for sessions and has never missed one. Frame changes have been few. She has not asked me any personal questions and I have volunteered no information about myself except that my field is social work. My counter-transference feelings have been consistently caring, sometimes strongly so.

When I first met Jen, she appeared as a bright and pretty woman in her early twenties. She had recently relocated from another state and had just begun a graduate program. At the opening of the first session, I asked her how I could be useful to her. She replied, "Every man I've been involved with has been abusive to me. I don't know why I'm attracted to men like that, but it's making my life miserable." She recounted that in the five-year period just past, she had lived with a man who had abused her emotionally and physically. During this period, she had provided financial support to him, had had three abortions, and had made a suicide attempt. During the first three sessions, I obtained a detailed history and I began setting the frame.

History—Jen is the fourth of six children. Her parents are professionals. She characterized her early childhood as happy. She remembered being close to her mother, holding onto her skirt. According to Jen, when she was in grammar school, her father was diagnosed as having a degenerative disease, but she and her siblings were not told of the illness. Jen recalled a subsequent shift in her father's mood to "grumpy" and withholding. She stated that she remembers believing that he hated her. At about this time, Jen's mother began to shift away from her role as a housewife and went back to school, ultimately obtaining a graduate degree. Jen recounted that there was verbal and physical conflict between her parents and that she received physical punishment from her father. This she characterized as "no big deal." Her parents were separated and later divorced when Jen was an adolescent.

During this next period of her life, Jen began sexual activity, drank heavily, was sometimes seriously ill, and made a suicide gesture while intoxicated. She lived with her mother until she finished high school. She then lived with the man, "Jim," with whom she maintained a long-term relationship. While attending college, she moved into her father's home, continued seeing Jim, and occasionally dated other men as well.

We agreed to meet weekly at a particular day and hour. We negotiated a fee which would be paid partly by her and partly by insurance. I told her she was responsible for missed sessions. I asked her if she had any objections to my tape-recording our sessions. She said she did not. Her therapy goal was to understand the reasons for and put an end to her behavior of entering into self-destructive relationships with men. In the first few sessions, Jen tended to deny or diminish the extent of the physical abuse by Jim and responded to my questions about it with, "I don't remember" or, "Well, I didn't go to the hospital." She ultimately broke through the denial.

> **Jen:** He punched me in the face. He kicked me when I was on the ground. I had bruises on my legs.
>
> **Therapist:** I think it's important that you acknowledge he actually beat you.
>
> **Jen:** I do, but it's hard to do that.
>
> **Therapist:** I hear that.
>
> **Jen:** (crying) He beat me up. He was a bastard.

Jen said that in spite of the abuse, it was "torture" to be away from Jim and that she longed for him when separated. After four sessions, I made a dynamic formulation. The self-destructive behavior suggested deficits had occurred early in her life. I hypothesized that she had not developed a strong enough sense of self during the early years of her life to enable her to leave a relationship that was harmful to her. I imagined that this derived from emotional deprivation and her growing up in a family where she witnessed and experienced violent behavior. Jen also had obvious ego strengths, namely, she could see her behavior as self-destructive and wanted to end it, she was very intelligent, and she had a pleasant personality. Also noteworthy were the following: anger was not readily available to her; she overidealized her father; she used intellectualization as a defence; she was counter-dependent, an obvious coping mechanism; and it was difficult for her to express sadness. Jen formed a quick attachment to me and looked to me for approval and mirroring. For about three months, Jen worked on breaking her emotional attachment to Jim and she began seeing another man, "Ken." She often spoke of her loneliness if she were not involved with a man.

From a psychosynthesis perspective, four major identifications, described below, were apparent at the beginning of therapy.

1. The Self-Destructive Subpersonality—This represented that part of her lacking in self-love that had driven her to abusing alcohol, suicidal behavior, and maintaining an abusive relationship. Although as the therapy progressed it became clear that this behavior derived from the child's (Subpersonality 2) need for love, at this early phase of therapy, Subpersonalities 1 and 2 appeared to be distinct. From a psychoanalytic perspective, Subpersonality 1 may be conceptualized as the source of Jen's masochism. Within this conceptualization, her difficulty in experiencing anger (i.e., aggression or sadism) can be understood as derived from the strong position of this subpersonality within her experience. Thus, if Jen began to experience and express more anger, the intensity of this subpersonality and the masochistic behavior would be diminished.

2. The Lonely Child—Jen tended to deny or denigrate the loneliness and dependency needs of the child, including its need for love. From a psychoanalytic and psychosynthetic perspective, it could be hypothesized that the root of this identification derived from a lack of early nurturing such that as an adult, Jen lacked the capacity to nurture herself.

3. The Counter-Dependent Subpersonality—This part of Jen denied need and made it difficult for her to express painful affect. Sometimes manifested as "superwoman," Subpersonality 3 was strong and able to handle everything alone. Jen feared that if she acknowledged needs or her vulnerability, she would lose her strength and become as weak and dependent as the child (Subpersonality 2). She feared dependency because, as the material which emerged later suggested, becoming dependent on someone had come to mean disappointment and hurt. I came to appreciate that from this subpersonality Jen derived her strength and courage. I hypothesized that if Jen could come to accept the dependency needs of the child and increase her capacity for self-nurturing, Subpersonality 3 would be freed as the source of genuine strength and thus integrated within 4.

4. The More Mature Subpersonality—This was that part of Jen which could see her previous behavior as self-destructive, wanted to end it, and had come into therapy with that stated intent. It appeared that Jen's will some-times was caught between Subpersonalities 1 and 4. I tried to strengthen the fourth by bringing it to her attention and thereby engaging her will whenever I noticed her moving toward Subpersonality 1 and losing awareness of the more mature part of herself.

In the tenth session, Jen spoke of seeing herself on a "tightrope" with Jim and said that she could go either way. I reminded her that she had said, "I'm not a punching bag," in an earlier session.

In the 11th session, she explicitly identified Subpersonality 1, saying, "The part of me that's self-defeating wants to go back to him. That's a mistake, a big mistake." Also in that session, in referring to her new boyfriend who had demonstrated his jealousy, she reported that she had said to him, "I'm not a possession," and with a big smile said to me, "You'd be so proud of me." This was an allusion to my encouraging her to express herself, particularly with respect to anger. Her wanting to please me suggested that a similar dynamic had existed with her parents when she was a child.

During this early alliance-building stage, I joined with what the psychoanalytic school would call the healthy part of her, while the psychosynthesis school would say I strengthened the most mature subpersonality. The work at this stage was almost entirely on the conscious and cognitive level and included development of her personal will. I call this a phase of personal psychosynthesis. Although not entirely free of the unhealthy attachment to Jim, after ten sessions Jen had made considerable progress in that direction and she was mindful of her experience and expressiveness with her new boyfriend.

I consider the 11th and 12th sessions as marking a movement to deeper levels. At the 11th, she reported the first dream. It involved her parents reconciling; her mother looked young ("the age was pulled off"). Jen was moved to call her mother after the dream. Jen took two important steps. She acknowledged more fully her sadness around her parents' divorce and, because of the conversation with her mother, Jen realized that her relationship with Jim was like that of her mother's with her father. Here, for the first time, Jen acknowledged the extent of her father's physical abuse of her mother. In the 12th session, she reported a recurrent dream:

> Something is pulling me in the room and I'm sliding off my bed. I feel like my hair is standing on end. Unnerves me. I can't wake up. I know I'm dreaming, but it feels very real.

Jen said she had had one dream recently and woke up feeling she was 6 or 7 and wanting her mother. She associated this age with the time of her father's withdrawal. But this time she also acknowledged that he was sexist and had a bad temper and further that she felt resentful toward her mother for returning to school and neglecting her children. Here Jen began to give greater expression to her anger.

At the 13th session, Jen reported that on her recent visit home she met with Jim and spent the night with him. That night she had a nightmare involving a bat that flew in through the window of the bedroom and became a vampire. I said that it was curious that she had a nightmare while she was sleeping with Jim. Jen acknowledged ambivalence to Jim, wanting him but fearing that she could never trust him again. Here again was the conflict between Subpersonalities 1 and 4, but 4 was stronger. At the 14th session, Jen focussed on her relationship with her parents:

> **Jen:** I feel my parents have let me down. They were into themselves. We brought ourselves up (crying). I can do it myself. I don't need them, but I want it and I won't get it. I had to learn to take care of myself.
>
> **Therapist:** You have a very independent side of you.

Jen: It was a way of surviving. There's also a part that isn't (crying). I can't depend on anyone but myself. I truly feel that way.

Therapist: That includes me?

Jen: You're different. You're here for a distinct reason, to help me and I depend on you. You're not a part of my life, you're outside. If I really needed to talk to you, I could call. Outside I can only count on myself.

Therapist: It's okay to call for help.

In this exchange, Jen could see both Subpersonalities 2 and 4 and she acknowledged the counter-dependency (i.e., Subpersonality 3) as something she had developed early in her life as a way to cope within her family. I used the transference to begin encouraging her to acknowledge need and to break the denial around dependency, that is, to disidentify from counter-dependency (Subpersonality 3).

At the 15th session, Jen expressed feeling disappointed by Jim around a planned visit that had not materialized. I returned to the nightmare about the vampire and asked her about the symbolism. She said, "He would suck me dry if I went back to him." In alluding to the dream, I brought to her attention Subpersonality 4 and what I saw as the warning from her Inner Wisdom. In the 17th session, Jen spoke of the "wall" that she used to protect herself from painful feelings. I said that the wall was cutting her off from the full range of emotional experience that was available to her:

Therapist: Trust that you can feel lousy and survive.

Jen: You just broke the wall (crying).

Therapist: You allowed it.

Jen: I don't understand why so many things hurt me.

Therapist: Because you've been hurt a lot.

Jen: No more than anyone else.

Therapist: You don't have to be superwoman all the time.

Jen: If I don't do for myself, no one else will. I have to do for myself.

Therapist: No reason you won't be able to. When you say "No more than anyone else," you close off the pain you've had all of your life. There's a lot of feelings around that stuff. You are strong, independent, and you can deal with the pain from the past. Trust yourself.

In this exchange, Jen allowed her defences to loosen up and give way to emotional expression. I encouraged her to trust her capacity to deal with pain which I knew intuitively she had. I believe she feared that if she allowed herself to feel and express pain, she would lose her strength and capacity to take care of herself. The work was one of trying to encourage the co-existence of Subpersonalities 2 and 3.

Between the 18th and 20th sessions, Jen expressed anger at her parents and at Jim, saying, "I was robbed by them and by Jim." She also reported that when she was about 5 she was sexually abused by a teenage boy in her neighborhood. She expressed feeling guilt and did not want to talk more about it because she said it was too humiliating. At the next session, she reported that all week she had had periods of feeling hyperactive and then very depressed. She said that one day she had nothing to do and she felt she might go crazy. She said, "I realize I can't be home alone with nothing to do for long. Losses sweep over me. I know I've been beaten again and again. I need to be loved." She also reported that there was a new man in her life, "Bob," and that the impulse to be with him derived from loneliness. The next week she was feeling better and reported a dream:

> I was in my bed, having that disembodied feeling. There was a guy sitting in a chair nearby. I had electrodes pasted on me, and he asked, "What does it feel like?" He kept bothering me, "What does it feel like, like you're on drugs or something?" I was saying, "Go away, I have to answer the phone." Then I woke up. Felt like I was dying. In all those dreams, feels like someone else is there. I'm being ripped out of my body or I get a prickly feeling and I'm scared. This time I wasn't scared, but annoyed. I felt disoriented, like I was being disembodied, my soul leaving my body. He looked like a doctor.

Therapist: Associations?

Jen: Electrodes, abortions, guinea pig. I felt like I was being experimented on.

Jen went on to describe her first abortion:

> It was a bizarre feeling, taking the baby out of you, ripping your stomach inside out, being sucked. I could not stop crying.

I explored the relationship of this dream to the recurrent one she had shared earlier:

> They started when I met Jim. It was a progressive dream. There's a force or power. I'm awake in the dream. I can't move, but something else is moving me, inside me and around me. It wanted to hurt Jim. The dream went away for a while. Now I feel it wants to take me away, pull me off the bed.

Therapist: I wonder about the molestation when you were a child—someone who was bigger and stronger than you. You were not in control of yourself, powerless.

Jen: I didn't have a choice.

Jen spoke about the early sexual abuse briefly, saying she knew it was wrong and wondered why she did it:

Jen: Maybe I wanted to be liked. Don't know. Just like I don't know why I let Jim hit me. If he tried that now, I'd kill him.

Therapist: You were 5.

Jen: Not sure. It's one of my first memories, 2½, 3½.

Therapist: Maybe the child needed to be loved.

Jen: I'm getting images of what happened. I'm reliving it (crying). I'm really angry. When I finally threw Jim out, I felt like tainted goods, a piece of trash. Why would I let somebody do that to me? I'm gonna be scarred for the rest of my life. I was raped when I was five and I was raped by Jim emotionally. Why did I let him do it? (Looked at me intently.)

Therapist: That needs to come from you. You hinted at it earlier.

Jen: Wanting to be loved? That's a stupid reason.

Therapist: You had need. Don't put yourself down for that. You lost your parents in a sense. Try to have sympathy for her (alluding to Subpersonality 2).

Jen: Hard to feel sorry for someone like that.

Therapist: It's hard for you to acknowledge need.

Jen: I want to work this through so bad. I feel like it's never gonna stop hurting me. I was so depressed last week. Three years ago, I would have killed myself. This time I knew it would pass.

Here the interweaving of affect around the two abuse experiences, one as a child, the other as an adult, can be seen, suggesting that a similar dynamic had operated. Also apparent is that it is the child and her need to be loved which is at the root of the self-destructive identification. In the next session, Jen acknowledged the humiliation she felt around Jim. Crying, she said, "I let him hit me. I needed him. I was alone. I was desperate." Here she was able to relive the feelings around her need and his abuse. Later in the session, she realized that the feelings which had led her into the early abuse, her need for love and her loneliness, were the same as those which led her into the abusive relationship with Jim. This was a clear indication of her moving to deeper levels of uncovering, realization, and integration.

At the 26th session, Jen began talking about her new boyfriend, Bob:

Relationships have cycles. At three months you make a decision regarding whether the person is worth an investment of feelings. After one year, there's a commitment.

I moved her explicitly to our relationship to deepen her experience.

Therapist: Is that true for us too?

Jen: It grows more positive. I owe you a lot (silence). I've had doubts and insecurities since childhood. My mother told me that my father beat her and that I saw it. I don't remember. She waited on him hand and foot. The house revolved around him particularly if he was in a bad mood. He was sexist, gave my brothers everything, me nothing. My older brothers would beat me until I started high school. My younger brother did until I left home. I realize what a hell it was growing up. That's why I ran away and then I went to the same thing.

Therapist: Did your father beat you?

Jen: Yes, but not bloody. Once he pulled my nightgown over my head and beat me with a belt on my bare back. I had welts on my back. My mother sat there and watched it, didn't try to stop it. She was a slave to him. I was a servant to Jim.

Jen cried over the loss of the family she wished she had had. At the 29th session, she reported that studying in her room alone reminded her of being a child, maybe 5 years old, and being sent to her room as punishment. She recalled in a moving fashion the sad, lonely, scared 5-year-old child. As she moved to deeper levels, she reported an earlier memory of being about 3 years old. She said she was in a crib near a window. Through the window she could see her brother and a friend playing outside. Her parents were out, there were no cars in the driveway. She cried, banged on the window, screamed, but no one paid attention to her. Eventually she fell asleep. This memory may be a composite of recurrent experiences of not being attended to rather than a single event. It appears to represent her experience of not getting her needs met and eventually learning that she could only depend on herself.

At the 30th session, Jen said that during the week she had read the book, *Prisoners of Childhood,* and that she had cried. She said that the material in the book reminded her of her childhood. She said that her mother had wanted lots of children to have "things to love her." A sister had told Jen that their mother had had an abortion and had been away in an institution, but Jen had no memories of these events. Jen said that she did remember that once she saw her mother sitting on the floor and crying for a long time. She said that when she first tried to leave home, her mother banged her head on the refrigerator and "flipped out." This was the first suggestion that her mother may have had emotional problems. As Jen moved deeper into her experience, she said:

> I was very, very good. I wanted their love. If anyone was sad or angry, I thought it was my fault. I never told anyone how I felt (sobbing). Why did they do that to me? I never did anything to them.

Here the superconscious quality, the innocence of the child, is manifested. Later in the session, she spoke of having told her boyfriend, Bob, that his seeming avoidance of her left her feeling hurt. Having said that she admitted, "I felt more like myself than ever before." Expressing her need and deriving joy from expressing it are indicative of her growth as a self.

At Jen's request, the time of our sessions was changed to a time earlier in the week. On the first of these meetings, I approached the waiting room on the way to my office some 10 minutes early. Jen was sitting in the waiting room. She immediately rose when she saw me and began following me. I felt uncomfortable asking her to wait and instead asked her if she wanted to begin early. She said yes. My impression of this dynamic was that of a little girl who was waiting for her mother and then followed her once she caught sight of her. This reminded me of her saying she used to hang on to her mother's skirts. Jen seemed very anxious that day. Since there was a change in the frame, I explored it with her. She said that her week starts on Monday, that the former meeting day seemed late, that meeting on this day was better because it was sooner. With this expression, she made me realize how important our relationship was to her. In this same session, she expressed anger at her parents for not helping her financially. From that, she moved on to express a deeper anger toward them for her childhood experience. She also gave expression to her awareness of her fear to express need, that this was due to fear of rejection.

A few sessions later, she again expressed feelings of shame around the early sexual abuse, but would not elaborate. She also gave expression to her joy as she was increasingly aware of her growth. She said she used to be like a "wounded puppy," hanging onto Jim when she was hurt, but now she saw herself as an eagle, strong, big, independent, and majestic.

I returned from vacation and met with Jen for our 37th session. She began:

> Several nights last week I found it hard to sleep. I finally realized that it was because you were away. I really missed you. I'm dependent on you. It's hard for me to say I depend on or need anyone, mother, father, you. I wanted to tell you.

I was impressed with this expression which demonstrated her increased capacity to allow need within her experience.

In subsequent sessions, Jen said that she had just realized that her boyfriend was in love with another woman and that, consequently, she had begun separating from him emotionally. She acknowledged the hurt she felt. She said:

> I need a male companion. Otherwise there's a void, loneliness, a feeling that something is missing. I have an incredible need to be loved. Why? I want to know why.

She also shared two dreams from the past. One occurred when she was 17 and involved her being in her father's bed in her bedroom just waiting for something to happen, for someone to come. The other occurred when she was about 10. In this dream, she was in bed and heard footsteps of someone approaching. She was terrified and hid under the covers. Then someone placed his hands over her mouth and pulled the covers down. She saw a faceless figure. Jen had few associations around these dreams except for the image of impending doom in both.

Jen has made considerable progress since the inception of therapy. She is capable of greater insight and emotional expression and she has freed herself from the domination of the lonely part of her that led her into unhealthy relationships. There may be more that will emerge around early abuse. She speaks about a part of her that is missing, that "dropped off" a long time ago. She may be alluding, as her dreams suggest, to abuse experiences of which she currently has no memory.

Conclusion

Although the therapy with Jen was done within the psychoanalytic model, I find it consistent with psychosynthesis work. Indeed, it can be said that psychoanalytic methodology enriches and expands the scope of Psychosynthesis. What I believe differentiates psychoanalytic work from a purely psychosynthesis approach is: (1) the developmental perspective which guides the therapist to early object relations, (2) the use of transference which enables the therapist to gain greater understanding of the client's early experience and to move the client on to deeper levels, and (3) the awareness of the importance of the frame in engendering trust in a relatively short span of time.

During the phase of therapy reported here, I chose to work within the transference experience of the client rather than the more purely psychosynthetic approach of disidentification techniques. This choice evolved from my belief that Jen needed to use me in a transference to have a reparative emotional relationship, one that included emotional experiences that presumably she did not have as a child. Further, given Jen's tendency for intellectualization and avoidance of emotional expression, I believe that more active techniques such as subpersonality work would have moved her into her "mind" and thus were contra-indicated.

Because of the deep work that she has done, Jen now has an increased capacity for self-observation and thus for disidentification. She also has an increased capacity to benefit from transference interpretations which make the connection between her experience of me and the important figures from her past. Both of these techniques, psychosynthetic disidentification and the psychoanalytic interpretation, will, I believe, help her move from a transference relationship to a real one. According to Yeomans (1986), Assagioli spoke of the progressive stages of therapy as "mother therapy, father therapy, co-worker therapy." In this, Assagioli seems to have been alluding to the evolution of the therapeutic relationship from transference to a real relationship, a movement that is recognized within the psychoanalytic school (Adler, 1980).

The clinical case presented above demonstrates the usefulness of psychoanalytic methodology in helping clients uncover unconscious material and thus releasing the painful affect associated with it. From the perspective of doing deep work with clients, the methodology can be integrated within the psychosynthesis model of the psyche.

Notes

1. Included within the psychoanalytic model of therapy are Freudian psychology, object relations theory, and self-psychology.

2. According to Horner, object relations refer to "intrapsychic structures" which come into being when the "infant organizes its world into . . . patterns" of self and other, i.e., primary care giver(s) (1984, pp. 4–5).

3. Names and historical data have been altered for reasons of confidentiality.

References

Adler, G. (1980). Transference, real relationship and alliance. *International Journal of Psychoanalysis*, 61, 547.

Altman, L. (1969). *The dream in psychoanalysis*. New York: International Universities Press.

Assagioli, R. (1971). *Psychosynthesis*. New York: Viking.

Blanck, G., & Blanck, R. (1974). *Ego psychology, theory and practice*. New York: Columbia University Press.

Chessick, R. (1985). *Psychology of the self and the treatment of narcissism*. Northvale, NJ: Jason Aronson.

Freud, S. (1966). On dreams. In J. Strachey (Trans.), *The standard edition of the complete psychological works of Sigmund Freud* (pp. 631–686). London: The Hogarth Press.

Friedman, W. (1984). Psychosynthesis, psychoanalysis, and the emerging developmental perspective in psychotherapy. In J. Weiser & T. Yeomans (Eds.), *Psychosynthesis in the helping professions* (pp. 31–46). Toronto: Department of Applied Psychology, Ontario Institute for Studies in Education.

Friedman, W. (1986, September). *Transference and countertransference in psychosynthesis*. Talk given at Northeastern International Center Psychosynthesis Conference, Amherst, MA.

Gill, M. (1982). *Analysis of transference* (Vol. 1). New York: International Universities Press.

Greenson, R. (1965). The working alliance and the transference neurosis. *Psychoanalysis Quarterly*, 34, 155–181.

Greenson, R. (1969, November). The exceptional position of the dream in psychoanalytic practice. The A. A. Brill Memorial Lecture.

Horner, A. (1984). *Object relations and the developing ego in therapy*. New York: Jason Aronson.

Langs, R. (1976). *The bipersonal field*. New York: Jason Aronson.

Rutan, J. S., & Stone, W. N. (1984). *Psychodynamic group psychotherapy*. Lexington, MA: D. C. Heath.

Winnicott, D. (1965). *The maturation processes and the facilitating environment*. New York: International Universities Press.

Wolstein, B. (1964). *Transference* (2nd ed.). New York: Grune & Stratton.

Yeomans, T. (1984, January). *Psychosynthesis for the helping professional training program*. Concord, MA.

Yeomans, T. (1985). Psychosynthesis: An introduction for the '80s. In J. Weiser & T. Yeomans (Eds.), *Readings in psychosynthesis: Theory process, & practice* (pp. 1–9). Toronto: Department of Applied Psychology, Ontario Institute for Studies in Education.

Yeomans, T. (1986, June). Lecture given at Advanced Training Summer Institute, Psychosynthesis for the Helping Professional, Concord, MA.

The Three Dimensions of Psychosynthesis

Thomas Yeomans

This article proposes a change in the theory of Psychosynthesis, namely that the process of psychosynthesis be conceived as having three rather than two dimensions and that these be termed "personal," "transpersonal," and "spiritual." This innovation entails drawing a distinction between "transpersonal" and "spiritual" and more fully delineating the issues of spiritual psychosynthesis. The change is proposed in the hope that it will shed light on the process of psycho-spiritual development and Self-realization as we are coming to understand it now.

Psychosynthesis, like all other theories, is a way of seeing human development and, so, is at best only an approximation of that reality.[1] Further, given the advance in our understanding of human development in this century, some of the ways of seeing within Psychosynthesis may be less useful in 1988 than they were in 1910 or 1937. This article seeks both to honor the early work in Psychosynthesis and to propose a modification in one aspect of its theory—a change which I think will help us better understand, and co-operate with, the process of psycho-spiritual development as we see it now. Time will tell the degree to which this new idea is useful; here I will only attempt to articulate it clearly so it can be examined more widely by fellow practitioners and theorists.

Background

When Roberto Assagioli first formulated Psychosynthesis, he posited two dimensions of human development—the psychological and the spiritual. This way of seeing and thinking about growth was powerful in that it acknowledged the full spectrum of human experience and supported the integration of these two dimensions in one lived reality. In 1910, this was an innovation in thought which did not achieve popularity until nearly 50 years later. Most work in the field of Psychology had stressed the psychological dimension and it was not until the advent of new thinking in the fifties and sixties that this way of seeing human development found some kin. Jung's work was, of course, the major exception to the general disregard for the spiritual dimension, as were some other minor schools of thought that developed during the first half-century.[2] But the dual formulation held up well over time, for it seems to describe accurately the process of growth that most people follow quite naturally—development along the personal dimension followed by an opening to the spiritual and subsequent growth

243

in this realm. What begins to make this theoretical distinction less precise and useful is the advent in the seventies of Transpersonal Psychology.

The development of the Fourth Force in Psychology has had several effects. One very positive outcome is a much fuller acknowledgment of spiritual development as an aspect of Psychology—an acknowledgment that has led to a far broader acceptance of spiritual phenomena within our culture. As this has happened, the terms "transpersonal" and "spiritual" have come to be understood as synonymous, and, in Psychosynthesis, for example, the Higher Self is now sometimes referred to as the "Transpersonal Self" or as the "Spiritual Self." Schools of thought and practice have emerged that recognize and seek to organize the phenomena of these two dimensions of growth as conceived in Psychosynthesis and in the spiritual disciplines of the East and those of native peoples around the world. This wealth of insight and practice has been the major contribution of Transpersonal Psychology to Psychology in the last 20 years.

Another effect of the development of the Fourth Force, however, has been less positive. As the seventies wore on and the eighties began, the term "transpersonal" was used increasingly to describe phenomena that were not necessarily spiritual in the sense that that term is used by psychosynthesists, and, in fact, by the early transpersonalists. These phenomena include psychic powers, trance, and shamanic states of consciousness, regressive and past life experiences, collective and archetypal material, channelling and sensitivity to mediums, and the opening to powerful superconscious energies. In the many versions of psychic healing and "energy" work, these are often confused with the energies of the Self. As the exploration of the human unconscious expanded, "transpersonal" increasingly became a catch-all for this vast spectrum of experience, with little attention paid to the different sources of experience within the unconscious and little discrimination as to their relative value and, at times, counter-indications for use. Specifically, the distinction between the Self and the Superconscious became blurred, if not lost, and the emphasis in therapeutic work was placed increasingly on awareness and the contents of consciousness. Less attention was paid to the development of the personal will and its alignment with the "higher" will, or will of the Self, which is a central aspect of spiritual psychosynthesis as Assagioli conceived it. In this context, spiritual work is reduced to transpersonal work in the sense that emphasis is placed on opening oneself to higher states of consciousness, or going deeper into the collective, thereby obscuring the very real issues around personal and spiritual direction, namely meaning, choice, and responsibility. It is as if the Self is merged with the unconscious, as shown in the egg diagram, and the "I" overshadowed by the dynamic energies of the psyche and the Collective.

This is perhaps an overstatement, but I think it points to a growing confusion about the spiritual dimension of work with clients. I would like to address this confusion here quite simply by proposing that we think of work with the process of psychosynthesis as differentiated by three, not two, dimensions—personal, transpersonal, and spiritual. In order to co-operate with the process of psycho-spiritual development, we need to make this distinction, both to acknowledge and to limit the transpersonal and to ensure that the spiritual dimension is honored and addressed in its own right as the core of the whole endeavor. "Transpersonal" can remain a more general term; we can still say Psychosynthesis is one of a number of transpersonal psychologies, but "transpersonal" in its use here is no longer synonymous with "spiritual." It is limited to describe work within the psyche, not with the Self.

The Personal Dimension

In the scheme I propose, the personal dimension is much as before. It contains the work of integrating the personality around a stable centre of identity and will, the "I." Work here is with subpersonalities, body, feelings, and mind identification, disidentification, and the development of the observing self. It also includes work with more unconscious aspects of the personality, early object relations and trauma, and an analysis of the functional and dysfunctional aspects of the personality as they are expressed in attitudes and behavior. Training of the personal will is also a central aspect of work in the personal realm.

The purpose of work in this dimension is to construct and/or cohere a personality structure and dynamic that is healthy and effective in both coping and expressing in the given environment.[3] Assagioli was clear that this work needed to precede opening oneself to the spiritual dimension—a conviction he shared with Jung. Western psychoanalytic and psychodynamic schools of thought concurred in this assessment, the difference being that they did not propose anything beyond this, as did Jung and Assagioli. Unfortunately, some forms of psychosynthetic practice ignored the need for thorough personal work and leaped prematurely into the spiritual. This was particularly true in the seventies when Psychosynthesis tended to be identified with the counter-culture in North America. Hopefully, this time is now past and a better balance exists between the personal and spiritual dimensions—a balance that honors the necessity of sound personality development as a foundation for spiritual opening and expression.

The Transpersonal Dimension

This is the new distinction. Previously this would have been subsumed under the spiritual dimension, but in the last 15 years the understanding of the realms of the psyche has grown and it seems more precise to differentiate this dimension of work from the others. Transpersonal work, as I am using the term, has to do with the expansion of consciousness beyond its normal limits into any realm (unconscious, personal, or collective). It entails the disciplined exploration of the various dimensions of the psyche, as portrayed in the egg diagram, for example, or work with the birth pattern and perinatal matrices as described in Stan Grof's (1985) work. Also included is work with what Jung termed the Shadow or with the Anima and Animus and their integration. It includes as well work with transgenerational patterns and past life phenomena, the emergence of psychic powers and parapsychological phenomena, altered states of consciousness, and the cultivation of superconscious qualities.

In short, the transpersonal is the realm of development that literally enables a person to know him or herself more fully and deeply, to become aware of aspects and energies that were not previously available to consciousness, and to integrate these into a more inclusive sense of identity. In all cases, the focus is on the expansion of awareness and the contents of consciousness. Obviously, a sound personality and personal will are prerequisites for doing this work safely. Neglect of the personal and a premature opening to transpersonal energies can generate further imbalance in the personality, ego inflation, and regression in behavior. Conversely, rightly used, the energies of the psyche can greatly enhance one's life, bring a fuller degree of self-knowledge, and heal, support, and foster the further development of the personality.

The Spiritual Dimension

As distinct from transpersonal work with the contents of the Unconscious, this dimension works directly with the energies of the Self, the energies of synthesis, the will of the Self, and the alignment of the personal with the spiritual will. The experience of the Self and spiritual will is central here, and this is distinguished from the transpersonal in that there is no content to this experience. The Self, this "contentless being," "suchness," "creative void," "Big Mind," whatever name the nameless is given, is seen as the context and guiding principle for the psyche and personality. Whereas psyche has content, and personality has dynamic structure, the Self is pure being which infuses the other two, much as the sun infuses atmosphere and earth. Self is not superconscious, it is not even soul, which is the experience of Self and psyche taken together, but it is an energy that permeates the entire life system and is the context for that system (see Hillman, 1975; Vaughn, 1986).

Work with the spiritual Self and its will has its own dimensions and issues, some of which I will speak of below. Spiritual work, in this sense, then, is not a matter of expanding awareness to get more content, high or low, but simply a matter of intensifying essential being, of removing obstacles to that being, and of making choices that allow that being to shine more clearly and brightly through the "lenses" of the psyche, of the personality, and of the body. Assagioli said that "the basic purpose of Psychosynthesis is to release, or let us say, help to release the energies of the Self" (1971, p. 65). The spiritual dimension works directly with these energies as they affect psyche and personality and with the experience of the will of the Self and its expression in life as a whole.

A simple model may help to clarify this distinction. If we visualize three concentric circles and posit that the innermost is the Self, the middle the psyche, and the outer the personality and if we hold that the Self is context for the psyche and the psyche is context for the personality, then we can see that the "light" of the Self will shine more fully into the world in proportion to the coherence of the "lenses" of the psyche and personality (see Figure 1). If the personality is disorganized, or the psyche chaotic, then the spiritual light of being will be blocked, distorted, or fragmented. Conversely, as the work of healing and growth goes on in the dimensions of the personality and psyche, this light will shine forth more coherently and the energies of the Self will be constructively released into the world.

The work of the personal and transpersonal dimensions is that of cohering and harmonizing the lenses, or inner systems, through which the light of being shines. The work of the spiritual dimension is that of affirming the reality of the light of being and reorganizing, through the personal and spiritual will, the outer environment so that this energy is fully released and expressed in the world.

Figure 1/ Self, Psyche, and Personality

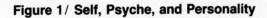
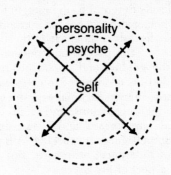

Implications

Some of the value of this distinction is immediately clear. First, because the Self is set at the very centre of work in Psychosynthesis, it becomes the context and the fruit of work in the other dimensions. Second, the distinction limits the work of expanding awareness within the psyche for what it is, and lessens the confusion between transpersonal phenomena and the experience of Spirit itself. Third, the distinction makes the will, both personal and spiritual, central to the work of Psychosynthesis. Rather than being relegated to something other than the two original dimensions, will is set at the centre of the whole process and endeavor of Self-realization as the thread of continuity that unites all three dimensions.

The distinction also allows for a more balanced conception of the process of psychosynthesis as a whole, honoring more fully the complexity and beauty of Life. Obviously, in actual work, the three dimensions are present, but at any particular time one will be in the foreground. Issues in the personal, transpersonal, and spiritual dimensions are different and should be treated differently, and when one is mistaken for the other, problems occur.

Below, I want to speak to some specific issues within spiritual psychosynthesis as it has been redefined here. As noted above, these issues in the past tended to be lumped together with transpersonal issues when in fact they are of a very different order. Coming up again and again in psychosynthetic clinical practice, they give a sense of the spiritual dimension of the work and its importance to the overall process of psycho-spiritual development. They are set under the headings of being, orientation, relationship, responsibility, and service.

Being—The experience of being is central to both the "I" and the Self. At moments of being in touch with these, there is no particular content to the consciousness, no coloration, no qualification, but simply a beingness that is both powerful and pervasive. This beingness is often accompanied by an experience of radiance, of being a source of light and life, an energy that permeates every aspect of psyche and personality and extends to others and the world. There is often an experience of being both universal and unique, having transcended all aspects of one's everyday self and yet at the same time being oneself more fully than at any other time.

This experience is radically different from being in touch with a superconscious quality, or a subpersonality. It has no content and yet it seems to hold, and be the context for, all content. It is the light out of which the coloration and the drama of the psyche and personality spring, the "unmoved mover" that is the guiding and organizing principle of inner and outer life events. Also, there is no "where" to go to have this experience; it is here/now. This contrasts to transpersonal experiences in which one journeys into a dimension of the unconscious, and seems to go far away or deep within. Being is present now/forever and is not dependent on change, growth, development, circumstance. In working with people, it is crucial to recognize and affirm this difference; otherwise, this central experience is reduced to just another aspect of the psyche.

Obviously, many spiritual practices, particularly those associated with some schools of Buddhism, aim directly at this revelation of being and bypass all content as simply "thinking, thinking; feeling, feeling." In Western psychotherapy and education, where there is more focus on content, this experience is only beginning to be recognized and cultivated (see Deikman, 1982). In Psychosynthesis, it is, and always has been, a touchstone for healing and human development, but it can be overlooked, or confused with very "high" content in the psyche.

Orientation—This issue concerns the basic life direction of the person or how the personality is oriented as a whole. It entails work with the alignment of the personal and spiritual will and the making of choices that energize and realize the deepest sense of direction, calling, destiny, and value that the person is aware of. It does not have to do with gaining more awareness— this is the work of the personal and transpersonal dimensions—but with choosing to choose on the basis of what one is aware of, to act in accord with what is felt as deepest and truest within one's soul. Many people avoid the issue of orientation by continuing to do personal and transpersonal work, mistakenly thinking that more work on expanding their awareness will help. Such work does not in and of itself help. What they need, rather, is encouragement to make real choices that will align their daily behavior with their spiritual will and help them recognize the intent of the Self so that they may give themselves to it fully. Issues of sacrifice, surrender, voluntary suffering, and self-forgetfulness all come to the fore here, and need to be treated seriously as spiritual struggles, not reduced to psychic or psychodynamic problems. A growing number of people who have integrated their personalities and have an ample amount of self-knowledge are struggling with these spiritual issues, and are hard put to find a therapist or counsellor who will acknowledge these issues in their own right.

A second area where orientation is of concern lies in what is sometimes termed a crisis of expression. Developmentally, this crisis tends to come after the growth crises of earlier life and the existential crises of mid-life, and it occurs when a person begins to recognize an expanded arena of expression that he or she is called to enter, leaving behind a familiar and often successful one. Again, this crisis is not resolved through expanded awareness, though some reworking of psyche and personality may be necessary to support the move, but rather through a series of choices that effect a move into this larger arena. This move entails personal sacrifice, but there is also a recognition of the "rightness" of the choice and a resultant increase in the flow of energies of the Self into the world. Accompanying the move is often a clearer sense and a fuller acceptance of one's place in the world, of one's strengths and limitations, and a recognition of one's involvement in and responsibility to the larger community. People in this crisis need support that recognizes these issues for what they are, and deals with them accordingly.

Relationship—As contact with the Self and the flow of the energies of synthesis grow, a new experience of relationship begins to emerge. Whereas earlier relationships involved a particular person or thing, often excluding others and reflecting some degree of attachment (or cathexis), at these moments the experience of relationship is of both detachment and kinship to all people and things, all aspects of creation. This lends an almost impersonal quality to relationships, even as they become, paradoxically, more immediate and intimate. For most, this is a matter of a moment only, an experience that comes and goes quickly; for a few, it becomes a fairly consistent experience. But the point is that it is *different*, whether it is built upon a relationship with one person or a number of people and things. It brings with it a realization of being inextricably interconnected with all Life and an awareness of the implications for "normal" relationships which tend in themselves to be exclusive and polarized. A common example of this realization is the recognition that occurs after intense work with one's own suffering as a child that "all children are my children."[4] The experience has no particular quality or specific focus, but it is an aspect of the touch of the Self and the inflow of a spiritual love that Dante had characterized as that which "moves the sun and all the stars." The experience needs recognition and validation in and of itself; it is an indication of the inherent participation of the Self in all life and of the universal aspect of identity.

Responsibility—The issue here concerns taking a stand in your life and doing your part in the world. It involves acting on what you know best at any particular time, being willing to make a mistake and to learn from it, and recognizing that only through choice and behavior can the energies of the Self be fully expressed. Responsibility is based on consciousness, but a response requires the transformation of consciousness into action. The action may be inner or outer, highly visible or known only to Self, but without it the process of psychosynthesis is blocked. Only by taking personal and spiritual responsibility, as expressed in behavior that is in line with one's calling, can the Higher Self express itself in the world.

If issues around taking responsibility are interpreted on a psychodynamic or transpersonal level and are treated as such, the opportunity for expression is delayed and the release of the energies of the Self impeded. Often work needs to be done at other levels to support taking spiritual responsibility, but this work is not the same as that of making choices, acting, and learning from the experience of Self-expression. The spiritual response requires a direct confrontation with the world, with those forces within and without that resist this action, and a willingness to be seen and heard in the light of one's deepest values. Taking spiritual responsibility in the world is the final flower of the process of psychosynthesis.

Service—The fruit, then, of the endeavor is service. Yet there is a great deal of confusion about the word and the experience. The most common mistake is to introduce service as a concept before work has been completed at the personal and transpersonal levels. This results in a forced experience of service, rooted in guilt and shame, inner or outer coercion, and intellec-tualized goodness, or its rejection as oppressive and arbitrary. The true experience of service is the deepest instinct and need of the Self. As a person matures, the impulse to be of service to others and the world natur-ally emerges, not as an arbitrary thought or as a concept imposed from a belief system, but as a natural outcome of life's development. The experi-ence of service is rooted in one's being, in presence to all life, a balance in the giving and receiving of love, and a recognition of the sacredness of all lives, including one's own. It is completely natural to the human being, and is the outpouring of the energies of the Self. That it is blocked in so many of us is only a measure of how disconnected we have become from the Self.

Service is seen quite often in children who are still connected to their deeper nature, in mature adults who have reconnected, and intermittently in the rest of us at those moments of Self-connection when we open to the reality of Self and "see the world" through its perspective. The need to serve is a spiritual issue involving the alignment of personal and spiritual will and the sustained release of the energies of the Self into the world. Work on personal and transpersonal issues is clearly prerequisite, but these issues are not to be confused with the experience itself and its acknowledgment and careful support.

Synthesis

The above gives a brief idea of the distinct clinical issues encountered in spiritual psychosynthesis. Clearly, the three dimensions, personal, transper-sonal, and spiritual, are inherently interconnected and in actual work all three are present in some proportion. But developmentally one is usually foreground, and if one dimension is mistaken for another, then difficulties arise in the work and the process is not fully supported. Conversely, if we can recognize each dimension for what it is, and address directly the issues that properly belong to it, then we greatly increase the precision of our co-operation with the Self in our work, and in this way are able to help release the energies of synthesis within the person for healing, growth, and service. The three dimensions, I believe, also apply to the development of couples, families, groups, organizations, and perhaps nations and the planet as a whole. For the moment, however, they are most clearly grounded in clinical practice with the individual. Should the distinction prove useful, then work can proceed in testing it at these other levels as well.

Psychosynthesis, like all systems of thought, all theories, or ways of seeing, is evolving, and I offer this one change as an aspect of its evolution. My hope is that it will allow us to see more clearly what is true about individuals and their development and to be of greater help in healing and nourishing both person and planet. If the idea is of use, then it will illuminate work in Psychosynthesis in a natural and common-sense way. What is needed now is the testing of its validity within the context of clinical and educational work. I invite fellow practitioners to this task and to the continuing examination of how we "see" and what its impact is on both our practice and our lives.

Notes

1. It is useful to remember that the word *theory* is derived from the ancient Greek *theorein*, which means "to see." A theory, then, is a "way of seeing" a topic, and different people will have different theories, depending on how they experience reality. Some theories will be more general, some more specific. All theories are biased and limited in some way. Therefore, the work of developing theory is to find a way of seeing that seems to fit the phenomena under observation and at the same time can gain enough consensus among fellow "seers" to be generally accepted. All theories are at best approximations and therefore never true in an absolute sense. They can, however, help us see what is "there" to the best of our knowledge at the time. As we "see" more clearly over time, we can modify our theories or we can reject them as they cease to be useful. At any point in time, certain theories will inform the "seeing" of the majority while other theories will have a more marginal existence, either because they are becoming obsolete or because they have not yet been recognized as holding a way of seeing that reveals reality. Examining a theory, then, involves studying how people see certain phenomena and assessing how useful this way of seeing is in its capacity to illuminate and explain the aspect of reality under scrutiny.

    At the moment in Psychology, a number of ways of seeing human development, function, and dysfunction exist side by side. The broad schools of thought in this century have been psychoanalytic, behavioral, humanistic, and transpersonal, but within each there have been many subschools with methods and techniques based on their particular ways of seeing. On the one hand, this has generated a fragmented and often conflicting array of possible approaches to healing and development. On the other, it points to the eventual emergence of a unified theory that will be capable of helping us see how the schools of thought are interrelated. This theory has yet to be found, but there are people working toward it. By the end of the century, we may have made a solid beginning toward a unified way of seeing human development in all its dimensions.

2. Victor Frankl's logotherapy is one example; Rudolf Steiner's thinking on education another.

3. In recent years, psychosynthesists have paid greater attention to psychopathology, recognizing that techniques for the various neurotic disorders were not appropriate for more severe dysfunction within the personality. This has led to the development of new techniques, still consonant with the principles of Psychosynthesis and appropriate for dealing with this level of pathology, and a consequent expansion of the dimensions of work in personal psychosynthesis.

4.   It is interesting to note that clinically this experience almost always follows the experience of the client's own particular pain. This is true also of outrage at world conditions, which follows from the release of personal anger about issues in one's own life. This would indicate that a true experience of "larger love" is rooted in a confrontation with personal suffering. Without this, the claim to this level of love can easily become platitudinous, superficial, and eventually used as a reaction formation to repressed and denied personal material.

References

Assagioli, R. (1971). *Psychosynthesis*. New York: Viking.

Dante, A. (1961). *The divine comedy*. London: Oxford University Press.

Deikman, A. (1982). *The observing self*. Boston: Beacon Press.

Grof, S. (1985). *Beyond the brain*. New York: SUNY Press.

Hillman, J. (1975). *Revisioning psychology*. New York: Harper & Row.

Vaughn, F. (1986). *The inward arc*. Boston: Shambala.

Psychosynthesis as Science

Douglas Russell

This article argues for psychosynthesis to become more scientific. The reader may, therefore, be surprised that I report rumors, I share my hunches, and I generalize, assuming that my personal experience can be applied to psychosynthesis as a whole. At the same time, I criticize the unscientific behavior of my colleagues. Notice I say "behavior," for I firmly believe that my fellow psychosynthesists have usually been dedicated and well-meaning, even when behaving at their worst. I wish to be the good critic, motivated by a quest for Truth—a quest that is fundamental to the values of scientists and spiritual seekers as well. Furthermore, my criticism is meant to be constructive, so I end on a positive note: I propose solutions to the problems I find in psychosynthesis today.

I write this as an open letter to my psychosynthesis colleagues, but it is intended for a broader audience. For readers who do not specialize in psychosynthesis, I want to stress that the central issue here is not limited to psychosynthesis; rather, it is the more general issue of whether *any psychology*, particularly a *transpersonal psychology*, can really be a science.

Psychosynthesis was described by its founder Roberto Assagioli as a spiritual psychology—a movement which aimed to develop a "science of the Self" (1965). Deikman points out that one can evaluate if a spiritual movement is genuine by "paying attention to how well a group's activities are suited to its stated aims" (1983, p. 9). I believe that if we are to become genuinely spiritual, our activities must indicate that we are developing a science.

I give many examples here of attitudes and behavior among my fellow psychosynthesists which are pseudo-scientific, anti-scientific, anti-theoretical, anti-intellectual. The spiritual idealists among us emphasize what works and are enthusiastic about the powerful effects of their training programs. They have at once a mystical dedication to the process of psychosynthesis and a mistrust of science. They attempt to integrate their mysticism and their pragmatism, but they fall short, reflecting instead the split in our culture between the spiritual and the scientific. They have not yet integrated recent developments in transpersonal psychology which point the way to our becoming mystical scientists, or scientific mystics (Tart, 1975). Thus we see evidence of weaknesses in psychosynthesis, both as a scientific discipline and as a spiritual movement. We aim to be a scientific psychology fostering transcendence and spiritual values. Yet we are not pursuing a thoroughly scientific quest for Truth. At best, we are an incomplete science at an early stage of its development. At worst, we have the features of a cult, emphasizing fear, greed, power, guilt, and vanity.

Our egocentrism sabotages the major goal of personal psychosynthesis: to facilitate identification with the personal self. We aim to be a movement fostering autonomous self-actualizers. But are we *really* empowering people to become autonomous? Deikman notes:

> Pressure toward conformity to group standards and ideals, inhibition of critical thinking, and reliance on the magic of the leader . . . work in the wrong direction. If the group does not inhibit or punish challenge and criticism, if it refuses to play parent to its members, and if it discourages their magical expectations, it can [enhance autonomy]. (1983, p. 15)

I give examples below to illustrate how our behavior has discouraged autonomy and attributed a magical quality to our founder. There is a lack of critical thinking and a lack of commitment to Truth. At the same time, we are sabotaging the major goal of spiritual or transpersonal psychosynthesis: to go beyond the personal self toward identification with the Transpersonal Self. Psychosynthesis aims to be a movement which fosters transcendence and spiritual values. Why, then, don't we pursue a thoroughly scientific quest for Truth—a transpersonal quality that we value?

> A genuine spiritual organization is run in such a way as to assist the student in making the shift from a self-centered life to one that is Truth-centered. An organization in which the methods of operation enhance selfish intentions can be adjudged dysfunctional. Such a group might do a good job of meeting other needs, but it is not actually engaged in spiritual development. (Deikman, 1983, p. 10)

It may seem paradoxical, but it is only by becoming more thoroughly scientific that psychosynthesis can realize its spiritual ideals.

Since this article focusses on scientific method, readers may be anticipating a heavily theoretical presentation. I assure you that there is some humor along the way and juicy criticism of my colleagues near the end. I am aware of the Native American saying, "Do not criticize unless you have walked a mile in the other's moccasins." But since I've found few psychosynthesists who own moccasins, I've decided to criticize anyway, without naming names, and being sure to criticize myself as well.

Is Psychosynthesis a Science?

The seeds for this article were germinated at a conference I attended in the summer, 1987, by a question posed by Dr. Ronald Jue, President of the Association of Transpersonal Psychology: Is psychosynthesis alive and growing, or is it being absorbed by other disciplines? (Stated differently, does psychosynthesis have a unique identity and place in the world, or is it merely a hodgepodge of ideas and techniques that are being used in various ways by many other types of transpersonalists, New Agers, and holistic healers?) At the time, I had no ready answer to this haunting question. I saw evidence suggesting growth and evidence suggesting dissolution. While in London in the summer of 1986, I saw the two large training institutes thriving. I also saw other signs of vitality in our ranks, such as the recent series of regional conferences on the east coast of the U.S. and the international conference in Italy planned for summer 1988. Yet locally, in California, training centres in Los Angeles and San Francisco had closed, and only a few small training programs remained. I knew personally of many people who had left psychosynthesis as a specialty, among them some of the most effective leaders in the development of psychosynthesis training programs.

It disturbed me that the question of whether psychosynthesis was growing or fading came from a man with so much knowledge of the world of transpersonal psychology. His question indicated that our growth in psychosynthesis was not being communicated to our professional colleagues. Also, I was troubled about continuing to invest energy in psychosynthesis as a writer and psychotherapist. Was I an adherent to some obscure form of psychology which had been unique 20 years ago but which was now being absorbed by the more recent developments in humanistic and transpersonal psychology? Why wasn't psychosynthesis known outside its own circle of specialists? Could it be that as psychosynthesists we had no unique identity, no contribution to make, and no future? Answers to these questions came to me from looking at psychosynthesis as a science.

The process of science is the growth and refinement of knowledge in a particular domain. If psychosynthesis is scientific, it has to be growing. It also needs some limits or boundaries defining its focus, its domain. It has to have a recognized body of knowledge, for it is the function of scientists to produce ordered knowledge (Marx, 1963). Assagioli himself once said that the major weakness of psychosynthesis is that it is too inclusive (1973). Yet where there is no boundary, there is no identity, no science. Some may rejoice in Assagioli's view of psychosynthesis as all-encompassing, but I recoil. Rather, I respond to the Assagioli who characterized his early work as an infant science.

Implicit in my other theoretical writings is the idea that, in fact, there *are* boundaries to psychosynthesis (Russell, 1981, 1982, 1985). Having a history with specific philosophical and spiritual roots creates one boundary: we are a movement, a tradition. As a "science of the Self," we focus on identity, particularly the personal self and its relationship to subpersonalities and the Transpersonal Self. And I also think there is another boundary: we explore the realm of soul, but not the realm of spirit. In Assagioli's words, "Psychosynthesis does not aim nor attempt to give . . . [an] explanation of the great Mystery—it leads to the door, but stops there" (1965, pp. 6–7). With the parameters of psychosynthesis thus delineated, we can affirm that there *is* a specific domain, and that we are indeed a particular aspect of modern psychology—a science which investigates certain levels of consciousness or identity.

If psychosynthesis is a science, then it should contain the elements outlined by Charles Tart in his transpersonal view of science:

> Scientific method can be reduced to four basic principles: (A) good observation; (B) the public nature of observation; (C) the necessity to theorize logically; and (D) the testing of theory against predicted, observable consequences. In a sense, this is "common sense." The scientist is someone who is more aware of and committed to these rules than the ordinary man. (1975, p. 22)

Tart sees the scientific search for Truth as a cyclical process which extends and refines knowledge. Observations (A) in a given field lead to theories (C) which are tested (D). This leads to more refined observing, more accurate theorizing, and further tests (research). The public nature of this investigation (B) means that scientists communicate their observations, theories, and experiments—primarily through conferences and publications. Other scientists can then validate, modify, or invalidate the conclusions and scientific knowledge continues to grow and be refined even further.

Applying this circular process to psychosynthesis, we can say that practice generates theory, and that theory guides practice. Examples from other disciplines help to clarify this. In physics, *Einstein's theories guided practice*. Researchers designed experiments to test those theories and thereby gained a great deal of new knowledge about sub-atomic particles. Data from test results led to new practical applications: for example, generating electricity with a nuclear reactor. Conversely, in music, *Bach's practices generated theory*. This music master had no theory of composition. He wrote intuitively, emphasizing practice. Two hundred years later, a musicologist analyzed the harmonies in Bach's chorales and found definite patterns which are now a part of modern music theory—the rules of harmony. Today this aspect of music theory provides composers with guidelines for adding pleasing harmonies to their melodies. To date, psychosynthesists have, for the most part, tended to emphasize practice—the applied, experiential, factual side of science. I believe we need to enhance our practice by refining our theories—the abstract, conceptual side of science.

It is clear that Assagioli's goal was to make psychosynthesis a part of Western psychology. Thus psychosynthesists would want to apply scientific method. While I criticize the current inadequacies of psychosynthesists as scientists, I agree with Deikman:

> Human activity is always flawed. It is expected that whatever personality flaws a teacher may possess, they will not be allowed to interfere with the teaching activity, and certainly not to determine it. Whenever inappropriate group behavior occurs it is to be noted and eliminated. The important and obvious point is that the behavior of the teacher and the group must contribute to achieving the stated goal. (1983, p. 17)

Assagioli gave us a mixed message when he attempted to place psychosynthesis in the field of psychology and yet resisted boundaries or definitions:

> Psychosynthesis is not a doctrine or a "school" of psychology; it is not a special or single method of self-realization, therapy, education, interpersonal and social (group) relations and integration.
>   It can be indicated (I do not use the word "define," because all definitions are limited and limiting) primarily as a general attitude of, and striving towards, integration and synthesis in all fields, but particularly in those just mentioned. It might be called a "movement," a "trend" and a "goal." (1981, p. 1)

Psychosynthesists have provided alternatives to these anti-scientific statements of Assagioli. For example, a distinction is made between "psychosynthesis" as a universal process of integration and synthesis and "Psychosynthesis" as a particular form of psychology that studies this process. I don't care for the capital "P," so I use the uncapitalized word to mean the tradition, the school of psychology, founded by Assagioli.* I believe that for my purpose here it is best called an "open system." I think of the general trend toward integration and synthesis as "evolution" (Russell, 1982).

Theories of the Self relate integration to the personal self and synthesis to the Transpersonal Self.

Is Psychosynthesis Growing?

Returning to the question, "Is psychosynthesis growing?", I now say, definitely yes! After some months of pondering this question, I focussed on the evidence for growth and found it convincing. Psychosyntheists have symbolized this growth as parallelling the development of a human being. In 1965, Assagioli wrote, "I consider (psychosynthesis) as a child—or at the most an adolescent." In 1983, Evans wrote:

> Psychosynthesis as a psychological and educational framework is in the early adolescent stage of development. The coming of age, the maturing, [is] rarely visible except among a few people who [are] willing to both question many of the established ideas and models and to see the need for serious research and debate. I think many of the existing psychosynthesis models have been taken too literally and are I believe often used somewhat naively today. I think we need at this time to be more rigorous in our thinking about psychosynthesis theories and models and particularly in how we use them. Perhaps through our willingness to consider the illusions in these models, the more spiritually pragmatic we become in our views of reality. (p. 7)

In 1987, I have concluded that as we heed Evans's call for serious research and debate, and as we become more rigorous in our thinking about our theories and models, we can actively foster the maturation of psychosynthesis into adulthood. I believe this can be achieved *now* through applications of all four aspects of scientific method. I also believe that when this is done we need no longer consider psychosynthesis an infant science or an adolescent movement. Instead, it will be revealed as a young adult, still immature but with a fully formed identity of its own. I feel it is up to us to be the kind of parents who support this growth beyond our family of specialists into the larger world of humanistic and transpersonal modalities.

As to evidence for growth in psychosynthesis, the development of training programs is one clear indication. Virtually unknown in the early 1900s outside Assagioli's base in Florence, Italy, psychosynthesis is now practised throughout the Western world. Training centres are established in Western Europe, the Americas, Australia, and New Zealand. The work has also been introduced in India, Japan, and the USSR. The fact that the number of training centres or groups has continued to expand since the 1960s indicates vitality in the movement. Though no accurate statistics have been kept, I estimate that there were less than 10 training centres active before 1970, more than 20 by the mid-1970s, and more than 50 by the early 1980s. Although a number of centres have closed, many trainers who worked in them are now conducting programs in new locations.

There is also strong evidence of growth in the body of psychosynthesis literature in the past three decades. By the 1960s, Assagioli had published some articles and one book, and the Psychosynthesis Research Foundation (PRF) in New York was publishing a series of monographs and reports of meetings. Perhaps only two authors besides Assagioli had published in professional journals. To my knowledge, few journal articles have appeared

since the 1960s, but psychosynthesists have self-published a great deal. By
the mid-1970s, Assagioli's second book and four issues of the periodical
Synthesis were published. In 1981–86, there were five issues of *Psychosynthesis Digest*. The 1980s have also seen publication of a newsletter, the
London Institute *Yearbooks* and monographs, and several major books
including Ferrucci (1982), Brown (1983), Weiser and Yeomans (1984, 1985),
Whitmore (1986), and Hardy (1987). There has also been a great deal of
literature generated by the training centres and their students since the late
1960s—brochures describing training programs, pamphlets, experiential
exercises, photocopied handouts, monographs, and student projects. Addi-
tionally, there have been many M.A. theses and Ph.D. dissertations completed in non-traditional universities.

The training programs and the proliferation of a psychosynthesis literature
are signs of observation and theory building, principles A and C, in Tart's
explanation of scientific method. As for our observations (A), I don't know
if they are "good." That is, I don't know if our observations about growth in
identity are useful, workable, predictive, life-enhancing. This needs to be
researched, but there has been almost no research or scientific testing in
psychosynthesis, principle D in Tart's scheme. There is a great deal of
psychosynthesis theory (C), although it is not particularly comprehensive
and may not have a consistent logic at this stage. As for the public nature
of our observations, principle B, much of our literature is unavailable! A lot
of material generated at the various training centres remains at those
centres. Also, while there are many training groups and individual
psychosynthesis specialists, most of their work has not been described in
print and thereby disseminated. Communication with our colleagues outside
psychosynthesis through established professional journals is almost nil. In
short, the activities of psychosynthesis today attest to haphazard application
of the four steps of scientific method. I conclude that we are long on observing and theorizing, but short on researching and communicating.

How do we remedy this situation? How do we make psychosynthesis a
more mature science? The remainder of this article addresses these questions by examining the principles of scientific method as they pertain to the
theory and practice of psychosynthesis. I examine each step in the most
natural and logical order: (1) research, (2) theorizing, (3) observation, and (4)
the public nature of the work.

1. Suggested Research

I believe that the first step in gathering more facts about psychosynthesis is
to locate the already voluminous literature. Is the rumor accurate that
Assagioli wrote over 300 articles? Only the Istituto di Psicosintesi in Florence is in a position to tell. When I visited the Istituto in 1977, I found that
it had "archives"—Assagioli's notes on little scraps of paper, catalogued and
available—but there was no mention of his unpublished articles. Scientific
investigators need access to a list of titles, an annotated bibliography, and
the articles themselves. Hardy's (1987) list is a promising beginning.

Another question: Who holds the copyrights to the *Synthesis* journals
published by the San Francisco Institute? Perhaps the former directors can
take the lead in making this out-of-print material available to all of us. In

addition, each psychosynthesis centre could gather a list of titles, prepare an annotated bibliography, and make all its printed materials available to researchers. I know this is a lot to ask of the centres, and I don't mean to imply that these groups are just sitting around and twiddling their thumbs. But I *am* saying that this contribution to the whole is sorely needed if psychosynthesis is to manifest its full potential as a science.

I believe the sum total of literature which is not catalogued or listed constitutes considerably more than half of all that we have produced. Alternatively, the following is readily available: The London Institute stocks all the old *PRF* monographs (which are public domain) along with several institute publications. The Psychosynthesis Press still has back issues of the *Digest* on sale. The newsletter and books mentioned at the beginning of this article are all currently available through their respective publishers. Dissertations and theses may be more difficult to track. Here in California, there are perhaps seven major alternative degree programs which probably could provide leads on obtaining psychosynthesis-based student projects.

I realize that this research—cataloging the extant body of literature in psychosynthesis—is a major project. It requires not only leadership, but also funding and personnel. However, it is definitely feasible, assuming that the psychosynthesis centres would co-operate. The extent of their co-operation is the extent to which psychosynthesis will be able to become all it can be as a scientific psychology in the near future.

In addition to making the whole of psychosynthesis literature available to those of us in the field there is also the issue of making it available to other researchers. Once it is catalogued, it could be placed in library computer data bases. I was appalled to hear that in 1987 yet another Ph.D. student attempted a literature search and the library computer indicated not one psychosynthesis-based article or book. Typical computer responses include, "Psychowhat?" and "Do you mean *photo*synthesis?" It is high time for our literature to come out of hiding so that psychosynthesis specialists, transpersonal psychologists, and others can examine its full range to date and thus contribute more intelligently to the evolution of the field.

A second major research thrust that I see as important and presently feasible is a study of the current psychosynthesis training programs. Would centres co-operate with researchers by having their trainers interviewed and by providing course outlines, handouts, and reading lists so that the nature of psychosynthesis training could be studied and communicated to all? This would go a long way toward defining the nature of psychosynthesis today.

A third major research thrust would be to identify and build on current research in psychosynthesis. The only research I know about has been reported by the International Association for Managerial and Organizational Psychosynthesis (IAMOP). In this research, Dr. John Cullen demonstrates that the basic psychosynthesis training course he adapted for MBA students *does* foster self-actualization. This research, using two scientifically-tested instruments, could be replicated in the basic training programs of other centres with the same simple pre- and post-tests of trainees. IAMOP researchers are also developing instruments to identify the seven psychological types, a psychosynthesis typology suggested by Assagioli (1973, 1983).

A fourth direction for research would come out of reviewing the complete literature and compiling a thorough overview of psychosynthesis theorizing to date. This abstract or conceptual side of our work is, I believe, already well-developed. A synthesis of extant theorizing would demonstrate that we have a coherent conceptual framework—that psychosynthesis is in fact a "system," not a hodgepodge of techniques. I think we would find common threads through all our literature indicating repeated use of a large number of constructs, theories, and scientific models. Recall that theory guides practice. The systematic presentation of psychosynthesis theory is the groundwork needed for generating hypotheses required for meaningful research in the future. Without this research we cannot honestly claim to be a maturing science with validated knowledge; rather, we remain prescientific with only "proto-knowledge."

2. Theory Building

Theory is the conceptual aspect of science. It is complementary to the empirical, fact-gathering aspect, observation. The interaction of theory and observation leads to meaningful research. The behaviorists describe theory as both a tool and a goal. As a tool, "systematic theory . . . guides observation and discovery. There are no raw facts" (Marx, 1963, p. 6). In transpersonal lingo, our belief systems shape our perceptions and our experiences. As a goal, "theory is useful because it provides an economical and efficient means of abstracting, codifying, summarizing, integrating, and storing information" (Marx, 1963, p. 6). In other words, theory supports integration and synthesis.

The word "theory" is used in different ways in science. The most common usage connotes its overall integrative function. This is akin to the concept of a system. For example, "psychosynthesis theory" refers to the set of concepts upon which the practice of psychosynthesis is based. A more technical definition of the word "theory" is useful to grasp the nature of theory building. In this definition, a theory is a hypothesis that has been verified, and a theory that has been verified repeatedly by independent researchers is called a "law." Thus we see a sequence in the refining of knowledge, moving from uncertainty toward greater degrees of certainty—from a hypothesis to a theory to a law.

A hypothesis is a conjecture or surmise that states a relationship among variables. A hypothesis is also a conjecture that can be tested. For example, Cullen's research on psychosynthesis training for managers tested the hypothesis, "Psychosynthesis basic training fosters the self-actualization process in our students." This conjecture grew out of Dr. Cullen's observations of psychosynthesis training and writings and was tested through the use of concrete pre- and post-tests.

Two other terms complete the basics of theory building—"construct" and "model." A construct is a special kind of concept. Simple concepts refer to things, or events, while a construct refers to "relationships among things and/or events, and their various properties" (Marx, 1963, p. 10). In my view, basic constructs in psychosynthesis theory are "synthesis," "personality," "evolution," "energy," "higher consciousness," "the Self," and "the will" (Russell, 1981). Marx, cited above, also points out that in the formative stages of a new discipline, the prescientific phase, constructs are often abstract and vague, but more specific concepts and hypotheses can be derived from constructs as the discipline evolves scientifically.

Unlike a hypothesis, a "model" in science does not require testing. Creating a model is "acting as if," or making an assumption which generates data, thus contributing to the growth of theory and practice. An example of a model is the egg diagram. We do not need to prove it right or wrong, but we assume that it is portraying something real. Then we design experiential exercises and generate concepts based upon it. In this way, the egg diagram has proved to be a very useful model indeed. Another example of a scientific model in psychology is Ken Wilber's (1977) "spectrum of consciousness" model. It has been very helpful for psychosynthesis theory in clarifying and defining the levels of the Self and the relationships between these levels.

In a prior article, I demonstrated how Wilber's spectrum of consciousness model is a most promising base for a science of the Self, as it readily suggests a psychosynthesis "spectrum of identity" model (Russell, 1983). Four hierarchical levels of the Self are "subpersonalities," "ego," "personal self," and "Transpersonal Self." This link to Wilber's model places psychosynthesis in the mainstream of Western psychology's most recent developments—the third force (humanistic psychology) and the fourth force (transpersonal psychology).

The spectrum of identity model relates psychosynthesis not only to the world of psychology but also to business and education. My latest efforts in theory building have not been in the therapeutic arena but in applications to manager training and organizational development (Cullen & Russell, 1987). Levels of the Self parallel the levels in Maslow's hierarchy of needs, a familiar model to managers and organizational consultants. The spectrum of identity model can also be applied to education as a developmental model, that is, a description of growth from a limited identity to more expanded levels of identity. We can draw parallels between our theories of the Self and theories of child development, cognitive development, and learning theory. Assagioli's vision of psychosynthesis applications in many fields is coming to fruition in psychology, business, and education through the utility of our spectrum of identity model.

While I have focussed on this particular model in recent years, other theorists have been exploring other important dimensions of psychosynthesis theory-building. For example, articles by McBeath and Wynne (1985) relate our ideas to general systems theory. Crampton (1980) makes many enlightening and useful points in her discussion of organismic theory. Caldironi's (1984) "Utopian Proposal" contains theory that can explain and potentially empower the current trend of networking. Hardy (1987) provides a broad historical perspective. All these hold great promise for the growth and refinement of the conceptual side of psychosynthesis.

I have noted in an earlier section that good theory guides good practice. A major implication of this section is that good theory also leads to good research—testing the value of psychosynthesis practices. Applications of psychosynthesis will be all the more practical and effective as their strengths and limitations are revealed through applying all four aspects of the scientific method—what Tart refers to as common sense. My own strong conviction is that psychosynthesists can build a more adequate theory by understanding the elements of theory building in the sciences—hypotheses, theories, laws, constructs, and models.

3. Observations

Our literature contains a great deal of observation—statements about human nature and descriptions of experiences with psychosynthesis techniques. In this section, I am going to emphasize my personal observations of psychosynthesis. I believe I am a qualified observer, having been involved in this work for two decades and counting among my acquaintances and friends many past and present psychosynthesis trainers and directors of centres in Europe and the Americas. I have been particularly active as a psychotherapist, trainer, writer, and publisher in the western U.S. I believe my observations reflect some important truths about psychosynthesis, but I hasten to temper this belief with the *mantra of humility*: one sits, preferably in the lotus position, folds the hands in the lap, closes the eyes, and repeats several times the phrase, "I could be wrong."

As I am about to launch into criticism of the behavior of some of my psychosynthesis colleagues, my "Mr. Nice Guy" subpersonality feels uncomfortable. He believes that criticism is bad. But the "thinker" comes to the rescue: "to be scientific involves sceptical attitudes and critical thinking." Wow! That got me centred immediately. If I start to get off-centre, I can now invoke the scholarly trick of quoting some authorities establishing precedents for doing this. Thus I can feel like a great scientist, standing on the shoulders of giants. For example, "The enemy is us" (Pogo). Gestaltists would encourage us to "re-own our projections." The Jungian attitude would be that we get into trouble if we ignore the "shadow." In 1982, James Fadiman addressed this issue in a letter to psychosynthesists:

> It will serve us all to keep the communication channels more open . . . to be the kind of friends to one another who can see faults and can tell each other of them. [Let's be] . . . informed of our successes as well as our failures so that we may understand that it is only by being human that we aspire towards personal and transpersonal integration. (pp. 87–88)

Since the first time I felt deeply hurt or angered by my colleagues, or critical of them, I have followed a principle I adapted from yogic teachings: "[The psychosynthesist] . . . understands the faults of others by seeing and studying them first in himself. This self-study teaches him to be charitable to all" (Iyengar, 1966, p. 27). Thus I proceed with some confessions:

1. I exemplify the Peter Principle. I was a good therapist who became a good trainer of therapists. Then I rose to my level of incompetence as a manager/administrator. First I became the director of a therapist training program and then the founder of a psychosynthesis training centre. Finally, as publisher of *Psychosynthesis Digest*, I lacked the organizational skills needed to meet promised deadlines and often delayed answering the mail.

2. I have not been immune to ego trips. Power struggles with a colleague at one point led to a parting of the ways which was hurtful to many of our students and to psychosynthesis itself. Also, I once tried to exercise control

over another group's training program. I asked a new centre to use training outlines that I had developed and pay me a percentage for doing so. To the group's credit, it refused my offer. I now call this franchising approach "Psycho McSynthesis."

3. I have been a naïve idealist. I have assumed that psychosynthesists always lived up to transpersonal values with no ego problems. I have failed in two major projects—founding a training centre and a publication—plunging ahead to manifest my ideal without the organization, planning, or funding that would have minimized the risk of failure.

I confess partly because I believe that many psychosynthesists share these weaknesses and may benefit by knowing of my experiences. I have learned first and foremost to see my strengths and weaknesses more clearly. Focussing on the strengths I have discovered, I can contribute to psychosynthesis more effectively. Knowing my weaknesses, I can better acknowledge my need to reach out to my colleagues and to affiliate with those whose skills and talents complement my own.

As publisher of the *Digest*, I found that others shared my limitations. When I wrote letters to the psychosynthesis centres, I found that over half of them didn't answer their mail. I attributed this in some cases to a lack of organizational skills. There is also an isolationist tendency, each group focussing locally and not participating in the larger whole. In some instances, I believe this lack of co-operation is due to a weak identity, a lack of confidence, and the fear of being somehow controlled or influenced by other centres or leaders.

An ego trip that gave psychosynthesis a cult-like flavor was demonstrated in the mid-1970s by a group that I shall call here the "San Fiasco Institute." A powerful group of trainers attempted to become the centralized authority controlling psychosynthesis training internationally. This aberration has been discussed briefly in print by Evans (1983). When this group's representatives came to our centre, which had been established for several years, they insisted that in order for us to affiliate with them, we would have to turn over the administration of our centre to them completely. They would train us and decide when we were ready to do the training right! Nothing could be further from good science than the imposition of authority and the attitude that "ours is the right and only way." Deikman has pointed out that this is an error for a spiritual group also.

I kept wanting to believe that affiliation with all my psychosynthesis colleagues was possible, and that, surely, when push came to shove, this group would invoke its highest values and transcend ego limitations. I invited San Fiasco staff members to observe one of my weekend training workshops. When it was over, one of them stood at a blackboard lecturing me on what I was doing wrong. In addition to being outraged by this person's behavior, I saw that my practice of psychosynthesis was essentially similar to his, merely presented in a different sequence and with different emphases. I was upset by this episode, mainly because it shattered my ideals about the centredness and spirituality of psychosynthesists. I was disillusioned. I also felt wounded by being excluded, separated from my colleagues, left out of their club.

As I felt so devastated by this distortion and its harm to the psychosyn-thesis movement, I travelled to Europe in the summer of 1977, where I met with many directors of programs who were more detached from the situation than I was. They were simply getting on with their work. I learned from them to trust in psychosynthesis principles, to believe that these would guide the movement, and that any personality distortions were ephemeral. My own observation was that this was not just a bad episode, a "learning experience" for those involved. It and other ego-based failures in our work have caused real damage to the health and family lives of individuals in the movement as well as to the standing of psychosynthesis with the public at large. Many disillusioned students have left the movement, talent has been lost, and the growth of psychosynthesis has thereby been retarded.

The reluctance to affiliate was at its height after the San Fiasco break-up in 1978. But gradually old wounds have healed, lines of communication have opened, and now networking is on the increase. I expect the 1988 International Conference to be an affirmation of our growing will to co-oper-ate and affiliate with one another as autonomous centres and groups. Net-working, both locally and internationally, is discussed theoretically by Caldironi (1984), and practical suggestions are presented by Evans (1983) and Yeomans (1984). The synthesis of various combinations of individuals and groups, with its cycles of death and rebirth, continues as a process in the movement.

Roberto Assagioli was a keen observer. He had a gift for translating mys-tical or spiritual teachings into the framework of Western psychology. Like Maslow, Assagioli made pioneering observations and formed constructs at a prescientific stage of a new discipline. Thus the body of his work can prop-erly be characterized by Maslow's term, "proto-knowledge"—ideas and observations which are untested, not scientifically validated. As scientists in the generations after him, I feel it is our job to define psychosynthesis constructs more concretely. This will lead to the formation of testable hypotheses and ways of articulating psychosynthesis theory that are closer to Truth and thus more effective in their application. Yet what I have observed in psychosynthesis is an attitude of adoration toward Assagioli that takes his word as law rather than as "proto-knowledge" to be refined and tested. (As new generations of trainers emerge who have had no contact with Roberto, this "cult of personality" is less of a problem.) Berne (1963) has called the phenomenon "canonization"—elevating a leader to superhu-man status when he dies. I see two major destructive tendencies in psychosynthesis arising from this.

First of all, elevating Assagioli, or any psychosynthesis leader, beyond a human level can actually feed low self-esteem in our students, preventing growth beyond ego. Instead of becoming empowered by the leader, one can become dependent and deluded—a starry-eyed follower and true believer, not an independent thinker. In this case, one projects higher consciousness out onto another human being and is cut off from one's own Transpersonal Self and superconscious. I once heard a well-respected trainer say to an audience with a faraway look in her eyes that Assagioli was not afraid of death; he was so enlightened that he accepted it joyfully when it came. The feeling of awe in the room was palpable. And I knew better. I had heard from another psychosynthesist who was actually with Roberto when he was on his death bed that a part of him resisted and fought against letting go to death.

I think truth is important here. That Assagioli had some struggle surrendering to death along with his mental and spiritual attitudes of acceptance makes him seem more real and human to me. As one who has worked in hospice with many dying cancer patients, I see that the most enlightened can effectively use their spiritual beliefs to make their dying a growth experience. However, to pretend that the most enlightened have no struggle at all can lead a person to feel guilty and unspiritual for not being 100 percent accepting. My observation is that at times in the dying process the spirit is willing but the flesh isn't. I believe I'm a more compassionate counsellor to the dying for acknowledging that resistance and struggle are part of the dying process at some stage. To pretend otherwise smacks of repression and illusion to me.

A second major destructive tendency coming from overvaluing Assagioli as an authority figure is the cutting off of psychosynthesis from its spiritual roots. Assagioli is said to have decided at some point to separate his personal spiritual beliefs from his work as a psychologist. It seems that before the 1950s in Europe he found he could not maintain professional credibility if he spoke openly about his interests in Eastern religions, Western mysticism, and esotericism. Therefore, to further the development and acceptance of psychosynthesis, he probably emphasized his credentials as a psychiatrist and the positive effects of his work with patients. He presented his observations in a scholarly way in professional circles, keeping his spiritual interests separate from his work of beginning a new science.

When I was introduced to psychosynthesis in 1968, I soon learned of this separation of personal spiritual interests from the public presentation of psychosynthesis, and I appreciated the rationale. It was a useful policy in a milieu where science and spirit were viewed as incompatible. However, I learned that to some it was seen as an order from on high to be obeyed forever. After all, this idea of hiding the spiritual background of psychosynthesis had come straight from the "horse's mouth"—that of Saint Roberto Eohippus Assagioli.

Whether psychosynthesis or Assagioli should be associated with esoteric and mystical traditions is a controversy in the movement to this day. For my part, I see keeping Assagioli's roots hidden as an erroneous policy for the late 20th century, particularly in America. It has limited our ability to understand and build on the streams of thought that he brought together to make psychosynthesis what it is today. Thus far, Hardy (1987) has provided the most thorough investigation of our roots.

One value of the "wall of silence" policy is that it created a needed boundary, making it clear that psychosynthesis emphasized not the mystical but the practical and the testable. Assagioli was signalling his intention to make psychosynthesis a science, a form of Western psychology. I agree that the policy was appropriate in our prescientific days, but to keep his sources hidden at this point limits the growth of psychosynthesis as a science.

We must consider the context if we are to keep psychosynthesis practical to the public. In the U.S., more than 50 percent of Americans surveyed by

Yankelovich in 1976 stated that they were seeking personal fulfilment, not just material goals. In modern America, spiritual groups are abundant and "New Age" practices are widely known. In California, my experience is that, quite contrary to the original intent behind separating the scientific and the spiritual, secrecy at this point gives the public false impressions. The sense that there is some hidden mystery in the movement gives us the appearance of a cult. It raises the possibility that psychosynthesis is not really a science after all, but a mystery cult masquerading as a psychology, and it makes Assagioli seem like a mystical guru/saint, pretending to be a scientist. In transpersonal psychology today, scientific work and spirituality are no longer considered incompatible (Tart, 1975).

I am not the only observer to note that separating one's personal spiritual beliefs from one's professional practice can create distortions. Szasz (1978) has pointed out that Freud was a Jew and demonstrated that this background covertly shaped Freud's thinking in his writings on psychoanalysis. What shaped Assagioli's thinking? He was also a Jew, an active contributor to the Jewish youth movement in Europe. He also had connections with mystics and with two radical psychiatrist contemporaries: Carl Jung, who studied alchemy and Eastern religions, and William James, who studied altered states of consciousness. Learning more about our philosophical and spiritual roots seems crucial, at least in California where the overwhelming majority of psychosynthesis trainers and trainees are exploring spiritual and esoteric paths. I have seen these people turn off to psychosynthesis when we refused to address their hunger for a spiritual quest and their wish to find ways of spiritual growth compatible with their practice of psychosynthesis. Since they perceived us as having something to hide, they felt we were untrustworthy.

Some would argue that people who want to emphasize the spiritual should leave the psychosynthesis movement. Robert Gerard (1973) is an example of one who has done this, founding an esoterically-based transpersonal approach which he calls "integral psychology." But, in my view, those psychosynthesists who want to explore further into the Mystery while continuing to contribute to psychosynthesis can enrich the movement. I firmly believe it would be more harmful to psychosynthesis to ostracize them than to make room for them. While finding its boundaries through science, psychosynthesis can also have explorers pushing beyond the limits of traditional psychosynthesis. If there is no room for mystical or esoteric psychosynthesists (and I am one of them), then the movement will lose some fine talent, dedicated leaders, and practitioners. I am convinced that such a loss will retard the growth of psychosynthesis. It will inhibit critical thinking and pressure individuals into unnecessary conformity. What's sauce for the prewar European goose is not sauce for the 1980s American gander.

Along this line of slowing growth, I have wondered why Assagioli has had a biographer for so many years without a biography forthcoming. Or is the rumor I heard in 1980 of a biographer a false one? I suspect the controversy about hiding versus making Assagioli's spiritual beliefs public is inhibiting the production of this book, and I wonder when psychosynthesists will stand up for Truth. Assagioli himself did so in his 1974 *Psychology Today* interview when he let it be known that he personally believed in reincarnation, though he also said that he did not make this a part of psychosynthesis. I firmly believe that an honest and balanced approach to discovering our spiritual roots would be enriching, not detrimental. Science itself has found that it is naïve to think that our personal beliefs can be totally separated from our professional work, that, in fact, our observations are a function of the beliefs we hold.

My own educational background as a social worker has influenced my perception of the development of psychosynthesis. When I was in graduate school, I saw that social workers were concerned about their place in the world as a unique profession and about appearing legitimate to other established professions. Were we a lot like psychologists? Or were we no different from untrained volunteers? Observation of actual social work practice and theorizing led to the conclusion that, in fact, we had an identity distinct from other disciplines. Social work became a profession when it had generated a body of knowledge that was transmitted in a recognized master's degree program. Similarly, we can say that psychosynthesis is well on its way to defining its place in the worlds of humanistic and transpersonal psychology. There are many graduate-level training programs in our centres, and in California there are non-traditional universities which give graduate credits for psychosynthesis training toward a degree in counselling or business.

Another parallel regarding psychosynthesis and the professionalization of social work is suggested by a medical social work director in a hospital who had been examining the problem of lack of regard for social workers as professionals. He made the point that among professionals, *acceptance and respect are gained by demonstrating competence*. I see the demonstration of scientific competence as a key to having psychosynthesis accepted by other psychologists. We need more than the many competent trainers and practitioners that we already have in our ranks. We also need competent psychosynthesis theorists, researchers, and writers. We need reliable, long-term psychosynthesis professional journals that are produced and distributed by professional editors and publishers.

Scientists value results, and we know that psychosynthesis training gets powerful results. Applications of psychosynthesis are clearly working effectively in many fields. But it is not enough for us as psychosynthesists to experience this effectiveness. We must demonstrate it to the larger field of psychology with good theory and research, and by making our body of knowledge public. I believe a major barrier here is that the reluctance to define psychosynthesis is manifested in our training programs as a reluctance to create boundaries in the training—a reluctance to allow anyone to graduate.

For those who resist limiting or defining psychosynthesis in any concrete way, I say let's acknowledge that various groups will continue to have different emphases but that we can find the commonalities that run through all major training programs. For example, I cannot imagine a psychosynthesis program that does not include the constructs "personal self" and "Transpersonal Self," the egg diagram model, and the model of a hierarchy of identity from subpersonalities to the Self. Is there a training program that does no visualization or that never mentions Roberto Assagioli? In line with my suggestions above about research on our extant literature, theory, and training, I am hypothesizing that, regardless of wide differences in the style of various training programs, certain theories, models, and practices exist that are being transmitted in all these programs. If my hypothesis proves correct, we can say that these common threads constitute a defined body of knowledge and that psychosynthesis does have a unique identity in the world of psychology—it is a young adult and no longer an adolescent.

This does not really limit us but empowers us. Like all knowledge, ours can still be evolving, even if we have defined training all the way through the equivalent of the master's degree level. In traditional education, the master's degree means mastery of knowledge and practice in the field as it currently exists. One learns the field's history, its theories, its methods, its issues, and its future directions. To go on to the PhD level means to make a unique contribution to that field. Various academic institutions have different emphases. Compare, for example, the university with a behaviorist-oriented psychology department and a non-traditional college that has a humanistic psychology emphasis. Similarly, psychosynthesis training programs are already differentiated, many focussed on therapy and some on education or business. Some present more theory and require more reading; some emphasize experience. Some bring in spiritual or esoteric studies while others emphatically exclude these.

The resistance to define or limit psychosynthesis means that the training could go on without end—a needlessly prolonged adolescence. The fear among some leaders of having students graduate is that the students may not do a good job, and that they will thus reflect negatively on their trainers, their centre, and the movement. This fear has been manifested in the addition of demands to the training. I know of more than one major training program in which students could not get a concrete idea of how to complete the training. They were put off repeatedly until many gave up in disgust. As recently as two years ago, a major training centre added an extra year of study at the intermediate level, much to the dismay of students who had already invested some years in their training and had been led to expect that they would graduate in one year.

I have heard that Assagioli did not have these fears. The story goes that after spending a couple of weeks with Assagioli a person went out to start his own psychosynthesis training program. An associate of Assagioli was very upset, but Roberto said, "He can do no harm." To me, this means that those training programs which demonstrate competence will grow and have influence but those which don't will not last; psychosynthesis will remain of a high quality even if some do not represent it adequately. Would that all psychosynthesists had Assagioli's confidence that psychosynthesis is strong and good and that competence will prevail. It is my conviction that the best protection for the integrity of the movement at this point in our history is to demonstrate our competence as scientific psychologists—to present truthfully our history and our knowledge base, and to research and refine both our theory and practice.

4. Communicating Who We Are: The Public Nature of Observation

I stated early in this article that psychosynthesis has a large body of observations and theories but is lacking in the other two aspects of scientific method—testing/research, and the public nature of observation. I have indicated that a great deal of the psychosynthesis literature is not readily available to the public or to us as psychosynthesists. I have noted that there has been a considerable amount of "in-house" publishing but a lack of psychosynthesis articles in established professional journals. I have also commented on the tendency of psychosynthesis groups to isolate themselves from one another and to fail to communicate.

At the same time, I have acknowledged a tendency to organize more conferences and to do networking, and publishing, and I have noted the beginnings of empirical research. I implore all of you who value psychosynthesis to allow it to be exposed to the larger world of Western psychology. Let's not be like the parent who is afraid to let the adolescent grow up. The time has come, I believe, when psychosynthesis is strong enough and mature enough to thrive in the public arena. I ask the various groups to cease hiding away our literature, our history, and the details of our training. Let's have the confidence Assagioli had, that psychosynthesis can stand on its own merits. Where it is competently presented, it *is* being accepted. Let's demonstrate to our professional colleagues and to the public that it does, in fact, bring valuable and effective results.

In closing, I return to the question, "Is psychosynthesis growing or fading away?" My final response is that *it is up to us*. We can put psychosynthesis on the map by going beyond the fears and other ego-oriented problems discussed above. Let's use our common sense. Let's be good scientists communicating our theories and practices to each other and to the world. Let's demonstrate the courage to face the truth about our successes and failures, our strengths and weaknesses. We have nothing to fear from public exposure and everything to gain by openly dialoguing about our commonalities and differences as psychosynthesists. We know in our hearts that we specialize in psychosynthesis because it is good, because it is worthwhile. We know it is worthy of our love, our respect, and our trust. In all these years since 1910 we have not always measured up to the ideals of psychosynthesis. There have been failures and embarrassments, but the principles we believe in have proved to be sound. Thus I remain convinced that we have nothing to hide—that the continuing quest for Truth in psychosynthesis is a scientific and spiritual quest that indeed empowers our movement and ultimately sets us free.

Editors' Note

*Readers will note that this distinction is made by the Editors of this volume and that the convention of capitalizing "Psychosynthesis" when it refers to a school of thought has been followed in the other articles.

References

Assagioli, R. (1965). *Psychosynthesis*. New York: Viking.

Assagioli, R. (1973). *The act of will*. Baltimore: Penguin.

Assagioli, R. (1983). *Psychosynthesis typology*. London: London Institute Monographs.

Bailey, A. A. (1936). *Esoteric psychology I*. New York: Lucis.

Bailey, A. A. (1955). *The light of the soul*. New York: Lucis.

Berne, E. (1963). *The structure and dynamics of organizations and groups*. Philadelphia: Lippincott.

Brown, M. Y. (1983). *The unfolding self*. Los Angeles: Psychosynthesis Press.

Caldironi, B. (1984). From the agony of the planet to the collective self. *Psychosynthesis Digest, 2*(2), 7–17.

Crampton, M. (1980). Organismic process. *The American Theosophist, 68*(5), 132–149.

Cullen, J. & Russell, D. (1987). *The self-actualizing manager*. Thousand Oaks: IAMOP.

Deikman, A. (1983). Evaluating spiritual groups. *Journal of Humanistic Psychology, 23*(3), 8–18.

Evans, R. (1983). Mirages of the mind. *Yearbook Vol. III*. London: Institute of Psychosynthesis.

Ferrucci, P. (1983). *What we may be*. Wellingborough: Turnstone.

Gerard, R. (1973). *Cosmos in man*. Agoura: Aquarian Educational Group.

Goble, F. (1970). *The third force*. New York: Pocket Books.

Hardy, J. (1987). *A psychology with a soul*. London: Routledge & Kegan Paul.

Iyengar, B.K.S. (1966). *Light on yoga*. New York: Schocken.

Marx, M. (1963). The general nature of theory construction. *Theories in contemporary psychology*. New York: Macmillan.

McBeath, B., & Wynne, D. (1985). Integrating systems in psychosynthesis: Applications to work with families, groups, and organizations. In J. Weiser & T. Yeomans (Eds.). *Readings in psychosynthesis: Theory, process, and practice* (Vol. 1). Toronto: Department of Applied Psychology, Ontario Institute for Studies in Education.

Roberts, R., & Nee, R. H. (Eds.). (1970). *Theories of Social Casework*. Chicago: University of Chicago Press.

Russell, D. (1981). Psychosynthesis in western psychology. *Psychosynthesis Digest, I*(1), 39–53.

Russell, D. (1982). Seven basic constructs of psychosynthesis. *Psychosynthesis Digest, I*(2), 51–79.

Russell, D. (1985). Psychosynthesis as a spectrum psychology. In J. Weiser & T. Yeomans (Eds.), *Readings in psychosynthesis* (Vol. 1). Toronto: Department of Applied Psychology, Ontario Institute for Studies in Education.

Szasz, T. (1978). *The myth of psychotherapy*. New York: Anchor.

Tart, C. (1975). *Transpersonal psychologies*. New York: Harper & Row.

Weiser, J., & Yeomans, T. (1984). *Psychosynthesis in the helping professions*. Toronto: Department of Applied Psychology, Ontario Institute for Studies in Education.

Weiser, J., & Yeomans, T. (1985). *Readings in psychosynthesis: Theory, process, and practice* (Vol. I). Toronto: Department of Applied Psychology, Ontario Institute for Studies in Education.

Whitmore, D. (1986). *Psychosynthesis in education*. Wellingborough: Turnstone Press.

Wilber, K. (1977). *The spectrum of consciousness*. Wheaton: Theosophical Publishing House.

Yeomans, T. (1984). Politics of the spirit. *Psychosynthesis Digest*, 2(2), 1–6.

Organizational Development

Attitude in the Outplacement Process: A Psychosynthesis Approach

Lida E. Sims

In the past ten to fifteen years, outplacement has emerged as a counselling and training modality in many large industries. In its various forms, it has been used to help individuals or groups who are involved in a major career transition, primarily the loss of a job. Generally, outplacement encompasses career counselling, training in job search techniques, and limited support or counselling to help people deal with the emotional stress of losing their jobs.

For being a relatively recent consulting area, outplacement has grown tremendously in the last few years and is used increasingly by industry as a way to deal both with individuals making career changes and with displaced groups. Recently, outplacement has responded to the need to handle large reductions in the work force due to the proliferation of restructurings, take-overs, mergers, acquisitions, and plant closings in various industries. Twenty or thirty years ago, there was a high probability that a person would spend his or her entire career with the same company. Reflecting the changing atmosphere in the work force, a person today, on average, spends less than five years in a company before making a career change either voluntarily or involuntarily.

Reasons that a company provides outplacement range from self-interest to humanitarian concerns. With widespread job loss resulting from the growing need to reduce the work force in many companies, outplacement is provided to form a bridge from one job to another. It provides workers with needed job search skills, support, and counsel in a time of crisis. Provided by the company, it is an add-on benefit to the severance package they receive on leaving the organization.

Not only does outplacement give needed assistance to the individuals involved, but it also tends to create positive feelings about the company. The company then retains a more positive image both with exiting workers and in the community. It sometimes minimizes the risk of lawsuits and gives assurance to remaining workers that there is a concern for individuals on the part of the company. It is often a gesture of thanks and acknowledgment for years of service, particularly when individuals or groups are leaving as a result of structural changes that have caused major adjustments in personnel needs.

In the early days, outplacement was provided almost exclusively to individuals in middle to upper management. In these cases, the situation was generally one in which the direction of the company had changed and a person did not have the necessary skills to meet the new demands of the organization or was no longer able to perform to satisfactory standards. The other common need for outplacement arose when new management decided to replace an old team, either to accommodate the changing business of the company or to bring in more compatible personalities and experiences.

Outplacement has grown from these particular applications to handling individuals and groups at all levels of an organization from upper management to hourly workers. It now ranges from intensive individual counselling to standard two- or three-day training programs provided to large groups. A typical individual program of outplacement is paid for by a company which is terminating an employee. The individual works with a consultant/counsellor until he or she is placed in a new job, a process that can take months. From the time that one enters such a program, there is approximately a month of search involved for every $10,000 that he or she makes. A person making $50,000 to $60,000, for example, can anticipate five to six months of search before finding a comparable job. This can be shortened or lengthened by other circumstances such as the person's age, whether he or she is limiting the search to a particular geographic area, and the general health of the industry in which he or she is looking.

The following is an overview of the program provided by Drake Beam Morin, Inc., the world's largest outplacement firm, with 32 domestic and 30 international offices. Drake Beam Morin has already assisted over 300,000 individuals.

Individual Executive Outplacement

The Drake Beam Morin individual executive program is divided into three phases. The first phase of the program is one of assessment, focussing on what has happened in the past as a way to build criteria for what clients will be looking for in the future. It is used to build the working relationship between the counsellor and the client and to deal with feelings about the transition. Clients are asked to list activities they have been involved in, what has been of interest to them, and what they would see as areas of outstanding performance. In addition, they are asked to look back on their career and rate activities in terms of personal satisfaction. In this way, they begin to pinpoint marketable skills and to highlight both high interest and high performance areas.

This assessment phase takes place through written exercises and through a battery of psychological instruments and interest inventories which augment the written exercises. Through the discussion of the exercises and the review of the results of the assessment package, the counsellor gets to know clients and their skills. Since the job loss often affects their confidence and self-esteem, the assessment phase aids in rebuilding self-esteem by allowing them to see objectively what they have accomplished in the years they have been working and what skills they have developed. Very often, clients remain unaware of the skills and talents they have developed over the years and take for granted many of the strengths of their particular skill base. By making clients more objectively aware of their strengths and skills, the process prepares them for marketing these skills. This first phase of the program gives clients the objectivity they need in order to conduct an effective search.

The second phase of the program is concerned with actual training in job search techniques and includes help in the writing of a resumé and developing communication and interview skills. Since there is only a 20 to 30 percent chance that clients will find a job from an ad or through search firms, they are encouraged not to depend on these as the source of jobs. They are taught to target companies that might have a desirable position and to make contact with the company to uncover potential openings prior to their becoming published. This activity involves researching potential companies, writing letters to them, and gathering information within an organization prior to any formal interviewing process. This trains clients in the various components that make an efficient and effective job search. This phase concludes with a highly structured plan for their search.

In addition to time with their counsellor, clients are provided with office space and secretarial services to support them in their search until they find a new job. Not only does this provide needed administrative support, but it also provides a structured environment for them to work in during their search. Clients report that the structured office environment and the ongoing support of the counsellor aid enormously in dealing with the discouragement and frustration they experience. They are also provided with the support of a peer group, since they are interacting with others in the same situation.

The third phase of the program is the implementation phase of the search. In this phase, the counsellor acts as a sounding board as clients evaluate the positions they are looking at. The consultant, at this point, is part of the support system, familiar with the search, knowledgeable about what the client is looking for, and skilled in helping with the evaluation process which will decide whether the company and the position are consistent with the client's ideal job parameters. The parameters are the client's criteria for judging the company and its compatibility with his or her interests, skills, and personality.

In the final phases of interviewing or negotiating, the consultant adds skill and objectivity in the sometimes difficult task of closure. This can be an emotionally intense time as the person commits money and resources to the risk of a new business venture or negotiates a salary. It is hard to attach a monetary value to one's worth and skills. This ends the process with another transition, whether going into a new job, starting or buying a business, consulting, or retiring.

Attitude and Job Search

As a counsellor, I have become increasingly aware of the importance of attitude in the search process. The person who can deal with the emotional shock that comes with the loss of a job and who can quickly regain confidence tends to have a shorter and more successful search. The person who has trouble dealing with the emotional impact of the search and who pulls away from the heavy interpersonal interaction that a job search demands is far more likely to be discouraged and to deal poorly with the rejection that is part of the search process.

The primary focus of outplacement has traditionally been on the job search, with the counselling component as a secondary focus. Outplacement provides the necessary skills for finding a job; it is not therapy and is not represented as such to the buying company or the client. The purpose of outplacement is for the individual to find a job. The degree to which a person needs to look at him or herself and feelings and attitudes has to be considered within this context. This emphasis has resulted in a lack of clarity as to how to deal with the emotional issues that are attendant to the job loss and that surface during the search.

The degree to which counselling is brought into play has not been clearly defined, and often consultants feel that the counselling that does take place is a hidden agenda. For most people involved in these programs, any suggestion that they should do any work on themselves implies that there is something wrong with them, a delicate point when their self-esteem is already suffering. This presents an added difficulty. The counselling component is then usually limited to offering a listening ear and words of encouragement when a client is discouraged. At the same time, the part that attitude holds in the success of a job search is a growing area of interest. It is now believed that a good attitude toward a search may be essential to the duration of a search and its ultimate success.

Coming to outplacement with a background in Psychosynthesis, I found a natural fit between psychosynthesis techniques and the outplacement process. The exciting thing is that Psychosynthesis offers a model for individuals to work with in a context that is not pathological. It gives individuals a way to manage their attitudes, beliefs, and feelings in a language that is not threatening. In addition, Psychosynthesis can aid clients in gaining clarity of purpose and can teach them to use their will in achieving defined goals. Psychosynthesis has complemented my work with existing programs, adding a new depth to processes already in place. Psychosynthesis can also add new dimensions to the outplacement process. Below I discuss the applicability of Psychosynthesis both to the more typical individual outplacement programs and to a recently developed program for work with groups.

Individual Outplacement Case Study

Since 90 percent of individual clients are men, reflecting the ratio of men to women in management, the "typical" client described here is male. Following this description is a discussion of the influence of Psychosynthesis on my outplacement practice as it presently exists.

"Joe" is in his forties and is in middle to upper management. He is married and has children. His income is approximately $50,000 a year. He has from five to twenty years work experience, perhaps all with the same company, and had expected to retire from the company which has just terminated him. He is conscientious, works hard, and is strongly identified with his job. The loss of the job is a tremendous blow to both his identity and self-esteem. Joe has the additional pressure of being the sole provider for his family and feels tremendous guilt that he is failing in this role.

278 *The Outplacement Process*

Dealing with a transition this major is a source of great stress for Joe, setting him on an emotional roller coaster ride through shock, anger, depression, and loss of self-esteem as he adjusts to the reality of what has happened. Since Joe has been released from his job involuntarily, he feels out of control and powerless. In an effort to regain a feeling of control, Joe quickly rationalizes the situation, saying that the company had to make a business decision, that he had seen it coming, that it had nothing to do with him personally. This is to cover up the feeling of having been betrayed by the company and to minimize the self-doubt that enters as his mind tries to find a rationale for the event. Since there was no clear reason given for the termination, it is important for Joe to realize that creating a reason often necessitates a rationale that finds him at fault. This can intensify the feelings of self-doubt and the tendency to dwell inappropriately on what he could have done differently.

In this initial period, Joe may speak of feeling numb, of having no idea what he should do next. To regain control, he might express a willingness to take any job he can find so as to be working again and to re-establish his sense of identity. This is discouraged by the counsellor who points out that now is a time for Joe to reflect on the past, re-evaluate his career, and create a clear intention for his next step.

The psychosynthesis model gives Joe a conceptual framework for building a sense of self apart from his job. And in separating himself from his identification with his job, Joe can begin to separate losing his job from being a statement about who he is. Psychosynthesis can help him build a sense of self while aiding him in disidentifying from his job role. The idea that Joe is more than his role in the job, and more than his thoughts and feelings about the situation, can help him begin to disidentify from the role and to build a "centre" from which to deal with the things that he is feeling. Here the model of Psychosynthesis, the identification with the "I," is essential. Working from his centre, it is easier for Joe to look at the transition in the context of a re-evaluation of his life situation.

In the existing outplacement process, this work is complemented by the assessment work in the first phase of the program. The feedback from the psychological testing is used for discussion to focus on strengths and personal attributes. This helps Joe list accomplishments and pinpoint activities in his career history which demonstrate his particular strengths. It is seldom that an employee or a company acknowledge the good work that takes place on a daily basis.

As the process of disidentification takes place and Joe begins to gain perspective on his situation, he may find that he has new insights into what has happened. In many cases, the job loss is symptomatic of a greater life change that is taking place. (In some cases, the loss of the job *is* solely due to circumstance, such as an entire company closing.) Often Joe finds himself talking about his loss of job satisfaction, disillusionment with the company, a change in management or policy that he could not agree with. He can see the termination as something that has forced him to deal with a situation that he was not happy with, but was staying with because of the security and the inertia associated with having been somewhere for a long time. He may even admit that his performance on the job had been affected. Joe has had little opportunity in his career to know what other jobs might be available. This has created a fear of the unknown that made it harder to leave a safe, if unrewarding, situation.

From a psychosynthesis point of view, it is a time to look more deeply into the transition in terms of underlying purpose. Is Joe's career taking him in the direction that he wants to be going, both in his career and his life? Joe will often say that he "ended up" in his career without really choosing it. The first job out of college established his career path within the same company or the same job function and industry. As Joe reflects on his past job in the outplacement process, he does so to build his ideal job parameters, the criteria that he will use to create his list of companies that he will target as he begins his job search. At one level, this is done to point out that a job search needs to be a pro-active search, not passively waiting to see what appears in want ads or through search firms.

Here Psychosynthesis offers Joe a larger context in which to look at what is going on in his life, giving him the opportunity to see his career as a reflection of who he is as a person. This is a change from seeing his career as defining who he is as a person. At a deeper level, Joe sees that where he works and what he does is something that he can choose and have some power over. Even if he finds at the end of the assessment phase that he would like to continue in the same kind of job, he often finds that he can recommit himself to this direction. A deeper sense of purpose will then guide clear goals for the future.

If Joe feels that he would like to make a change in his career, there are many forms that this may take. He may change industries but stay with the same job function. For example, if he has been an accountant in a large accounting firm, he may choose to look for a job as comptroller, treasurer, or chief financial officer in a small manufacturing firm.

The career change may be more drastic. Joe may choose to leave the structure of working for an organization and buy or start a business of his own. This kind of change requires a period of exploration in order to establish what is available and to evaluate the various possibilities.

It is important for Joe to see the job loss as the end of a cycle and to accept that there may be a transition period in which the future is unclear. Joe may feel that he is in a void and he will need to work creatively with this time. There is no doubt that for many people outplacement is a time of crisis. Since it is a time of change, it is helpful for them to understand the nature of change.

Nature is an easily understood metaphor for change. Joe is in a winter cycle where there is nothing showing in the world of form yet tremendous creative potential in the darkness. Winter is a time to be open to the little things pointing to the next cycle—images, ideas, thoughts, feelings, and fantasies. It is not a time for Joe to be overly practical as he looks again at dreams he has always had of starting a business or as he reconnects to the sense of purpose he identified with when he initially chose his career path. Given the concrete, pragmatic, results-oriented atmosphere that most clients come out of, it is often easy to dismiss possibilities which seem far-fetched and impractical without giving them time to develop. Joe is encouraged to consider all possibilities at this time. This reflective re-evaluation process generates the material that then becomes the criteria Joe will be looking for in his next job, business plan, or plan of action for buying a business.

As a model for dealing with change, Psychosynthesis emphasizes the need for both awareness and the use of the will to effect change. In this case, Joe needs to be aware of himself, to listen to the subtle signals coming from within his own being indicating what the next step is going to be. He also needs to acknowledge the current situation and to have an awareness of what is going on, both intellectually and emotionally. Developing this awareness is often more important than the application of the will in the implementation of a change. Joe is quite adept at effecting change, since his role in business has been results oriented, and perseverance and determination are qualities he is familiar with. What he may be unfamiliar with is the skilful and creative use of the will through self-acceptance, confidence in his abilities, and holding to a positive vision for the outcome of his search.

Change involves two elements. The first is that in order to change Joe has to be clear about the outcome he wants. Establishing a sense of purpose will aid him in dealing with the uncertainty of the situation. Yet this is sometimes difficult for Joe because he is used to highly structured environments where results are usually production goals or performance goals.

The second element in change is that the clearer Joe is about the outcome, the more he has to deal with the fear of not achieving it. Dealing with this fear takes courage, willingness, and ability to confront feelings that might arise. (The opposite view is to assume that the power for change is in external circumstances, a view which easily causes a person to fall into an attitude of powerlessness.) The involuntary life change that Joe has experienced reinforces his belief that he cannot effect change in his life. This blow to his self-esteem can make it difficult for him to feel confident in his ability to find the job or situation that he wants. Since one of the key elements in the job search is taking a pro-active role, and being clear about the outcome that he is looking for, it is crucial to work with any attitudes or beliefs that may get in the way of accomplishing this purpose. By emphasizing the importance of attitude in the job search and by showing that it can have an effect on the outcome, the counsellor can help Joe create the outcome that he wants and deal with what might be getting in his way at an emotional level.

What Psychosynthesis puts in place is a practical model for working with inhibiting feelings and beliefs in the context of achieving a clearly defined goal. If Joe is motivated by fear of not having a job, or not being good enough, it is easy for this to become a self-fulfilling prophesy, as he creates a subpersonality that will work to bring this into manifestation. The same anticipation of a negative outcome is also anxiety-producing and the degree to which he anticipates a negative outcome will influence both the level of anxiety and the potential outcome. The use of a subpersonality model here can help point out to Joe that a part of him might unconsciously believe that he cannot accomplish the task. By identifying with the "I" and strengthening his sense of purpose, Joe has a clearer place to work from in dealing with the feelings and actions of this subpersonality.

Joe is under a tremendous amount of stress, and the underlying attitude with which the search is approached is a great contributor to either increasing the amount of anxiety and stress or helping him manage it. If Joe approaches the search with a clear intention of what he wants to happen, psychological energy is not being lost to the fear of a negative outcome. An example of the importance of attitude is provided by different approaches to using the phone as a way to contact potential employers. If people assume a high probability of rejection, they are likely to be tentative and apologetic and not make themselves clear about what it is they want to happen. Even in the simple act of a telephone call, the ingredients should be there—a clear objective and a model for monitoring and dealing with negative feelings of anticipation.

As Joe progresses with his search, he should have in place concepts and tools for dealing with disappointment and discouragement. Remember that his search will probably last five months—a long period to deal with uncertainty and rejection. Looking for a job means dealing with rejection in many different forms. Joe can have difficulty getting someone to talk to him at a company that he thinks he would like to work for. It often happens that Joe will be interviewed for a job, experience it as a good interview, and then find out that the job is going to someone else because of personal chemistry or because his skills were apparently not what the company was looking for. Joe may be interviewed several times by the same company only to find out that the company has decided not to hire anyone. There are many things that happen in the search process that can cause Joe to feel rejected and discouraged.

But when Joe is placed, there will be a good match both in terms of skills and the personalities involved. One of the important things that Joe will learn is that he is interviewing the company as much as the company is interviewing him. Sometime in his search, Joe will find that not only will he be rejected as a candidate for a job, but he will also reject companies which do not offer the job satisfaction that he is looking for. This may be discovered through tangible factors such as scope of responsibilities or salary. But it may also be that Joe will reject an opportunity because he does not feel that he could work productively with the personalities or commit himself to the company's product.

In this, we see a change in Joe. At the beginning of the process, he was willing to take anything that came along; at the end, he has come to a clear sense of purpose about where he and his career are going and a willingness to look until he finds the situation that will give him the job satisfaction he is looking for. When Joe accepts his new position, he will begin a new cycle of his career. He will enter the new position aware that he cannot always count on the job to be there. He will go into the new company committed to what he is doing and aware of the potential impermanence. He will monitor the new job to see if it continues to meet his needs for job satisfaction. He will be willing to take responsibility to make the job work and to make a change should that become necessary.

Joe represents a fairly typical client whose financial situation and skills allow him the luxury of looking for a position that will give him a high degree of job satisfaction. Other clients are not so fortunate. Some have a limited time frame in which to look due to limited financial resources and are less likely to turn down a position. Others have skills that are not easily marketable, forcing them to choose from a more limited pool of available jobs.

From Individual to Group Work—It was in working with individual clients that I became aware of the elements that are important in dealing with feelings and beliefs around a job search. Out of this awareness, I developed a more structured program with specific exercises and techniques and presented these at workshops to interested individual clients at our office. The groups were well attended and the evaluations showed enthusiasm for the program.

Recently, in addition to work with individual clients, I have been involved with the development of a Drake Beam Morin program, now in the pilot stage, which utilizes a variety of techniques including Psychosynthesis to help clients deal with feelings, beliefs, and attitudes in the job search process. In 1987, the program was used in eight offices; if adopted corporate wide, the program will be used by 250 to 300 consultants and become a standard component of the outplacement process serving approximately 6,000 to 7,000 clients a year.

Some consultants in the firm had been developing an awareness of the work being done in attitude management, but in different fields, such as sports, stress reduction, and the psychology of achievement. In the fall of 1986, under the direction of Dr. Don Monoco, a task force was created with consultants from offices around the country to create a pilot program dealing with this area. My program, the only one that had been designed specifically for our clients, served as a base for the design. The program itself used many disciplines as well as Psychosynthesis. In addition to contributing to the overall design of the program, my specific task was to design the exercises. Below, Optimum Performance Training, a pilot group program for Drake Beam Morin clients, is described. The program is done in two parts, each lasting between two and two and a half hours.

Optimum Performance Training

In the first session of Optimum Performance Training, the emphasis is on the history and rationale of the program. It is first pointed out that visualization, or mental rehearsal, can affect behavior. Recent publications in sports, business, medicine and stress management, behavioral science, and the psychology of motivation are cited in order to show clients the convergence of techniques that contribute to the achievement of excellence. Being exposed to a number of disciplines, including Psychosynthesis, they are given a model for how thinking and feeling can influence behavior. The work of Charles Garfield, in particular, contributes a model for achievement in the business environment.

Emphasis is put on the fact that negative "self-talk," both conscious and unconscious, can have an impact on behavior during a job search. Clients are asked to become an observer of the inner dialogue they experience that might negatively influence their job search.

Exercises in this session include the basic technique of visualization, a longer relaxation exercise, and the creation of a "Favorite Place" image for use in the next session. Clients are given an audio tape of the exercises in the program.

As an assignment between sessions, clients are asked to keep a journal of negative messages that impede their search process. They are told to use the Relaxation/Favorite Place imagery when they feel they are under stress and want to approach a particular situation in a more relaxed state.

The second session uses the foundation of the first, the visualization technique, to help clients focus on the successful outcome of their job search. They are also given hints on how to adapt the exercise to more specific aspects of their search. The session begins with processing the work from the last session. There is discussion of the inner dialogue and beliefs and feelings that may be negatively influencing the job search. Seeing that attitudes are held in common gives clients permission to accept them and to feel less alone when they have an occasional difficulty. A discussion of the qualities that are associated with the experience of success precedes the exercises.

The first exercise focusses on remembering a time of success. This experience is then processed and used to bridge the next visualization exercise which builds a symbolic picture of the successful outcome of the job search. This will then serve as a focus point and motivator for the search itself.

Clients are told they can use the processes they have learned in the workshop to deal with more specific search-related activities. In conclusion, they are asked to look at any action they need to take in their search to incorporate the understanding and experience gained from the workshop. The exercises are described in more detail below.

Session 1: Relaxing and Creating a Favorite Place—This visualization exercise enables one to relax and to go into the altered state of consciousness needed to do other visualization exercises. It is an induction exercise preparing clients for the creative work of the program. The more often a person works with this exercise, the easier it is to go to the Favorite Place and the easier it is to do the other exercises. The exercise can also be used on its own for relaxation and stress reduction.

When using the Favorite Place visualization as a foundation for other exercises, the end of this exercise is where all the other exercises begin. That is, future exercises begin with an instruction to go to the Favorite Place, eliminating the need to begin with a long induction and relaxation.

Let's begin by closing your eyes, which is simply a way to focus your awareness inwardly instead of outwardly. As you close your eyes, become aware of the chair you're sitting in—just to make sure you are sitting comfortably and then take a deep breath, exhale, and relax. You may want to move your head around a little bit to help you relax.

Focus your awareness on your breathing so that you're noticing as you breathe in and breathe out.

Now, I'd like you to imagine that each time you exhale, you're going to relax just a little bit more—letting the chair hold you as you relax into it.

I'd like you to imagine that you're walking down a flight of stairs. Each time that I call out a number, imagine that you are taking one more step down, and with each step down you will also become more and more relaxed.

Now, beginning at the top, take one step down. That's 10, 9, 8, as you become more relaxed. And 7, 6, 5, with each step, you are becoming more and more relaxed. That's 4, 3, 2, you're feeling very relaxed now, letting the chair support you. One. You are at the bottom of the stairs, feeling very relaxed, very comfortable, with your breathing very even.

Now, I'd like you to imagine a place in nature that you find particularly beautiful. This may be a place you remember going to. It may be a place that just appears in your mind's eye. But it is a place that you find particularly beautiful, relaxing, and peaceful. It might be at the top of a mountain; it might be near water. Just whatever—it is a place in which you feel relaxed and at peace. Take a moment to let this image or impression form.

What is this place like? Turn around slowly, taking in all that you would be seeing. What does it look like? What things are you seeing? What colors are there? What time of day is it? What is the quality of the light? Are there any sounds? Be aware of where you are sitting or standing. What season is it?

Take a moment to fix your impression of this place. As you breathe, imagine you are breathing in the atmosphere of this place. And be aware of becoming more relaxed as you breathe in the quiet, the peace, and the beauty of this place.

As you do this, be aware of how your body feels—as you relax, breathe in the atmosphere of this place.

Now, as you breathe, inhale more deeply the peacefulness, the relaxation, and the beauty of this place.

Now, take a moment to be aware of how it feels in your body.

Hold these feelings, the sense of relaxation and peace and the impression of this place. Bring these with you as you slowly bring your awareness back to the room. Keeping your eyes closed, take a moment to be aware of the chair and the room and of the feelings of your favorite place which you have brought with you.

Open your eyes and stretch to help bring yourself back to the room.

At the end of this visualization, clients are given a few minutes to write down what they have experienced in order to fix the experience in their conscious mind. You should begin the discussion by asking if anyone couldn't do the exercise. Be sympathetic and suggest that they will find it easier with practice and that they might find that hearing about what others have experienced will help. Then let several people, who were able to do the exercise easily, describe what happened for them. Out of the discussion you will want to emphasize that they should be feeling relaxed as a result of the exercise.

A short version of the Favorite Place exercise is done next to demonstrate how much easier it is to reconnect to an image created previously. You should point out to clients that in the future they will use the same image.

Now, close your eyes again. Take a deep breath. As you exhale, imagine once again being in your favorite place. Take your time to re-create what it looks like; what the air is like; what sounds you are hearing.

Take a deep breath and once again breathe in the atmosphere of the place as it relaxes you. (long pause)

Now, bringing those feelings with you again, bring your attention back to the room and open your eyes.

This discussion is very brief and simply intends to demonstrate that it is easier to go back to an image. Since the exercise focusses on relaxation, it can be of great value to clients for stress reduction. Suggest that they use both the tape and their image when they need to reconnect with feelings of relaxation.

Session 2: Remembering Success—This portion of the program begins to move toward the creative uses of visualization. In the Remembering Success exercise, you want to access a memory of a past achievement or success. In order to set the stage, you should discuss what success is. What you are looking for are examples which demonstrate the characteristics of successful achievers as outlined in the discussion with which the program begins. Clients should be using words like "motivated" and "energized" while stressing that the person is "relaxed," for example, an energetic and busy person does his work effortlessly.

A deeply relaxed state makes available a stronger "felt sense" of an experience, allowing a person to access memories that may not be easily brought to mind. By creating a strong sense of what it feels like to succeed, the second part of the exercise goes on to re-create that same feeling in a situation where clients have not felt successful. In asking them to think of such an incident in their recent job search, make sure that it is something that is not too traumatic or emotionally charged. It should be a minor event. In bringing the feeling of the first successful event to the second part of the exercise, you are helping clients create a model for using their felt sense of success in situations where they need to access those same positive feelings.

Close your eyes and take a deep breath and relax as you exhale. Then focus your awareness on your breathing so that you're noticing as you breathe in and out. Imagine that each time you exhale, you're going to relax just a little bit more. Let the chair hold you as you relax into it.

Now, take a moment to imagine that you are once again in your favorite place, a place of beauty and peace.

Take a moment to let yourself be there, seeing the things that you would be seeing and breathing in the atmosphere of the place. Let your body relax as you feel what it's like to be there.

Now, I would like you to take a moment to remember a time when you were successful, feeling energized, relaxed. Everything seemed almost effortless. Take your time and allow the memory of this experience to come back to you.

Notice what thoughts you are having. Notice what you are feeling. What are you feeling in your body?

Are you in the situation or are you observing the situation? As you do this, allow your memory of this experience to grow stronger.

Re-experience now what it felt like in your body to be successful. Take a deep breath, and as you exhale allow all the feelings to deepen.

Allow the sense you have of yourself to grow stronger.

Now, staying connected to this feeling, bring your awareness back to the room. Keeping your eyes closed, become aware of the chair you are sitting in and become aware of feeling successful.

Again, take a deep breath, and as you exhale relax into being here experiencing the feelings of success.

Open your eyes, keeping that inward feeling of success as you look around the room. Close your eyes again. Reconnect with those feelings of success. Now, take a deep breath and allow those feelings to deepen. And open your eyes again. Make some notes about what you experienced.

Now, remember a small incident in your recent job search in which you felt like you weren't successful. It might be a phone call or talking with someone. As you look at this picture, be aware of the thoughts and feelings you were having.

Now, take that picture, put it to the side for the moment, and focus on reconnecting with the feelings of being successful.

Remember what it felt like, what it looked like, and any sounds connected with it. Take a deep breath, exhale, relax, and allow that successful feeling to be present. As you do so this time, be aware that the feelings are stronger as you re-experience in your body the sense of effortlessness and ease.

Now, look at the picture of what happened recently and imagine yourself being in that same situation, but feeling as you do right now.

Take a minute and become aware of the changes that you would make in the situation. What would you be feeling that would change the picture? What would you know or feel that would make a difference?

Let go of the picture, reconnect to the feelings of being successful, and staying connected with that feeling bring your awareness back to the room.

In discussion after the second part, you will find that those who did the exercise thoroughly will have a sense of what the self-defeating attitude or thought was that made the event a "failure." Clients should also be able to see the change in the "unsuccessful" situation; they should have a clear idea of what they could have said or done differently. You will also notice that those who have done the exercise successfully will feel successful and energized and have a sense of the exercise's possibilities for use in other situations.

The third part of this session works with the image of success again. The memory of success created in the last exercise is connected with an image or symbol for a successful outcome of the search process. This symbol can provide emotional force for the day-to-day activity of the search.

Now, we're going to use the image of success again, drawing on it as an energy source. What you have done before, you can do again, and this will help you connect to that energy as you conduct your search.

Take a moment to focus on your breathing and relax. Remember how it felt to be successful. Remember what you were doing and connect to what you were feeling at the time. Take a moment to feel again the energy and relaxation that you felt. Reconnect to all the feelings, the exhilaration, how easy and inevitable it was that you would succeed. Even before you started, you somehow felt it was an accomplished fact. Take a deep breath and allow the feelings to grow stronger. This is a great source of energy. Let your connection to it grow stronger.

Time has passed and I now want you to imagine yourself in your new situation. Let the picture or symbol appear that will represent that future success.

See what is around you. Are you in the picture or looking at it? What represents the outcome? Is it something that you feel, something that you see, or something that you hear?

Now, bring all the energy that you felt in your previous success into the present situation and feel all the same feelings in this same situation. Breathe it in and let the experience grow stronger. Create around you what you would be seeing and doing. Is it something that you see that makes you know, or is it something that someone is saying to you? Perhaps you are on the telephone telling someone or listening to them congratulate you. It may be a feeling—what is it?

Allow the impression to deepen and grow stronger. Then, bringing all the feelings with you, bring your awareness back to the room.

Take a moment to make notes. These are clues you will want to use again.

Program Evaluation—Most of the clients who participated in the Optimum Performance Training pilot program submitted evaluation forms. They were, for the most part, unfamiliar with the concepts that were used. Only 23 percent said they had any significant degree of familiarity with the material. Most had some limited exposure to stress management techniques and some were aware of the use of visualization and attitude management in sports. Although they had no prior experience to draw on, they felt, however, that the program was an important factor in how they were doing in their job search. Some felt they had been highly successful in their prior job because of their attitudes but that they were unable to translate these attitudes into the process of the job search.

Asked if they felt the program had been or would be useful to them in improving their search, 57 percent reported that they felt it would be either very helpful or extremely helpful. The other 43 percent said they thought it would be of considerable help. When asked to comment on whether they felt committed to continuing with the techniques, a surprising number said they were quite committed to continuing with the use of the techniques, although they were under no obligation to do so.

A brief overview of the results to date were presented to all the Drake Beam Morin consultants at the recent annual conference. This presentation was followed by an optional break-out session that presented the program in more depth. There was considerable excitement about the program reflecting the growing awareness of the importance of the client's attitudes in the job search process. It has often been noted that attitude is particularly important for clients whose search extends beyond the normal time frame. One of the potential merits of the program is, in fact, its ability to impact "dwell time" or the length of the search.

There was some concern that the use of visualization would be unacceptable to some clients and to some companies that Drake Beam Morin works with, associating the company with such things as meditation and hypnosis. The general feeling in this group was that the program was "flaky" and of no practical value in the job search process. There is no doubt that some clients will simply not be willing to participate in such a program, and, like anything else in the outplacement program, it must be optional.

Others who participated in the program were aware of their own resistance which affected their ability to do the exercises. Because the program is only four to five hours long, it presents a very limited framework to learn the concepts and techniques. For those who do not grasp the concepts and techniques easily, utilizing the program is difficult.

The audio tape mentioned above, a composite of the basic visualization exercises used in the program, gives the client one method to continue to work with the exercises after the program is complete. What amount of time will be structured for follow-up or ongoing group meetings has not yet been decided. There is interest on the part of clients to continue with the process although the workshops have been poorly attended largely due to the fact that clients get involved in their job search and see the program as a low priority. Interest in the program is rekindled when the client finds he or she is having a difficult time.

Programs and techniques such as the Optimum Performance Training Program at Drake Beam Morin, designed to help people manage the feelings attendant to a job loss and a job search, are in their infancy. Potentially, they offer a strong additional service to the task of helping a person make a difficult life transition.

References

Assagioli, R. (1965). *Psychosynthesis*. New York: Penguin.

Assagioli, R. (1974). *The act of will*. New York: Penguin.

Bandler, R., & Grinder, J. (1979). *Frogs into princes*. Moab, UT: Real People Press.

Benson, H. (1975). *The relaxation response*. New York: Avon.

Benson, H. (1979). *The mind body effect*. New York: Simon & Schuster.

Ferrucci, P. (1982). *What we may be*. Los Angeles: Tarcher.

Fritz, R. (1984). *The path of least resistance*. Salem, MA: Stillpoint.

Garfield, C. (1986). *Peak performers: New heroes in American business*. New York: Morrow & Co.

Gendlin, E. (1981). *Focusing*. New York: Bantam.

Kubler-Ross, E. (1969). *On death and dying*. New York: Macmillan.

Kubler-Ross, E. (1975). *Death: The final stage of growth*. Englewood Cliffs, NJ: Prentice-Hall.

Maslow, A. (1968). *Toward a psychology of being*. New York: Van Norstrand.

Maslow, A. (1971). *The farther reaches of human nature*. New York: Viking.

Morin, W., & Cabrera, J. (1982). *Parting company*. New York: H.B.J.

Morin, W., & York, L. (1982). *Outplacement techniques*. New York: PEM.

Robbins, A. (1986). *Unlimited power: The new science of achievement*. New York: Simon & Schuster.

Birthing and Rebirthing Peace-Building Communities: Experiments in Social Psychosynthesis

Judith Bach and Helena Davis

In *Psychosynthesis: Individual and Social,* Assagioli wrote:

All human individuals and groups of all kinds should be regarded as elements, cells or organs (that is, living parts) of a greater organism which includes the whole of mankind. Thus the principle of, and the trend to, synthesis carries us from group to group in ever wider circles to humanity as an integral whole. The essential unity of origin, of nature and of aims, and the unbreakable interdependence and solidarity between all human beings and groups are a spiritual, psychological and practical reality. It cannot be suppressed, however often it may be negated and violated through the numberless conflicts in which men, foolishly and painfully, squander their precious energies and even deprive each other of the sacred gift of life. (1965, p. 9)

As spiritual beings, we are devoted to peace on an inner level. We have skills and knowledge which enable us to move toward peace within ourselves and, in a small way, to promote world peace by contributing positive attitudes and qualities to our global environment. Yet our experience shows us that this alone is not enough to create a peaceful world.

We who have begun to learn to create inner peace can apply our knowledge to wider foci; we can use these same skills and experiences to help families, communities, and institutions create peace.

We have chosen to write this article because we strongly believe that the most effective way to bring peace to our world is through the principle of synthesis. Ferrucci (1982) describes synthesis within the psyche as the harmonization of diverse elements into successively greater wholes. Through the process of attaining inner wholeness through "balance and synthesis of opposites" (Assagioli, 1965), we attain not only a state of inner harmony, but also the capacity to do our work more effectively in the world.

We have worked with this principle of synthesis within individuals and in process groups. We are convinced that it can be applied to promote peace in families and communities as well. Thus, our present endeavors involve the development of models and interventions which will help communities grow and flourish in the direction of greater creativity and harmony:

289

It is imperative that we encourage the growth of peaceful communities in order to promote world peace. If we are to achieve world peace, we cannot address our problems on a few levels and ignore the remainder. We cannot teach the skills of peace just to ourselves or to mediators and government leaders; education must take place at all levels, from the smallest child in a poor rural village to the most powerful heads of states. The global transformation we are trying to achieve can only take place if the values of peace are woven into the fabric of Earth's cultures. If such systemic change is to occur, skill levels and awareness must increase from the grass roots upwards—from the intrinsic motivation of ordinary citizens to the moral imperatives they can engender in the heads of state. (Davis, 1986, pp. 1–2)

As we move toward synthesis in our own lives, sooner or later we feel the need to transform the context in which we live; we yearn to transform it to support continued synthesis for ourselves and others. As we and our immediate environment move closer to synthesis, the energy released creates a ripple effect that is felt through the other systems to which we belong: from self, to family, to community, to town, to state, to nation, to planet.

If we are to transform our communities to support further synthesis, how do we assess success? How do we discriminate which segments of the environment have evolved toward synthesis? Once we have identified the "evolutionary state" of a particular segment of the community at large, can we set realistic goals for transformation or determine the most effective interventions to achieve those goals?

This article explores the use of a model to study the evolution of communities. The model is briefly described and case studies are presented to demonstrate how it works.

Theory

In the same breath that we offer this model, we want to caution the reader about the danger of "pigeon-holing" or categorizing that is so prevalent in the field of psychotherapy these days. This same danger exists in relation to social systems. As we attempt to understand and work with communities, we must approach each group of people, not only with our skills and knowledge, but also with awe and humility as we join with others to reach toward the best within all of us.

Our model is based on Assagioli's (1965, p. 17) map of consciousness: the lower-unconscious realm, the personal or self-conscious realm, and the transpersonal or superconscious realm. It is not such a great stretch to parallel the unintegrated, lower-unconscious primitive and instinctual drives of an individual to a community in which the dominant mode of relating includes unconscious, unreflective, impulsive expressions of basic human drives. The self-conscious level is equivalent to consciousness, awareness, and the capacity to function adaptively and reflectively in daily life. For a community, it is the ability to mediate conflicts, to take responsibility, and to plan and achieve goals. The transpersonal level for a community is its capacity to uphold a value system that speaks to and lives a consciousness of the whole. Such values as co-operation, sharing, and good will are implicit in such a world view.

We must also be able to determine the "ego strength" and personal will development of a community. Ego functioning can be measured by how the community carries out its daily business. Does snow get removed? Are potholes filled? Is the mail distributed efficiently?[1]

The community psychosynthesist is, most effectively, a small group whose role is to evoke the creative spirit within the community in order that it may design its own future in the direction of stronger ego-functioning and spiritual psychosynthesis. From this perspective, the "design group" can be seen as the temporary I-consciousness of the community, with the capacity to observe, reflect, and choose appropriate courses of action without being caught up in limited identifications (Assagioli, 1965). Throughout this process, it is essential for the design group to encourage continually the development of a healthy community I-consciousness. We are defining "community I-consciousness" as the capacity of a critical mass of the members of the community to disidentify from their own narrow viewpoints and to work toward the betterment of the whole.

It is through the process of design itself, that is, through creating new organizations and reorganizing old ones that peace building can happen. Through consensus methodologies and group creative thinking, each member of the community not only has the opportunity to participate in the process of design, but also to learn how to achieve harmony in group interaction. For such a transformative process to happen, it is essential that the initial design group hold the attitude of sensitivity and concern for the inclusion of all of the members of the larger group. Decision making must be approached with creativity and concern for the whole and the *process* of decision making must be considered as important as the product.

The group's concern must be that everyone experiences freedom of action and thought. Each point of view must be contained within the whole. There must be a wise tolerance of each person's beliefs. No one has the right to interfere with even the humblest person's belief system or to influence personal opinion. Any other attitude will lead to distortion and dissension. The end must never justify the means. The secret behind such an "ideal" group model is that it is precisely the differences that, if handled creatively, can lead to harmony, not only in relationships, but also in terms of purpose and goal orientation. So long as unity exists on the level of purpose, differences in details can—and must—be worked out. As the design group learns to work harmoniously and creatively, it becomes the model for the rest of the community as different groups take over parts of the design process that pertain to their own interests. We believe that the process of self-organization, using consensus methodologies, is self-empowering for people and is truly transformative on both group and individual levels.

Once the community has achieved a relative degree of personal (ego) integration and the potent organizations or subsystems within the community are reaching higher values, then the community has begun to move into a state of self-transcendence, or spiritual psychosynthesis. By this time, there are enough individuals to take responsibility for the spiritual direction of the community. A critical mass has been achieved that, in the long run, can affect all of the members of the community, whether or not they are consciously participating in this evolutionary process.

292   *Peace-Building Communities*

Case Studies

From Chaos to Co-operation—The first case study looks at an elementary school selected in 1982 as the pilot site for a training program to provide teachers and students with conflict management and mediation skills. This pilot program acted as the catalyst which enabled the school to strengthen its I-consciousness and thereby synthesize its diverse elements into successively greater wholes. As synthesis occurred, harmony and creativity increased. In two years, the school's ambience changed from chaotic, rugged individualism to joyful co-operation.

The school is located in a low-income urban neighborhood and students come from modest, single-family dwellings and city-subsidized apartments known as "the projects." Students and staff represent approximately 15 nationalities or ethnic groups and speak an equal number of languages. At first glance, one is immediately aware of a great many Latinos, Blacks, Filipinos, and Pacific Islanders.

The youngsters are very active and the playground is too small to adequately accommodate their energy. In perpetual motion, students often bump into each other; they seem like molecules bounding in a hot frying pan. The noise is almost deafening. It is no wonder that the principal reports that more conflicts occur on the playground than anywhere else.

Upon returning to class, students find it difficult to settle down and work because they are still carrying the frustrations from incidents which occurred outside. It is difficult to do anything more than to survive one day at a time when classrooms are crammed with 35 to 40 active youngsters, all of whom have special needs. Children compete for space and scarce materials, as well as the teacher's attention. Many children lack adequate nourishment and sleep; they need far more affection and security than they can hope to get at home. Spending 30 minutes on the campus evokes such phrases as: "law of the jungle," "every man for himself," "sink or swim," and "survival of the fittest."

This community had little to offer its members in 1982. Physically, the building was adequately lit and heated; there was ventilation, there was pleasing visual stimulation. However, there was a severe lack of playground and classroom space. Texts and basic tools such as pencils, crayons, and scissors were also in short supply.

Emotionally, this community needed help. Most feelings emitted were negative. Many adults and children felt isolated, irritated, discouraged; they perceived themselves as being harassed by peers, other community groups, and the central administration. Conflict among students and between students and teachers happened in almost every classroom, every hour. In the teachers' lunchroom, faculty gathered in small cliques to gossip and complain; some sat by themselves. There was no positive sense of community; there was no sense of hope. Students' behavior at lunch and recess was similar. There seemed to be no sense of co-operation or belonging to a community. There was only survival.

For the most part, planning and decision making took place at the administrative level. While some effort was made to include staff in decision making and co-operative projects to improve the school, these overtures were often met with cynicism and apathy. A small handful of staff did most of the work. Planning in the classroom was reactive; it often took place in a moment of crisis or a few minutes before "zero hour" because life in the classroom seemed to be one crisis after another.

Many staff and students felt isolated from the community at large and, in fact, did not feel that there was a community. Communication, for the most part, was either manipulative or aggressive and was delivered in the form of verbal put-downs or memos. Normal conversation between adults and students or among adults tended to be superficial. Staff seemed to have little sense of purpose other than their common goal of trying to survive one more day by getting all the paperwork done and going home without a splitting headache.

The spiritual aspect of the school was not apparent. There seemed to be no sense of common purpose or co-operation. One observer was reminded of a saying: "When you're up to your eyeballs in alligators, it's hard to remember that the initial objective was to drain the swamp." At this stage in its development, Assagioli might have said this community was dominated by lower unconscious dynamics, without a strong "I," or centredness, and without a sense of alignment with superconscious qualities and values.

In 1982, we convened a meeting to introduce the staff to a training program. After formal introductions, teachers participated in an exercise in which they described what school was like for them. All descriptors were negative. Next, teachers offered descriptors about how they would like the school to be. Finally, as we reviewed the second group of statements with the group, they identified which things could be changed and which things they most wanted to change. Increased discipline and less fighting were at the top of the list. Faculty also expressed a strong need for affirmation for staff and students and the need to feel like part of a community. A short time later, the principal and a small group of teachers were trained as leaders for the new conflict management program. In effect, this group became the I-consciousness of the school community.

After intensive work with students and staff during the 1982–82 school year, not only did the training program flourish and begin to function independently, but the school community as a whole used its new skills to create a community that worked interdependently to fulfil common needs and goals. Indeed, the entire school environment seemed far more positive than it had in the fall of 1982.

According to final program evaluations, the most notable changes occurred in the types of goals set by individuals and the community at large. People were no longer interested just in their own survival; they wanted to improve the quality of life for everyone. Students and staff, alike, expressed wants and needs assertively about 80 percent more frequently than in 1982. Listening skills improved almost as much. On the playground, which once seemed like an armed camp, student mediators complained about not having enough work to do. Adult playground monitors looked a little bored rather than frazzled. Classrooms were calmer and students settled into the business of learning. Relationships between students and teachers improved significantly and classrooms seemed more like cohesive groups than mere collections of individuals. On the whole, staff responded to adversity in pro-active, problem-solving modes rather than complaining or gossiping and feeling powerless. Faculty and student groups spent less time arguing and complaining; they devoted time and energy to thinking of new ways to improve the school environment so that it would support everyone's growth efforts. This school became a community where individuals and groups could determine their own needs and initiate their own changes in response to those needs.

In Search of Spiritual Identity—Our second case study is about a small New England village community which we will call Cranfield. Cranfield, with its population of 800, can be viewed as a community that is in search of its spiritual identity and collective consciousness, reflected in such values as good will and co-operation.

If you drive into Cranfield, you are likely to be on the other side of town before you know it. The ambience is New England white clapboard (with a few brown and green houses thrown in for variety), the obligatory spartan white church, general store, and post office. Next to the general store beside the river is the library.

The community is rural-residential, with several working farms. There are two lakes which attract a summer population, increasing the town size to about 2,000 each summer. This population is a strong subgroup, coming primarily from New York City and the Boston area. Cranfield is in one of the major cultural areas in the East, featuring music, dance, and theatre in the summer. As a result, the area contains a heterogeneous population of intellectuals, artists and writers, and "old-timers," leading to a greater level of sophistication among the villagers than one would find in otherwise similar New England towns.

In the business district of the village, there is a general store; a luncheonette, managed by a therapeutic farm community for former mental and drug patients; a New Age bookstore, a car-repair garage, and a combination health food and wooden toys store. There is also a thriving cottage industry in the community. For example, one young couple runs a successful goat-cheese farm. Another family sells maple syrup, makes and repairs musical instruments, and plays for dances in the area. There are also potters, artists, odd-job men and women, carpenters, teachers, psychotherapists, secretaries, store clerks, and construction workers.

At this point in the town's life, there is an integration process happening between the various factions of the community. Fifteen years ago there were schisms between the oldsters and the newcomers; today such separations have been largely healed. At a planning board meeting recently, an old-timer was heard to say that the community must be open to the fact that the town is changing and that new people are moving in. This statement was in dramatic contrast to what this resident said five years ago when she was very fearful about change and resistant to alterations in the town.

If we hope to co-operate in the evolution of our communities, we must reframe our attitudes about instability, or crisis. These crisis points happen organically in all living systems and almost invariably precede and accompany growth (Jantsch, 1980). How the system responds to crisis or instability determines whether or not pathology or synthesis will result. For example, pathology can occur when the pain from crisis is suppressed. Conversely, when pain and difficulty are acknowledged and consciously worked with, there is an opportunity for integration and synthesis. While a small community allows for more cohesive decision-making and action than a large complex social system, it is also more subject to shock waves generated by crisis situations.

In most communities, when crisis occurs, the ensuing polarizations often take years to heal. This was also true of Cranfield, until one person, the minister, moved to town. How he helped heal one crisis and contributed to the evolution of the community to a new level of consciousness is a powerful example of the positive power of one individual in a community. In the early seventies, a group of young people moved to town who were interested in buying land and becoming self-sufficient. The old-timers had become paranoid toward these young people, fearful that they would introduce drugs into the community. Had this situation run its course without the intervention of the minister, the healing, if it had happened at all, might have taken years. With his intervention, the illness was aborted. He invited the young people to participate in a monthly "alternative life-style supper" in the church basement in order to meet and inform other community members of their intentions and plans. He then invited everyone in town to attend these suppers to discover what "alternative life-style" was all about. After about six months, a monthly community supper evolved out of this idea which, 15 years later, continues. It is a time for old and young, traditional and non-traditional members of the community to eat together and participate in a program after the supper.

Since that time, such active, conscious interventions in the ongoing life of the community have been applied in a fairly regular manner by a design group. As community designers, our approach has been to identify, draw forth, and enhance the most evolutionary possibilities that exist in the community and, at the same time, facilitate the integration of these possibilities into the community as a whole.

Our first intervention was to invite 40 people to a community-building meeting. To our astonishment, 42 people showed up on a blustery, rainy evening. This group ranged in age from 11 to 90 and included both those whose families had lived in town for generations and newcomers to the community.

First, we asked each person to share what he or she felt about the community. The effect was a warm, group-building experience. We then asked people to think about the values they would like to see upheld and worked for in the town. "Brotherhood," "sharing," "the spirit of co-operation" were some of the statements expressed. And, finally, we asked the group to respond to the question, "What do you think needs to happen in this town as an expression of these values?" Ideas such as a community garden, transportation for the elderly, a community bulletin board, and a children's play group emerged in response to this question.

We then created working groups around each of these central initiatives. These groups met over a period of time to actualize these projects. Some of the projects materialized quickly, some more slowly, and some have yet to be realized. The most powerful aspect of the meeting was the message that we could effect change if we mobilize the will of the group in relation to a stated value system, a phenomenon often experienced in psychosynthesis psychotherapy.

Another intervention of the design group was to initiate an annual "I Love Cranfield Day"—an event that was built around a theme that expressed some aspect of good will. The first such event was called "A Festival of the Earth." This was a day of celebration of the planet, ecological principles, and sound energy use and planning. The seed was planted. Just one month later, the Cranfield Energy Committee was formed, which became one of the most effective in the state.

Within the community, there has grown an increasing sense of global consciousness, linked to concerns about nuclear proliferation and peace-education efforts. At a meeting of community members in 1985, it was suggested that this group of 20 people focus prayers and healing visualization on Ethiopia. The issue was raised by several people that perhaps we had better concern ourselves with poverty at home. The discussion continued all evening. The questions raised and the ongoing discussions were crucial to the establishment of seeds of global consciousness within the community.

One of the most important dynamics happening in the community accords with Banathy's (1984) statement that "traditional values, transcendent values, and individual values are dynamically interrelated with design to form unique amalgams of humanly purposed systems" (pp. 3–23). The current challenge in Cranfield is to integrate the emergent values, as represented by the New Age group, with individual and traditional values. The New Agers introduced a new crisis and opportunity for growth when they started moving into town about seven years ago. Although their belief systems are divergent, they are principally united around a suspicion of traditional religious practice and a commitment to a holistic life-style, such as health food, meditative practices, and alternative forms of healing. They have a deep commitment to spiritual growth, whatever form that takes for them individually. Many traditional-thinking townspeople have had their ideas stretched throughout this process; the New Agers are also learning that they can be as "dug in" and separative as anyone else. However, the integration is beginning to occur.

An example of how this polarity became resolved on a higher level of integration is the general store. (See "The Balancing and Synthesis of Opposites," Assagioli, 1972.) A good general store must be a confluence of all the strands in the community, satisfying material needs from cleanser to soup to nails. Fifteen years ago, an elderly couple ran the store. It was a traditional old-style country store. When they retired, it was sold to a young man who ran it very ineptly. People stopped coming. To walk inside was a dreary experience. Then, with the first wave of New Agers, the store was bought by several members of this group who tastefully remodelled it, threw out the cleanser and the nails, installed health food and a restaurant, and waited for customers. They never came. An angry relationship developed between the owners and many of the villagers who refused to support it because they just weren't interested in health food; those who wanted health food were in the minority and couldn't support the store by themselves. It became clear to the design group that the store was not representing the community.

We tried to talk to the owners, who stubbornly defended their position, angered that the community was not supporting them. The position of many townspeople was, Why should we support a store that refuses to carry what we really want? Ultimately, the new owners gave up, and it was bought by a man in town who was committed to the needs of the whole village. The general store now stocks sugar *and* health food and is serving the needs of the whole community. This is a concrete expression of good will.

Another arena for the integration process has been the church itself. With a long tradition of community involvement, the church is one of the most powerful social forces in town. When the minister retired several years ago, the church was thrown into crisis. Up to that point, many newcomers had not felt that the church met their more eclectic spiritual needs, and so had stayed away. In order to take advantage of the possibilities for growth, we inaugurated a series of three meetings with the parish council, the governing body of the church. Through an envisioning process, members were encouraged to create their ideal church. (See Assagioli, 1965, on the "ideal model.") These images were separated into spiritual images, such as purpose and values, and structural images, such as forms of worship and placement of pews. There was so much enthusiasm generated at these meetings that the church council itself became the design team that facilitated moving the process out into the larger church community in order to generate more communication and feedback. Small "cottage" groups met several times, led by members of the council, to discuss desired changes in the church. Out of these discussions, one of the members of the council put together the results, which became the basis of the "profile" provided to applicants for the ministry.

The primary effect of this process was to suggest to the church community that it could design its own future. The result was an unparallelled amount of energy and creativity in the group, the development of a lay ministry, and a series of weekly discussions before and after church services engaging the entire congregation. Discussions ranged from questions of whether or not baptism should be optional to deep spiritual sharing. The more traditional members of the church community and the New Agers began to discover in each other the same spiritual commitment, even though their forms of worship differed.

Further evidence of value-based changes in the community can be seen in the annual town meetings. A new spirit of good will has entered this process. For example, a bridge collapsed in the village. The issue arose about whether to use available state funds to build a concrete bridge or to raise money to build a more ecologically sound, aesthetic bridge. Five to ten years ago, this issue would have led to heated and probably explosive exchanges at the town meeting. The discussion during this particular meeting was good-humored and polite, each side presenting its case with clarity and reasonableness. The implications of the fact that the townspeople voted state funding down by a two-thirds majority are that the community must develop self-sufficiency, not as a retreat from the world, but so that it can cleave to the values that are important to it.

Another crisis was presented by a woman who moved to town with a long history of psychosis. She began to act out, wandering into people's houses, creating havoc in the stores, and disrupting meetings. Instead of calling the police, people tried to respond in a caring way. When this didn't work, an informal support network was formed. For example, the clerk in the store would call a psychotherapist in town to get advice, or just to vent. Finally, a group of community members, along with the woman, went to a family therapist outside the community, who demonstrated how to set the boundaries that she obviously needed. His comment to her when she complained about us to him was that this was his first experience of a community reaching out to try to resolve such a situation rather than just throwing her out. The learning for the community was "tough love."

At this time in Cranfield's history, the original design group has been absorbed into the community. There is now enough I-consciousness so that whenever there is a new crisis (and there are always crises), there is a spirit of willingness to work with it and learn from it. The people of Cranfield are becoming more open to facing their pain and vulnerability and, thereby, learning to become more loving and caring.

Conclusion

As we look at communities in general, it seems that they consist of fragmented aspects of the whole, much like an individual. What is often lacking in the dysfunctional community is an "I" with sufficient strength and knowledge to transform and integrate distorted subpersonalities or fragments. If psychosynthesists can intervene and facilitate transformation and I-consciousness on a social level, then other community members, through their own involvement and evolution, can nurture the growth of the community as a whole.

The implications of applying social psychosynthesis to disenfranchised communities, such as refugee groups, the rural or urban poor, and villages in the Third World countries, are far-reaching. The possibilities for empowerment of the most powerless are tremendous. The positive transformation of several small communities in a given area would certainly have a potent effect on the region in which they exist, and as regions change, their wider contexts change as well. Such change can occur peacefully through evolution rather than violently through revolution.

Where there is true good will, where people learn to co-operate in designing their own future, the ground is prepared for the emergence of a consciousness of the whole. One can no longer think only of self, but experiences the self as part of a greater landscape in which all of us are intimately connected, pulsing with the one Life that lies hidden within our hearts. It is when we move more into relation to that Life that we experience our connection with everything on earth. Imagine the effect of communities around the planet expressing these values of good will!

Note

1. Miller (1978) has developed a comprehensive scheme which derives from the assumption that all living systems, from the cell to the supra-national system, have sets of common properties, even though each system occupies a different hierarchical level. His Living Systems Theory provides us with an approach which is useful in assessing the ego strength of a social system (Bach, 1985).

References

Assagioli, R. (1965). *Psychosynthesis: Individual and social*. New York: Psychosynthesis Research Foundation.

Assagioli, R. (1972). *The balancing and synthesis of opposites*. New York: Psychosynthesis Research Foundation.

Assagioli, R. (1977). *Psychosynthesis*. New York: Penguin.

Bach, J. (1985). *A systems study of the psychology of a small community*. Unpublished Master's thesis. Saybrook Graduate School, San Francisco.

Banathy, B. H. (1984). *Systems design in the context of human activity systems*. San Francisco: International Systems Institute.

Davis, H. (1986). *Culturally relevant conflict management training: A participatory design approach*. Paper presented at the Third National Conference on Peacemaking and Conflict Resolution.

Ferrucci, P. (1982). *What we may be*. Los Angeles: Tarcher.

Jantsch, E. (1980). *The self-organizing universe*. New York: Pergamon.

Miller, J. G. (1978). *Living systems*. New York: McGraw-Hill.

Inquiring Into Organizational Systems: Psychosynthesis Spawns a Methodology

Bruce McBeath

Psychosynthesis principles long useful for the understanding of individual psychodynamics have recently been incorporated into a methodology for discovering how organizational systems are perceived and experienced by individuals within them. This methodology represents another step in a continuing effort to understand the interrelationship between individual and organizational dynamics. In this article, some of the efforts to understand the linkages between individual experience and organizational dynamics are profiled followed by a description of a psychosynthesis-related methodology for understanding the individual/organization interface.

In his recent contribution to organizational theory *Stakeholders of the Organizational Mind* (1983), Mitroff identifies the key roles played by what he terms the "internal stakeholders" of various organizational members. Internal stakeholders look very much like what we, from a psychosynthesis perspective, identify as "subpersonalities." Mitroff speculates about how various relationships between an individual's internal stakeholders come together to form the culture of an organization. Mitroff draws on Jung's concept of the archetype to develop the idea that organizational archetypes emerge that interact with and variously reinforce individual patterns of stakeholding in the system of the organization.

I found Mitroff's work particularly helpful in developing an integration of the principles of depth psychology with those of systems science (McBeath, 1986). Human systems theory has characteristically been expansively conceived to describe the dynamics of collectives apart from the subtleties of individual experience. Depth psychology, and here I would include Psychosynthesis, has placed phenomenal importance on the intrapsychic character of individual experience. (Assagioli [1965], calling Psychosynthesis a "heighth psychology," referred to it as making a major contribution to the "depth psychology" of Freud and Jung.) Generally depth psychology has disregarded the impact of larger collective, or conjoint, experience. There are few theoretical constructs that incorporate depth (or heighth) psychology into systems perspectives, though Mitroff does so to some extent using Jung's typology, as does Maccoby (1976) who turns his attention to the psychological dynamics motivating organizational leaders. The often quoted though perhaps little understood Bateson (1979) has provided the source for several recent forays into systems discussions that touch on individual

300

dynamics (e.g., Maturana and Varela, 1980). These are useful but essentially theoretical stabs at understanding the individual-within-the-system.

I sought to generate a methodological approach that would describe from a subjective point of view the relationship between intrapsychic process and group or larger organizational process. Assagioli's techniques, related to images, symbols, and metaphors, were key aspects in my effort to capture the conjoint experience of persons united within a common organizational system.

Purposeful Imagination Within the Organization

Assagioli (1965) described the "purposeful imagination" and its role in the integration and spiritual synthesis of the personality. Assagioli, Jung (1955), and more recently Lifton (1976) characterized the imaging process as an important aspect of an internal guidance system that influences the ongoing development of the individual. The systems philosopher Jantsch went even further in developing the idea of a "guiding image" that functions as a universal archetype in influencing the development of persons, societies, and the evolution of culture (Jantsch & Waddington, 1976).

At the individual level, Assagioli's "ideal model" exercise elaborates a psychosynthesis technique that uses images to enhance individual development. This exercise illustrates how the imagination can function as a mirror reflecting one's internal psycho-spiritual "condition" at a given moment in time. Subjective images are taken that reflect both deflated and inflated experiences of the self as related to self-perception and the perception of others. The ideal model exercise "catches" these various subjective impressions so that they can be harmonized and integrated within an emerging positive image of the self. In the exercise, even inflated images have a particular relationship to the model that is finally evoked. As with most experiences with imagery work related to personality development, the ideal model becomes real as it becomes the focus of sustained creative mediation, that is, as it is incorporated into oneself and the essence of that image is expressed in everyday life.

The use of imagery to reflect group process is a fascinating new area of study. At this point, organizational applications of a reflective imaging process have been only partially developed and are often used haphazardly. Thus the development of an ideal model process for larger systems might help us tap into the subjective experience of persons and systems. This would seem a useful extension of Assagioli's earlier applications with individuals.

The structured use of mental imagery as described in the ideal model exercise provides a starting point for the design of a larger methodological framework to explore the person/system interface within organizational settings. The larger approach described below uses imagery and other facilitative processes to characterize organizations in ways that capture both the depth of subjective individual experience and the breadth of the collective system.

Bridging Psychosynthesis and Systems—Individuality and collectivity come together at the juncture of person and system. Jantsch (1980) uses the analogy of a stream to describe the boundaries that the individual maintains between self and other in a particular system. Covering the perspectives identified by Checkland (1981), Jantsch says that one can observe the stream, or ride its surface (experience the flow "on the stream"), or become the stream itself (identify oneself "as the stream"). From this last perspective, identification with the system becomes an expansion of self-identification and a definition of a larger experience of "self."

The fundamental construct of the egg diagram designed by Assagioli (1965) has permeable boundaries that suggest transpersonal possibilities for the further expansion of the identity of the self. The diagram can be extended to describe the purposeful, evolutionary nature of the interaction between individuals as members of a larger constellation of relationships. Images help us explore how an individual's subjective experience of connection to others colludes with the subjective experience of others to form images of the larger system. This evolving network of interindividual images becomes what Jantsch and Waddington (1976) refer to as a "guiding image" that determines the composition and evolution of the system (i.e., relationships, families, or organizations). Theoretically, these system images influence the development of the individual's self-image as well.

Description of the Methodology

Inspired by Assagioli, Jung, and others regarding the power of imagery (especially Assagioli's methodology relating to the progressive clarification of an image as an ideal model) and augmented by Checkland's description of an interactive systems methodology, I designed an approach that integrates imaging into a broader interactive systems methodology. This methodology was further developed and refined through its application in several organizations. Assagioli's view of how a network of images constitutes the experience of the self is reflected in the methodology; its purpose is to evolve a conscious description of a system as it is experienced by its members (the image of the system as-it-is) and to use this description as a link to the evolution of the system in the future (the image of the system as-it-might-become). The stages in this methodology are outlined below in an abbreviated fashion.

Before beginning the systems characterization process, an individual "baseline" or starting point is established for exploring the self/system interface. An abbreviated form of Assagioli's ideal model exercise is used here to evoke images of self. First, individuals reflect on self-image distortions in both a positive and negative direction, and then they are led to evoke a more realistic yet positive self-image. This becomes the individual's baseline image characterizing his or her subjective experience before moving into his or her experience in relation to the system. The three individual images of the self—as deflated, as inflated, and as functioning well—comprise a subjective scale that can be used to rate how well an individual perceives his or her relationship to the system at various points in the systems characterization process.

Following the formation of an individual baseline image, a fourth image is tapped that reflects an individual's general experience with the organization. This is also a baseline impression, without regard for any particular problem situation within the organization.

After the initial "image taking," a process of characterizing person and system is employed that relates systems images to personal images. This is an interactive, dialogic process through which the subjective meanings of individual and collective images are amplified and examined. Finally, a realistic and positive ideal model image of the organization is elaborated. (For a more detailed presentation of this methodology, see McBeath [1986].) The ideal organizational model that results becomes a basis for designing action strategies to make the ideal image an actuality. This process is similar to grounding in work with individual ideal model images. Its purpose is to make an organizational image or model viable and real.

Example—The following example illustrates how this process was used with one particular organization. The participants were the management staff of a small company that had experienced very rapid growth. The company president was aware that the growth spurt had created job stress for the managers. The management staff had no previous familiarity in working with imagery techniques, nor had they previously attempted to look systemically at organizational problems. They also had little familiarity with group process techniques, although they had been meeting as a management group for over two years.

Imagery was used to help make conscious and available for discussion aspects of individual experience with the system that might not have otherwise emerged. At the first meeting, the managers were asked to generate a series of images of how they experienced themselves functioning in general; then they were asked to evoke personal images that characterized how they functioned in relation to a particular subsystem (the management staff) and to the organization as a whole. They were also asked to generate images which characterized their relationship to organizational issues that were drawn from responses to a set of prestructured questions (a part of the methodology). Initially, they "imaged" their individual relationship to these issues with some difficulty and awkwardness, possibly related to their unfamiliarity in accessing and sharing internal perceptions with each other and the uncertainty they had about trusting this kind of information in the group.

During the second meeting, the managers began to fashion a definition of a system that would contain the issues they had elaborated at the first meeting. In accordance with the methodology I was using, I introduced a focussed discussion that was intended to characterize these issues systemically. I wanted this discussion to result in problem-solving strategies which would address the more systemic problems, not simply the symptoms of those problems (which is what usually happens when organizational issues are not systemically addressed).

In attempting to help the managers think systemically about the issues they had identified, I was aware of their high level of fatigue, which was only enhanced by our late afternoon meeting. In order to enliven the session, I invited the managers to play with organizational images which captured their perspectives regarding the interrelationship of the various issues they had described. A rush of energy arose when they began to synthesize individual images into "corporate images" that integrated their collective personal experiences of the organization. One manager who had imaged herself "tiny" and "intimidated" began to view the organization as an infant whose needs were overwhelming her capacity to supply them. Through continued discussion, the organizational images began to coalesce around one particular theme—that of the developing child. The organization was characterized as a child experiencing a growth spurt. Parts of the organization's development (growth, co-ordination, capacity to make decisions, ability to manufacture its own resources) were out of balance with other parts. The managers used the language of the image to talk about how a rebalancing of the organization would allow development to even out.

The use of this organizational image prompted managers to identify personal images that characterized their individual experience with the organization in relation to this theme (i.e., issues generated by the growth spurt). Personal images were shared that related to being, "expected to run when I'm just learning to walk," or "a small child with a headful of curiosity who is still trying to get his body to work right."

These images stimulated an elaboration of the organizational ideal model. The managers decided that the organizational climate needed to be a safe one for the "child's" continued development to occur. This led to a discussion of how a nourishing work climate and appropriate staff expectations could be structured. Earlier the managers had abstractly (and metaphorically) described the need for a management focus on establishing a nourishing work climate; now they saw that such a climate would have to provide direction and support for the "child" (organizational staff) if it was to help it through a stressful time in its development. Providing appropriate nourishment translated into revising staffing patterns and job performance expectations and providing sufficient preparation and on-the-job training so that a well-developed (or developing) staff would result. Thus, the image of the developing child became the basis for an organizational model that presented a unified perspective on how the organizational system would appear if it were providing an appropriate, nourishing environment.

This collective image of the organization captured a particular insight for managers because it conveyed the idea that the organization was a *developing* business and that it had different needs from a *developed* business. The managers determined that a legitimate need for external assistance existed in the short run, and broadened their consideration of strategies to support the development of such assistance. Imaging themselves as a developing organization altered their perceptions both of how they actually "were" as a system and of the strategies they might employ to move from unbalanced development to greater maturity. For example, the managers' stance regarding available external sources of contract funding softened. They had formerly been unwilling to consider various loans and government-sponsored business-assistance programs that were available to the newer, more fledgling divisions, preferring to demonstrate their capacity to run each of the divisions "solidly in the black." This pervasive emphasis on fiscal independence had in part resulted in a restrictive and punitive reaction to issues resulting from "down time" (mechanical or human in origin), even when employee errors could be simply viewed as an expected part of the process of learning to do the job. Management's punitive response contributed to the staff morale issues that were captured metaphorically in the image of the child "running before he can walk." This image helped the managers characterize a systemic issue (the need for the appropriately supportive development of the organization's capacity to "grow" into its expanded services) rather than focus on an isolated symptom like down time or staff morale. Further, the image was a model that provided some direction about possible and desirable changes that would contribute to a systemic "solution" to this problem.

Further Discussion

Several authors (Assagioli, 1965; Campbell, 1972; Hillman, 1983; Jantsch & Waddington, 1976; Jantsch, 1980; Jung, 1959, 1961; Lifton, 1976) attest to the power of the image as a vehicle that can both contain and communicate to others essential elements of the psychological or, more appropriately, psycho-spiritual experience of the self. From the perspective of human systems, images are tools that capture the *emerging* nature of a system as well as the evolving nature of the self.

Self and system demonstrate an interconnected pattern of mutually reinforced, reciprocal development that has been theoretically described by writers demonstrating the breadth of systemic approach (e.g., Churchman, 1977) and those probing the depth of the structural foundation of the human psyche (e.g., Assagioli, 1965; Jung, 1959). Both the breadth of the systemic perspective and the depth of human experience are contained in the collective and intersubjective experiences as represented in the corporate images of organizations. Guiding images or ideal models serve as vehicles for achieving shared understanding regarding complex problems and can illuminate the steps in the transition from problem to resolution, from today's issues to tomorrow's potential.

References

Assagioli, R. (1965). *Psychosynthesis*. New York: Viking.

Banathy, B. (1973). *Developing a systems view of education*. Seaside, CA: Intersystems Publications.

Bateson, G. (1979). *Toward an ecology of mind*. New York: Ballantine.

Campbell, J. (1972). *Myths we live by*. New York: Bantam.

Checkland, P. (1981). *Systems thinking, systems practice*. Chichester: John Wiley & Sons.

Churchman, C. W. (1977). *The systems approach and its enemies*. New York: Basic Books.

Hillman, J. (1983). *Healing fiction*. Barrytown, NY: Station Hill.

Jantsch, E., & Waddington, C. (1976). *Evolution and consciousness*. Reading, MA: Addison-Wesley.

Jantsch, E. (1980). *The self-organizing universe*. New York: Pergamon Press.

Jung, C. G. (1955). *Modern man in search of a soul*. New York: Harcourt Brace Jovanovich.

Jung, C. G. (1959). *Aion: Researches into the phenomenology of the self*. Princeton, NJ: Bollingen Series, Princeton University Press.

Jung, C. G. (1961). *Memories, dreams, reflections*. New York: Random House.

Lifton, R. (1976). *The life of the self*. New York: Simon & Schuster.

Maturana, H., & Varela, F. (1980). *Autopoiesis and cognition*. Boston: Reidel Publishing.

Maccoby, M. (1976). *The gamesman*. New York: Simon & Schuster.

McBeath, B. (1986). *Exploring the interface between human systems and human beings: A methodology for characterizing human systems*. Saybrook Institute: San Francisco.

Mitroff, I. I. (1983). *Stakeholders of the organizational mind*. San Francisco: Jossey-Bass.

World Order

Reflections on Psychosynthesis and Non-Violence by a Therapist Turned Peace Educator and Activist

Anne Yeomans

In our era the road to holiness necessarily passes through the world of action.

DAG HAMMARSKJÖLD (1964)

In 1980, something happened which no longer made it possible for me to limit my work to being a therapist sitting in a room listening to and supporting the healing and growth of my clients. I had seen a film about Helen Caldicott called "Eight Minutes to Midnight" and it shook me to my core. It awakened me to the reality that the world could be destroyed by nuclear war before I would die a natural death, before my children could grow up, before any of the world's children could grow up. I felt her message all the way through me, and it left me terrified and anxious for weeks to follow. I continued to live my normal life as wife, mother, therapist, but inside me there was a panic raging. When anyone, family or friends, talked about future plans, hopes, and dreams, in my mind the thoughts would be, "But maybe we won't be here."

I felt I must do something. I even felt that if I didn't do something the world would be gone. This fear mobilized me and catapulted me into action.

Many different actions followed. The first was a gathering at my house in San Francisco on January 1, 1982, to show another film, "The Last Epidemic," about physicians talking of the effects of nuclear war. Later, when we moved to the East coast, I worked on local fundraising for the campaign to stop the Euromissiles and helped organize a town meeting to prepare educators and parents for the showing of the film "The Day After." I also worked with parents and Educators for Social Responsibility and got involved in the usual marches and petitions. It felt better to be active, to be participating, but I still didn't have the sense that I had found my "place" or that I was using myself, or being used, in a way that I could make my best contribution.

What about Psychosynthesis, I wondered. What about those last ten years as therapist and trainer? What about all that I had learned about how people grow and change, about how the inner transformation happens, about how inner wars and conflicts are healed, about the birth of the sacred self? Did I have to put all that aside and be an activist now? Was there a use for what I had learned as a therapist in the world of action and in relation to the challenge of peacemaking?

Throughout my explorations and efforts, the aspect of peace work that continued to draw me the most was non-violence. When I read Gandhi, Martin Luther King, Cesar Chavez, Dorothy Day, Jim Douglass, Adolfo Pérez Esquivel, and others, I found myself uplifted and deeply moved by the commitment to *life* that their lives expressed. What was my relation to non-violence, I asked myself. Was I brave enough to commit civil disobedience and go to jail? Was that even the best use of myself? How would I know?

A turning point came after being with Jim and Shelley Douglass, activists from Bangor, Washington. I had just finished reading Jim's powerful book *Lightning East to West, Jesus, Gandhi, and the Nuclear Age* (1984) in which he writes of our era as being an end-time. Yet he also says that "an end-time can be a beginning." Again I asked myself how I could respond, and an answer came. I decided to create a workshop on the psychological and spiritual foundations of non-violence. Here was a way to respond to the peace challenge and at the same time bring with me the learning of all those psychological years. Excitement came first and then very soon doubt. Still, with the support of a couple of friends and strengthened by what I have come to call "inner civil disobedience" (going ahead even though the voices in your head are saying, "You can't"), I began.

My goal was to weave together non-violence and Psychosynthesis, to see what they had to do with each other. In what ways, I asked, could psychosynthesis thought and methods contribute to the inner transformation that leads to non-violent action in the world? Psychosynthesis, as I had known it, focussed on methods which supported the healing and transformation of individuals. Although Assagioli (1965b) had suggested that the principles and methods he used in working with individuals could be applied to the relationships between individuals and between groups, an inter-individual psychosynthesis is not been well developed and articulated. As far as I knew at that time, the relationship of Psychosynthesis to social and political action had not been explored.

Goals for the Teaching

I started my project by trying to define what my goals in teaching about non-violence were. How did I plan to approach this vast subject? This is what I came up with:

1. I wanted to teach about non-violence in a way that many people could relate to, not just people considering civil disobedience.
2. I wanted to find ways to explore non-violence as a way of life, not only as a social and political action or tactic.
3. I wanted to show that non-violence toward oneself was part of peacemaking and that a violated self only violates others.

4. I wanted to show that non-violence could be practised at the level of self, relationship, community, and world and that right action at any level affected all the others.

5. I wanted to help people reframe what they were doing in their personal lives, in their families, in their neighborhoods, at work and to see where they were already doing the work of peacemaking.

6. I wanted to be straight about the seriousness of the challenge we were facing, about the urgency of this time, and to emphasize that each of us is called to find our way to respond.

7. I wanted to help participants in my workshops explore the relationship between the world of contemplation as expressed in prayer, meditation, and other practices of self-awareness and the world of social and political action.

8. I wanted to find stories of thinkers and activists who tried to integrate action and contemplation in their own lives. I also wanted to balance stories of discouragement and despair with stories of hope and inspiration.

9. I wanted to support people finding their own individual way of responding to the peace challenge of our era. This necessitated, among other things, challenging some stereotypes of what social action looks like.

A Search for Principles—The first thing I tried to do was to discover some of the basic principles of non-violence. Through reading Gandhi (1962, 1965), King (1963), Esquivel (1985), Douglass (1984), Goss-Mayr (1985), and others, the following emerged:

1. *Non-violence is based on the sacredness of all life and the absolute worth of every single individual.* Here are two basic assumptions about the spiritual nature of life and the value of each individual, even those we might call our adversary or even enemy. These ideas are totally consistent with the principles underlying Psychosynthesis, and are at the heart of non-violence.

The reference to sacredness immediately raises the question, how do we live so as to keep in touch with an experience of sacredness, particularly in a culture which is so secular, so driven to activity and acquisition, so outer-oriented? What choices, what life styles, and what spiritual practices contribute to this?

2. *Ahimsa (non-violence) is in accord with the truth of human nature* (Gandhi). This suggests to me that the consciousness out of which true non-violent action springs already exists within us. It is there to be discovered rather than created. This idea parallels the psychosynthesis concept of the Self as who we are and who we have always been. Many people refer to the experience of connecting to their Self as an experience of "coming home." Might we imagine non-violent action, which can be thought of as an expression of the Self in the world, as an extension of the experience of coming home?

3. *The first principle of non-violence is non-co-operation with anything humiliating* (Gandhi). I work extensively with this principle because it emphasizes the justice aspect of non-violence. It suggests the spirit of liberation and connects us with a tradition of non-violent action in which people without worldly power have used non-violence as a way of fighting injustice and human rights abuses. This principle expresses power, refuting any notion that confuses non-violence with being weak and ineffective. It challenges us to look at personal humiliations as well as humiliations and violations going on in the world today. This principle allows us to see that work with all these issues, from the personal to the global, is part of the work of peacemaking and non-violence.

I believe that the extensive work that is going on today in America in the areas of addiction recovery, treating adult children of alcoholics, and sexual abuse is all part of peace and justice work.

4. *Non-violence seeks lasting gains, not a rapid win. It always wants improved relations with the opposing party, never its submission* (Nagler, 1982). This principle is at the centre of non-violent action, making it unique as a way of fighting for justice and for human rights. The non-violent activist doesn't want to win by diminishing the other party in any way; he or she wants freedom for all parties, not freedom for one at the expense of the other.

Within Psychosynthesis, parallels can be made with the intrapsychic work of liberating one part of the personality from the domination of another, and ultimately working to let all parts, or subpersonalities, find their rightful place. This often includes learning how to look through distorted behavior to the deeper need or concerns it masks.

This principle can be applied to the work for justice within an individual, a family, a neighborhood, a country, or between countries. In asking myself what kind of consciousness approaches conflict and injustice in this way, and how it can be awakened, I was led to learn more about "win-win" and non-adversarial approaches to conflict.

5. *As the means are so the end* (Gandhi). This principle suggests the importance of *process*. It reminds us to honor all aspects of the process of peacemaking. In the words of A. J. Muste, "There is no way to peace. Peace is the way." This principle is particularly important to me because of my personal experience with the destructiveness and pain that result when means are ignored for the sake of ends. This principle is crucial to the true spirit of non-violence and is a safeguard against the fanaticism which so often arises in approaches which try to work with "the truth." This is an area where a tremendous amount of learning and practice is needed.

6. *Non-violence comes from within*. This principle suggests the primacy of the inner life in the preparation for non-violent social action. It also suggests the need for some kind of contemplative practice, like meditation and prayer, as well as self-awareness. In Gandhi's (1962) words, "In spite of despair staring me in the face on the political horizon, I have never lost my peace . . . that peace comes from prayer. . . ."

Clearing Up Some Misunderstandings—It became very clear in one of the first workshops I taught that the word "non-violence" created tremendous problems and misunderstandings for everyone, suggesting the absence of something rather than the living presence and expression of something positive. Non-violence is, of course, much more than the absence of violence, just as true peace is much more than just the absence of war. Yet because we have so little experience of a peace or non-violence that is more than just the absence of something, it is hard for us to understand or even speak of it in a way that reflects its real nature.

In order to deal with the confusion that the word created, it seemed important in my teaching to introduce the word used by Gandhi, *Satyagraha*. *Satyagraha* means soul force, truth force, holding fast to the truth. It comes much closer to conveying the living force, the active love, which is embodied in the actions and teaching of the great non-violent activists. I think the expression of the soul force of a King, Gandhi, Esquivel, or Dorothy Day touches us deeply because their expression of this force resonates with the soul force latent in each one of us.

I also found helpful in clearing up these misunderstandings Gandhi's writings on the non-violence of the weak which he describes as a "policy of passive protest or a cloak for impotent hatred which does not dare to use force." To this "false and cowardly non-violence," Gandhi (1965) says he would prefer "an honest resort to force." The idea of a non-violence of the weak seems very much like what Assagioli describes as love without will, and true non-violence seems very much like what psychosynthesists have known as the synthesis of love and will. In one of the workshops, some participants and I roughed out a synthesis triangle (see Figure 1) which suggests that non-violence of the weak should not be confused with *satyagraha* or true non-violent action and that on a psychological level non-violence must include the acceptance and the transmutation of one's own "dark side," one's own aggressive energies, one's own capacity to violate, retaliate, and get back. It will not last if it is based on repression and denial.

Figure 1/Synthesis Triangle

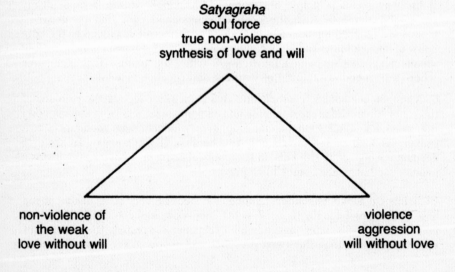

Satyagraha
soul force
true non-violence
synthesis of love and will

non-violence of
the weak
love without will

violence
aggression
will without love

The acceptance and transformation of aggressive energies thus began to be an important part of my teaching. I found it was particularly useful to some activists or "would be activists" who were very identified with peace and saw the military mind as something foreign to them. The emphasis was also helpful to those who had tried to work with the aggressive side of their nature through a spiritual approach and who had few psychological tools and methods. It seems to me that this whole area of work is in much need of research and study, particularly by psychosynthesists who have both a psychological and a spiritual perspective on the acceptance and transmutation of aggressive energies. In the words of Assagioli (1973), "The transformation of combative and aggressive drives has a central importance because it constitutes one of the most effective, perhaps the most effective, means of eliminating interpersonal conflicts and preventing war."

There has never been a workshop in which the question of anger and non-violence didn't come up, clearly a question on many people's minds. At a retreat I attended, Adolfo Perez Esquivel, the Argentinian non-violent activist and 1980 Nobel Prize winner, gave one answer which I have found very useful: "I think that those people who don't become angry and rebellious can't truly become non-violent because we have to rebel against injustice with all our strength . . . but as Martin Luther King has taught us, we can hate segregation and not the segregationist . . . we must struggle against injustice but with profound respect for all human beings." Esquivel reminded us of the reality of the deep rage that exists when there has been injustice and at the same time of the need to direct it, not at the person, but at the forces of darkness, ignorance, and separation which limit us all.

The challenge is to put these ideas into practice. What degree of psychological or spiritual maturity does it take to be able to do this? What methods, skills, ways of communicating contribute to it? Clearly, a tremendous amount of learning is needed.

Gandhi also spoke about anger in a way which has a lot of psychological implications: "I have learnt through bitter experience the one supreme lesson to conserve my anger, and as heat conserved is transmuted into energy, even so our anger controlled can be transmuted into a power which can move the world" (cited in Black, Harvey & Robertson, 1973). It is, of course, impossible to know exactly what he meant by the word "conserve," but the point is he did not say deny or repress. It is my sense that non-violence based on denial or repression will not last, especially when it is tested or challenged, nor will it have the transformative power of non-violence based on a thorough knowledge of one's psyche. This is not meant to suggest that we should wait until we really know ourselves before acting (even if this were possible), for certainly much transformation and self-knowledge happen in action. Rather, there is a need to balance action and self-reflection. Michael Nagler (1982) implies this in his book *America Without Violence*. When the British did not respond, Gandhi often withdrew to do work within his own movement.

The Workshop

These then are the ideas and principles I have tried to teach. Translating

314 Reflections on Non-Violence

them into a workshop form has been challenging, and the workshop itself has evolved and changed over time. When I started, I had very little idea of *how* I would do it, only that I *must* do it. Below I describe the workshop in the format of four 3-hour sessions, though I have also done it in both shorter and longer sessions.

Session 1: Introduction

Goal: Set the context. Clarify the dimensions of the exploration. The three circles: self, other, world. Introduce the basic principles of non-violence.

Besides the usual workshop beginnings of introductions and group-building exercises, my goal Friday evening is to set the context for the exploration of non-violence at this time in history. I use the image of the whole earth (with a beautiful photograph I have) and remind participants that this is a relatively new image. (It is only since 1967 that we have been able to see the whole earth.) At the same time, I remind them that it is also unprecedented in the history of humankind to have weapons powerful enough to destroy civilization as we know it. I'm not saying anything that everyone in the room doesn't know but it seems important to say it and say it and say it. It is a fact too enormous to be assimilated, and it is no wonder that the extent of our denial is tremendous.

As well as confronting the nuclear threat, I also try to talk about ecological issues and human rights abuses, putting out enough facts to call forth the seriousness of the situation we are in, and to make it real. I always find this hard, and have to confront my own denial every time I do it. On the other hand, I try not to introduce so many "heavy" facts that I drive people into numbness and panic. How I balance this varies from group to group.

There are different ways of trying to set the context and I have experimented with various approaches. Sometimes I take the lead in putting out facts, sometimes I have group members talk about both those issues which move and trouble them and those which give them hope. I also try to make room for feelings and emotional responses.

The release of feelings about life in the nuclear age is not my primary goal, however. This work is done very completely in the Despair and Empowerment Workshops of the Interhelp Organization (Box 331, Northampton, MA 01061). Yet I have found if there is no room for some feelings, a kind of deadness sets in. At the core, we feel so deeply about this topic that to come alive to it we must feel how we feel.

The other thing I do the first night is present a very brief history of non-violence and introduce the principles described earlier in this article. I have them written up on large pieces of newsprint in the front of the room.

I also put up a drawing of three concentric circles—self, other, and community or world—and say that one can practise non-violence at any of these levels, that action in any one sphere affects all the rest (see Figure 2). This introduces the idea of non-violence toward ourselves, which for many is a new idea. I point out that when we are violating ourselves, whether it be through self-hatred or self-criticism, through overactivity, or denial of our feelings or of our deepest values and concerns, we soon begin to violate others. People seem to understand this very readily, and yet find it a new way of thinking about the applications of the principles of non-violence. I talk as well about the courage and power of non-violent action, introducing the principle of non-co-operation with humiliation as a way of clearing up any misunderstanding around non-violence being weak or passive.

Figure 2/Levels of Non-Violence

Session 2: Personal Dimensions of Non-Violence

Goal: Explore some of the psychological aspects of non-violence (including the issue of non-violence toward oneself) and also the acceptance and transmutation of aggressive energies.

On Saturday morning, I begin to work with some of the personal dimensions of non-violence, with what Esquivel (1985) calls "discovering you are a person." Two exercises have been useful for this—(1) Interaction with a Partner and (2) Writing and Reflecting on Non-Co-operation with Humiliation.

Interaction with a Partner is a dyadic exercise which begins with the expression of demands by each partner, moves through self-assertion of one's own worth and one's right to be listened to, and ends (hopefully) with an experience of compassionate listening that comes not from obligation but from an inner place of strength and wholeness.

This exercise usually brings out vitality, aliveness, and deep contact. Many people who have not had the experience of making self-assertive demands and who have only known the non-violence of the weak feel empowered. Others come to an awareness of how unfamiliar they are with their own aggression.

One person said at the end of the exercise how wonderful it was to be listened to by someone who knew she was worthy. This led into a discussion of listening and how much better we listen when we feel whole and connected to ourselves, and how sometimes listening is used not to hear the other person but as protection or even self-defence.

Writing about Non-Co-operation with Humiliation, the second exercise of the morning, involves answering several questions about the experience of humiliation. I ask participants to look first at humiliations they have experienced personally, then to notice whether they continue to commit the same kinds of humiliations against themselves. I also ask them to see if there are people in their lives whom they have humiliated and violated or whom they would like to humiliate. I ask them to notice what humiliations and violations in the world today trouble them the most.

This takes participants to the personal roots of violence and humiliation and points to how one violation leads to another—the chains of violence of "you get me" and "I get you back." I am careful to define violence as much more than physical. I talk about psychological and emotional violence, verbal and mental violence, and institutional violence.

Session 3: Non-Violence in Relationship

Goal: Explore non-violent approaches to the resolution of conflict. Final hour—Martin Luther King film. Discussion of the moral challenge his life and teachings raise.

To set the contrast between win-lose and win-win approaches to conflict, I stage an argument on Saturday afternoon asking participants to stand in two lines facing each other. Line A is to argue that the way to a more peaceful world is through social and political action. Line B is to argue that the way to a more peaceful world is through prayer, meditation, and inner work. After a period of time, I ask participants to switch and argue the opposite point of view. The final step is to step back (to disidentify) and to see the problem of peace on the floor between them, then to work co-operatively on it. I warn them to guard against a premature harmony, a "premature peace," but to represent assertively their point of view until they feel it has been adequately included.

In watching this last step of co-operation, I have noticed that the atmosphere in the room totally changes; it becomes focussed, steady, and sometimes even healing, a place for creativity and clear thinking. I end the exercise by having each person talk to their partner about what they learned. Then the whole group brainstorms about both the quality of relationship and the quality of thinking in win-lose and win-win approaches to conflict. I follow this with a very brief introduction to win-win conflict resolution. (This part I have now developed into a 6- or 9-hour workshop on conflict resolution which I can present on its own.)

I end the afternoon by presenting a video of Martin Luther King's life and a 30-minute talk on the feelings it touches in us. It is an old black and white film and of quite poor quality, but it includes a brief history of the civil rights movement and clips from a number of King's speeches. The effect is always powerful, moving the issue of non-violence to its full moral and spiritual depth in a way that nothing I can say or do does. I have learned to trust the power of this film and to give the group time to do the same.

Session 4: Resources for Making and Sustaining a Commitment to Peace and Non-Violence

Goal: Connection with a source of inner wisdom, finding a meaningful next step. Raising the issue of self-care for social activists.

I often begin this last Sunday morning with a long guided meditation called Dialogue with the Whole Earth. The idea is to become aware of one's feelings for the earth and for the different kingdoms of life on earth, almost as if one were doing a Wise Person imagery in a more traditional psychosynthesis workshop. I have participants dialogue with the earth, and eventually I suggest that the earth will give them a gift, something that will help them in their work for peace and non-violence. I then give time for writing and drawing and sharing about this image.

I see this exercise as allowing an expression of the deep inner wisdom we all have to respond to each person's journey as peacemaker. Profound insights have been gained through this exercise. It has been particularly meaningful for people unfamiliar with ways of accessing inner wisdom.

I also take some time this last morning to do some teaching on the theme of self-care. How do we keep ourselves whole for the task? What happens if we don't? I make reference to Thomas Merton's words: "There is a pervasive form of contemporary violence to which the idealist fighting for peace by non-violent methods most easily succumbs: activism and overwork." I draw on the teachings of the Vietnamese Buddhist monk Thich Nhat Hahn (1976) who considered that a day of mindfulness each week was essential for anyone doing social action. I also relay other stories of activists who seemed to know about the need to balance action and contemplation. I remind participants that all the great non-violent activists have had regular periods of meditation and prayer. At the same time, I talk about what a radical act it is to make a commitment to such a practice in the secular and overactive American culture that we live in. I suggest support groups or even a linking up with one or two others in the workshop as a way of building support for this kind of inner work. I usually find people nodding in agreement, and very eager to discuss self-care.

Most people who have been active for any length of time have struggled with burnout. The questions are often raised, At a time when action is so greatly needed, can we afford to slow down, to stop for renewal? If we don't stop for renewal, what kind of consciousness do we bring to our action?

I have found helpful Jim Douglass' thought that this is a time calling for an "urgent patience." I also often remember Assagioli's saying, "Make haste slowly." I sometimes speak of Mother Teresa who celebrates mass every morning and says that out of this all else comes. I often ask participants, What is your own mass? What is your way of connecting to inner sources of strength and renewal? How do you find not just physical rest, but "spiritual rest," to quote another non-violent worker for peace and justice, Dom Helder Camara of Brazil. I often quote my friend Ann Eno who after a peace vigil at the AVCO plant in Wilmington, MA, said, "Now I am going canoeing so I can remember why I am doing this." Yes, it seems essential to remember why we are doing this, to keep alive in us what it is that motivates us to act and to speak out for peace and justice at this time.

I end the workshop by returning to the three circles—self, other, and world—and by asking participants to think about what their next steps are, asking them to choose both an inner step and an outer step, and to share it with another participant in the workshop.

We close with a final meditation and a circle of silence.

Future Directions

I don't know for certain in what direction this teaching will take me. So far, it seems to have had a life of its own, leading me to teach and speak about non-violence and related topics to a number of groups who have no prior knowledge of or experience with Psychosynthesis. I have also become increasingly interested in conflict resolution as a way to anchor the principles and attitudes of non-violence in daily life.

The teaching has also made me want to learn more about the process of enemy making and how projection of our disowned qualities, usually our "dark side," leads to warring in both personal and political ways. This area is one in which I believe the psychological community can make a great contribution.

There are also a number of other areas and issues within Psychosynthesis that I want to integrate in my teaching about non-violence. One is the issue of identifications which, applied to social action, raises the question of where from within does a person's action come—for example, action from a proud and self-righteous part masked as a martyr, or action from a pleaser who is seeking approval from some real or imagined authority figure, or from a rebel unconsciously working out anger at a parent perhaps, or perhaps action from a more centred place. How would one know? How would these various identifications limit or contribute to the action taken? These are all questions that interest me.

I would also like to do more work helping people clarify their core values and finding ways to make their actions expressions of their most deeply held values. I believe a tremendous amount of courage and strength is released when this kind of value-based action is taken.

A central part of non-violence which I feel I have not yet found a good way to teach about is sacrifice and voluntary suffering—the commitment of the non-violent activist to take on suffering rather than impose it, to endure harm if necessary for what seems right. The civil rights movement in the United States guided by Martin Luther King, Jr. and the life and leadership of Mahatma Gandhi remind us forever of the power of this commitment. And yet I know there is much confusion and distortion about what it means for each of us. Sacrifice from what place in ourselves? Sacrifice for what? To whom? There is also what someone described to me as a "movement macho," a pressure to be "cool," which might lead one to act for the wrong reasons. At the same time, these very questions can be used as rationalization for not acting when it is time to. In this light, I appreciate the work of Jim and Shelley Douglass who in training people for non-violent action help them first look carefully at their motivations.

These discernments are difficult and maybe they can only ultimately be answered within one's own soul. In any case, I would like to find a way to raise more of these issues in the teaching I am already doing.

Final Reflections

I know this work is far from finished. Mine is a small beginning, but it is a beginning that has allowed me to keep my sanity these last few years. I sleep better most nights because I have finally found a way to talk about what is really on my mind. I have found a way to be connected to the peace challenge of our time and to bring to it what I have learned through my life and my work. I know my understanding of non-violence has deepened and

I am grateful to those who have explored this area with me, both participants in the workshops and a few close friends.

I still struggle with the voice in my head that says, Who do you think you are to teach about non-violence? He (and I think it is a male voice—the patriarchy within perhaps) dies slowly. I have come to see that when I listen to this voice, I not only cancel my trust in myself but I also add a bit more violence to a world which already has too much. I have decided the only remedy is to go ahead. This is my "disobedience" for now. And by going ahead, I have put myself in a place where I can share what I do know and learn what I don't know. This is clearly a better option. In the words of Martin Luther King, Jr., "The choice is no longer between violence and non-violence. It is between non-violence and non-existence."

References

Assagioli, R. (1965a). *Psychosynthesis*. New York: Viking.

Assagioli, R. (1965b). Psychosynthesis, Individual and Social. In Psychosynthesis Research Foundation (No. 16). London: Institute of Psychosynthesis.

Assagioli, R. (1973). *The act of will*. Baltimore: Penguin.

Black, Harvey, & Robertson (1973). *Gandhi the man*. San Francisco: Glide.

Douglass, J. (1984). *Lightning East to West*. New York: Crossroad.

Esquivel, A. (1985). *Christ in a poncho*. Maryknoll, NY: Orbis.

Gandhi, M. (1962). *The essential Gandhi* (Ed. by L. Fischer). New York: Vintage.

Gandhi, M. (1965). *Gandhi on non-violence* (Ed. by T. Merton). New York: New Directions.

Gandhi, M. (1966). *The mind of Mahatma Gandhi* (Ed. by Prabhu & Rao). Ahmedabad-14: Navajivan Publishing.

Goss-Mayr, H. (1985). Active non-violence. In T. Coninck (Ed.), *Essays on non-violence*. Nyack, NY: Fellowship of Reconciliation.

Hammarskjöld, D. (1964). *Markings*. New York: Knopf.

King, M. L. (1963). *Strength to love*. Philadelphia: Fortress.

Nagler, M. (1982). *America without violence*. Covelo, CA: Island Press.

Nhat Hanh, T. (1976). *The miracle of mindfulness*. Boston: Beacon.

Teixeira, B. (1987). Comments on *Ahimsa* (non-violence). *Journal of Transpersonal Psychology*, 19.

Four Questions for Guiding Peacework

Molly Young Brown

Let us imagine that we are sitting together at some sort of planetary conference. We have decided to consult our inner wisdom about some basic questions in order to better focus our deliberations. To prepare, we each assume
a comfortable position, relaxed and alert, and take a few minutes to focus
attention within ourselves. We close our eyes and breathe slowly and
deeply. We gently move our awareness to a place deep inside where we
each feel safe, private, quiet. In these inner places, we can ask questions
and receive responses from our deepest wisdom. The answers may come in
words, but more likely they will come in impressions of various kinds, such
as visual images, sounds, sensations, emotions, tastes, smells, or combinations of these. So we prepare to be receptive, patient, and non-judgmental,
simply observing whatever happens inside in response to each question.

We will ask ourselves four questions.[1] The exact wording is not so important as is the general direction of the inquiry:

> The first question we ask is, Where are we now in our life as a species? Or,
> Where are we (humanity) now in relationship to our planet Earth? After
> observing our inner responses, we attempt to draw or write about them. Then
> we return to our meditative state and ask a second question, What is our
> highest vision for ourselves as a species? Or, What is emerging for us now;
> what is our next step in growth? Again, we draw or write out our responses.
> Now, holding a sense of that vision, we ask a third question, What is getting
> in our way of moving toward that vision or next step? What might hold us
> back? After observing our responses, including our feelings about them, we
> draw or write them out once again. We now prepare for the fourth and last
> question, taking time to quiet any emotional upsurges from the previous ques-
> tions. Now we ask, What do we need to develop, collectively, to move toward
> our potential? What qualities do we need now to move past our blocks? Again,
> trusting whatever comes, we record our responses in drawing or writing.

If we were indeed sitting together at a planetary conference, we could now
create a very rich synthesis of our wisdom, visions, and perspectives by
sharing our various responses to the four questions. We could go on to
brainstorm ways of developing needed qualities, and plan an array of
activities to do so. These four questions can form the framework for
peacemaking and transformative projects, just as they do for individual
psychosynthesis.

This process can be used to address more specific situations, adapting the
questions accordingly. For example, we might ask, Where are we Americans

320

now in our relationship to the Soviet Union? Or, Where is the peace movement now? What is our next step (Questions 1 and 2)? The four questions could also address one's personal involvement in peacework: Where am I now in my contribution to world peace? What is emerging for me in this work? What holds me back from a more effective or satisfying contribution? What do I need to develop?

These four questions represent an attitude toward growth which is of far greater significance than the specific methodology described here, however useful a tool it may be. This attitude is the willingness to perceive and work with all aspects of a situation—its here-and-now totality, its potentials, its problems, and its inherent growth challenge. Almost any problem or situation, from personal to planetary, may be elucidated by approaching it with this attitude and with these questions. Let's look at each question in more depth to discover its special value to the process of growth, and to see how its perspective contributes to a whole, balanced, and effective transformation.

Question 1: Where Are We Now?

The first question begins the process of conscious growth by exploring where we are now; its purpose is to expand and clarify our awareness of the scope, quality, and interrelationships of the current situation. We cannot hope to find solutions to problems—or even to know clearly what the problems are—unless we first give our attention to "where we are now." All too often, we react to a life crisis by putting on Band-Aids without apprehending the whole situation. Political leaders often react this way to national and world crises (reflagging oil tankers in the Persian Gulf, for example, or sending arms to prop up an unpopular government). Personally or politically, the Band-Aids often do more harm than good because the needs and dynamics of the whole have not been taken into account.

Along with understanding the whole, we also need a sense of acceptance of the present situation, with all its pain and beauty. This does not mean resignation, only a realistic recognition of things as they are and a willingness to work from that base. Acceptance is always the first step, so that we begin from *where we actually are now*, not from where we would like to be.

I know from my own experience that the complexity and profound dysfunctioning of our present world situation are part of what make it so difficult to acknowledge and accept where we are now as a species. It seems that whenever I begin to explore this question, to find out more about what our world situation is, the information I gather is so painful to accept that I often turn away from knowing more. So it seems important to balance the bad news with the good, to include in our explorations the sustaining, creative, and healing forces which are alive in our world as well as the forces that are destructive and confused. It is also necessary to breathe, to open our hearts, to take our time, and to return often to our inner place of quiet and peace.

There is a great deal of useful literature on the state of the planet that can be consulted as part of exploring Question 1. I recommend especially *Staying Alive: The Psychology of Human Survival* by Roger Walsh (1984), *Gaia: An Atlas of Planet Management* edited by Dr. Norman Myers (1984), and *Peace: A Dream Unfolding* edited by Penney Kome and Patrick Crean (1986). Walsh's book summarizes in very brief and dramatic terms our world problems, focussing primarily on the arms race, hunger, and major environmental crises, and goes on to outline the major psychological dysfunctions underlying these problems. *Gaia* provides in-depth, graphic documentation of environmental resources, crises, and management alternatives. *Peace* is a collection of writings and illustrations on the search for peace throughout history and on the nuclear threat and on efforts to create peace today. Of course, there are many other helpful books, films, periodicals, and resources.

Whatever study materials are used, it is very important to bring the information within oneself and to allow the unconscious to expand and synthesize it all. Only in this way can we create the living images we need to guide us intuitively and imaginatively toward new perspectives and commitments.

Question 2: What Is Our Vision for Ourselves?

The second question addresses an often neglected step, one that is essential to creative transformation. Our tendency seems to be to burrow into our problems without first noticing where it is we want to end up. What is on the other side of the problem? What is our vision of what is possible? By asking for a vision of our potential, or even more specifically for our next step, we allow ourselves to connect emotionally with a purpose or goal. A vision or sense of purpose can energize the problem-solving process; it gives us a positive reason for going through the often painful or tedious steps that lie before us.

Few of us have a coherent vision of what is possible for humanity. We tend to think in terms of absence of problems rather than holding visions of positive potentials. We may imagine peace, for example, as the absence of conflict rather than as an exciting, enjoyable arrangement in which conflict is used creatively. Of course, there are various ideological visions in the world, but many of these tend to divide and alienate one group from another. We need to synthesize our visions of the future and create images for the dynamic possibilities which a peaceful world could hold, images which transcend particular socio-economic systems or religions. Now, for perhaps the first time in history, large groups of people are becoming capable of this scope of vision. More and more people are awakening to the perception that our common humanity makes us more alike than different, and that our differences can enhance our world rather than threatening to destroy it.

So, like Question 1, Question 2 is worthy of time and attention. Resolving the problems which might come up in actualizing the visions comes later. First we must create and energize the visions, and commit ourselves fully to making them possible. Only then will we have the fire within—the will—to meet and resolve the inevitable problems.

We can create images of our potential in various areas of concern. We can imagine a world without war; we can imagine a world without hunger; we can imagine a world of self-reliant people living side by side within their own communities of faith and culture. We can create images of an adequate water supply for everyone, or of mobility without traffic noise and pollution. We can imagine people of the First, Second, and Third Worlds learning from one another and sharing resources equitably. One source of inspiration here is the quarterly journal *In Context,* which describes itself as "a cooperative project exploring and clarifying just what is involved in a humane sustainable culture—and how we can get there." Each thematic issue inspires hope and vision for me.

Broadly brushed images seem to work better than those tied closely to a form. Believing that we can only save the world through capitalism, for example, may prevent us from seeing the value and truths in other systems and approaches. At this early stage, we need to focus on qualities and flavors more than mechanisms and structures. And this is not easy for those of us trained to be "practical" by a technologically oriented educational system.

Our images need to be "realistic" as well, but we cannot limit our creativity with pessimism. It is better to have to revise an overly optimistic plan than to labor along under the limitations of "can't" or "that won't work." Unfortunately, realism is usually based on our collective past experience, which in turn has been determined by our collective beliefs of how the world works. The challenge of the second step in this process is to break free of our past limitations of belief and create new inspiration and hope for ourselves and our world.

Question 3: What Might Get in Our Way?

The third question now moves into the "problem" by uncovering the blocks to growth and change. Notice, however, that the question "What gets in our way? What might hold us back?" focusses the exploration on the specific blocks to the vision or goal of Question 2. This is very different from asking, "What's wrong with me (or us)?" When we ask what's wrong, we open up a "can of worms"; self-criticism, guilt, fear, self-blame, and denial can come wriggling out. By asking what gets in the way, on the other hand, we address patterns, beliefs, or problems which block the immediate path. There is no need for us to worry about limitations or faults which are not holding us back from our purpose.

Moreover, the question of what gets in our way implies no judgment; a pattern, behavior, or belief which blocks us in one endeavor may actually help us in another, or it may be a carry-over from the past when it did indeed serve our welfare. So we don't need to feel bad about ourselves; we only need to observe dispassionately what may be getting in our way and take steps to change that within the current circumstances.

It is a temptation for many of us when asking this question of ourselves to look for external conditions beyond our control to blame for our dilemma. Many people in the U.S., for example, apparently believe peace is not possible as long as communist states exist. Unfortunately, this brings the process to a dead stop and puts us into a position of helplessness and defeat or of constant belligerence. It is far more empowering to consider the ways in which we hold ourselves back. These can be changed; we have power over the ways we act and respond to life's demands. And generally when we take the responsibility (not the blame) for our self-imposed limitations, we find many of the external blocks disappearing as well. We can also often find ways to use constructively the blocks which don't disappear, or at least we can work around them.

About two years ago, I saw a television documentary about a small town in India which demonstrated these principles dramatically. The town transformed itself from a starving village into a thriving agricultural community. If the villagers had been asked several years before what had gotten in the way of their making an adequate living for themselves, I imagine they would have blamed the rocks in their fields and the monsoon floods. The vision of one man inspired them to use those hated rocks to build a dam and to store the flood waters of the monsoons to irrigate their crops year round. Their own sense of hopelessness and impotence had held them back.

This example demonstrates another principle as well. Had the leader criticized the villagers for their hopelessness, had he lectured them about their shortcomings, it is doubtful that any positive change would have resulted. They would have either resented his scolding or felt even worse about themselves (or both!). The same is true when we examine our own patterns of self-limitation; we need to hold an attitude of compassion and detachment. "Yes," we might say to ourselves, "this way of acting or this belief seems to be getting in my way now; it is probably time to change it."

It seems to be an enormous undertaking to examine the collective beliefs and behaviors which are now getting in the way of planetary peace. We need to address the question a little at a time, noticing at each step on our journey what gets in our way rather than trying to encompass all at once our collective shortcomings.

When we examine our inner blocks, whether individually or collectively, a lot of painful feelings are likely to be brought to the surface; we might become aware of hurt, fear, grief, anger, and other uncomfortable emotions which we have been suppressing. As we begin to notice the many ways we as a species have stood in our own way of growth, have held ourselves back from our potential, we may feel very badly about it all. A very necessary part of this third step is to experience these feelings fully. I am convinced that when we cut off our feelings of grief and anger and anguish about the human condition, we cut ourselves off from our strongest source of energy to change. We may need to weep and wail together in order to experience our common humanity. Joanna Macy and others leading the Despair and Empowerment Workshops have found collective expression of pain to be a powerful release of commitment and power (Glendinning, 1987; Macy, 1984). Figuratively speaking, we need to create a planetary self-help group, like Alcoholics Anonymous, to acknowledge our common despair and to commit ourselves collectively to healing.

The third step in the process of conscious growth is to recognize without blame or negative judgment the beliefs, patterns of behavior, and attitudes which hold us back and get in the way of our collective growth. The step includes the experience and appropriate expression of the feelings which may arise through this recognition. Often, the very process of recognition and emotional release allows the beliefs and behaviors to change spontaneously; they have been held in place only by our denial and ignorance.

Sometimes, however, we need to explore these patterns in more depth, seeking their origins within our history and unravelling their complex inter-relations with the various dynamics of our lives. Then, the fourth step can facilitate the needed transformation.

Question 4: What Do We Need to Develop?

The fourth question asks, not what we should *do*, but what we need to develop. It seeks a needed quality rather than a specific plan of action. This is a departure from the way many of us have traditionally solved problems. We tend to ask what's wrong and what should we do about it. In this psychosynthesis process, we ask what is possible (Question 2) and what needs to change or to grow within ourselves to remove the blocks to the possible.

If what is in our way to peace is hopelessness and a sense of impotence, what qualities do we need to develop in ourselves to move forward? Logically, it would seem we need hope and self-empowerment, and these indeed may be on the mark. But sometimes the contemplation of this question yields surprising responses. We may need courage, or love, or commitment. We may need faith.

Often, when confronted with words like "courage," "hope," or "faith," we feel embarrassed or inadequate. Just as we have tended to suppress our feelings of fear and pain, we also suffer from "the repression of the sublime" (Haronian, 1967). We may fear that we will fail if we strive for such ideals, or we may have been disillusioned as children by the preachings of hypocritical adults. Yet as we look around us, we find inspiring examples of these admirable qualities in action, and we can see the benefit they bring to the world. If we look within, moreover, we find deep yearnings to realize higher values in our lives.

We need to learn more deeply and fully the meaning and scope of the qualities we see as valuable to our world. What is courage, for example? How does it feel to be courageous? What is its opposite? What kind of experiences tend to develop courage in people, and what experiences *dis-courage* people? Who are some models for courage in our world, either historical or living now?

Question 4 is based on the premise that, once we have identified qualities we need, we can develop them within ourselves through study, meditation, imagery, imitation, and practice. We can begin by examining what we already understand about a quality and how we have experienced it in our lives. Just thinking about a quality in this manner begins to activate it within us. And we can expand what we already know by reading, talking, listening, imagining, imitating others, and by trying things out. Roberto Assagioli observed that whatever we give energy to, grows; the simple act of giving attention (energy) to desirable qualities brings them more actively into our lives. Attempting to teach others about these qualities, and how to develop them, can also help us do the same for ourselves.

Question 4 challenges us to identify what qualities we need to develop as peacemakers or as Americans or as First World citizens, and to set about doing so. Of course, just as an individual can only develop something which already lies latent within, so the qualities we need are already in existence in humanity and in some cases are highly developed. Each culture of our human family has special qualities and gifts to offer as well as undeveloped dimensions and limitations. So Question 4 may be answered differently for different people. And, in many cases, we may need to seek the help and guidance of another culture to help us develop certain qualities within our own culture. We see this recognition, for example, among young people in the United States who are eager to learn from Native American traditions. This process promises to bring together the various peoples of the world on new terms.

The mechanisms for developing such qualities already exist within our social structures: schools, media, churches, social and service organizations, to name a few. Projects which endeavor to develop qualities may even experience a greater sense of success because they are not fixed on specific quantitative goals. Moreover, we can carry out our qualitative education without threatening political structures because our strategies need not be focussed on them. Few governments would object to their people developing courage, for example; yet as their people became more courageous, changes within the political structure would surely follow. Such changes would tend to be evolutionary and harmonious rather than sudden and violent; they would occur at all levels of life and not be aimed at just one particular institution.

I offer this process to groups and individuals seeking to generate transformation in our world today—transformation vitally needed for our common survival and for improving the basic living conditions for most of our human family. Such transformation will also inevitably lead to the flowering of our vast human potential. I believe that many human projects naturally follow these principles and that our work can be made more effective and more joyful by using them consciously. Whether or not the questions are formally addressed as outlined here, projects can be planned with the same steps in mind. As we work with them together, we will no doubt expand and refine them so that this process too will evolve in the service of planetary synthesis.

Note

1.   A description of these four questions applied to individual psychosynthesis work appears in my book *The Unfolding Self* (pp. 69–70).

References

Brown, M. Y. (1983). *The unfolding self: Psychosynthesis and counseling.* Los Angeles: Psychosynthesis Press.

Gilman, R. (Ed.). (1982–1987). *In Context*, 1–17. (P.O. Box 2107, Sequim, WA 98382).

Glendinning, C. (1987). *Waking up in the nuclear age.* New York: William Morrow.

Haronian, F. (1967). *Repression of the sublime.* Psychosynthesis Research Foundation.

Kome, P., & Crean, P. (Eds.). (1986). *Peace: A dream unfolding.* San Francisco: Sierra Club Books.

Macy, J. R. (1983). *Despair and personal power in the nuclear age*. Philadelphia: New Society.

Myers, N. (Ed.). (1984). *Gaia: An atlas of planetary management*. Garden City: Anchor/Doubleday.

Walsh, R. (1984). *Staying alive: The psychology of human survival*. Boulder & London: Shambala.

Contributors

Robert A. Anderson, M.D., graduated with honors from the University of Washington School of Medicine, has taught medical students in the clinical program of the Department of Medicine at the University of Washington, is a diplomate of the American Board of Family Practice, and is a Fellow of the American Academy of Family Physicians and the American College of Preventive Medicine. He is past president of the American Holistic Medical Association and the King County Academy of Family Physicians. Dr. Anderson completed certification of training in Psychosynthesis in 1979, and is the author of *Stress Power! How to Turn Tension into Energy* (1978) and *Wellness Medicine* (1987).

Judith Bach is Founder and Director of the Berkshire Center for Psychosynthesis where she is engaged in a counselling practice. She is also a founder of the Psychosynthesis Institute of New York. Currently involved in Ph.D. studies in systems science at the Saybrook Graduate School, she is synthesizing Psychosynthesis and systems theory in the area of peace development. She is currently involved in designing an International City, a project of the Center for Peace through Culture.

Elinor Berke, D.Min., is a pastoral counsellor and Unitarian-Universalist minister now back in Chicago after serving counselling centres and churches in New England. She is a graduate of the Chicago Theological Seminary, Psychosynthesis for the Helping Professional, the Gestalt Institute of Chicago, and the Oasis Facilitator Training Program. She teaches in Chicago and has a private practice.

Joan Borton, M.Ed., practises psychotherapy in the Cape Ann area north of Boston. Her interest and creativity centre in work with young children and healing the child within the woman. Most recently her groups on menopause have become a source of learning and growth. Joan leads retreats for women, spiritual growth groups, and meditation retreats with her husband who is a minister of the United Church of Christ in Rockport, Massachusetts.

Molly Young Brown offers workshops and counselling in Marin county, California. She has worked in Psychosynthesis for 17 years, including study at the Psychosynthesis Institute in San Francisco and with Roberto Assagioli in Italy. She is author of *The Unfolding Self: Psychosynthesis and Counseling* (1983) and of various articles on psychosynthesis and peace topics. She was Co-Director of Intermountain Associates for Psychosynthesis in New Mexico until moving to the San Francisco Bay Area in 1986. Her interest in peace psychology will take her to the Soviet Union in September 1988 as co-leader of a psychosynthesis delegation.

Jack Canfield is the President of the Foundation for Self-Esteem in Pacific Palisades, California. He has been a classroom teacher, college instructor, and teacher trainer. He has consulted with over 300 school districts in the United States, Canada, Europe, and Australia. He is a member of the

California Task Force to Promote Self-Esteem and Personal and Social Responsibility and of the Board of Trustees of the National Council for Self-Esteem. Jack has written numerous books and curriculum guides in the area of holistic education, including *100 Ways to Enhance Self-Concept in the Classroom* and *Self-Esteem in the Classroom: A Curriculum Guide*.

Therese Caveney is a licensed marriage, family, and child therapist in private practice in Los Gatos, California. She specializes in healing the wounds of adults who were abused as children and offers training in Psychosynthesis for helping professionals with special emphasis on healing the inner family.

Helena Davis is a teacher, trainer, and pioneer in the field of conflict management and mediation training for children and youth. She is exploring ways to integrate psychosynthesis principles and techniques with both systems theory and interpersonal communication techniques to heal dysfunctional families and communities. She currently has a pilot community project underway in Costa Rica. Helena is also designing non-violent parenting workshops.

Kathleen Denison is the Executive Director of God Accepting the Exiled (The G.A.T.E.). She is a former Sister of Mercy who received her MA.S. in Applied Spirituality in 1979. She had nine years of teaching experience prior to receiving training in Psychosynthesis in the Boston area. In 1984, she was accepted into a national internship for prison chaplains. Through this work, she began to form a clearer understanding of the power of inner healing for this population. Her chaplaincy has evolved into the formation of a non-profit organization which continues the inner healing work with the incarcerated.

Vincent Dummer, Psy.D., is a licensed psychologist in private practice and Director/Trainer at the Kentucky Center of Psychosynthesis. He grew up in the Netherlands and graduated in 1979 from the Catholic University of Nijmegen. He received his psychosynthesis training from the London Institute of Psychosynthesis and moved in 1983 to the U.S. to join the Kentucky Center of Psychosynthesis. He has been treating clients with multiple personality disorders and other dissociative disorders since 1982.

Cherie Martin Franklin, Ph.D., is a writer, educator, and therapist specializing in women's issues. She was trained in Psychosynthesis at the Synthesis Graduate School in San Francisco and received her Ph.D. in Counselling Psychology from Ryokan College in Los Angeles. Dr. Franklin is a member of the faculty of the graduate program of Immaculata College and Co-Founder/Director of The Psychosynthesis Center in Uwchlan, Pennsylvania, where she is in private practice.

John Franklin is a psychosynthesis educator and psychotherapist trained in Montreal and San Francisco. He is Co-Director of the Psychosynthesis Center in Philadelphia. He is also Director of the Fathers' Center, a non-profit agency that educates and serves new fathers in the development of nurturing and active child-care participation. He is the co-author of *Father-birth: The Challenge of Becoming a Male Parent*. He lives on a farm with his wife and two girls.

Will Friedman, M.A., is Co-Founder and Director of the Psychosynthesis Institute of New York. He is a psychotherapist in private practice and has taught Psychosynthesis to professionals in London, England, and throughout North America. His past publications have focussed on both the clinical and social applications of Psychosynthesis.

Michael Gigante, Ph.D., received his training in Psychosynthesis at the Psychosynthesis Institute in San Francisco. He is currently working in private practice as a psychotherapist, teacher, and consultant with the Psychosynthesis Center of New Hampshire. Much of his practice focusses on individuals with developmental disabilities and the agencies that serve them as well as with Gay and Lesbian clients.

Mary Greene, Ph.D., has been Director of the Kentucky Center of Psychosynthesis for seven years. She is a psychologist who devotes over half of her private practice to working with dissociation and multiple personality disorder. Her recent creative efforts have consisted in developing seminars for the Center's Professional Training Program and in assisting other professionals in their work with multiple personality disorder.

Jonathan P. Kessler, L.I.C.S.W., is a psychotherapist in private practice. Jonathan is a recovering addict and is dedicated to helping people heal themselves and their addictions. He is currently working on a book about the integration of spiritual practice in recovery. He draws on his training in Psychosynthesis (with Tom Yeomans), psychodynamic therapy, meditation, and other paths to self-awareness, transformation, and personal healing. He is the past Clinical Director of NUVA Inc., in Gloucester, Massachusetts.

Sheldon Z. Kramer has a B.A. in psychology and religion, an M.A. in counselling, and a Ph.D. in clinical psychology. He is currently Assistant Professor of Psychology and Assistant Clinical Training Director of Psychology at United States International University in San Diego. Over the years, Dr. Kramer has been integrating psychosynthesis theory and practice with family systems theory. He has a private practice in San Diego and is Director of the Mission Valley Psychosynthesis Center where he counsels and trains people in psychosynthesis theory and application to individuals, couples, and families.

Mary Marcus is a nurse educator in the New York City area. She completed training at the Psychosynthesis Institute of New York.

Bruce McBeath, Ph.D., is Founder and Core Faculty with the Psychosynthesis Institute of Minnesota, adjunct professor at St. Mary's graduate school, and a psychologist in private practice. He is particularly interested in the integration of principles from transpersonal psychology with systems perspectives. When not meandering through trout streams, Bruce resides in St. Paul, Minnesota.

Maria T. Miliora is an educator, scientist, and psychotherapist in private practice. She has a Ph.D. in chemistry and an M.A. in social work. She has been on the faculty of Suffolk University in Boston for over 20 years and is a Professor of Chemistry. She has done advanced training in Psychosynthesis, principally with Tom Yeomans, and postgraduate training in psychoanalytic psychotherapy at the Boston Institute for Psychotherapies.

Douglas Russell, M.S.W., is a licensed psychotherapist and consultant in private practice in West Los Angeles, California.

Bonnie Gulino Schaub, M.S., R.N., and **Richard Schaub,** Ph.D., C.R.C., both have extensive professional experience in the psychotherapy and rehabilitation of chemically dependent adolescents and adults. With years of experience in mental health clinics, hospitals, and graduate school teaching, the Schaubs are currently teachers and therapists at the Psychosynthesis Institute of New York.

Kay Lynne Sherman is a psychotherapist in private practice in Seattle. She worked with disturbed adolescents and their families for 12 years in the public school system in California, and has been using Psychosynthesis in her work since 1980. More recently, in her private practice, she has concentrated on life issues: birth, death, and grief. Kay Lynne was a member of the Findhorn Foundation in Scotland from 1978-1981, and while living there wrote *The Findhorn Family Cookbook*.

Lida E. Sims is a Vice President of Drake Beam Morin Inc., an international human resource consulting firm. Ms. Sims has extensive experience as a trainer and consultant both in the U.S. and Great Britain. She has an M.A. in psychology and has done advanced training in Psychosynthesis. Prior to joining Drake Beam Morin, she was director of a specialized training and counselling centre for professionals in the fields of psychology, education, and business.

Victoria Tackett, M.A., Ph.D. candidate, is the Founding Director of Synthesis Institute in Palo Alto, California. She has been in private practice as a psychosynthesis guide since the early 1970s and teaches Psychosynthesis at John F. Kennedy University. She wrote the 1983 monograph, *Domestic Violence: A Primer for Psychosynthesis Practitioners*. In addition to her counselling and teaching activities, she is also a graphic artist who provides services for non-profit and educational organizations. Victoria convened the 1987 West Coast Psychosynthesis Advanced Training Reunion.

Jane E. Vennard is ordained in the United Church of Christ to a special ministry of teaching and spiritual direction. She is a guest lecturer at the Iliff School of Theology in Denver, leads retreats for church communities, conducts workshops, and sees individuals for spiritual direction. Jane was educated at Wellesley College (B.A.), Stanford University (M.A.), and San Francisco Theological Seminary (M.Div.). She completed her psychosynthesis training in San Francisco in 1978.

John Weiser, Ed.D., psychologist, educator, and psychotherapist, teaches in the Department of Applied Psychology at the Ontario Institute for Studies in Education, Toronto. He was co-convenor of the Psychosynthesis International Conference in Toronto in 1983 and is Co-Director of the Toronto Center for Psychosynthesis.

Anne Yeomans, M.A., has been a teacher and a therapist in Psychosynthesis since the early seventies. Since 1985, her teaching has focussed on the issues of inner and outer peacemaking, non-violence, and conflict resolution. She is currently in private practice in Concord, Massachusetts.

Thomas Yeomans, Ph.D., is Director of Psychosynthesis for the Helping Professional in the Boston area. Since 1970, he has been a therapist, teacher, and trainer of professionals in Psychosynthesis. In 1983, he was co-convenor, with John Weiser, of an international conference on Psychosynthesis in Toronto, and is co-editor, also with John Weiser, of the two previously published books *Psychosynthesis in the Helping Professions* (1984) and *Readings in Psychosynthesis, Volume I* (1985).

Penelope Young has been a psychotherapist since 1971. After completing her M.A. in psychiatric social work at Fordham University in New York City, she completed a four-year internship in marriage and family therapy at Albert Einstein College of Medicine in New York City. She then trained in Psychosynthesis with the Montreal and San Francisco institutes for five years. She studied Sacred Psychology with Jean Houston for two years in New York City and completed training in "Heart Centered" Therapy at Spring Hill in Ashby, Massachusetts. Ms. Young moved to San Diego in September of 1984 with her son Adam. In addition to maintaining a private practice for individuals, couples, and families, she is engaged in teaching Psychosynthesis throughout the United States.